AN EYE FOR AN EYE

OTHER BOOKS BY JOHN SACK

The Butcher
From Here to Shimbashi
Report from Practically Nowhere
M
Lieutenant Calley
The Man-Eating Machine
Fingerprint

AN EYE
FOR
AN EYE

John Sack

BasicBooks
A Division of HarperCollins*Publishers*

for all who died
and for all who because of this story
might live

Some of this book first appeared, in much different form, in *California* and *The Village Voice*.

Copyright © 1993 by John Sack. Preface to the Paperback Edition copyright © 1995 by John Sack. Published by BasicBooks, Inc., A Division of HarperCollins Publishers, Inc.

Library of Congress Cataloging-in-Publication Data
Sack, John.
    An eye for an eye / John Sack.
       p.   cm.
    Includes bibliographical references and index.
    ISBN 0-465-04214-7 (cloth)
    ISBN 0-465-02215-4 (paper)
    1. Blatt, Lola Potok Ackerfeld, 1921- . 2. Jews—Poland—Bedzin—Biography. 3.
Auschwitz (Poland: Concentration camp) 4. Holocaust survivors—Poland—Biography. 5.
Prison wardens—Poland—Gliwice—Biography. I. Title.
DS135.P63B5467 1993
940.53'18'092—dc20
[B]
                                          93-27369
                                            CIP

95 96 97 98 ◆/Dunn 9 8 7 6 5 4 3 2 1

CONTENTS

PREFACE TO THE
PAPERBACK EDITION

This book had a glaring error when it was published in November, 1993. The error appeared in the Preface, where I wrote that in 1945 some Jews who'd survived the Holocaust killed thousands of German civilians: German men, women, children, babies. That allegation was accurate, but I then wrote, "I knew that if I reported it, I'd be exhibiting, well, call it *chutzpa*, for I could guess what the world would say." By then I'd worked seven years on *An Eye for an Eye*, and I truly believed that the world could say nothing I hadn't already guessed. It may seem paranoid, but I'd even guessed that on some 40-watt radio station somewhere, someone from the extremities might phone in and call me a Nazi, and this indeed happened on a small station in Rutherford, New Jersey, but never in my wildest speculations did I suppose that an eminent intellectual on a television network would refer to "a man called John Sack" and another intellectual would say, "Well, first of all, these people are anti-Semites, second of all they're neo-Nazis." Ten years earlier, I'd done an exposé of the Nazis on Channel 2 in Los Angeles—I was still on the Nazi hit list, and I hadn't foreseen that scholars would call me one.

When I wrote *An Eye for an Eye*, I hadn't guessed that people would call it a monstrous lie. A lot of it, after all, had been fact-checked by three major magazines and a paper whose editor said, "It may be the most accurate story in the history of American journalism." A lot had been fact-checked by *60 Minutes*, which found eight eyewitnesses who I hadn't and

1,580 death certificates signed by a Jewish commandant, so I hadn't guessed that the titles of some reviews would be *False Witness* and *The Big Lie*. One noted Jewish paper said, "Sack is transparently writing docudrama" and "Sack is trafficking with imagined reality," and it then argued that Lola, the central character, couldn't have commanded the prison for Germans that is the central locale in *An Eye for an Eye*. Lola herself had told me, "I was the commandant," thirty-five people (among them the current commandant) had corroborated her, and I had the document appointing her and a document signed by her as the *naczelnika*, or commandant, but the paper argued, "The unlikelihood is overwhelming." Another review referred to Lola as "Lola," as if I'd concocted her.

When I read these stories, I felt I was being lectured by Groucho Marx, who was asking me, "Who do you believe? Your own two eyes or me?" But also I hadn't guessed there would be *reviewers* who'd lie, reviewers who'd write, "Sack never adequately estimates the number of Germans slaughtered," when I'd demonstrably estimated this in Chapter 9, and reviewers who'd write, "Only in Sack's notes does he reveal that [Czesław] was a Catholic," when I'd demonstrably revealed this in Chapter 11. Other reviewers wrote that I'd written things that I hadn't, wrote, "Dare anyone who has even a modicum of respect for language use an expression like—" whereupon the reviewer, a rabbi, quoted some words that I'd never written anywhere, ever. In Chapter 4 of *An Eye for an Eye*, I'd said that three-fourths of the officers—the lieutenants, captains and majors—in the Office of State Security in the city of Kattowitz in February, 1945, were Jews, but a magazine said that I'd said that three-fourths of all the Office in all of Poland were Jews, and a newspaper said that I'd said that three-fourths of all the "factotums" in all of Poland were Jews. Having devised this statistic, the reviewers went on to refute it, a Harvard professor writing, "We *know*,"

> We know how many Jews were in the Office of State Security. According to a tabulation of November 21, 1945, by Bolesław Bierut, then President of Poland, the Office of State Security had 438 Jews. 438! Not Sack's 75 percent but 1.7 percent.

Now, I'd gone to Harvard, whose motto is *veritas*, truth, and I'd never expected this. Let's forget that the Harvard professor didn't deny that the head of the Office was a Jew and all or almost all the department heads were Jews. Let's forget that this year a Polish professor found a secret directory of the 447 top officers in Warsaw from 1944 to 1953, and thirty percent were Jews. In my innocence, I'd thought it enough that I'd said in *An Eye for an Eye* that Jews left the Office "as early as June, 1945," that "hundreds of Jews escaped from the Office" by September, 1945, and that "all but a scattering of Jews returned to the Torah and Talmud and fled from the Office by December, 1945." If, as the Harvard professor wrote, there were 438 Jews in the Office as late as November 21, 1945, that's sixty times more than I'd ever mentioned in *An Eye for an Eye*—and also I'd never guessed that I'd not be allowed to report this fact until now. When I wrote a letter to the editor of the Harvard professor's outlet, the editor wouldn't publish it, and when I bought a $425 ad, the editor wouldn't publish *that*. I then bought an ad in the student paper at Harvard, but the students wouldn't publish it.

To be sure, there were honest reviewers and reporters in *New York, the New York Daily News, Newsweek* and *The Progressive* and on public radio and *60 Minutes,* but most reviewers seemed to be in determined denial. "Some Jews," they allowed, "became murderers," but they called them "a small group of Jewish survivors" and "one Jewish woman and a handful of Jewish men" who essentially weren't Jews at all. They were "more communist than Jewish," a University of California professor wrote—they were "communists from Jewish families," "communists from Jewish backgrounds," "communists of Jewish origin." Now, I'd known these people seven years, and I'd never thought I would read that. I'd interviewed twenty-three Jews who'd been in the Office, and one, just one, had considered himself a communist in 1945. He and the others had gone to Jewish schools, studied the Torah, been bar-mitzvahed, sometimes worn *payes*. In German camps, at the risk of their lives, some had made *matzo* on Pesach, and in 1945 they had lighted candles on Shabbas, held seders on Pesach, stood under *huppas* at weddings, sounded *shofars* on Rosh Hashanah, and fasted on Yom Kippur. By whose definition weren't they Jews? Not by the Talmud's, certainly, not by the government of Israel's or the government of Nazi Germany's. Had they died in the Holocaust, I'd have guessed that the world would count them among the six million.

But clearly I'm not good at guessing games. I've been asked, but I can't explain why the world has turned itself inside out to avoid confronting this book. Denial, we're told, is our first response when the doctor announces we're going to die, and maybe the Jewish establishment fears that if I report that Jews are normal human beings, that Jews can love, hate and take revenge just as anyone can, then I trumpet the end of the Jewish religion or Jewish race, perhaps at the hands of the neo-Nazis. Or maybe the Jewish establishment fears that if I report that Jews aren't always pitiful victims who Catholics, Protestants and Moslems, their constant oppressors, owe reparations to, then I trumpet the end of Israel.

Maybe the men who (along with God) oversee the Jewish community feel that the Day of Atonement, Yom Kippur, is some sort of sting operation and Jews who are caught confessing to

> *The sin we've committed in Thy sight*
> *By oppressing our fellow man*

are *ipso facto* not Jews at all but felons of Jewish origin.

I don't believe this. The news that Jews aren't saints is right in the Bible, which says of King Solomon, even King Solomon, "He did evil"— the news is two thousand years old and Jews have hardly suppressed it. Why, then, for fifty years did people suppress the news of Shlomo (Solomon) Morel? I'd have thought that a man who commanded a concentration camp, who Jews and Germans testified killed thousands of prisoners, who was wanted in Poland but (as happened last year) who fled to the Middle East—I'd have thought that Shlomo's story was well worth telling, but Shlomo's not German but Jewish, he didn't flee to Syria but Israel, and for almost fifty years not one American newspaper mentioned him. After this book appeared, a dozen papers asked about him, even wrote stories about him and told me the stories would run the next day, but for a year they never did. At last, today, as I write this, one ran in the *New York Times,* and the *Times*'s reports of beatings, tortures and murders at Shlomo's camp confirm what the Harvard professor called the "more outrageous claims" in *An Eye for an Eye.*

I welcome the *Times*'s candor, however tardy. I don't know anyone, even survivors of Shlomo's camp, who can't sympathize with a man whose father, mother, brothers (there were no sisters), uncles, aunts and all but one cousin died in the Holocaust, a man whose anguish in 1945 drowned out the Torah's words "Do not take revenge." But many, many people, including me, were dismayed when the very papers that told us each year of the Hun of the Year, of Barbie, Demjanjuk, Bousquet, Touvier, the papers that said "Dog Bites Man" didn't also say "Shlomo Bites Dog," and many, many more would have been dismayed if the normal response of denial had lasted until, after fifty years, it wouldn't be distinguishable from an old-time political cover-up. I note with pride that the *Times*'s publisher and the *Times*'s executive editor (like me, my agent and my own editor at Basic Books) are Jews. If the day ever comes when the race that taught the civilized world to love its neighbors has no *rachmanis* except for its own and is no more enlightened than Serbs and Somalis, then that, I believe, and not *An Eye for an Eye,* will herald the end of the Jewish religion, the Jewish race, and Israel.

Considering this, I must thank you, the reader, for not caving in to reviews with titles like "DO ME A FAVOR—DON'T READ THIS BOOK" and for reading at least this far. If you read on, I hope you'll observe what so few reviewers did but what, quite curiously, almost all the readers who've written me did: that this is a book on the saving grace of the Jewish religion—which, when Lola returned to it, brought her redemption and love. I hope that in spite of the hullaballoo, you'll observe that no one, no Jew, German or Pole who was present in 1945 (except for the people who say "I didn't do it") has ever denied anything that I wrote in *An Eye for an Eye* or its Notes. I had some minor errors, yes—the Polish word is *któż,* not *który,* there is no tunnel under the Brenner Pass—and I thank the people who pointed these out, but I've not corrected them in this paperback printing lest I be accused of my own little cover-up. The book that incensed so many reviewers is exactly the one you're reading, right down to those sad, unsuspecting words "I could guess what the world would say." Please turn to the Preface.

John Sack
November 1994

PREFACE

My mother's mother was from Cracow, thirty miles from Auschwitz, and I must assume that if she (and my other grandparents) hadn't left in the 1890s and sailed to America, that I'd have been sent to Auschwitz in the early 1940s. I'd have been about twelve years old. Like other boys then, I'd have been wearing a drab gray suit and a flat gray "golfer" cap, and I'd have stepped from the train with my mother, father, and freckle-cheeked sister, nine years old, and onto the concrete platform inside of the Auschwitz wires. As it happened, I didn't go to Auschwitz until four years ago, when I was almost sixty and it was safe to do so. I stood on the wide concrete platform, and I stared at the tracks where the train would have been, but I couldn't picture myself getting off it. I tried, but the "when, where and what" of Auschwitz were so remote from my own remembered world that I felt I was trying to see myself as I or my atoms were just before the Big Bang.

I'd read about Auschwitz, and I knew that Mengele would have been on this platform that day, and I went to where he'd have stood. I knew he'd have told my mother and father, "Go right," and my sister and me, "Go left," but I still couldn't picture it. I went to the ruins of the dressing room—the undressing room—then of the cyanide chamber, which now had no roof and was full of old roof components, of dirt, grass and dandelions, and (as I looked closely) of tiny white chips of bone that, in the 1940s, had fallen there from the sky. Again, I tried to picture my sister and me in this cyanide chamber, undressed, our two bodies touching and one thousand people around us, all screaming, the gas coming down upon us, and I simply couldn't see it, my mind had no hook that could hold it, I might as well have been groping for "Why does the universe exist? What if it didn't?" I left without taking notes, but I remember that I felt some sympathy for the men and women who say that the Holocaust didn't happen. The people who say it are fools, maybe worse, but I can commiserate with them. The thought that the Holocaust did, indeed, happen is too enormous for one little volleyball brain.

I'd come to Auschwitz, and this part of Poland, to research this book. I had heard of a Jewish girl, Lola, who, after one-and-one-half years at Auschwitz, had turned the Holocaust upside down by becoming the commandant of a big prison for Germans at Gleiwitz, thirty miles away, and, in some ways, imitating the SS women at Auschwitz, and I wanted to write about her. Lola wasn't in Poland anymore, but as I spoke to Jews, Poles and Germans about her and as I studied documents in a cobwebbed cellar in Poland and a concrete castle over the Rhine, I slowly became aware that the truth was much, much larger than Lola. I learned that hundreds of Jews who'd been on the platform at Auschwitz (or the numerous places like it) in the early 1940s could picture things that I couldn't and, in fact, could *do* things that in the 1930s they couldn't even have pictured. When the Holocaust ended, I learned, a number of Jews became commandants like Lola. I understood why, but the Jews were sometimes as cruel as their exemplars at Auschwitz, and they even ran the organization that ran the prisons and—as I learned—the concentration camps for German civilians in Poland and Poland-administered Germany. Once again, I felt that I was confronting something too big for one little three-pound brain, for I was learning that, yes, the Holocaust happened, the Germans killed Jews, but that a second atrocity happened that the Jews who committed it covered up: one where the Jews killed Germans. God knows the Jews were provoked, but I learned that in 1945 they killed a great number of Germans: not Nazis, not Hitler's trigger men, but German civilians, German men, women, children, *babies,* whose "crime" was just to be Germans. Through the wrath of Jews, however understandable, the Germans lost more civilians than at Dresden, more than, or just as many as, the Japanese at Hiroshima, the Americans at Pearl Harbor, the British in the Battle of Britain, or the Jews themselves in all of Poland's pogroms: so I now learned, and I was aghast to learn it. This was no Holocaust or the moral equivalent of the Holocaust, but I knew that if I reported it, I'd be exhibiting, well, call it *chutzpa,* for I could guess what the world would say. Even so, I felt I'd be doing the righteous thing both as a reporter and as a man who's a Jew.

I'm not a Biblical scholar, but I went to Saturday school (I was voted the "most religious") and I knew that the Torah tells us to bear honest witness, tells us, indeed, that if someone sins and we know it and *don't* report it, then we're guilty too. The men (and the woman, a scholar says) who wrote the Torah didn't cover up Jewish misdeeds. Even when Abraham, the father of the Jewish people, sinned—God told him to go to Israel, but he went to Egypt, instead—the Torah reported it. It reported that Judah, whose name is the source of "Jew," made love to a harlot, and it reported that Moses, even Moses, trespassed against the Lord, who then didn't let him into the Promised Land. The people who wrote the Torah (or according to Orthodox Jews, the God who wrote it) believed that we Jews couldn't proclaim, "Thou shalt not covet," "Thou shalt not steal," "Thou shalt not kill," if we ourselves did it and covered it up, and I, as a Jew doing research in Europe, felt that I must report what the Jewish commandants did if Jews were to keep any moral authority. I suspected that some Jews would ask me, "How could a Jew write this book?" and I knew that my answer must be "No, how could a Jew *not* write it?"

When I came back from Europe, and when I started writing, I still chose to concentrate on the intimate story of Lola and Lola's circle. To write a whole formal history such as the Germans wrote, from the German viewpoint, omitting all mention of Jews, in a three-volume work in the 1960s, would demand a battalion of historians who, even then, probably wouldn't turn up the truth of a secret organization from 1945. For myself, I didn't want to write something like "The Jews did this," "The Jews did that," "Well, weren't the Jews just awful," just as I hadn't written like that in my three books about the American soldiers in Vietnam and as I hope I wouldn't write if I ever wrote about the German SS. I decided that in *An Eye for an Eye,* I wouldn't report that a Jew had beaten a German, tortured a German, or killed a German until the reader could understand why the Jew had done it and even could think, *If I'd been that Jew, I'd have done it myself,* and I hope with all my heart that I've succeeded. I also decided that *An Eye for an Eye* wouldn't just be about the Jews who strayed from the Torah but also about the Jews who prevailed upon them to return, and I hope I've succeeded here too. In the end, I hope that *An Eye for an Eye* is something more than the story of Jewish revenge: the story of Jewish redemption.

A word to those readers who, in the 1990s, get understandably lost at the borders of document, docudrama, and drama on documented matters. The people in *An Eye for an Eye* are real. The events in *An Eye for an Eye* really happened. The quotations in *An Eye for an Eye,* with three minor exceptions that I describe in the Notes, are not "reconstructed" but are what people really recalled or, very rarely, would have to have said, and the thoughts in *An Eye for an Eye* are what people reported or, very rarely, would have to have thought. At the end of *An Eye for an Eye* are sixty-five pages of Notes and Sources, and among these is the documentation for the number of Jews in the German-imprisoning organization, the positions that the Jews held, the number of prisons for Germans and concentration camps for Germans, and the number of Germans who died inside them and Germans who died all in all. If, despite this, a reader still feels that he or she is standing on some strange platform in Poland thinking, "I can't believe this," I can well sympathize, for I've been on that platform myself. I can just promise that I'm a careful reporter and *An Eye for an Eye* is true.

John Sack
August 1993

AN EYE FOR AN EYE

1

At five o'clock in the morning on Friday, January 12, 1945, the silence along the Vistula River in Poland was broken by thousands of loud commands of "Fire!" Thousands of Russian officers cried, *"Ogon,"* the wind sent their words to the Russian gunners' ears, and in seconds the earth seemed to split apart as twenty thousand cannon, rocket and mortar shells exploded over the sleeping soldiers of Hitler's army. "Lock! Load! Fire!" the thunder of twenty thousand more, "Fire!" "Fire!" "Fire!" one hundred thousand now, and the shells rained down on the Germans for one hour, forty-five minutes. When the noise stopped, the Germans who weren't dead were like punch-drunk people, the blood coming out of their ears, noses, and open mouths as Russia's three million soldiers rolled over them. On the Russian tanks were the painted words NA BERLIN! TO BERLIN!

Six days later, the Russians had rolled a hundred miles west, and now their shells shook the windows of the House of the Armed SS in the willow-filled town of Oświęcim, or Auschwitz. Inside were the men and women of Hitler's private army, the SS, who for years had been feasting on pork, pike, duck, roasted hare, and red cabbage, washing them down with Bulgarian wine and Yugoslavian schnapps. After dinner, the SS men had pulled out the chairs from under the SS women's *popos,* the women plopping onto the floor, roaring, the men vomiting onto the Persian rugs, betting that the next vomiter would be Hans, whoever, the fat and red-fleshed women roaring along with the men. As the Russians got closer, though, the SS had rolled from the House moaning, *"Hitler kaputt,"* swilling its Yugoslavian schnapps. *"Alles ist aus!* Everything's lost!"

And tonight the SS was panic-stricken by Russia's guns. God in His heaven! What clemency could an SS man or, worse, an SS woman in Nuit de Paris perfume expect from the Russian infantry? Nor was the SS soothed by the orders of Himmler, its Hitler-mustached leader in Berlin, to flee to Gross Rosen, Germany, two hundred miles west, and to bring along the 64,438 murderers, robbers and Jews who, for years, had been doing slave labor at Auschwitz. What worse impediment to any hell-bent retreat than the slow, stumbling feet of its sixty thousand slaves? But cursing them, the SS snapped on its hats with the jolly-roger insignias and by boot, bike and motorcycle descended on the vast stables where the sixty thousand lived, two or three dozen to every stall.

"Aufstehen! Get up!" the SS shouted, as the rats that were snuggling by the men and women scooted away. *"Stinkende schweine!* You stinking pigs! *Heraus!* Get out!" the SS continued, stomping down the wet aisles, stepping in the diarrhea, swearing, wiping its boots on the sack-of-straw mattresses, booting the half-asleep prisoners. To avoid their lice, the SS didn't touch anyone except with a boot, strap, bullwhip, or, in one woman's hand, a whip with a bead-encrusted handle. *"Schneller!* Faster!" the SS shouted, shooting its Lugers at all who were tired or had typhus, killing them, and it then watched as the sixty thousand snatched up their only possessions, their shoes, and ran to the red-tinted open air. *"Aufstellen!* Line up!" an SS sergeant shouted. *"Appell! Appell!* Head count!" he shouted, laying about with a wooden club. "No, there isn't time!" the others shouted. *"Wir marschieren jetzt!* We're marching!" they cried, and the prisoners went past the wires, the whine of 6,000 volts, the gates of Auschwitz, and the inscription of ARBEIT MACHT FREI, WORK MAKES YOU FREE, to the cadence of *"Links! Links! Links!* To your left!"

One of them that winter night was Lola Potok, a Jewish girl from Poland. She was not quite twenty-four.

It was ten below on the road to Germany. It was snowing, the snow congealing to ice on Lola's eyebrows. Not far behind her, the Russians had copies of *Pravda* inside their boots, the SS was using the *Abendpost* but Lola was walking in two left shoes, her feet killing her, her knees knocking one another, becoming raw, and the blood dripping an inch or two before freezing on Lola's bare legs. Behind her, the Russians in fur-lined coats from America muttered, *"Sabachi holod!* It's dog cold!" but Lola wore an old dress and a coat with the sign of a slave on its shoulders: a cross of rigid red paint. The cold crept through it, through skin, through bones, till the only ember was Lola's heart.

Her family was all she thought of. Born twenty miles away in Będzin to a father and mother versed in the Torah, Lola had had ten older brothers and sisters: a boxer, a foreman, a CPA, a couturier, a pop band leader whose hottest song was *Blue Skies (Smiling at Me)*, a philologist and a pilot among them. But when, in 1943, the Germans smashed in her family's door shouting, *"Schmutzige Juden!* You dirty Jews! *Heraus!* Get out!" and cattle-carred many of these brothers, sisters, nephews, nieces, and Lola's mother and Lola's daughter to Auschwitz, the only one who the Germans considered able-bodied was Lola, then twenty-one. The rest were selected by Mengele, the SS's whistling doctor, to be gassed (or, in one case, hanged) and be cremated in the ovens whose sickening smell had the SS sneering at Auschwitz as *Anus Mundi.* Among the condemned was Lola's daughter, age one.

And now, one-and-one-half years later, as sixty thousand people moved like the Doomed, as SS in black woolen cloaks cried, *"Weiter!* Go on!" as SS dogs in black woolen blankets snarled, as SS in pell-mell retreat shot the people who, for any reason, stopped, as waste matter ran down the other people's legs, and as Lola shuffled by one, two, three hundred corpses—now, Lola just thought of Ada, of Zlata. Straggling beside her, Ada and Zlata, the wives of two of her brothers, were, to her knowledge, her only surviving relatives. She had kept them alive at Auschwitz by spooning the ill-smelling soup (was it turnip? nettle? rutabaga? the Jews believed it was poison ivy) into their mouths saying, "Eat it," Ada and Zlata crying, "I can't," Lola yelling, "Swallow it!" and Ada and Zlata downing it, holding their noses. At Auschwitz, Lola had yelled like a drill instructor in her determination that the Potok family should survive. And now, she sneaked from the slow-moving column to dig up four frozen potatoes to pass to Ada and Zlata, who put them under their armpits to thaw before wolfing them down. *They need me,* Lola told herself, for her will to live depended on her two sisters-in-law.

At dawn the black became gray. The air and the earth were the same cardboard color, and the homes by the road were just darker blotches. It was so cold that some firing pins cracked as the SS shot hundreds of Jews. At noon Ada cried, "I see some meat!" and ran to a snow-covered meadow where a dead animal lay, but before the SS could shoot her, she ran back saying, "No, it's human." At twilight, the SS finally said, *"Stehen bleiben!* Stop!" and as Zlata slumped to the snow, starting to eat it, Lola knocked on a German's door, saying, "We need some bread." What she got, she shared with Zlata—just Zlata, for Ada had disappeared. Ada's shoes had fallen apart and had fallen off.

Lola's shoes tortured her. She sat in a roadside shed with Zlata and pulled them off. Her feet were blue and, on being released, started to swell up. Zlata cried, "Put your shoes on! Or you'll never be able to!"

"Zlata, I'll get gangrene. . . ."

"No, put them back on!" Zlata cried, and she almost held Lola down as she jammed her in. All night Lola lay in agony, attributing this to Zlata. In the morning, the SS said, "We're moving on," and the sixty or fifty or forty thousand resumed the funeral march.

By twilight Lola couldn't take it. She was in Germany, somewhere south of Gleiwitz. It was fifteen below, and her feet seemed to be in iron torture devices. She weighed sixty-six pounds. Despite surviving at Auschwitz, the SS women maiming her, her back surviving sciatica, her hand surviving gangrene, her body surviving typhus and 104 degrees, and Mengele even condemning her to the cyanide chamber—despite this, the will to live wasn't there anymore and Lola gave up. She whispered to Zlata in Yiddish, "I'm not walking another step."

"What else can you do?"

"I've had it, I'm walking away."

"They'll kill you!"

"If that's what my destiny is, it will happen right here."

"No, I'll never see you!"

"Whatever will be. . . ."

"Don't do it! They'll kill you!" said Zlata. "Be careful!" she cried, as Lola moved off from the Hosts of Hell.

Now, alongside the road observing the passing parade were some German civilians, and Zlata saw Lola move toward them. In the dim light, the Germans didn't see the red cross on Lola's coat, but as Zlata looked on in horror, an SS man with a Luger, a leash with a snarling dog, and a jolly-roger, skull-and-bones, head-of-death insignia—an SS man charged up to Lola shouting, "Sie, gehören Sie dazu? You! Do you belong with the Jews?" Zlata couldn't hear what Lola replied. As she moved on, Zlata heard the crack of a Luger and thought, Lola's dead! She was wrong.

That night, Zlata and one thousand others went to a railroad station and, at dawn, into railroad cars—into coal cars, exposed to the cold air. The train started up and went north, south, east, west, up and down mountains all January and February, eluding the Russians. In the open cars, the people on top froze to death, the ones at the bottom suffocated, and the SS kept shouting, "Die körper hinaus! The corpses outside!" the dead going overboard. Zlata, in the middle layer, stayed alive by eating the snow and the bread that the Germans at one of the stations gave her. She wasn't let off at Buchenwald, but she was let off at a concentration camp near Denmark, and she stayed there all March and April. She ate the same soup as at Auschwitz but avoided the sandy spinach, knowing that Lola couldn't tell her, "Eat it!" and she mended the bullet holes in

German uniforms till the Americans freed her on Wednesday, May 2. With seven other girls, all Jews, she then headed back to Będzin, and she was in Gleiwitz, Germany, near Lola's walkout in January, when someone reported that Lola was living in Gleiwitz at 25 Lange Reihe. "Lola Potok?" said Zlata.

"Yes, from Będzin."

"It couldn't be," Zlata said. But she and the others walked past the German parade ground, where, in the war, the horses had caracoled every day, and turned onto Lange Reihe. A ways down this cobblestoned street was a pretty red tulip bed and a "25" on a tile-gabled house. In the door was a small square window, and the lace curtain parted almost as soon as Zlata knocked. In its place were the peering eyes of a German woman, thirty years old, who opened the Tudor door saying, "You must be Zlata." She led the mystified girls to the living room and, as they stared at the paneled walls, the oil portraits, and the baby grand piano, made a telephone call in German. Soon there was a roar outside, a German motorcycle pulled up, and a man in a uniform jumped off. He wore a Luger, hurried into the living room, and, as the girls watched, astonished, whipped off his goggles and eagle-insignia hat. A shower of dark blonde hair came down, and Zlata gasped, "Lola! It's you!"

"Zlata! You're alive!"

The girls were stunned. Lola, for that's who the "man" was, was half again heavier than in January, weighing about a hundred pounds. She was almost robust, and her face even showed some baby fat. Her jacket of olive drab had a row of brass eagle-insignia buttons, and on her high collar were what the Americans called scrambled eggs: a splatter of silver embroidery. On each of her shoulders were two silver embroidered stars. On her chest was a sam-browne belt, on her hip was a holster and gun, and her skirt, olive drab, came down to her gleaming black cavalry boots, like General Patton's. Still striding, Lola reached out but Zlata shrank back, for she'd never known a man or woman in uniform who'd tried to embrace her.

"Lola, your clothes—"

Lola shrugged. She half-turned to her right and left, as though modeling them. Her hand, which was on her hip, pulled out her Luger, displaying it like some trophy.

"Lola! I'm scared!" said Zlata. "Put that away!"

"Don't worry about it," Lola said. She put her Luger back, and she turned to the German woman, saying, "Gertrude! Get them some food!" Gertrude went out.

"Lola, what are you in? The Russian Army?" Zlata said.

"No, I'm an officer in—" and Lola rolled off some initials that Zlata didn't know the meaning of. But then, Lola rolled off the names of some other officers in the olive-clothed organization, and Zlata recognized them. So-and-So from Auschwitz. So-and-So also from Auschwitz. So-and-So from school in Będzin. Even as Gertrude was coming back with some German sausages, Zlata detected a pattern among those names.

"Everyone's Jewish."

"Eat something. Yes."

All that hour, the girls ate and Lola told them about the olive-clothed people. To listen to Lola, hundreds of Jews were operating in all of Poland and Poland-administered Germany. Their leaders were Jewish generals in Warsaw, to listen to Lola. Their mission was to hunt for SS, Nazis, and Nazi collaborators, to punish them and, if appropriate, execute them, and, in this way, to take revenge against the Jew-killers of Germany. Or so Lola said.

Zlata couldn't buy it. She knew that at Auschwitz, everyone's dream was to do what the Germans did: to force the Germans to stand in the wind, rain and snow, hour after hour, naked, their hands overhead in a "Saxon greeting," beating them, whipping them as they cried, "No!" and marching them to the cyanide to the cadence of *"Links!* To your left!" But the dream disappeared every day at the call of *"Aufstellen!* Line up!" and now Zlata wondered if wish and reality weren't mixed up in Lola's mind. "Lola," said Zlata. "Are *you* in charge of any Germans?"

"A thousand. About a mile from here."

"Well, what do you actually do?"

"The same things the Germans did to us."

"Lola, what does that *mean?*"

"Do you want to see it? Come," Lola said.

2

Lola was born in Będzin ("Ben Gene") on Sunday, March 20, 1921. To get to Będzin, one boarded the train at Kattowitz, the central city of Silesia, the coal-mining part of Germany, and ten minutes later the soot in the air disappeared and one was in Poland, in Będzin. From the station, one strolled up the cobblestone streets where the peddlers called out in Yiddish, *"Bagel!" "Zemmil!" "Lemonad!"* and the peddlers with poles across their necks and two metal buckets at the ends called out, *"Vasser! Tsen groshen!* Water! Two cents!" At the top of this gentle hill, one saw the only "sight" of Będzin, the Góra Zamkowa Castle. As castles go, it was small, the size of a Disneyland one, and its walls were in ruins and its moats full of fluffy dandelions. No one was living inside it in 1921, but the boys of Będzin would storm it sometimes, and the girls would draw hopscotch boards on the castle's approaches, hopping from the אs to the ךs.

Będzin had had Jews ever since the Crusades. They had come in the 1200s, and they were twenty thousand strong by the 1920s. They didn't look like the cast of *Fiddler on the Roof,* for they worked as doctors, lawyers, owners of zinc-plating plants, and not as people who sat on stools, sewing the parts of men's pants together. True, there was a Shlomo the Tailor in Będzin, but the man used sewing machines, and his smart double-breasted suits were the last word even in Germany. After work, Shlomo would light a Silesia cigarette, letting it sag at an I-don't-care angle, looking sensationally like Humphrey Bogart, and, in his boots, breeches, tweed jacket, and tie, would drive down to Germany to tango the night away on the Carioca's rotating floor.

By the 1920s, a fiddler on any of Będzin's roofs would be out of earshot, for the houses were several stories high, like in most small cities of Europe. In one such town house on Modrzejowska Street, the Potoks—mother, father, two daughters, and eight shouting sons—were residing when Lola was born. Their street-level flat was a stronghold more than the castle was. The eight brothers knew the Torah, sure, and the Torah commanded them to love their neighbors, but woe unto him who called any Potok boy *"Głupku!* You dope!" *"Kretynie!* You cretin!" or, God help him, *"Parszywy Żydzie!* You boil-covered Jew!" A black eye, a bloody nose, or a few missing teeth would be the consequence of these antipotokic sentiments. Nor did the brothers let any boy harm their sisters, going so far as to ask every gentleman caller, "Who are you?" "What does your father do?" "What . . .?"

The father of this little minyan was a beer brewer, and the mother was a woman well read in the Torah and Talmud. At Passover, Rivka would teach her most recent children the words to *Dayenu,* at Purim the words to,

> *Oh, today we'll merry, merry be!*
> *Oh, today we'll merry, merry be!*

and on Fridays she'd light the two Sabbath candles. Rivka's husband would hold up the wine while hurrying through the Sabbath prayer, but Rivka would say it conscientiously, finishing last. ". . . Has given us Thy holy Sabbath," Rivka would pray. "Blessed art Thou, O Lord, who hallows the Sabbath. *You,"* she'd then tell her husband and children—"you take the express and I'll take the local. But you'll still have to wait for me."

After that, Rivka would serve the fresh-baked *chala,* the chicken soup, the gefilte fish. At times there'd be sounds on her windowpane, the pitter-pat of pebbles there, and her sons would yell, "It's the Polish boys!" Her sons would start to run out, but Rivka would stop them.

"No," she would say. "It's the Sabbath. We'll live as the Torah tells us. We aren't like them." Her sons would sit down, their fists still clenched, and Rivka would tell them, "No, listen. Do you know about the man and the Polish policeman?"

"No, Mama. . . ."

"The man," and Rivka smiled mischievously, "was standing on the street making pee-pee. And the policeman told him, 'You! You with your thing out! You better stop it and hide it!' You know what the man answered him?"

"No. . . ."

"The man said, 'All right, I hid it—but I didn't stop it!'" The boys laughed and Rivka went on. "And you. All that hate. You hid it but you didn't stop it. Your hate can't hurt the Polish boys. It only hurts you. It corrodes your soul. So just stop it."

"All right, Mama."

And then this wise woman would serve the dessert: the honey, raisins and carrots. "One more child? I can handle it," Rivka told people when Lola was due. "I'll put some more water in the chicken soup." Her oldest daughter was twenty-one, her other daughter sixteen, her sons were seventeen to four on Sunday, March 20, 1921, when Lola was born in Rivka's lace-curtained bedroom.

That same day, the Germans across the border went to their polling places in compliance with the Treaty of Versailles. The question on their ballots was, Do you want this area to be in Germany or Poland? The Germans voted for Germany but Poland invaded them, and Kattowitz, all its coal mines, and all its inhabitants became part of Poland.

In March, 1933, Hitler became the leader of Germany and Lola turned twelve. She was very attractive, blonde-haired, brown-eyed. Her red cheeks embarrassed her, and sometimes she'd say, "Oh Mama! I look like a farmer's daughter!" ("Someday you'll thank me for it"), but her high cheekbones were less like a Polish peasant's than an Indian princess's. She was eager, energetic, cheerful, and she went to school singing songs—well, so did the other girls, but the others sang in Hebrew and Yiddish, in German and Russian, and in Polish for the latest hits like *Pani Maryśka, Telefonistka (Miss Mary, the Telephone Operator)*. Lola, while skipping to school, sang in the most exotic tongue of all,

> *On the Good Ship*
> *Lollipop,*
> *It's a sweet trip*
> *To a candy shop,*

and other songs from the hit parade, though Lola didn't know a lollipop from a polliwog. She got her far-out lyrics from her youngest brother, who played the piano and trumpet and led the Melody Makers, a band with its name on its big bass drum in English.

One day in 1933, Lola's father, a diabetic, passed away, and her brothers became an eight-headed father for her. The brothers danced when the older sister married a quarry owner near Cracow, but they rent their clothes when the other sister eloped with a dairy owner in Königshütte, a German who wasn't a Jew. In time, the barrel-chested brothers went to the dairy owner's home and, as they leaned over him like gorillas, told him, "We're taking her," and then took his weeping wife away. As for

Lola, the brothers did the "Who are you?" bit if Lola as much as entrusted her Polish, history and geography books to some virtuous lad. One summer night, Lola wasn't home at six, and her brothers scattered to all eight corners of Będzin asking, "Have you seen her?" They were still frantic when Lola came home at midnight, for she'd fallen asleep at the movies while watching all the four screenings of *Rose Marie* and memorizing the *Indian Love Song*.

The next day, Lola was skipping to school singing,

> *When I'm calling you-ou-ou,*
> *Will you answer too-oo-oo,*

gazing uphill like Nelson Eddy. She didn't dream of America (she wanted to stay in Poland, where the Potoks were), but her American repertoire was the envy of all the other girls, whose list of romantic ballads ended at *Dovid un Donia*, a song in Yiddish about a Yeshiva student and his Ukrainian *shiksa*. "Teach us," the others would beg, and Lola would write out a new acquisition in Polish phonetic letters,

> *Bifor da fydlers hew fled,*
> *Bifor dej esk as tu pej da byl,*
> *Ęd łajl li styl hew da częs,*
> *Lec fejs da miuzyk ęd dęs.*

"Um. . . ," the other girls would say.

"Before the fiddlers have fled," Lola would patiently tell them, and the girls would stumble along till Lola came to the rousing coda, "Let's face the music and dance!"

Now, one little girl who Lola shared songs with was Ada Neufeld. Ada was Jewish, but her songs couldn't be further from the *"Dayenu"*'s and the "Merry, merry be"s. Ada, who lived near a Catholic boy, who loved the boy's colorful religion, who knew the words to "Our father who art. . . ," and who told the Catholic priest, "When I grow up, I'll be a nun," the priest patting her on her shoulder, saying, "Good girl!"—Ada sang Christmas carols. It might be summer, but Ada went to school singing,

> *W żłobie leży,*
> *Który pobieży,*
> *Kolędować. . .*

her hands clasped like a Carmelite nun. Intrigued, Lola once checked out the Catholic church, a fourteenth-century edifice with an onion dome, a spire above that, a ball above that, and a cross above all.

It was Sunday. The door was six inches thick, but it slowly swung open at Lola's touch. She peeped in at the churchgoers, glorious in the stained-glass light. The windows depicted a blue-cloaked woman holding a gold-haloed baby, up front were the same two people, painted, above them a pair of caryatids held up some saints, and on top were some swords, a cross, and a book whose title was GLORIA PATRIA FILIA ET SPIRITU SANCTO. In the wood-tasseled pulpit in red gold-embroidered robes was Ada's priest, giving a sermon about the Jews. "They degraded our Lord," Lola heard him say. "They reviled Him and had Him crucified. They aren't good!" His small round glasses reflected the golden light as the priest said, "The Jews are the Antichrist!"

Lola fled. She ran past the church's chestnut trees to her haven on Modrzejowska Street. She still sang American songs, not Christmas carols, at her eighteenth birthday party in 1939.

In 1939, Kattowitz still was in Poland, and Germany was twenty miles west at the picture-postcard city of Gleiwitz. The city had one hundred thousand inhabitants. At its center was a quaint city hall full of whale-shaped gargoyles, the rainwater running from the whales' lips. In the square around it, the children played at a statue of Neptune, and the mothers sat on the benches chatting or reading the *People's Observer* (WAR MOBILIZATION IN POLAND). Three jets of water spouted from Neptune's trident, sprinkling the children's heads and the god's bronze belly, changing it to the color of old gold coins. At the sides of the square, the four-story homes had such whimsical things on their pastel facades as Ionic columns or deer-antler trophies, and the street-level signs said CAFE, RESTAURANT, APOTHEKE. From here the city of Gleiwitz spread in concentric circles, and a sort of Toonerville trolley took the merchants, the coal-mine-company clerks, and the many soldiers and SS to and fro for eight cents each.

In the evening, the people of Gleiwitz went to the opera house to listen to their all-time favorites, *Il Trovatore* and *Tannhaüser*, while the children of Lola's age checked in at the hall of the Hitler Youth and its counterpart, the Union of German Women. Here they were taught to shoot wooden guns and to sing patriotic songs like,

> *Wach auf, wach auf, du Deutsches land,*
> *Du hast genug geschlaffen!*
> *Bedenk, was Gott an dich gewandt,*
> *Wozu er dich erschaffen!*
>
> *Wake up, wake up, you German country,*
> *You have slept enough!*

> *Consider what God intended for you,*
> *And why He created you!*

and, as the evening ended,

> *Um Deutsche erde kämpfen wir!*
> *Für Adolf Hitler sterben wir!*
>
> *We fight for German soil!*
> *We die for Adolf Hitler!*

On the way home, the trolley cars rolling like tanks, almost plowing the cobblestones up, the boys looked in awe (and the girls in adoration) at the soldiers and SS, telling them, "We shot a gun in the Hitler Youth!"

One day in August, 1939, the SS in Gleiwitz got a telephone call from Berlin saying, "Grandma's dead." Putting on Polish uniforms, the SS drove to the edge of the city, where, like a crazy erector set, a mass of creosote-covered logs and of L-shaped angle irons rose to form a radio tower twenty stories high. In the studio under it, a German working for Goebbels, the Minister of Propaganda, was broadcasting to Poland when the SS attacked. The SS shot bullets into the ceiling, seized the microphone, shouted in Polish, "Attention! The tower now is Polish! Long live Poland!" and, four minutes later, left, but it left behind what it called canned goods: a number of corpses in Polish uniforms. The next day, Friday, September 1, the mothers at Neptune's statue read of the Polish provocation in the *People's Observer*. "It was clearly the signal for a general attack," the paper said, but Hitler counterattacked that day and started World War II.

In two days the Germans were in Będzin. As the half-tracks rolled in, Lola was scared but a number of Jews were waving, believing the bombings were over. They weren't. On Friday as Jews at the temple welcomed the Sabbath by saying the 92d Psalm, "At the work of Thy hands I sing glad song," the temple suddenly caught fire, the flames climbing up the white curtains and melting the gold stained glass. In the smoke, the Jews tried to rescue the Torah, the scroll with the first five books of the Bible, traditionally written by God, but others rushed out the temple doors, where the SS shot them. The cries of the worshipers were like an enormous scream. Eight hundred died, but one hundred fled next door to the Catholic priest, who hid them in spite of the law that a Pole who harbored a Jew would die. The priest who had said, "The Jews are the Antichrist," was the bishop now, and the priest in Będzin was someone new.

By mid-September, Lola had to walk on the street, not the sidewalk, and sit in the center of Będzin's own Toonerville trolley. She tried to avoid going out, for the streets of Będzin—of Bendsburg, the Germans called it—were worse than the streets of Shanghai. Every day, the SS would snatch up Lola's schoolmates, hand them some shovels, tell them to dig up the dirt, whatever, or send them to farms and factories in Germany. At age eighteen, Lola was an obvious choice for the faraway labor camps that the SS called concentration camps. She was 1-A and she knew it.

Now, this was early in World War II. The girls the SS was picking up didn't know what a concentration camp was. In the first contingent, the girls were whispering, "Shh. Don't tell anyone. We're going to a chocolate factory." As they walked west, the SS saying, *"Die arme ruhig.* Don't swing your arms," the SS not saying why, the arms at every girl's sides like in a parade of wooden soldiers—as they walked, the girls started laughing, "We will eat chocolate now," and they thought of their mothers' noodles, on top of the noodles chocolate bars, the heat of the noodles melting them. Not till they got to Gleiwitz to a room full of rows of gas burners did Lola's schoolmates say, "This isn't chocolate."

In fact, they were in a soot factory, a factory that made soot. The word that came back to Lola was, the girls had to work from eight to four, four to midnight, or midnight to eight every day to keep the flames at 707 degrees. As the soot drifted down, the girls sucked it up with vacuums, packed it in 50-pound sacks, tied it with wires, labeled it "P" for *pulver,* powder—it would be used in gunpowder, the SS said—carried it to conveyor belts as the SS shouted, *"Schnell!"* and loaded it on. The soot went into their ears, their eyes, the spaces between their teeth, and in minutes the girls were unrecognizable, calling out, "Abba?" "Anna?" "Aviva? Where are you?" By the end of a shift, the girls were as black as chimney sweeps—as Negroes, they'd say, and one girl even sang sadly,

> We look as if our mothers were black,
> Some of our children will be black,
> Some of our children white. . . .

As they went to the shower room, the commandant stood at the door, leering, and the girl who was Senior Jew, the *Judenälteste,* came in her boots when the girls were soaped up and turned off the showers, shouting, "Out!" The Senior Jew, a girl with a face full of chicken-pox pits and an envious personality, had got her position when an SS woman asked, "Who wants to be Senior Jew?" Her hand shooting up, the girl with the pits was excused from the soot-making work and got her own shower, too.

But that wasn't all. The word Lola got was, the girls at the camp were being hurt by the rubber clubs of the SS commandant and the Senior Jew. Lola was anxious to stay in Będzin, and one day Rivka, her mother, told her, "I know how you can," for Rivka had seen that the girls who the SS abducted had one common characteristic: they were unmarried. A husband and children made a girl draft-exempt, it appeared to Rivka. A friend of Lola's had married a brother of Shlomo the Tailor, and Lola's friend Ada, who'd gone to a Catholic school, who'd been number-one in Polish class but, as a Jew, had been made number-two, and who'd given up Christmas carols for Zionist songs like,

Sea of Galilee! My Sea of Galilee!
Are you real? Or are you a dream?

—Ada had married one of Lola's brothers. Another girl in Będzin had married another brother, and the best chef in Będzin, Zlata Martyn, had married another one, and Rivka observed that the SS hadn't abducted them. She said to Lola, "Get married."

Inquiries were made. Now, Rivka had a friend whose nephew was a Będzin bachelor. Although thirty-five, he was irresistible to women, who often phoned him and told him in Yiddish, *"Ich hob dich leeb.* I love you," and who even downed bottles of iodine in his living room in the hopes of dramatically dying for him. Lola and the Casanova met, her predicament and his passion intertwined, and in August, 1941, in a small ceremony in Będzin, Lola was married to Shlomo the Tailor, a man whose last name was Ackerfeld. "Now the Germans won't take you," Rivka said. "But hurry! Get pregnant!" In fact Lola already was.

She gave birth to Itusha, or Itu, in April, 1942. A mother at age twenty-one, she was also eight brothers to Itu, for she believed that a girl should be sheltered, and Shlomo, her husband, didn't do it. Lola wrapped Itu, breast-fed her, and sang lullabies to her in Hebrew,

Lie down, lie down,
Your daddy's working,
The jackals are howling
Far away. . . .

but there was no work for Shlomo, for the SS was closer now. Itu was one month old when the SS sent some older people to Auschwitz, and she was crawling when the SS sent her, Lola, Shlomo, and the rest of the

Jews to a ghetto outside of Będzin. Itu lived in a room with twelve adults
as Lola still sought to be her mother/brother.

By now, the SS was killing people. The first was a sweet-smiling friend
of Lola's, Pinek Mąka—or so Lola heard, though in time she'd learn that
he was alive and a very important officer in the olive-clothed organization, the SS's nemesis. The false report of his death was a blow to Lola,
who'd grown up on Pinek's street, played with him at the dandelion castle, and sat around fires with him at a Zionist summer camp near Czechoslovakia. The sparks had climbed up as Lola sang in Yiddish,

> *Arum daym fayer,*
> *Zingen mir leeder,*
> *Dee nacht iz tayer,*
> *Un mir vern nisht meeder,*

> *Around the fire,*
> *We're singing songs,*
> *The night is dear,*
> *And we aren't tired,*

and as Lola looked past the flames at Pinek's cherubic face, as red and as
round as the harvest moon. Some nights as Lola slept, Pinek had crept to
her cabin and done the most dastardly deed he was capable of: had drawn
a mustache on Lola's face, and Lola had woken up saying, "Oh!" In
twenty years, Lola had never known a mean or malevolent bone in
Pinek's body. The boy was pure good, and the world had never forgiven
him for it.

After graduating in Będzin, Pinek, a student of metal engineering, had
gone to Warsaw Polytechnic. One day his math professor had gone to the
blackboard and drawn a geometric curve, the cissoid of Diocles, say. The
professor then wrote the formula for it, $r = 2a \tan\theta \sin\theta$, and then asked,
"Who knows what the tangent would be?" Pinek raised his hand eagerly,
but the professor said, "We don't need any Jewish answers."

Pinek wasn't discourteous. He said very sweetly, "Sir? If you don't
need any Jewish answers, why—" and he held up his copy of *Analytic
Geometry* by Professor Henryk Mąka of Stefan Batory University, in
Wilno—"why are you using my uncle's textbook?"

"You sonofabitch! Sit down!" the professor shouted, and as the class let
out, the other students used wooden bats on Pinek's head till Pinek
passed out.

The next year, the Germans were in Będzin, and the chief of the Jewish police came to Pinek's home. He wore a blue-and-white armband and

a blue-and-white visored hat with a Star of David, and he carried a whip that the Germans had given him. "We need volunteers for the camps," he said to Pinek.

"No, I work for the Germans here in Będzin," Pinek explained.

"The hell you do! You want to live soft like before the war!"

"No, Julek, I work very hard," said Pinek, who did indeed work in a German factory, making knives.

The fat round face of the chief turned red. "Well, I'm sending you to a camp!" he cried, cracking his whip on Pinek's cheek. "I'll show you who's boss!" Instinctively, Pinek seized the chief's tie, but the chief and his four policemen fell on Pinek, beating him and calling him, "*Hacher!* You troublemaker!" "*Huren zeen!* You sonofabitch!" "*Shaigitz!* You Christian!" Pinek passed out, and the chief dragged him off and delivered him to the German police while slapping each hand on the other as though saying, "I'm rid of that *dreck!*" But then the knife-factory director arrived. He told the German police, "Look at his hands!" at Pinek's hands, and "Look at that *schweinehund*'s hands!" at the hands of the Jewish police chief. "And tell me who's working for us!"

The Germans sent Pinek home. Pinek's last feud with the anti-good elements was in 1942, when he worked in a German factory making the nuts and bolts—the real nuts and bolts—for German tanks. One night, the bolt machine broke down. The factory director, a Nazi, was frantic till Pinek fixed it, but still someone blamed it on Pinek, and the SS secret police, the Gestapo, came and arrested him. It took him to Kattowitz, its sooty headquarters city, to an office as big as a Hollywood set. Three crystal chandeliers hung in the office like in *Hotel Berlin,* and a collection of Nazi flags, emblems, and cavalry sabers covered each wall. On the farthest wall was a portrait of Hitler, beneath it a big mahogany desk, a brown leather chair, and a Gestapo colonel. "Why did you arrest me?" Pinek asked him.

"You sabotaged the bolt-making machine," the colonel said. He wore his black cap aslant like a Frenchman's beret, and he looked at Pinek crookedly.

"No sir, I didn't," Pinek said.

And wham! A man who had Pinek's arms in a grizzly bear's grip held on, but another let go and struck him. "Admit that you did it," the colonel said.

"No, I worked every day for the German Reich!"

And wham! Day after day, Pinek was brought to this room and the slant-hatted colonel. The two Gestapo men beat him with fists, sticks, and wooden clubs. They punched him in his stomach and, as he gasped for air, punched him in his stomach again. "No, I have witnesses!" Pinek said,

but it didn't help. The two men took little pins, pushing them up his fingernails like surgical instruments in spite of Pinek's screams. He passed
out, but the two men slapped him to consciousness, and his blood
dripped on a rubber mat as they continued to torture him. At last Pinek,
his forehead bloody, his fingernails black, his body the color of rotten
meat, his head telling him, *Why prolong it? Whatever I do they'll kill
me*—Pinek lied to the colonel, saying, "I did it." The colonel gave him a
fountain pen and a two-page confession in German,

*I, Pinek Mąka, willingly and without duress, confess that I destroyed
the machine at the Silesia Factory. I did this to sabotage the war effort
of the Third Reich, and . . .*

and Pinek signed it.

At that the colonel practically sighed. The set of his jaw relaxed, as
though an ordeal were over for *him*. "Now, that's the boy," the colonel
said. "All this time I've been saying you did it. You see, I was right." Pinek
had no time to contemplate why a German colonel needed a Jew for cor-
roboration, for the man sentenced him to the gallows and had him carried off. The word in Będzin was, Pinek was dead, and as Lola mourned
him, she told herself that if Germans could kill the gentlest person there
was, who wouldn't they kill? Herself? Her husband? Her baby?

Itu was fifteen months old and could say *mama* and *papa* when the SS
sent her and her mother and father to Auschwitz. The day before, on Saturday, July 31, 1943, the Jews were warned that the SS was coming.
There was in Będzin a German uniform factory where Ada and Zlata, the
wives of two brothers of Lola's, worked, cutting up camouflage-colored
wool, stitching it into clothing, and sewing the buttons on, and that day
the factory director, a German with wavy black hair, told some of the
Jews, "Tonight will be the *Judenrein*," the cleaning-out of Będzin's Jews.
"Get your family. Bring them here, and I'll hide them." By night there
were four hundred people under the German camouflage, but Lola and
her dapper husband weren't among them. "They'll kill us at Auschwitz!"
Lola had told him, but Shlomo had answered, "No, that isn't possible."

The SS came after midnight. As soon as Lola heard shouts outside,
she, Itu and Shlomo went into a secret potato cellar, closing the trap door
behind them. The smell of potatoes enveloped them. A half dozen other
people were there, the Hassidics praying, the babies wailing, the mothers
clapping the babies' mouths saying, "Shh!" the babies suffocating, dying,
the mothers looking aghast. Above them, the SS kicked in the door,
shouted, "*Juden heraus!*" and stomped like a cattle stampede, the dust in

the cracks of the ceiling settling on Lola's and Shlomo's heads. In seconds, the trap door opened, a flashlight beam like a lightning bolt hit, and
the SS shouted, *"Heraus!"* Lola and Shlomo climbed up, an SS man
pulling them by the hair, booting them, beating them, calling them
"Schmutzige Juden! Dirty Jews!" Lola wanted to yell at Shlomo, "Do
something!" thinking, *My brothers would!*

She held Itu tight in her arms. As the sun came up, as she and the others marched to the station, and as the SS gloated, "At last this city is
Judenrein!" the SS took some babies away to rip in two pieces or pitch at
the walls or toss in the air and catch like quoits on their bayonets—but
Lola held Itu tighter. At the pretty yellow-brick station, a girl put her
newborn boy by the statue of the Virgin Mary in the hope that a Polish
woman might find and adopt him—but Lola held on. Then, the Jews
marched into the station with its INFORMACJA information booths and its
KASA BILETOWA ticket booths and up the wide granite stairs onto the train
to Auschwitz, Lola holding Itu come what may. *I'll never let her go,* Lola
thought.

3

That same day, the Jews underneath the camouflage at the uniform factory came out, and the German director went to the Gestapo commandant in Będzin. "I have four hundred people," the young director said. "I need them for the German war effort."

"Where did you get them?"

"What matters is, I got them," the director said, and he soon had the four hundred cutting, stitching, sweeping, etcetera, sleeping on cots and eating cakes, the gifts of the German soldier guards. No one there knew if Lola was still alive, but two of her brothers and Ada and Zlata, their wives, were still sewing buttons as Ada sang *Sea of Galilee* and Zlata, a round, jolly, outspoken girl, told Yiddish jokes.

Ada was pregnant, and she was six months pregnant in January, 1944, when the Gestapo imprisoned the factory director and the rumor went round that the Jews were going to Auschwitz. By then, Ada knew that at Auschwitz a child was an albatross, dooming itself and its mother to cyanide, and Ada paid $1,200 to a Polish doctor to come to the factory and to abort her first child by Caesarian section. Ada still wasn't well on January 20, 1944, when the Gestapo assigned Lola's brothers to far-off concentration camps and Ada and Zlata to Auschwitz, twenty miles south. "Auschwitz. My convalescent home," Ada told Zlata wryly.

A truck picked Ada and Zlata up. As it drove off, Zlata rolled up a canvas side, and a blast of winter air whistled in. In the van with her, the German soldiers from the factory fingered their rifles warily, and the other seamsters and seamstresses said, "Are you nuts? They're going to kill you!" "Well," Zlata said, "if they kill me, I'd rather be looking out-side," and she gazed at the low, rolling, snow-covered hills and the crows scratching lines across the sky. The crows disappeared as Ada and Zlata drove through an arch into Auschwitz.

All around them were barbed wires, and a number of girls were marching by and singing in German with Yiddish accents. Zlata, still look-ing out, had heard that the SS had spared some Jews to help kill the Jews who followed them, and, in fact, the girls going by were in the baggage *kommando,* the baggage crew. As soon as a Jew was dead, the girls would go through his or her baggage to take out the soap, toothpaste, tooth-brush, and circular tins of Sambo, Bison or Egu shoe polish ("Your shoes look fine, With that Egu shine"). The girls were now marching home, and Zlata peered out to see if one might be Lola, alive. None was, and Zlata turned to a German soldier, asking, "What work do these women do?"

"Don't talk! They're going to kill us!" the others said.

"So what can I lose? What work do they do?"

"I don't know," the soldier answered. "But you're going to do that work too."

"We aren't going to the crematorium?"

"No," the kind soldier said.

But they stopped at a building with a disproportionate smokestack. Ada, in her galoshes, Zlata, in good leather boots, and the fifty-five others got off, and the German soldiers escorted them to a room with a row of old pitted faucets, like a shower room. The door closed behind them, and the Jews concluded correctly that they were in a cyanide chamber. One girl swallowed a poison pill, and the others started to wail in Yiddish, *"Nisht aroys!* We'll never get out!" In fact, half of these people would live to tell about this, for the SS man who usually furnished the C-ration-colored cans with the GIFT! or POISON! inscriptions, who usually used a hammer, chisel, and can opener to open them, and who usually dumped them into a vent while laughing, *"Na, gib ihnen schön zu fressen.* Well, give them something good to eat"—the SS man wasn't there, for the SS didn't want to use up insect exterminator on a room just three percent full. It told the German soldiers to watch the Jews until the next train pulled in.

So the door opened, and a strange night began. *"Hat jemand hunger?* Is anyone hungry?" a German soldier said, and, when the Jews said yes, the Germans gave them some boiled potatoes, also some wine. *"Zigarette?"* the Germans said, and as Zlata stood smoking one, a Ger-man told her, "I'm worried about my wife and my children in Germany."

"Why?"

"All that bombing. I haven't had any letters from them."

"Ah. . . ."

As the night wore on, Ada and Zlata heard the sound of iron scraping on iron near by. It came, in fact, from the grates of the crematorium ovens, as Ada and Zlata learned when a Jew on the oven crew opened the hatch to their gray-walled room. He seemed surprised to see people living, sleeping and snoring there, and he said to Zlata, "Where are you people from?"

"From Będzin."

"Well, you'll all be hamburgers soon."

"Oh, we will?" Zlata said. She was wearing culottes, and she put her foot on a bench so her knee could confront the impudent boy. "I know a woman in Będzin. She makes sausages there. Is that what you do?"

"Zlata. . . ," the others began.

"Just wait," said the oven-crew boy. "We're going to make meatballs from you!"

"And you? You think you'll be made into something else?"

"Zlata, don't goad him," the others said.

"Why not?" Zlata said. "We're going to die anyway."

At that point, a second boy on the oven crew came to the hatch with a look of "What's going on?" He looked at Ada, age twenty-two, and Zlata, a little older, and said to the German soldiers, "You can't have these people gassed. They aren't *selected* yet." He then hurried off, and he returned at dawn telling the Jews, "Mengele's coming. So pretty up."

"Why?" Zlata asked. "Is he going to marry me?" But she put her lipstick on and set her hair in two buns like mickey-mouse ears, the mode then in Poland. Ada got ready too, and one girl put on some rouge while shooing her four-year-old and six-year-old sons away. She told them, "Don't tell them you're with me."

A man now appeared. He was wearing white gloves, black boots, and an SS green uniform as tightly tailored as something from Saville Row. The man, who indeed was Mengele, the top doctor at Auschwitz, immediately asked, "Are there tailors here?"

"Yes!" Since every adult was from the uniform factory, every adult said, "Yes!"

"Good. We need tailors," Mengele said. He then started pointing to Jews saying, "Left," or "Right." The old people, mothers and children, including the four-year-old and the six-year-old boys, and one girl of Ada's age who wanted to stay with her mother went to the left, twenty-nine people. Ada, Zlata, the mother of the four-year-old and the six-year-old, and the girl who'd swallowed the poison pill—the pill was old, and it hadn't worked—went to the right, twenty-eight. "*Aufstellen.* Line up," the SS men with Mengele shouted to group number two, and Ada and

Zlata were happy as people pulled from the sea as they marched to an Auschwitz reception center.

There, their "I hit the jackpot" emotions continued as the SS told them, *"Die kleide herunter!* Undress!" Zlata pulled off a 100-deutschmark bill glued to the sole of her foot, giving it to the SS, but another girl who had bills inside her vagina didn't take them out. *"Zum haare schneiden!* To the haircuts!" the SS said, and a man cut off Zlata's mickey-mouse ears and Ada's long hair, except for the two wild tufts under the arms of her glasses. "Ada, you're like a religious boy," Zlata said of the new scruffy sideburns. *"Zu den duschen!* To the showers!" the SS said. *"Einseifen!* Soap up! *Abwaschen!* Rinse off! *Hinaus!* Get out! *Schneller!"* the SS said, swabbing a foul-smelling fluid on Ada and Zlata. *"Anziehen!* Get dressed!" the SS continued, handing a size-six skirt to Zlata, who wore size ten, and another mismatch to Ada. Then, the SS had Ada tattooed with a "74729" and Zlata, close behind her, with a "74731," and, their pin-pricks burning, their bald heads freezing, the two girls in too-big shoes clomped off to their beds in a low wooden building.

And fell asleep. At about three, Zlata awoke to a tap-tap-tap on her window and to the whisper of "Zlata!" She sat up and peered through the rime-covered pane at a bald-headed girl in the frosty night air, and Zlata then gasped, saying, "Lola?"

"I'll come back tonight," Lola whispered. And hurried away.

Soon after that, Ada, Zlata, and the 1,500 other women in their building awoke to a reveille call of *"Aufstehen!* Get up!" Their building was a stable whose prior inhabitants were the horses of Germany's Africa Corps. On the walls were the big iron rings that the horses had once been tethered to, as well as such signs as ALL MANGY ANIMALS MUST BE CULLED OUT. To convert this to human use, the SS had tacked up additional signs like NO SMOKING IN THE BARRACKS, CAPS OFF IN THE BARRACKS, and QUIET IN THE BARRACKS, and it had built shelves in each of the stalls so one dozen women could sleep on the ground, one dozen more on the lower shelf and one dozen more on the upper one. The upper one was the best one, for the air was less fetid there and the rain that came through the roof trickled down to the lower shelf and the ground, a "bed" of permanent mud. The space between shelves was two feet, six inches, not quite enough for a woman to sit in, so Ada and Zlata had to slide out like caterpillars at the call of *"Aufstehen!"*

The head count lasted till dawn. As it counted, the SS used rubber and wooden clubs on the women who weren't motionless, yelling, *"Du schmutziger hund!* You dirty dog!" *"Du mistbiene!* You dung bug!" *"Du arschloch!* You asshole!" For breakfast, the women each had a pint of some yellow fluid, and the rest of the day they stood, sat, or lay on the snow while the sun crept across the sky. Around them, Auschwitz spread out for three hundred acres. Zlata was in good spirits, considering, but Ada was still depressed from her Caesarian abortion. The girl who had told her two sons, "Don't tell them you're with me," kept staring at the smoke coming out of the smokestacks and coasting like rain clouds across the sun. She kept repeating, "There are my children, there. . . ." Though almost all Jews at Auschwitz went, as they said, up the chimney, the ones in Ada and Zlata's group would soon have the job of sliding them into the ovens, cutting the diamonds out of their prayer shawls, piling up their granny glasses, etcetera. But now they were still in quarantine, milling around until they had a supper of four slices' worth of black bread apiece, with oleo.

The meal didn't appeal to Zlata. She had run the best restaurant in Będzin, and to her the bread tasted disastrous. She didn't eat it—until like an apparition at her window was Lola again. Lola yelled, "You've got to eat it!"

"Lola, I can't. . . ."

"You might as well kill yourself then! You might as well throw yourself on the electrified wire!" Now, Lola actually *yelled* this. Her face was red, and it turned to rose as her breath turned to frost on Zlata's window. To Zlata, Lola seemed to have metamorphosed into one or all of her brothers, yelling, "Do this!" "Do that!" And truly she had, for Lola was now alone at age twenty-two and now was her own big brother.

Her loved ones, Lola had learned, were dead. When the *Judenrein* happened in August, Rivka, her mother, was hiding at a Polish friend's, but the Germans announced that the Poles who were hiding the Jews would die, and Rivka had gallantly turned herself in and, together with Lola's nephew, Zlata's five-year-old son, had died in an Auschwitz cyanide chamber. By then, Lola's oldest sister and her quarry-owner husband had also been cyanided, as had their delicate five-year-old daughter. Their other daughter, a sixteen-year-old who had often dressed up in her mother's *haute-couture* clothes, saying, "Someday, I'll inherit this," had been alive in Auschwitz till recently. She had then caught typhus, and Lola had crawled through the wires to bring her a dab of Rivka's all-purpose remedy, mustard. "It wakes your heart up," Lola had said, but her niece lay in bed exhausted till she was "selected" by Mengele and sent to a cyanide chamber by Hössler, the good-natured commandant of the Auschwitz women's camp. Three wives and three other children of Lola's brothers had died in the cyanide chambers, but the brother who was a CPA was still alive at Auschwitz, reportedly. So was Shlomo, Lola's ineffectual husband, who in August had stared at the smokestacks as people told him, "They're burning the Jews." He'd answered, "Are you sick?" and he still hadn't believed it in September, as the gray smoke floated over him and tiny white chips of bone fell into the mud around him. As for Itu, their baby girl—well, Lola just couldn't remember. Itu had been with her the morning of Sunday, August 1, when Lola arrived at Auschwitz, and hadn't been with her at night, but Lola couldn't remember why. In all, thirteen people in Lola's family were dead, and Lola had chosen to act like her brothers to keep the others alive.

"Eat it!!!" she screamed to Zlata, and Zlata ate the Auschwitz bread.

Night after night, Lola came back like the most emphatic of Jewish mothers, yelling, "Eat!" Whatever daytime work she did, she didn't do on Sunday, apparently, for she showed up in Ada and Zlata's stable that day. She was thin, maybe eighty pounds, and her dishrag dress dangled like one on a wire hanger, but she had something that Ada and Zlata didn't: a look in her eyes of "I shall survive!" Indeed, some of the girls from Będzin were already dead. The girl who had told her two sons, "Don't tell them you're with me," had killed herself by walking into the electrified wire. Ada was wasting away on her shelf, staring at the splinters above her or, at night, dreaming of the Catholic boy's home in Będzin. In his parlor, in Ada's dream, was a baby grand, on top was a vase of red lilies, on the stand was a book of Christmas carols, and Ada was singing along. And then she'd wake up in Auschwitz, her hair gone, her head chilled, her mouth full of chili peppers: of sores from the sawdust bread. She lay like a dying patient on her mattress—till Sunday, when Lola hurried over.

Lola didn't quite do what her brothers would've done. She didn't stuff the black bread in Ada's mouth, but she yelled, she *yelled*, at Ada, "You've got to eat it!"

"I can't. . . ."

"If you don't eat the bread, you'll die! You'll die of hunger, you'll die of typhus, you'll die!"

"It burns. . . ."

"You'll die!"

That didn't matter to Ada. She wanted to die, but she wanted more for Lola to stop annoying her. Still crying, she ate the bread—but Lola didn't stop.

"Get down from your bunk! Get down!"

"I'm sick. . . ."

"You're spoiled! My brother spoiled you!" said Lola, jealous that Ada's husband, Lola's brother, had chosen to spoil his bride instead of his little sister. "My brother isn't here for you!" said Lola, whose brother wasn't there for Lola, either. "You've got to take care of yourself now! Get down!"

Ada climbed down and Lola left. Ada had diarrhea now, and her mouth was a fire eater's. She sought to soothe it by singing softly,

> Maybe these things never happened,
> Maybe I never woke up in the morning,
> Maybe I never immersed myself
>   In the Sea of Galilee.
> Oh, Sea of Galilee! My Sea. . . .

Some other girls in the stable gathered around her. One sang along with her, but another one shouted, "Shut up! Let her sing!" The barracks boss, a Jewish girl with a wooden club, came by. "Why all the noise?" she shouted but, on hearing the singing, said, "It reminds me of Płońsk," her village in Poland. "My brother was in the Zionists there. Go on." Ada went on, the barracks boss bringing her hot milk and honey, and Ada did this every day. She and Zlata survived.

The quarantine ended in February, 1944. Normally, Ada and Zlata would now be assigned to a crew like the baggage crew, but Lola, who didn't work in such ghoulish jobs but in a German factory, managed to get them assigned there. One day after roll call, Ada and Zlata, with hundreds of other girls and Lola, marched out at five in the morning, singing,

> Von der Maas bis an die Memel,
> Von der Etsch bis an den Belt,
> Deutschland, Deutschland, über alles,
> Über alles in der welt!
>
> Germany, Germany, over everything,
> Over everything in the world!

"Lauter! Louder!" the bosses cried to the freezing girls. The bosses weren't SS but other women prisoners, not Jews but common criminals, who used hard rubber and wooden clubs if a girl wasn't singing, if her arms were swinging, or if she was eating garbage along the way. Many bosses were Polish and Czech, but the top one was German, a red-headed freckle-faced prostitute with a cry that made cracks in the icy air, "Schweinehunde Juden! Dirty Jews!" She walked like an ape, as if she might land on all fours—and she did, for she fell down in the snow once, weary from beating a Jew.

Ada and Zlata took Lola's word that they had it good, comparatively. After walking three miles, they got to a place called the Union Factory.

Ada was assigned to use a small spoon, smaller than an espresso spoon, to put black powder in small metal pellets, and Zlata was assigned to screw hot screws in small metal cones. The other girls from Będzin had to put nuts on bolts after oiling them with hot oil. The oil splattered on their arms, scalding them, so they sold their bread to buy paper sacks with the label ZEMENT, CEMENT, to wear like a knight-in-armor's brassarts. As for Lola, she stood drilling holes of a fifth-of-an-inch diameter in the nose of the small metal cones, but she was a foreman, too, and she told the girls and even the German engineers, "Do this! Do that!" She now had the take-over temperament of her brothers, and her one imperfection was one she shared with the colonel in *Bridge on the River Kwai*. Like him, she didn't stop and say, "What am I doing?"

For the factory made ammunition. It was started by Krupp in April, 1943, at the order of Hitler, who had been grumbling, "I have 150,000 convicts making slippers." A half year later, the SS went to the Krupp people saying, "Your deadline is up," and hired the Union people instead. Soon, Union was making the fuses for 37-millimeter anti-aircraft shells. In each hole that Lola drilled went a wooden hammer, which, when it hit the bottom of an Allied bomber, sent a steel striker into Ada's black powder. This then exploded, and the steel that Zlata had screwed together could bring down a Flying Fortress. Her eye out for Ada and Zlata, Lola didn't see how counterproductive she was. She traded her bread for galoshes for Zlata, she taught the trading arts to Ada, she fed the smelly soup to Zlata, telling her, "Hold your nose!" she nursed her nearest and dearest when someone beat them—and she made anti-aircraft shells. She saw her short-range objective, that's all.

All around her, the girls were working slow. If the SS wasn't watching them, they sat on their benches reading communiqués in the newspapers some of their bosses wrapped up their sausages in, or sat writing to "boyfriends" at Auschwitz, letters like,

> *My Dear Heniek,*
>
> *I was embarrassed when we first met at the wire fence. My looks didn't appeal to anyone else but you. A shaved head, a striped dress with a filthy cord, and a pair of wooden shoes that banged on the pavement loudly. But nevertheless. . . .*

or sat gossiping. "She said she was raped," a girl would say. "The lawyer in Sosnowiec asked her how. So she lay down, and she pulled her underpants off!"

"In the lawyer's office?"

"Yes!" And the gossip went on, the girls engrossed, the SS not noticing, the screws for the anti-aircraft shells lying in the bins like dead flies, and Lola hurrying by on one or another endeavor.

Her in-laws were soldiering too. Zlata kept falling asleep, and she once had the *chutzpa* to tell the SS, "My tooth hurts," the SS incredibly getting her a bed, blanket, aspirin, and a warm anti-aircraft fuse to put on her cheek. Ada was singing in German *Lili Marlene*, in Polish *Pani Maryśka, Telefonistka*, in Russian *Katushka*, and even in English,

> *Sweetheart! Sweetheart! Sweetheart!*
> *Will you love me. . . .*

while inspecting the holes in the small metal cones. She also was doing something the SS could hang her for. Unknown to Lola, Ada had been in the underground in Będzin, and she was now putting the cones with the too-big holes in the PASS instead of the FAIL container. In battle, the air that whooshed through the holes threw the strikers against the gunpowder prematurely. The shells exploded, killing or wounding the German anti-aircraft men.

Lola didn't know about this. Not until summer, 1944, did a look of "What am I doing?" come over her. One day, her cousin, her mother's sister's child, a short girl who worked at a bowl of black powder, gave her a bit of cloth as small as a spitball to smuggle from the Union Factory. Not arguing, Lola hid the cloth in her short blonde hair. She walked out at six o'clock, the SS searching the girls ahead of her and behind her but Lola getting by. Her head scarf was on securely as she marched through the mud singing, *"Deutschland, Deutschland,"* as Ada and Zlata sang too, and as the bosses shouted, *"Lauter!"* beating the Jewish *schweinehunde*. One hour later, Lola got to her stable, and she, Ada, Zlata, and many other girls took the cloths out of their hair, mouths and vaginas, rolling them open. Inside each one was a pinch of black powder—gunpowder— that the girls jiggled into a bag and slipped like an illegal drug to the oven-crew boys. All summer long, the girls left the factory doing this. Sweetheart. Sweetheart. Sweetheart.

The eight hundred oven-crew boys hid the gunpowder in a crematorium ceiling. At the ovens beneath it, they used a long iron fork to push the dead people in and poke the dead cinders off. In each combustion chamber were three people, in each oven two or three chambers, and in each crematorium either two or five ovens, so as many as forty-five people were burning in any one crematorium at any one moment. At the five crematoriums, the flames of all this humanity roared out the squat, square-sided chimneys like the flames of enormous torches. They turned to billows of smoke that, as the damp autumn weather came, didn't rise to the sky but spread like a tarpaulin over the women's camp and, across the train tracks, the camp for men. There, a Jew named Adam Krawecki, who, like Lola, would soon be an officer in the olive-clothed organization, stared at the smoke every evening, perplexed.

What puzzled him was the extent of it. Maybe, just maybe, the SS had enough hate in its soul to fill up that whole vast canopy. But then the clouds drifted off, and the SS had enough hate to fill up the sky the day after that, and the day after that. What, Adam asked himself, was the source of such inexhaustible hate? In school in Konin, where he'd studied philosophy, he'd grown fond of Spinoza, the Jew who had laid out the qualities of love, hate, etcetera, as neatly as equilateral triangles and, like Euclid, condensed them to propositions, corollaries and QEDs. "Proposition XIII. Note," wrote Spinoza, and Adam still remembered it. "Hate is pain accompanied by the idea of an external cause." All right, Adam thought, the SS had pain, accompanied by the odd idea that the Jews had caused it. But *that* much pain? As deep as the sea in Thor's cup? So deep that the sky wasn't wide enough to empty it in? "Proposition XX. He who conceives that the object of his hate is destroyed will feel pleasure." Yes yes, Adam thought, the SS had pleasure, but ten seconds later the SS had even more pain, more hate. It welled and it welled from—where? At Auschwitz, Adam wondered about this.

One evening as Adam contemplated the hate made manifest over him, a prisoner who was a Catholic priest—indeed, a Catholic bishop—walked by, and Adam fell into conversation with him. Now, Adam was not yet twenty-four. His limpid eyes and his half-open lips said to everyone silently, "Yes, I'm listening." The bishop was a much older man, and as they walked through the mud, Adam took the novice's role. "Why do the gentiles hate the Jews?" Adam asked.

"It's this way," the bishop said. "A lion is lying in the woods, glutted and gorged, and a deer comes along. The lion isn't hungry, and the deer isn't going to harm it. But still the lion pounces on it."

"But why?"

"The lion has a bestial instinct, you see, an instinct that tells it to kill that deer. The same with the gentile against the Jew. The Jew isn't going to harm him, but the gentile still calls him a *Schweinehund Jude*. He has this instinct against the Jew."

"But where does the instinct come from?"

"Maybe," the bishop continued, "the gentile receives it when he receives his mother's milk. He hears from the day he's born that if you don't eat, the Jew will get you, if you don't sleep, the Jew will get you. Maybe that."

Adam thought not. His own mother in Konin had told him, "Eat. Or the *policeman* will get you." Adam had grown up disliking police, but the thought of shoving just one of those bogeymen into a cyanide chamber, a crematorium oven, and a fire of 1,800 degrees so as to neutralize him was so disproportionate to Adam's misgivings about him that the two thoughts couldn't fit in Adam's small skull. If one thought was in, the other was out, and Adam just thanked the well-intentioned bishop, going to sleep in his stable perplexed.

Well before dawn, he marched out of Auschwitz singing in German and whipping his cap off for the SS. By six he was back at work in the Union Factory. His mission in the gunpowder plot was to keep an eye on the smuggler girls in case the SS should catch them. But also, Adam stole a pair of pink-rubber-handled shears that a man or woman could use to cut electrified wire, and he gave these to a girl to smuggle past the SS. The plan was, the oven-crew boys would use the powder to blow up the crematoriums, saving the lives of ten thousand people every day. That done, they'd use the shears to cut the barbed wires, and all sixty thousand slaves would escape. The rebellion was set for October, 1944.

In October, Adam still worked at the Union Factory. He sharpened Lola's drills, Lola drilled holes in 37-millimeter fuses, and Ada inspected Lola's holes. *"V'od.* And also," Ada was singing in Hebrew now,

> *And also another secret!*
> *I have been burned by a flame.*
> *They say there is love in this world.*
> *How do I know love's name?*

Her voice in this place was a sprinkle of cool water, and, in gratitude, another girl gave her a jar half-filled with jam, and another a slice of bread after using an anti-aircraft bolt to scratch in the oleo, KOCHAM CIĘ, I LOVE YOU. On her twenty-third birthday, a boy in the factory gave her the buttercups he'd seen on the road while marching in. Her boss, a one-eyed professional murderer, a German, told her, *"Du bist mein gold.* You are gold," and another boss, a Pole, actually kissed her. Even some SS, whose usual musical pastime was to stand at attention on Sunday evenings singing, *"Deutschland, Deutschland,"* and then to sit on folding chairs listening to Wagner—even the SS nodded along with Ada sometimes, as she tossed the FAILs into the PASS container.

But one day, Ada heard shouts behind her. She turned and saw an SS woman holding a box of anti-aircraft parts from the German army. "Who inspects Part Number Nine?" the SS woman shouted.

"I do," Ada said hesitantly. And slap! the woman gave her a violent slap, and the girl next to Ada started crying. "Don't cry," Ada whispered in Polish.

"What did you say?" the SS woman shouted, hitting her and ordering her, "Report to the SS office!" Ada's throat went dry as though from a desert wind. The words really meant, "Report to the SS office, where the SS will beat you, torture you, move you to Barracks Eleven, and hang you."

Happily for Ada, the one-eyed murderer told her, "I'll fix it." He did, somehow, but the SS had ended her one-woman war and, a little later, ended the whole rebellion at Auschwitz. On Saturday, October 7, the oven crew threw one of its bosses into an oven, killed the SS men Josef, Rudolf and Willi, blew up a crematorium with a powder-packed sardine can, cut the barbed wire with the pink-rubber shears, and, singing the *Internationale* in Russian, Polish, Czech and German, escaped to the birch trees, where the SS machine gunners killed them all, 250 boys. Their last gasp was in code to Auschwitz,

4 3 24 3 2 6. 7. 40. 14 5 11 16 11. 24 27 31. 7 27 26. . . .
The desperate men fell on the SS. . . .

Two days later, the SS, who'd caught the girl with the shears, caught four of the gunpowder smugglers, including Lola's cousin. The SS beat her, whipped her, and tortured her, crushing her hands and feet like walnut shells, but Lola's cousin didn't tell them Lola's name. The girls couldn't walk, so the SS carried them to the gallows outside of Lola's window. It carried them up the gallows steps and was putting the nooses on when one of them cried in Yiddish, "Avenge me!"

Lola was at her window, watching. As the trap gave way and the girls dropped through it, a mass of hot matter welled up in Lola like in a volcano's core, and it pressed on her skin in search of some way out. There wasn't any. A girl on Lola's shelf whose sister was one of the ones who was hanged started screaming, but Lola pushed her into her mattress, whispering, "Shh!"

A stifled scream.

"They'll hear you!"

The boys at Auschwitz, like Adam, also saw the bodies drop like four counterweights. But the boys had an outlet for the hot matter inside them, for in one of their barracks lived the boy who'd ratted on Lola's cousin, a Jew known as Little Leon. "We're celebrating New Year's," an older prisoner said in December, 1944. "Let's celebrate without Leon." That night, Adam and the others hid in the toilet room, and as Leon came in, their hate burst out, and they threw a blanket over him and strangled him. It was strange: the hate expended itself, but at dawn it again bubbled up from some unaccountable source. At the sight of the garbage cans and of Leon's pitiful five-foot body near them, the boys weren't full of joy but of even more loathing, more hate.

As for Lola, the lava inside of her sloshed around, it smashed at her stomach, intestines, heart, it exhausted her. She felt that a wolf was caged up inside her and chewing her internal organs. By the night of Thursday, January 18, 1945, when the SS stomped into Lola's stable beating her, shouting, "*Stinkendes schwein!* You stinking pig! *Heraus!* Get out!" Lola just couldn't budge. She told Zlata, "Let's hide under the bed."

"No, Lola! They'll kill us!"

Zlata pulled Lola outdoors, and Lola in two left shoes started walking to Germany. Her family was all she thought of. Her mother, father, child were dead, her husband unbearable. Her brothers and sisters, except, perhaps, for the CPA, were, as far as she knew, also dead. Ada was unaccounted for, and Zlata was the fiend who'd put the shoes on Lola's blue feet, telling her, "Put them back on!" In time, the last little drip of endurance drained out of Lola's bleeding knees. At twilight on Saturday, she said to Zlata, "I've had it."

"They'll kill you!"

"I'm walking away."

"*Be careful!*" said Zlata, and threw her a little packet as Lola slipped into the German crowd.

At once, the SS man with his Luger, his leash with his snarling dog, and his jolly-roger, skull-and-bones, head-of-death insignia accosted her. Now, the men with the German shepherds were the scum of the Auschwitz SS. Half the SS had volunteered for the "dog-*führer*" work, and the sergeants had gotten rid of their undesirables by telling them, "You, you, you." Even the Auschwitz commandant, Höss, who'd invented the cyanide chambers and who'd sent one or two million people there— even he had complained that the dog-*führers* sicced the Jews just for fun. The one tonight was a tired and hot-tempered man, and his mouth had a rectangle shape as he yelled at Lola, "*Sie, gehören Sie dazu?* You! Do you belong with the Jews?" His dog strained forward, snarling.

"*W*as, sind Sie verrückt? What, are you crazy?" Lola screamed in her Union Factory German. Now, Lola was down to sixty-six pounds, but her overcoat hid her. Her hair, as short as a brush's bristles, was invisible under her simple scarf, and her face wasn't pale but red from exposure, red as a farmer's daughter's would be ("Someday you'll thank me," her mother had told her). Her sunken cheeks could be those of a high-fashion model, and the fear in her eyes could be indignation at being considered a Jew. *"Nein! Ich gehöre nicht dazu!* No! I don't belong with them!" Lola screamed, and the genes of her brothers gave her the strength to spit the word *them* like a pellet of rotten meat. Briefly, the SS man stared as though saying, "Hey, lady, you don't intimidate *me*," then he and his dog moved on.

All around Lola, the Germans hadn't said boo. Maybe they hadn't seen the rigid red paint like an old graffito on the back of her brown cloth coat, or maybe they thought the war was practically over, or maybe they pitied the Jews, Lola didn't know. She turned to a man standing next to her in a shiny black raincoat, saying in German, "May I have your coat? Mine has a mark, and I want to cover it."

"No, you can not!" the man snorted. "I've just come from a labor camp too!" Lola said nothing, and two minutes passed. "But this I can give you!" the man said suddenly, and he reached in his pocket for one mark, fifty pfennigs: about sixty cents.

"Danke, mein herr," said Lola, and after the column of Jews and SS had gone like a chain gang past her, she trudged through the hem-high snow to a coal shack in someone's back yard. Inside, she pulled off her two left shoes and collapsed, an old soot-stained rag.

In the morning the roosters awoke her. She sat up as slow as a body on Judgment Day. She was frozen, her hands were blue and in places purple, and her feet were without sensation. She picked up her ice-covered shoes and, in her stockings, stumbled outside. She was in one of the villages that in 1921 had voted to stay in Germany, had been invaded by Poland, and now was in Germany again. Nearby was an old wooden house, and an old man with a mustache came out and stared at his uninvited guest.

Lola was desperate. "Sir," she said in Polish. "I'm thirsty. Do you have some tea?"

The man stared some more. He then went inside, but he came back with a tin cup of coffee and a piece of tea-cake.

"Thank you," said Lola. *It must be Sunday,* she thought as she ate the newly baked cake and drank the coffee. "Sir, I'm cold," she continued. "I need to warm up."

The man still stared. He then said, "All right," and guided her up the rickety stairs to a little parlor. He seated her at a pot-bellied stove as a woman in the bedroom shouted, "No, don't let her in! She's a Jew!"

"I'll do what I want to."

"She'll get us all killed! She'll. . . ."

"Shut up."

"I'll leave as soon as I can," Lola promised. She asked the man for a pair of scissors, thimble, needle and thread and, on getting them, used them with shivering fingers to cut the coat bottom off and sew it on top of the red cross, concealing it. She then put the coat back on. Her head scarf was dirty, her stockings stained by her blood, but in Zlata's little packet was a new scarf and new stockings, and Lola put them on. She put on her shoes, the man gave her a sandwich, and Lola left, saying, "Thank you, sir."

It was Sunday indeed. The bells were ringing, and all the Germans were on the road, walking to Mass. Lola went with them into a Catholic church, but the priest looked at her as though the word JUDE were stamped on her head, the whole congregation turned around, and Lola backed out. She walked west until, at a railroad crossing, she saw something out of Dante's *Inferno*. In the snow were the Jews from the evening before. There were maybe one thousand, living, dying, dead—the living screaming, the dying crying, the dead ones kneeling, their hands on their heads, their bodies as white as snow statues, frozen solid. On the tracks were some open coal cars, and the SS, shouting, "*Hinein!* Get in!" was using its rifles as cattle prods to herd people on. To the ones who couldn't climb, the SS said, "*Knien!* Kneel!" and abandoned them in the ten-below-zero cold. The colors were those in a steel engraving, black and white: a drawing of the last ring of hell.

Lola fled. She didn't look for Ada and Zlata. The two were dead, Lola thought—if not now, then surely soon. She rushed through the village in random directions, a frightened fish in a hammerhead's tank. She ran past the grocer's, butcher's, pharmacist's stores. In their windows her image kept pace with her, and Lola caught sight of this pale-colored *doppelgänger* once. It rattled her, for she looked like a model, a junior miss, in a rush to an eight o'clock shoot. *My God!* Lola thought. *Who am I? What will I do? Where will I go?*

I've one place to go, Lola thought, and she started walking east. The sky was blue, and the snow went crunch! underfoot, like a wafer of melba toast in a person's mouth. To her sides, the elm and acacia trees were as barren as skeleton bones, and the fire tower east of the village was bare-boned too. It had been built of logs and ladders slapped to each other as randomly as a set of pick-up sticks, rising for floor after floor, lurching to the left, right, left, and rallying till, at six stories high, it tottered above the potato farms like a man on some giant stilts. It was grotesque, looking to Lola like a giant watchtower for the SS. High on this edifice was a crow, an Erlkönig peering at her, stumbling below.

A sign on the road said MYSLOWITZ 50 KILOMETER, and Lola turned in that direction, northeast. Ahead of her she heard people singing in Russian, and her heart leapt up and then down again as they passed her, for they were all Russians in Hitler's army, retreating. They wore metal hats from World War I, and they called out to Lola, "Cutie! Come with us!" and then serenaded her,

> There were some Cossacks from the Don,
> Going to war!
> They saw a pretty girl, Galya,
> They took her along!

I don't believe this, Lola thought, and, for safety's sake, she fell into step with a German woman beside her.

"*Guten morgen.* Good morning," the German said. "I'm going to Myslowitz. My brother was wounded there." She carried a heavy straw shopping bag. "What about you?"

"The same," Lola said. She took a handle of the woman's bag.

"Thank you. How come you're empty-handed?"

"I have nothing left."

"How come?

"I was bombed out."

"Oh, I was bombed out too. . . ."

The women walked thirty miles. That night in Myslowitz, Lola used her one mark, fifty pfennigs, for the slow train to Kattowitz and the trolley to Königshütte. On board were a couple of German men, who asked her, "Who are you? Where are you coming from? Where are you headed to?" in their relentless effort to pick her up. "How can I contact you?" one German said.

Lola said nothing. The trolley stopped, and the German conductor got out and ran ahead. He used a two-foot "key" to switch the trolley tracks from the direction of Hermann Göring Place to that of Königshütte East. He got back on, the trolley wobbled along, and the Germans came on to Lola again. The trolley stopped and Lola got off, but the Germans did too. She got back on, but so did the two German Romeos. At last, Lola jumped off on Bismarck Street and took the next trolley to Königshütte. There, she got off and stumbled up a dark street to a German home. She knocked, and the German who opened the door was her only known living relative: the dairy owner, the one who'd been married to her sister, the one who her brothers had done their gorilla bit on, saying, "We are taking her!" On seeing Lola, the German gasped, and Lola passed out on his welcome mat.

4

She came to a few hours later. The first thing she saw was the German's face. He was standing above her, and his tears were streaming down his red cheeks. He had carried her to a couch, apparently, for her spine was sinking in something soft, and he had put a warm blanket over her. He now brought her a bowl of hot soup, which coursed through her to her toe-tips, and a feast of meats, cheeses, vegetables. He put some ointment on her raw knees, and he drew her a bath where the pain in her bones receded into the water like sighs. He gave her a fresh set of clothes, and he led her to his garden and to a bunker where, in the lantern light, she discovered six Jewish families. All during the war he'd hidden them here, and Lola would hide here too. He said good night, and she lay down in the smell of the soil.

And fell asleep. The sounds of the shells didn't awaken her, but they unnerved the Germans who still were at Auschwitz, twenty miles off. Like frightened fish—like Lola that day—the SS ran in every direction or drove through the turned-off traffic lights. Höss, the commandant, wasn't there, but Hössler was snatching up fat brown folders, and Mengele was looking for Jews who still hadn't left. Two thousand Jews were dying of thirst at the hospital, but the SS wasn't about to use two thousand bullets to silence them. Some others were in a warehouse under a pile of shirts, skirts and trousers, their throats dry and their lips blue-black because of their drinking ink, and the SS finally found them. "You are spies!" the SS cried, and it locked them in a lamp-lit room in its whorehouse, telling

them, "We will shoot you," "No, we will ship you out," "No. . . ." But one
Jew the SS didn't find was Adam, the Spinoza-intoxicated boy, who, with
some others, was hiding in Barracks Eight.

By Wednesday, January 24, the SS was beside itself. On its radios it
had heard of the Russian advances, and it was shouting now, *"Schnell!*
Hurry up!" *"Lass das!* Don't bother with that!" *"Aus dem scheisswagen,
raus!* Let's get out of this shitcart!" By three the SS was gone, but an
olive-colored car full of Germans drove up, a four-star general got out,
and Adam, in the barracks, announced he was going out too. Adam wasn't
quite like Esther, in the Old Testament, who announced that she'd try to
save thousands of Jews by going to King Ahasuerus. Esther said, "If I perish, I perish," or, as one commentator put it, "I will sacrifice myself for
Israel," but Adam simply said, "Someone must do it."

"I hope you'll come back," the others said.

Then, Adam and another boy, a former middleweight fighter, a Jew,
went out of Barracks Eight. Both were in the Auschwitz fire company
and in black clothes with a bright red stripe on each arm and leg, and the
general looked at them curiously, asking, "What place are we in?"

"Auschwitz. Our concentration camp," the middleweight said.

"Auschwitz. . . ?" The general seemed not to know of it.

"Yes."

"And you're prisoners? Well, you'll be liberated any day."

"Herr General," Adam interrupted. "We need something from you.
Do you see that swimming pool? We're in the fire company, and we need
to put our pumps and hoses there."

"What for?"

"The hospital has no water, and we need to pump some in."

"So. . . ?"

"We need protection, Herr General. If the SS catches us, it will kill
us."

The general frowned. He was six foot two, a Prussian perhaps, and he
seemed to have little love for Hitler's SS. "Go do it. *I* am in charge of this
front now," he said, and he remained at Auschwitz till Adam and the middleweight were at the pool, pumping away. The middleweight had a
spade-shaped chin, a firm underline to his wide and warmhearted smile.
He worked the two-handled pump in the tough but, oh, so gentle way of
a man who's giving a seesaw ride to a half-dozen neighborhood kids. He
was from Miechów, near Cracow. He had fought in amateur matches and
ridden in the Polish cavalry till the Germans shot the horse under him in
September, 1939. In his first week at Auschwitz, he had punched out his
German boss. "I'm going to kill you!" the German cried, lying on the
floor, bleeding, but the middleweight said, "If I'm dead, then you're dead

too," and the German didn't even try. By now the middleweight was an Auschwitz underground leader. And two weeks from now, he'd carry a Luger and, at a Kattowitz restaurant, be shooting it out with the SS, killing them all, for he was the first boy—or girl—at Auschwitz who would enlist in the olive-clothed organization. His name was Barek Eisenstein.

On Saturday, January 27, the Russians came running into Auschwitz— actually running, for they were rushing from tree to tree in their snow-colored camouflage clothes. In Barracks Eight, Adam, Barek, and the other boys found a red tablecloth and mounted it on a mopstick: a Russian flag. The girls who Adam and Barek had found, forgotten, in a lamp-lit room in the whorehouse combed their hair and cut some squares from the tablecloth, putting them on as red head-scarves. The boy with the tablecloth then put it cautiously out the door and, when the Russians didn't fire, ran out and waved it in figure-eights like a man at the head of the May Day Parade. A cheer went up, and the boys and girls burst out the door, running to the white-clothed soldiers, hugging, kissing, giving them all their worldly goods: a comb, whatever they had. Barek felt like a man who'd won by a KO. A minute later, a Russian battalion rolled in in trucks, shouting, "You're free! You're free! No more Germans! No more SS! Go home! It's over! You're free!"

Then something surprising happened. The joy just stopped like a popped balloon, and the Jews started crying. The boy with the flag let it sag, and a girl from the lamp-lit room went to her barracks and fell on her bed, sobbing. That day her mirror had cracked when a Russian shell went over her, and now she wondered if that was a warning sign. Outside, a very bewildered lieutenant colonel said in Russian, "Why are you people crying?"

"My nie mamy domów!" Barek cried in Polish.

"I don't speak Polish!" the colonel cried. He was tall, slender, close to Barek's age, twenty-seven. "Kto govorit po Russki? Does someone speak Russian? Redt emitser Yiddish? Does someone speak Yiddish?"

"Yo!" Barek and thirty others cried.

"All right! I'm a Jew! What's going on?"

Barek and the others told him. "You freed us. We were happy about it. You told us, 'Go home!' And then we remembered: we have no home to go to!" And they started weeping again, Barek too—his mother, father, and his two sisters were dead at Treblinka.

The colonel ran up the barracks stairs. He called for a chair and stood on it. "Comrades!" he cried to his soldiers. "This place is Auschwitz. My mother, father, and our fellow soldiers perished here. All that's left are the people you see. What a victory that we have freed them! But we mustn't take gifts from them. We must *give* them gifts." Like children, the Russians gave back the combs and gave the Jews bread, cigarettes and vodka. "Now we've another job to do!" the colonel cried. "To go to Berlin!"

"To Berlin! To Berlin!" the Russians repeated, their arms in the air as though waving down a Berlin-bound bus. There were tears in their eyes from the colonel's speech. "How far to Berlin?" they kept asking the Jews, and they peered to the west to see it, out past the ARBEIT MACHT FREI sign.

The colonel gave Barek a horse and wagon, and two dozen people got on. Adam stayed back to help the two thousand invalids, but Barek went east, then west, then north, then south through the low rolling hills. Nearly everyone else got off, but Barek remained the Wandering Jew. He got soup at a Catholic convent, slept at a Catholic's home, made a few dollars by selling the dear departed's clothes that he had picked up at an Auschwitz warehouse. For days he didn't see a Jewish face. "The people from the concentration camps. Where do they go?" he asked the Poles, but the Poles said, "No one survived. The Germans killed all the Jews." By the end of January, Barek saw that the Germans had stolen not only his war years but his whole future, too.

He hated them for it. "My blood is boiling," he told the one girl still with him, and he wished that he had a petcock to let out the scalding steam. The month before that, he was at Auschwitz when one of the bosses, an Austrian, told the Jews piling up soap, toothpaste and tooth-brushes how not to burst apart from hate. The man had stood on a chair and, as eighteen hundred prisoners and an SS lieutenant listened, had shouted, "Friends! The war will soon end. Be patient, and we'll soon take revenge on the Germans." "Hans! Do you know what you're saying?" the SS lieutenant gasped. "I do. And you can put handcuffs on me if you don't like it," the Austrian said. He then stepped down, but Barek had suddenly seen an outlet for his hot blood: he could use it to boil the Ger-mans in.

It wasn't in fact inconceivable. As the war moved west, the SS didn't melt into soap like the Jews of Danzig, apocryphally. It ran off to Ger-many, but sometimes it hid in sewers and cellars and, in assumed identi-ties, in farms and factories in Poland and Poland-administered Germany. To smoke out the SS, the Nazi party members, and the Nazi collaborators and to give them their due (in some cases, the firing squad) was a priority of the Polish Provisional Government in Lublin. To that end, the Poles were putting together an organization called the Office of State Security. Its personnel, some of whom were called generals, dressed in olive-drab uniforms, as well as black holsters with the Lugers they used doing mop-ups. Already, as Barek had learned, the Office of State Security was recruiting in Kattowitz, and Barek assumed that as a high-school gradu-ate, middleweight fighter, veteran, and underground leader he'd be a shoo-in if he were a Polish Catholic. But a Jew?

He went to Kattowitz anyhow, spending some of his last coins for a trolley ticket there on Thursday, February 1. Kattowitz looked like a ghost town, for it had just fallen to the Russians and a lot of German inhabitants seemed to have fled to Breslau, Berlin, and points west. For once, it was also devoid of soot and a smell like that of charred wood, for the Germans who ran the steel mills were gone. Barek walked from the trolley into a building on Beate Street. The only clues that it wasn't deserted were a couple of men who were sitting at desks, solitary as sawhorses, amidst the broken windows, cracked plaster, and peeling paint—a couple of men and dozens waiting for interviews with them. The men at the desks were recruiters for the Office of State Security, and as Barek approached them, his one uncertainty was *Will they let in a Jew?*

W ill the New York City Police let the Irish in? The first man who Barek approached was a Jewish grocer from Miechów, Barek's home-town. Barek saw him and cried out, "Moshe!"

"Bolek!" The man responded to Barek using his Polish name, not his Jewish one. "You're alive!" the man said, embracing him. "But don't call me Moshe now, I'm Max." He took Barek to the second floor to meet other officers—lieutenants and captains—in the Office of State Security, but Barek already knew them. Many were Jewish boys from Miechów, though few of them used the names that Barek knew them by. Some oth-ers were Jews from Landwirtschaft, his first concentration camp, and sev-eral were Catholics who Barek didn't know. Or were these "Catholics" also Jews? "Oh, Bolek's here, Bolek's here!" the man who was Moshe/Max kept saying. Not even stopping to swear him in, the man said, "Bolek will work with us!"

"Good!" "Great!" "Welcome!" the others said. The abundance of Jews was a nice surprise, a wonderment even, but Barek wasn't surprised that the Jews would use Polish names in a Polish paramilitia. He himself said he'd adopt the name of a Miechów butcher and be Bolek Jurkowski. "And your girlfriend?" said Moshe/Max, for Barek had admitted being in love with the girl who'd stayed on the cart with him.

"Her name is Regina, so she'll be Resia," Barek said.

He started work on Monday, February 5. He was given an office on Beate Street, as well as a sunny apartment a German had left behind. In his job as a second lieutenant, he was soon raiding the sewers, throwing grenades into one by the Savoy Restaurant and killing three men in SS gray. More often, he was talking to German informants, and, on their say-so, bringing in German suspects. After work, Barek and the other officers met in apartments to listen to round-dialed radios. "The troops crossed the Oder southeast of Breslau," the announcer might say. "To cross it. . . ."

"They aren't in Breslau yet. They should bomb it," a boy would say.

"Even if they bomb it," another would say, "the troops will have to go house to house."

"If they bomb it, there won't be a house to go to."

"Sure there will."

"Shhh."

". . . and Soviet units established a few small bridgeheads." The news would end, and, while waiting for it to begin again, the boys would drink vodka out of the goblets the Germans had left behind, slice up some sausages with the Germans' knives, raise a rumpus, and, as a boy with a pear-shaped mandolin sang the verses, sing the chorus with him,

> *It's good in the army,*
> *The girls come all day!*

> *Hopai-shupa! Hopai-shupa!*
> *Hopai-shupa! Dana!*

> *Once they put out on the sofa,*
> *Now they put out in the hay!*

> *Hopai-shupa! Hopai-shupa—*

And again, the news would come on, and the announcer would say, "Our infantry, armor and artillery streamed toward the bridgeheads. . . ."

"Good. They have Breslau encircled," the mandolinist would say.

The talk was in Yiddish, mostly. By the grace of God or of some good fairy, about three out of four of the officers—two hundred rowdy boys—in the Office of State Security in Kattowitz were Jews, and they felt their blood boiling, or their muscles curling, or their bones aching with hate for the German murderers. Some, like Barek, had been liberated at Auschwitz. Others had been marched out of Auschwitz but had hidden in houses or snow-drifts or run to the woods while the SS was shooting the boys running with them. Still others had jumped from the coal cars while the SS was shooting the boys with *them*. At the parties in Kattowitz, the survivors didn't talk of Auschwitz, but sometimes they stopped during a Yiddish song like *The Bells of the Village*, sobbing, remembering life in

Będzin, wherever. They used names like Stanisław Niegosławski, a name
that belonged to a Pole at a Będzin salami store.

Not every Jew in the Office of State Security was from Auschwitz.
Some were from other camps, and some had been hiding during the war.
Others, who now were commandants of the many prisons and, for the
overflow, the cellars and camps full of SS, Nazi and Nazi collaborator suspects, were from the Polish army or Polish partisans. At the parties, they
were the toughest bunch, quite like the Potok boys in Będzin. One whose
left arm had been mangled by "friendly fire" in the partisans always flared
up at arguments like "They should bomb it," "No, they shouldn't," and
used his good arm to seize his opponent's collar or punch his opponent's
nose. And even the mandolinist, who had fought in the Jewish partisans,
who now commanded a camp full of German suspects at Schwientochlowitz, near Kattowitz, and who was usually singing hopai-shupa,
would also sing,

> We will point our guns
> At the enemy's heart. . . .

At these parties were also girls. Barek would bring Regina, the girl
he'd found hiding, not hustling, in the SS whorehouse and who was now
living in his apartment in Kattowitz, locking her door lest a Russian soldier come up and try to rape her. Other officers brought other girls, and
one day the mandolinist came with a short-haired blonde he'd met in
Kattowitz. She weighed eighty pounds from her year-and-a-half at
Auschwitz, and the boy introduced her as Lola Potok.

Some girls were smooching, but Lola wasn't. She sipped from a jigger of
vodka while the boys downed a bottle each, and she gazed up at them,
impressed, as they recounted their deeds in the Office of State Security.
She didn't join in their songs,

> I will die,
> And no one will know
> Where they'll bury me,

for she had never heard them. She said very little, as if she were practic-
ing being alive. After coming to Königshütte, she'd spent seven days in
the bunker before being liberated, and then she'd gone to Kattowitz to
put in a word for the dairyman, that he wasn't a Nazi. She'd also gone to
Będzin to see if any of her brothers were somehow in their pre-war home
on Modrzejowska Street. None were: the home belonged to a Pole now,
nor had a brother sent a wire to Będzin saying, "I'm alive." The brother

who was a CPA and who'd been at Auschwitz hadn't shown up in Będzin either. And never would, Lola learned at this party in Kattowitz.

The bearer of this bad news was a Jew from the camp at Gintergrube, twenty miles from Auschwitz. It was a coal mine, the boy reported to Lola, and the healthiest boys at Auschwitz had been taken to it in October or November, 1944. Among them was Lola's brother Ittel, the CPA, who'd been a miner there until the SS swarmed into his barracks at midnight, shouting, *"Appell! Appell!* Head count!" It called out Ittel's number, took him to a torture room, and tied him around a pole like an oven spit, spinning, beating and whipping him till he cried out, "Yes, I tried to escape from camp!" It then built a gallows and, as the other miners and Lola's informant watched, paraded him to it. His next-to-last words were in Hebrew, *"Shema Yisroel!* Hear, O Israel! The Lord our God, the Lord is One!" and his last words were in Yiddish, *"Ir zolt nekume nemen!* You must take revenge!" He was then hanged.

Now, Ittel had been fourteen when Lola was born. He hadn't played with her but had kicked soccer balls even if he was wearing his shiny new shoes for Passover. He had done accounting on an adding machine with an iron handle, like on a slot machine, as Lola sat learning her one, two, threes. He wasn't close, but in death he did what the other brothers and sisters hadn't. On hearing how Ittel said, "Take revenge," Lola felt the lava well up but not lodge inside her. The heat she'd suppressed at Auschwitz at last erupted, and she screamed, "No!" Her fingers curled on her glass as though wringing the vodka out, but she really wanted to wring the neck of an SS man—of Höss or Hössler or Mengele. The next day, she went to the broken-windowed building on Beate Street and asked for a job in the Office of State Security.

She was black with hate. She was given a four-page form with the word SECRET on top and started filling it in. Name? In pen and ink, Lola wrote, "Lola Potok." Father's name? Lola wrote, "Abram Potok." Birthday? "20 March 1921." Birthplace? "Będzin." The form didn't ask for Lola's sex, for women didn't often apply to the Office of State Security. Nationality? "Polish of Jewish origin." Citizenship? "Polish." Education? "Grammar and trade school." Occupation? Lola wrote, "Cutter," for she'd once worked at a tailor's shop in Będzin. Religion? Lola wrote, "No religion," for God had been gassed at Auschwitz. Military service? "No." Partisans? "No." War wounds? "No." Medals? "No." Political parties before the war? "None." Political parties during the war? "None. I was in a concentration camp." Parents' address? "They're dead." Brothers' and sisters' addresses? "No family in Poland." The form didn't ask if Lola was married, for women didn't often apply to the Office of State Security. How many possessions? "Nothing." How many children? "None."

Next, Lola was asked for a résumé. In pen and ink, and with some mis-spellings, such as the Polish word for *I*, Lola wrote, "I was born in a mid-dle-class family in Będzin. We were eleven children, so conditions were hard. At seventeen I started work as a cutter, but the war broke out and I didn't work long. I was married during the war, but two years later there was a great deportation and I lost my whole family. I went to the concen-tration camp at Auschwitz, where I went through a Gehenna," a place in the Bible, the site of some human sacrifices in Jeremiah. "My whole life until then hadn't been so rich in experiences as those two horrible years in the hands of the German criminals. I witnessed my brothers' and sis-ters' executions, and I avoided this by a miracle. We worked in a factory making ammunition, and we were organizing everyone's escape. To do it, we carried gunpowder out. Unfortunately, we were betrayed, and my nearest ended up on the gallows. We were moved from Auschwitz toward Breslau ahead of the Russian army, but I escaped along the way. And now I want to cooperate against our German oppressors."

After filling the form in, Lola signed it, and someone put it with hun-dreds of applications from men. But then Lola did what the men hadn't needed to and walked to the Silesian government building, on Bernhard Street, to make an in-person pitch to the Secretary of State Security. The building was full of French windows, and the Secretary's office as big as a Hollywood set. It was, in fact, till a couple of weeks earlier, the office of the Gestapo commandant, and was the place where the sweet-smiling boy who was Lola's playmate—Pinek—had been tortured in 1942 and taken to a German gallows. The sabers were still on the wall as Lola walked in, but there was a shiny square where the picture of Hitler had been, and at the big mahogany desk was a Polish captain who was the Secretary now. Lola had heard who the captain would be, but he himself wasn't expecting her, and as she walked up, he jumped up and cried out, "Lola!" His eyes were moist as he hurried toward her and hugged her. The captain was Pinek.

In 1942 he'd been saved by a German. Pinek, while growing up, had been beaten by Polish students, Jewish police, and the Gestapo, remem-ber. He'd signed a two-page confession in Kattowitz,

I, Pinek Mąka, willingly and without duress, confess that I destroyed the machine at the Silesia Factory...

and had been dragged away, when at that eleventh hour the German fac-tory director hurried into the Gestapo office. "You're accusing a Jew. It's easy enough to accuse a Jew, but I can't run the factory without him," the director hyperbolized. "Our boys will suffer if I don't have him." Not killing him, the Gestapo put Pinek in a hospital until, three weeks later, his skin was flesh-colored again and his nails were growing back, and it sent him back to Będzin after warning him, "If you tell anyone, we'll arrest you and kill you."

Pinek kept mum. At his ghetto home, he said nothing to his mother, father, and pretty sister but "I was interrogated." But his sister's boyfriend, a sort of interrogator himself, wouldn't let up. He kept harping at Pinek, "What happened in Kattowitz?"

"I told you."

"But what did they do?"

"I don't even tell my sister that."

"You're hiding something."

"Why would I be, Chaim?"

"You are." Pinek's sister's boyfriend had so many questions that one or two had to hit their mark. "You're planning something, aren't you? Are you going to hide in Będzin? Are you going to South America?" The boy was Jewish, but he had icy eyes like the Gestapo colonel.

"South America! It's easier to go to Russia!" Pinek said.

In fact, Pinek was in the partisans now. At the Kattowitz hospital, another patient, a Pole, had studied his black-and-blue blemishes, had told him, "A man who survives the Gestapo will be good for us," and had given him the address of some partisans north of Będzin. And now, Pinek was making a bolt every fifty seconds at the Silesia Factory and, at night, was giving the partisan unit the ID cards he'd stolen during the day.

"Why won't you tell me?" Pinek's sister's boyfriend said, but Pinek didn't do it. On Saturday night, July 31, 1943, when the SS cried, "*Juden heraus!*" and carried off Lola, Pinek was with the partisans raiding the German police, and one year later when Lola, to little avail, was gathering up gunpowder like diamond dust, he was using machine guns to kill the SS and get even more machine guns. He was shot in the leg, dug out the bullet, recovered, and became the commander of three hundred men, an acting lieutenant colonel. His men and the Russians liberated Będzin in January, 1945, and soon after that he was handed an onionskin paper that said, "We hereby appoint you the Secretary of State Security for Silesia." The province was all Southwest Poland and Poland-administered Germany: close to five million people, as many as in Massachusetts, and twenty thousand square miles, as much as in Massachusetts, Connecticut, Rhode Island, and the lower half of Vermont and New Hampshire. Pinek, whose turf this now was, was six months younger than Lola, twenty-three.

A lieutenant drove him to Kattowitz. A major showed him to his office and his big mahogany desk, and Pinek felt a certain *déjà vu* as he stared at a pipe rack there. It was round, it had six brown pipes, it—"Oh, my goodness!" Pinek cried. "I was almost killed here!" He burst into tears.

"You were. . . ?" the major said.

"The Germans!" Pinek cried, and he told what happened in 1942. The major, also in tears, hugged him and kissed him, and Pinek sat down quite stunned in his new three-chandeliered home. The light flooded through the French windows, and he found himself thinking that he was here through the will of God. But where others might think that God wanted them to do what the Germans did—to do it to Germans, eye for eye—Pinek believed that God wanted him to do the reverse and to set the times right again.

He hadn't changed. He still was pure good, for he hadn't suffered what Lola had. His father had died during the war of a foot infection, but his mother, sister, and her inquisitive boyfriend had hidden on a Polish farm that Pinek had found outside of Będzin. One brother was in the partisans, and the other had escaped from the Markstädt concentration camp in May, 1944, during an SS interrogation. "Your brothers are partisans!" the SS man had shouted, beating up Pinek's brother until the blood ran from his mouth, dumping him into an SS car, driving him off, and telling him, "Olek! It's me!" for the "SS man" was Pinek's other brother in SS drag. Any anger that Pinek had felt during the war had expended itself in blowing up German depots and German trains. It hadn't congealed into hate, as Lola's anger at Auschwitz had, and now Pinek wasn't about to let the wild dogs of revenge—of hate in action—loose in his little part of the post-war world. He sat in his office, determined to use it for his fellow men, for the life, liberty and happiness of everyone hurt by the Germans: his family, his friends, the Jews, the Poles, and (well, except for the Germans) the war-ravaged people of Europe.

"I want revenge," Lola told him. She was wearing a dress she'd found in a closet in Königshütte and was sitting stiffly at a coffee table in Pinek's office—stiffly, for she was wearing a steel-ribbed corset to ease the sciatica pains from the SS beatings at Auschwitz. A secretary (there were girls in the government, apparently) had poured her some tea, and Lola was holding the cup rather awkwardly, for her thumb had been mangled by one of the anti-aircraft machines at Auschwitz. Pinek was sitting with her and weeping again, for Lola had just reported that her mother, daughter, and at least twelve of her sisters, brothers, nieces, nephews and, in a sense, much of Lola herself had been executed at Auschwitz or, in Ittel's case, Gintergrube. Pinek had just heard her say, "I want revenge."

The word wasn't new for him. Pinek had heard it a hundred times from the Jews who wanted to work in the Office of State Security. He had always pooh-poohed it, for mayhem and murder weren't what the Jews he'd known in Będzin ever did. It wasn't how Jews were brought up, and Pinek himself, on killing a German during the war, had just felt guilty about it. "Oh, Lola," Pinek said. "You're not a murderer, you're not a person who'll go around in the streets shooting guns. Do you really want revenge?"

"Yes."

"Well, how will you get it?"

Lola didn't know. In her mind's eye, she'd seen herself choking the life out of Höss, Hössler or Mengele, but she hadn't put any details in. Would she really put her hands on his throat and use her two thumbs, her good and her mangled one, to suffocate him? Or would she use the scarf she'd found in a closet in Königshütte? Or the belt she'd found with it? Höss, Hössler or Mengele would put up a struggle, surely—would she ask the Jewish boys at the Office of State Security to hold him down as she killed him? Or to tie his arms to his chair so she could kill at her leisure? Would she cremate him too?

"You couldn't do it," Pinek said. "You're not a Nazi."

"I want them to suffer like us," Lola said.

Pinek regarded her. She was sitting straight and was holding her cup in a strangler's grasp. *She's a tough little girl, a Cossack—a Potok,* Pinek thought. Once in Będzin, the SS had come to his house to pick up his old and bed-ridden mother's mother, but a Potok boy had jumped into bed with her and pulled up the blankets over her and, as the SS came in, had lain with a look of "It's only me." He had saved her, and now Pinek looked at Lola thinking, *She's tough like him,* the right personality profile for the Office of State Security. He wanted her in it.

Now, Pinek wasn't the good fairy who was allotting three-fourths of the jobs at the Office to Jews. The Office of State Security was a Polish *national* organization, and as Secretary of State Security for the province, or state, of Silesia, Pinek was like a Secretary of the Army, Navy or Air Force for an American state. He had no lawful authority, for the olive-clothed people didn't work for him but for someone appointed by Warsaw, and he couldn't lawfully pick up his phone and say, "Arrest So-and-So. Schedule a trial for So-and-So. And hire Lola Potok." But the laws were still being written in 1945, and Pinek usually got his way. He'd already hired his two brothers and his sister's icy-eyed boyfriend, who, not unreasonably, he'd made an interrogator in Kattowitz. He'd also hired girls, like a Jewish secretary at a Warsaw insane asylum who'd told him, "I'm going crazy there," who he'd made a secretary in Kattowitz.

Lola could be a secretary, too, but Pinek saw her as officer material. He had openings in all five sections of the Office of State Security: in Intelligence, Interrogation, Imprisonment, Prosecution and Implementation. The people in Intelligence, like Barek, rounded up SS, Nazis and Nazi collaborators and so were sometimes under fire: no place for Lola. The people in Interrogation, like Pinek's sister's boyfriend, sometimes had to use duress, and the ones in Imprisonment, like the mandolinist, had to contend with hundreds of suspects in any facility at any particular time. The people in Prosecution were attorneys, and the section for Implementation—or, as everyone called it, Section Five—was also not for a Jewish girl, for it mostly consisted of firing squads. After thinking about it, Pinek concluded that Lola should be in Imprisonment at one of his many prisons, most of them small as a cellar, some as big as Alcatraz. He told her, "I've got the job for you," and added for safety's sake, "It's one where you can say, 'I'm the boss now. Whatever I want to do I can do—*but I won't do it.*'" He looked at Lola levelly, Lola didn't look away, and he offered her the commandant's job at the prison in Gleiwitz, the city where the Germans started World War II.

It was Tuesday, February 13, 1945. Lola was just short of twenty-four. Two weeks earlier, she'd lived on a cot in Königshütte, and two weeks before that on a shelf at Auschwitz. Her eyes were still pits, and her hair still mirrored her hairbrush. But she was a Potok, as qualified as anyone else in Kattowitz during the war. She didn't need to ponder on Pinek's offer, for she assumed that in Gleiwitz she'd find a way to blow off the hate inside her. She saw she could turn the hierarchy of Auschwitz upside down, and she even hoped she'd catch and do God-knew-what to her three wanted men, Höss, Hössler and Mengele. She saw she'd be well-fed, well-housed, well-paid as a first lieutenant in the Office of State Security—call it simply the Office. Lola accepted the job.

5

Gleiwitz was occupied now. On Tuesday, January 23, the Russians had rolled to the quaint city hall and to Neptune's statue. Long before that, the Nazi party brass—the "golden pheasants" in fine brown uniforms—had fled toward the setting sun, and the common people were in the cellars, waiting. The mothers and fathers were lying on bumpy potatoes, and the children were playing with Christmas presents like Messerschmitt planes made of swastika-covered wood. "*Ba-ba-bang!* You're Russian! You're dead!" the children cried till on Tuesday they heard the Russian shells, and the mothers and fathers put the Messerschmitts and the pictures of Hitler into the furnaces, saying, "We must, or the Russians will kill us."

The first shells landed on Kaiser Wilhelm Street and killed two German schoolgirls. In the days after that, the Russians—all Asiatics, covered like so many coat-racks in fur, concertinas, guns, and X-shaped bullet belts—killed the people of Gleiwitz practically aimlessly. They shouted, "*Du Gitler!* You Hitler!" and they shot policemen, firemen, postmen, and train conductors in navy-blue uniforms, even a man in whose home was a gold-braided epaulet from World War I. They shot some doctors, lawyers, tailors, nurses, carpenters, sculptors, coiffeurs, auditors, watch-store owners, cigar-store owners, shoemakers, bookbinders, principals, miners, even a few escapees from Auschwitz, even Jews. In their cellars, the Germans poured schnapps down the drains so the Russians couldn't become drunker, and the women cut off their hair so the Russians wouldn't rape them. "*Frau komm!* Woman come!" the Russians said anyhow, as they lined up to rape even eight-year-olds and eighty-year-old nuns.

To the people of Gleiwitz, it seemed like the Hun Occupation, but the worst hadn't happened yet. At dinner in Tehran, Iran, in November, 1943, Stalin had asked for all Eastern Poland, and Churchill had put down three matches representing all Russia, Poland and Germany. He had then moved the Russian and Polish matches toward the German one and proposed that if Russia got Eastern Poland, Poland should get Eastern Germany. Roosevelt had said yes, and by January, 1945, the plan was for Gleiwitz, Breslau, Stettin, Stolp, and 44,000 square miles of Germany to be handed to Polish officials like Lola. But early in February, when Stalin, Churchill and Roosevelt met again at the czar's summer palace in Yalta, on the Black Sea, Stalin had also asked for ten billion dollars and—it turned out—for two hundred thousand laborers from Germany. On Wednesday, February 14, Lola's first day in the Office of State Security, the Russians put up a poster in Gleiwitz,

1. *All male Germans between the ages of 16 and 50 must report, within 48 hours, to the Labor Conscription Office. . . .*

2. *All must bring at least two complete sets of winter clothing, blankets, cooking utensils, and food for at least 10 days. . . .*

Since the Labor Conscription Office was the Gleiwitz prison, Lola didn't go to Gleiwitz immediately. She waited in Kattowitz for the Russians to do their "selection" and for the prison to pass to Polish control.

Meanwhile, the Germans of Gleiwitz reported in. If they didn't, the Russians went to their homes telling them, *"Mitkommen.* Come with us," or snatched them off of the streets even if they were seventy-five. At the prison, the Germans moved in counterclockwise circles until they got on the cattle cars, 120 per car. Like the Jews before them, most of them had to stand up, eat the crumbs, and sip the water condensing on door rails as they rolled to camps in Russia five hundred miles past Moscow, where they dug the peat in 120 degrees or the snow at 65 below. But some Germans went to a camp much closer to Gleiwitz. "We were in Auschwitz," a coal miner wrote to a Catholic priest. "In the dismal moonlight, every lamppost looked like a gallows, and every pool of water like a pit that was waiting for us. We were sure we'd never get out of this hell alive."

Auschwitz by now was a tourist town. In truck after truck, the Russian and Polish soldiers came to learn about their enemies. They were met by a tour conductor, a Jewish survivor of Auschwitz who was none other than Adam, the Spinoza-devoted philosopher. "Now, here's where the train came in," Adam would say as matter-of-factly as someone in an INFORMACJA booth. "And here," he'd say as he walked along, "is where the train stopped and the old people, mothers and fathers, and children got out. It was chaos here. Everyone screaming, 'Jacob!' or 'Josef! Where are you?' and everyone being screamed at, '*Schnell!*' The men went here," Adam would gesture and say, "and the women here. They were wondering, *What's going on?* And that's when a German told them, 'Good morning. On behalf of the Administration, I welcome you all. We want to avoid epidemics here, so we have some showers. . . .'"

"Those sonofabitches!" a Russian or Polish soldier would say.

"Over here was the shower room," Adam would say, and he'd lead the crowd to a red brick building the SS had blown up in November, 1944, so the world wouldn't know. Adam would stand at the edge, gesturing down at the ruins of the 55-yard-long undressing room, and he'd say, "Then the German said, 'Please undress. Put your clothes on one of the hooks, and please remember the number on it. . . .'"

"Those bastards!"

"Those barbarians!"

"I'd like to kill them!"

"Well, I can't believe it!"

"You can't?" At comments like that, Adam would lose his philosophic composure. He'd point to the bones around him and say, "Take your clothes off and experience it. And then maybe you'll believe it."

One Sunday in March, Adam was holding forth for a number of Polish soldiers, including a Jewish major. The man was small, his lips were lemon-rind thin, his eyebrows were even thinner, and his forehead rose to the top of his head before encountering hair. In his high-collared uniform, he looked like an alien space man, but as Adam finished he came up and introduced himself as Major Jurkowski. He didn't say, "I can't believe it," but said he'd seen something like it on rolling into the Płaszów concentration camp. On the ground were a hundred bodies, above them a hundred logs, and the bodies, logs, bodies, logs rose for a half-dozen tiers that the SS had burned like a funeral pyre till a man couldn't tell if some of the char was animal or vegetable. "And you," the major continued. "You were at Auschwitz?"

"Yes," Adam said.

"What plans have you now?"

"None at all."

"Well, I work in Kattowitz," the major said. "We're building there a New Poland." Now, Adam knew that a *new* anything was a communist term, and he concluded that the major was an old communist. That didn't disturb him, for Stalin had freed him, and when the major proposed, "You should come to Kattowitz with me," Adam said yes.

He drove there in the major's black car and stayed at the major's home. His *landsmann* gave him new clothes after burning his old lice-infested ones, and Adam went out to see the city's wonders. It was a crisp winter day, the air still clean but the pus-colored smoke from the steel mills starting to blur it. Near Beate Street, Adam spotted a girl he'd known from the Auschwitz gunpowder plot, and he called out, "Lola!"

"Adam! You're alive!" Lola said.

She ran up and hugged him. She was stronger now, and her weight was in the high double digits. She was still living in Kattowitz, impatient to get to her prison in Gleiwitz. By day she was eating, at night romancing the mandolinist, the commandant of Schwientochlowitz. She'd been issued an olive-colored uniform with the two silver stars of a first lieutenant, but, not comfortable in a man's pants, she'd made a skirt to wear with black boots, a style she'd seen on an SS woman in Auschwitz. She'd also been issued a Luger, and she often shot at coffee cans as the Gintergrube boy, the one who saw Ittel, her brother, hanged, told her in Polish, not Yiddish, "*Ściśnąć*. Squeeze." She was in her civvies as Adam hailed her and as they hugged, kissed, and told each other their wondrous tales.

"Where are you staying in Kattowitz?" Lola asked.

"At some major's house."

"What major?"

"At Major Jurkowski's."

Lola gasped. Her hand flew up in astonishment, and she said, "Oh! Do you know who he is?"

"No."

"He's chief of the UB!" Lola said. She pronounced this in Polish, *"Oo Bay."* The letters stood for Urząd Bezpieczeństwa Publicznego, or Office of State Security, but they weren't familiar to Adam.

"What's the UB?"

"It's like the Russian NKVD!"

"I don't understand."

"It's like the Gestapo!"

"Oh," Adam said.

Later that day, Adam saw Barek, his middleweight friend, at the Office of State Security, and also stopped at the Jewish major's opulent office. The man, who indeed was the chief for Silesia, proposed that Adam should work with him. "We can build a New Poland, New Europe, New World," the Jewish major said. At age thirty-three, he was an old communist, indeed.

He had been born in Lublin to Orthodox Jews. He was three when
he'd gone to Jewish school, twelve when he'd been bar-mitzvahed. He
had worn *tsitsits*, put on *tefillins*, wrapped the black leather straps into
the שׁ7׳ shape of God's holy name, put on a *tallit*, and said every day,
"Baruch ata. Blessed art Thou." No one had ever called him *"Parszywy
Żydzie.* Boil-covered Jew," for he didn't look like a Jew and his Jewish
name, Josef Jurkowski, was Polish if he simply *zzz*'d the Josef. But sometimes the Poles at a Lublin firehouse said "Boil-covered Jew." to Josef's
brother, beating him up, and Josef was eager to end antisemitism in
Poland. At age fifteen, he discovered how in a book by a Jew, Karl Marx,

*What is the worldly cult of the Jew? Haggling. Very well! A society that
abolishes the preconditions of haggling renders the Jew impossible.*

No capitalism meant no haggling, no haggling meant no Jews, no Jews
meant no antisemitism, said Marx, and Josef wasn't offended by Marx's
argument. He thought of his hours bound, like a sado-masochist, in black
leather straps, and he agreed that the Jewish religion was the Jews' opiate.
He joined a communist cell in Lublin. He stopped saying, *"Baruch
ata,"* and started using words like the Inevitable Victory of the Prole-
tariat. Events like the fall of Rome or even of Poland, to Germany,
seemed to Josef like minor tremors ahead of the Great Day to Come. In
fifty years, what would the world remember about them? Just that the
Vandals were vandals and the Germans counterrevolutionaries. Josef
himself, being communist, was in a jail when the Germans invaded, but
the jailers fled and he unscrewed his bed, battered his cell door down,
battered the office door down, took out the keys, unlocked all the cells,
shouted, "We're free!" and, just ahead of the Germans, walked to Russia.
Russia was Marx's dream. It wasn't antisemitic, as far as Josef could
see. Jews near China were building a Jewish Republic, a home for Yiddish literature, Yiddish theater, and Yiddish art, though not for Jewish
haggling or Jewish religion. Molotov's wife was a Jew, Kaganovich ("the
Son of Cohen") was Stalin's pal, and Stalin himself had told a Jewish
reporter, "Antisemitism is cannibalism." It got the death penalty in Russia, Stalin had said, and Josef had promptly volunteered for the Russian
army. He fell back to Stalingrad, switched to the Polish army, and led his
battalion across a world of brick chimneys—everything else was in
ruins—to Warsaw. He was appointed chief of the Office of State Security
for Silesia, opened an office in Kattowitz, put up a picture of Stalin, and
put Jews in charge of Intelligence, Imprisonment, etcetera, and in three-
fourths of the other officers' jobs. But still, Josef was not the good fairy.

The good fairy was Stalin. Stalin's fondness for Jews wasn't strange to the Jews, who assumed that he wanted the Germans pursued by the hounds of hell: themselves. In fact, Stalin wasn't a German-hater. At age thirty-three, he had lived in Vienna as Hitler was painting postcards and antiperspirant posters nearby. Hitler's army was one hundred miles from Moscow when Stalin proclaimed, "Hitlers come and go, but the German people remain." Nor was Stalin serious when, in Tehran, he proposed that the Allies execute 50,000 German officers after the war. "Never!" Churchill retorted. "Fifty thousand," said Stalin. "I'd rather be shot myself!" said Churchill. "Well, 49,000," said Roosevelt, but Stalin was only pulling their legs. And now, Stalin was sending the Germans to camps in Russia whose signs didn't say, "All hope abandon," but "Hitlers come and go, but the German people remain."

Why then was Stalin so partial to Jews? Stalin didn't say. On Christmas Eve, 1943, he simply invited some Jewish and Catholic Poles who were living in Moscow to dine at the Kremlin. He served them Georgian wine, said, "To Poland," and declared them the Polish absentee government. On his orders, a Jew whose father had died at Treblinka would be chief of the Office of State Security, and Jews would be chiefs of all the departments, though from now on their names wouldn't be Jewish ones but "General Romkowski"s and "Colonel Różanski"s. In time, these people appointed all the security chiefs for Poland—including Josef, who now would be Józef, and who'd never wonder, *Why does Stalin like Jews?*

Neither would Adam, who now was sitting in Josef's imposing office. Adam's father had died, his mother was still in Belsen, his girlfriend in Ravensbrück. He'd recently given the eulogy at a mass burial in Auschwitz, saying, "I will take revenge," but his revenge so far was to manage the food, water and medicine at the hospital and to tell tourists, "Now, here's where the train came in." "How would I build a New World?" he now said to Josef, intrigued.

"We must first root out the Nazis," said Josef—though he didn't call them the Nazis, he called them the Fascists and, after that, the Bandits, Criminals, Enemies of the People, Agents of Reactionary Elements, Oppressors, Imperialists, and Counterrevolutionaries. "We must root out the Hitlerites, first."

"What would I do?"

"You would find them."

"And after that?"

"We would try them."

"All right," Adam said, and he became a captain in Interrogation. He took a one-week course from a Jewish lieutenant who said, "You may not use force. But," the lieutenant went on, a blackboard behind him, a half-battalion of students there, "if a German wants to hit you—well, they've hit us enough, and you may hit him back." Adam observed that the Jewish lieutenant didn't say, "If he hits you," but "If he *wants* to hit you." Adam, four more Jews, and one Catholic were the top students, and on graduation he was made chief interrogator in Lola's appointed city of Gleiwitz. He went there by Mercedes on Thursday, March 15.

Gleiwitz was the Wild West. The bad guys were the Russians—the Asiatics, and the criminals doing their time in the Russian army. On foot, canes, crutches and bicycles that, like broncos, tossed them into the snow, they came into Gleiwitz on one-day passes like Jesse Jameses. Up to their armpits and up to their *knees* were the watches they'd robbed by grunting like in the Stone Age, *"Urr!"* meaning *"Uhr!"* the German for "Watch!" They kept winding these as if, if they didn't, their limbs might stop like an animatronic man's at midnight in Disneyland. They also took lighters to light their fires, light bulbs to light their tents, and Nuit de Paris perfume in lieu of Smirnoff. *"Otvirai!* Open up!" they shouted at German homes and, on entering, robbed the men, raped the women, played with the children, washed in the toilet bowls, and got even drunker, telling the Germans to drink and say, "Long live Stalin!"

The Russians didn't care if a German wasn't SS. A squad of Russians would come to a block, take all the men over sixteen to Gleiwitz's prison, send some, most, or all to Russia, and hit another block. Since many Germans were miners, exempt from the German draft, there were as many as thirty thousand eligibles in Gleiwitz. They were still passing through the prison in March, and Adam had to set up his office outside it in Gleiwitz's old Gestapo building. He hung up his officer's hat in one old interrogation room, and he waited for Germans to interrogate and, if they flunked, to send to the camp at Schwientochlowitz and, in time, to the courts, prisons, and firing squads in Kattowitz.

He also went walking in Gleiwitz. The open-mouthed whales on the city hall were eating icicles now, and the city-hall square was full of slush, mop-water gray from the steel-mill soot. The street from the square to the railroad station was a ghost street now, for the Germans in Gleiwitz seldom went out. At intervals, a trolley or horse-drawn coach full of Russians went by and spattered the trees with the soot-colored slush. One such wet day, Adam, in civvies except for his half-hidden gun, was walking on this deserted street when he saw something strange: a civilian, a good-looking woman in thick black fur. She was too old for Adam, forty, but he stopped her and told her, "Excuse me. I'm from the police, may I know who you are?"

"Frau Sophie Schmidt." Or some such name.

"Have you any ID?"

"Of course." The woman reached in her purse, pulling out a letter from a Polish priest. It said something like,

To Whom It May Concern:
   This introduces Frau Sophie Schmidt, a member of the Church of the Holy Trinity in Lvov. I hereby certify that. . . .

But as Adam was reading it, a Polish policeman came up. Having seen the woman open her purse, he had concluded that Adam was robbing her, and he held his hand near his gun while demanding, "Who are you?"

"I'm from the UB."

"What's that?" The policeman didn't know, but the German woman did. In German, the Office was called the Staatlicher Sicherheitsdienst, or, inevitably, the Polish SS and Polish Gestapo, and the Germans were scared of it. The woman lunged in her purse for letters from Polish schools and Polish clubs, all the while jabbering to Adam, "I'm active in charities, too, and. . . ."

Adam became suspicious. He told the Polish policeman, "Okay. If you haven't heard of the UB, you can escort us to Teuchert Street." He led them past city hall to an ominous-looking building, ominous due to the rows of black bricks between the usual red ones. At the door, a guard let Adam and the woman in but kept the policeman out, and Adam brought her to his third-floor office, seated her in a wooden chair, and sat down opposite her. A gray light came through the windowpanes. "Who are you?" Adam asked.

"I told you. Sophie Schmidt."

"And you're from. . . ?"

"Lvov. As the letter says."

The woman was nervous. A bun at the back of her head pulled at her hair like a human hand, and the hair seemed to tug at her facial skin. At one point, Adam excused himself, and on his return the woman was gone. A crowd of employees stood at the open window, and Adam looked out to see some black fur on the concrete below, like a dead black bear. He said, "What happened?"

"She must have jumped," someone said.

She was dead. In time, Adam discovered that she'd been a Nazi's mistress, someone he might have sent to Schwientochlowitz, to court in Kattowitz, and to a prison run by the Office of State Security for—What? Two years? No longer than that. *She didn't have to fear us,* Adam thought. *She didn't have to do it.*

Lola had lost her patience now. She paced around Kattowitz as a prizefighter might if the other fighter doesn't come out. It had been six weeks!

Her prison wasn't for Coal-Miner Carl but for Höss, Hössler and Mengele! When the Russians were done with it, would anyone still be in Gleiwitz to be imprisoned in it? Stewing about it on Beate Street, Lola often went to the cellar and the cells with the skull-and-bones on their doors, chalked there by Jewish jailers ("It means they'll kill us," the Germans said). She studied the prisoners' faces lest any be Auschwitz SS, and she once behaved like a Potok boy and hit one. Ironically, her victim wasn't a German but a Jew, the former police chief in Będzin, the one who'd beaten up Pinek, called him, "You troublemaker!" "You sonofabitch!" "You Christian!" and handed him to the Germans while gesturing like Pontius Pilate. During the war, he'd paid six hundred dollars to hide with a Pole, but Pinek had now arrested him and, not waiting for a verdict of "Guilty," had decretally sentenced him to a Kattowitz coal mine. The man was being processed when Lola spotted him. She knew he'd once picked up Rivka, her mother, impounded her in a soccer field, told her and the other old people he'd send them to Auschwitz, but surrendered her to her dangerous sons ("I knew they would get me," Rivka had said). And slap! slap! as the jailers watched, the chief cowered in a corner and Lola got one small rock off in Kattowitz.

It didn't calm her. It made her more impatient to get her hands on the real guilty party, the SS. She chafed as she listened to radios with Russian communiqués like "We have captured the Hangman of the Polish People." At parties, she drank her vodka straight, and she danced on the tabletops at Kattowitz clubs like the Bagatelle as the band played the Allied war songs,

> It's a long way to Tipperary!
> It's a long way to go!

Her lover the mandolinist did the heavier drinking, knocking off vodkas as if it were closing time.

"Vodka! I want more vodka!" a boy would cry.

"Oh, drink your piss!" the one-armed boy.

"*Do rana pijemy!* We'll drink until dawn!"

Long after midnight, the mandolinist would drive to his home at Schwientochlowitz or to Lola's apartment near the Kattowitz station. But the night of Wednesday, March 28, was different from the other nights in Kattowitz.

It was Passover, and Lola was invited to Shlomo Singer's. Shlomo's first name was his only resemblance to Lola's vanished husband. He was younger, twenty-five, shorter, five-foot-five, rounder, too, and his teeth had a gap that gave him an I-couldn't-hurt-a-beetle smile. He was from

Będzin, and his parents were orthodox, but they had taught that the cap, the *tsitsit*, the arm-*tefillin*, the head-*tefillin*, the neck-*tallit*, the door-*mezuzah*, and the 613 duties of Jews were like so many strings-around-the-fingers to remind them of God's great presence. In time, Shlomo couldn't see a shooting star or a piece of bread without saying, *"Baruch ata.* Blessed art Thou," and his joyous awareness of God made light seem to emanate from him and to warm everyone around him, like the light through a temple's gold-stained glass.

He had been sent to Auschwitz when Lola was. He had kept the faith, saying his prayers on New Year's and fasting on the Day of Atonement. Sent on to Gęsia, in Warsaw, to chop the mortar off of old bricks, he had made plans for Passover, 1944. The important thing was the *matzo,* the crackerlike bread that the Jews had baked in their abrupt exodus from Egypt. Of course, there was no *matzo* at Gęsia, but Shlomo traded his black bread for four pounds of flour and, one midnight in April, crept to the washroom, where he and another boy wet the flour with the wash-room water. They kneaded this in a soup bowl, rolled it with a soda bot-tle, and set the slices on the hot washroom stove. "Hurry," said the other boy softly, lest the SS hear him.

"We need more wood," Shlomo said.

"But they'll see the smoke."

"No, it still isn't hot."

"All right. But hurry."

"You know?" Shlomo said, "We're making the *matzo* the same way the Jewish people did on their flight from Egypt."

"Yes, they hurried too."

"And I'm even more scared than they were," Shlomo said.

He made eight *matzos* before going back to bed and hiding them in his straw mattress. On Passover night, Shlomo said, "Blessed art Thou, O Lord our God, who has bidden us to eat *matzo,*" and he ate these crispy things instead of the black bread and flour-filled soup. The *matzo* brought joy to Shlomo. It reminded him how the Jews had been slaves before now, had even made bricks before now, but how God had freed them. The *matzo* still fed him—spiritually—while he was hiding in a Warsaw cellar from September, 1944, to January, 1945, when the Rus-sians became his Moses. Going back to Będzin, he found that God had given and God had taken away, for his father, mother, three sisters, and all his uncles, aunts and cousins were dead. "Blessed art Thou," Shlomo said, and he moved to Kattowitz the same holy man he had been when the Germans invaded.

He now made plans for Passover, 1945. This time, Shlomo got *matzo* from a baker and the other essentials—the eggs, apples, horseradish, parsley, sugar and salt—from a big, bear-like, roaring man he had met in Kattowitz, a Russian colonel, a Jew. The peas, carrots and potatoes came from the Kattowitz market, and the wine from a Jewish charity in New York. To the seder on March 28, Shlomo invited Lola, the boy who'd made *matzo* with him, Pinek, and other friends from Będzin. He also invited the Russian colonel—hesitantly, for the colonel had often come to Shlomo's apartment, overindulged, pulled out a gun, and chased a girl to the bedroom, roaring, "I'm good! I'm kind! I'm handsome! I *liberated* you! Why won't you sleep with me?" Often, Shlomo had told the mad Russian, "No, that's wrong."

In late afternoon, Lola and two dozen others showed up at Shlomo's apartment. On the walls were the oil paintings that the previous owner, an SS man, had left behind, and the table was set with the SS man's linen, chinaware and crystal, including one cup for the Prophet Elijah, in case of Elijah's welcome return. Everyone seated themselves, Shlomo said, "Blessed art Thou," and everyone drank some wine and ate some parsley dipped into salt. Then, Shlomo invited someone to read from a prayer book that a Jew had hidden during the war. "Why," the person began, "is this night different from all other nights? On all other nights, we eat both leavened and unleavened bread, but on this night only the unleavened bread. On all other nights. . . ."

In their eyes, almost all the Jews had tears, but they read the answer aloud. "We were slaves of Pharaoh in Egypt, and the Lord our God brought us forth with a mighty hand and an outstretched arm. . . ." But then the Jews who God had brought forth from the Holocaust started sobbing, and the Jews couldn't go on.

Shlomo put down his prayer book. On his right, crying copiously, was a broad-shouldered girl he was hopelessly fond of—hopelessly, for he was two inches shorter than she, and the gap was fatal to love 1940s-style. He touched her softly and told her, "Tell us about it, Rivka."

"I was in Auschwitz," Rivka said between sobs. "We were walking to Germany, but I ran away. I hid in a barn underneath the hay. But the farmer came, and he kept poking his pitchfork into the hay. He kept saying in German, 'Someone's here!' But praise the Name," Rivka said, for a Jew mustn't say, "God," except in a prayer, "the German didn't find me. My feet were frozen, though. I knocked on the German's door, and his wife opened it. She said, 'Oh, you're from the concentration camp!' She said, 'There are German soldiers here!' She took me to the pigpen and told me, 'Sit down.' With her knife she cut off my shoes, and she put my feet in hot, then cold, then hot, then cold, water, until my feet were alive again. She brought me hot milk, a piece of fresh bread, and a pair of her husband's shoes. I cried and I called her 'Angel' and started walking to Kattowitz. But a German bought me a ticket, and I took a train to Kattowitz. Praise the Name."

Rivka and all the Jews were crying. Shlomo wiped his own tears away, turning to Rivka's cousin, another strong-looking girl. "Now you, Adela," Shlomo said.

"I, too, was walking to Germany," said Adela. "I ran away too, and I hid in a house. But there was a German holster there, and I knew the German would come for it. I pulled out the gun, and I waited until the German came. Oh, I was scared!" said Adela, her fingers around an invisible gun. "When the German came, I pointed it. My arm was like this," like a Heil Hitler, "and shaking like this! I had never shot before, and I thank the Name that I didn't try. The man took the gun from me. He laughed and laughed," said Adela, and she laughed too, and she also cried. "My shoes, my clothes, my dirty face! Oh, I must have looked comical! A second man came and was laughing too. He gave me some women's clothes, he seated me on his bicycle bar, he pedaled me to the station, and he bought me a ticket to Sosnowiec. Praise the Name."

Now the Jews were crying and laughing, and Shlomo said, "Lola, now you."

"I ran away too," Lola said. "I saw an SS man and his dog. . . ." But unlike the other two, Lola was unemotional as she told of "May I have your coat?" "No, you can not!" "Do you have some tea?" "No, don't let her in!" *"Where will I go?"* "Cutie! Come with us!" and her long flight to Königshütte. Her sobs, her smiles, stayed stuck in her throat, and her words came out in a matrix of strangled rage. She couldn't praise the name of God. Her mother, her brothers, her sisters, the people she'd been with at Passover, singing with them, *"Dayenu.* It would have been ample,"

> *If He had given us riches,*
> *And hadn't parted the Sea,*
> *Dayenu!*

> *If He had parted the Sea,*
> *And hadn't taken us through it,*
> *Dayenu!*

> *If He had taken us through it—*

her loved ones were dead in Egypt, far from the Promised Land. For them, Lola thought, there was no Exodus.

Nor was she out of Egypt herself. As someone in State Security, she knew that the SS was lying in wait in sewers and cellars, calling itself the Werewolves. She knew that the Polish governor of Silesia had said, "I'd thought the Germans killed all the Jews. But the Jews are taking over," and that the mayor of Kattowitz had said, "We must stop them." She knew that Jews in the Office were being killed in Kattowitz. One had arrested a man who'd then dropped his handkerchief, stooped for it, pulled out a gun, and shot him, and the lieutenant who'd said, "You may not use force, but," had been murdered too. Above all, Lola couldn't celebrate till, like the sea, her wrath had washed over the Pharaoh and all his men. Her own escape wasn't ample.

"And that's how I came to Königshütte," Lola concluded.

"Praise the Name," Shlomo said. After everyone spoke, he lifted his wineglass, saying, "He led us from slavery to emancipation, sorrow to joy, mourning to celebration, darkness to light, bondage to freedom. We will sing a new song unto Him! Hallelujah!" Everyone drank, and everyone ate the bitter horseradish and the sweet sugar-and-apple dip. "Blessed art Thou, O Lord," Shlomo said, and everyone ate the Passover dinner. Shlomo shone like the sun, Lola gained another pound, the Russian colonel told her, "You're lovely," but he didn't try to ravish her. "Next year in Jerusalem," Shlomo said.

"Next year in Jerusalem," everyone said.

Then everyone left. For another month, Lola waited in Kattowitz, listened to round-dialed radios, went out with the mandolinist, went out with the Russian colonel, tangoed with them, and fired her Luger impatiently until, late in April, the Russians were done in Gleiwitz and she took a limousine twenty miles to 10 Kloster Street. She buzzed, a big iron gate ground open, and she beheld a five-story prison and, on each window, five iron bars. *"Dobry den.* Good day," a Russian said, and he took her to a first-floor office where the stern eyes of Stalin looked down on a desk, a chair, a row of wood wardrobes, and one single prison bed. After briefing her, the Russian and all the Russians left, and Lola took off her Luger and clothes before lying down in the bed, for one night the one inhabitant of her prison in Gleiwitz, Germany. Next year in Jerusalem. Next.

6

The next day, the Germans came. A truck full of men and women rolled in as Lola stood in the wet stone court, wet from the April rain. She wore her uniform but not her Luger, lest a German attempt to seize it. Standing with her was the Jewish boy who saw Ittel, her brother, hanged, and who was her adjutant now, as well as fifty people—some boys, some girls, some Jews, some not—who now were her prison guards. In their holsters were Hungarian cigarettes, though high on the walls, like high in the towers at Auschwitz, the guards carried rifles at Lola's orders. The truck stopped, and as the Germans got off, a Jewish guard cried in Polish, *"Szybciej!* Faster!" and clapped his hands rapidly, a gesture the Germans understood. But when the guard said in Polish, *"Mężczyźni tu!* Men over here! *Kobiety tam!* Women over there!" the Germans didn't move. *"Mężczyźni tu!"* the boy said louder, pointing around him. *"Kobiety tam!"*

"Ich verstehe nicht. I don't understand," one German who, like the rest, was wearing civilian clothes said in German.

"Głupku! You dope!" the boy shouted. He pulled the man to the men's position, and he then pulled the men and pushed the women until the Germans caught on. *"W jednej linii!* Line up!" the boy cried.

"Aufstellen. Line up," a German interpreted.

"Pierodolone Szwaby! You fucking German! *Cicho!* Shut up!" the boy replied, slapping the German linguist. The boy didn't know if the German's words meant "Line up" or "Attack," and, to punish him, he now ordered him, "Squat! Stand up! Squat! Stand up! Do twenty more!"

As the German complied, Lola watched him but didn't recognize him.

Her eyes went from one to another person that the Office's informants identified as SS, Nazis or Nazi collaborators. Some were sixteen, some were of SS age, apparently, some were quite old. Many wore overcoats, but a few didn't and, on this damp morning, stood like the men and women in soup lines, flapping their elbows like chicken wings. None was Höss, Hössler, Mengele, or anyone else from Auschwitz who Lola recognized, and she told her guards rather crossly, "Move them in."

"Yes, Madame Commandant."

Now, the prison had the shape of a T, and the stem was for German men and the crossbar for German women. *Do paki!* To the box!" the girl-guards said to the women, pushing them if they didn't understand, and the boys moved the men through a small barred door in the T-stem.

Lola followed the men. She was in a vast space like the nave of a Catholic cathedral, extending in front of her two hundred feet and up to the frosted skylights fifty feet over her. To her left and right, where the windows would be, rose tier after tier of gray catwalks, the high ones suffused with a gray, rainy light, the middle ones dimmer until, down at Lola's level, the place was almost basement black. By available light, a guard at a table collected the Germans' money, watches and rings and, as Lola kept watching, told the Germans, *"Zdjąć ubranie!* Get undressed!"

"Ausziehen. Get undressed," the Germans whispered.

"Do łaźni! To the showers!"

"Zum baden. To the showers," the Germans whispered.

Lola didn't leave. She knew that the Germans might have lice, the near-invisible carriers of typhus, the disease that had decimated the Jews at Auschwitz. Even in Lola's stable there'd been a sign that said, ONE LOUSE—YOU'RE DEAD, and Lola didn't want one in her own lodgings in Gleiwitz. She watched while the Germans showered, dried, and painted themselves with Lysol, and while a German barber cut off their hair and, his clippers in hand, then left to the women's prison to cut off the women's hair, too. "Get dressed!" a guard said, and the Germans put on the clothes they'd come in. A guard sent a German to cook some potato soup and to bring it, in pails, to the others, who he put into cells along the two walls, four to a cell, one on each lower bunk and one on each upper one. He then closed the doors, put a six-inch key in the locks, used another key as a lever to turn the six-inch one, and locked the new prisoners in as Lola took their money, watches and rings to her office-apartment, padlocking them in a sort of wood pirate chest.

Later that day, Lola got another truckful of Germans. By early May, she had close to a thousand, eight or more to a cell, two or more to a bed and on the floor, too. The cell doors were solid as church doors, but Lola could see the Germans if a door was opened to let in the potato-soup pails or let out the excrement pails, or if she lifted a tear-shaped tab in the center of any closed door. At such times, Lola could see the Germans by the cell-window light or, at night, the cell light bulb. Their bunks would be folded up, and they would be sitting on stools and the floor and using the 7s through 10s, the face cards, and the aces for a game known as "Dog" or chips of wood for "A Man Isn't Angry." Of course, Lola knew that the Germans weren't convicted or even indicted yet, and that they might be as innocent as Auschwitz's Jews. Even so, she was incensed to see them leading the life of Riley, comparatively, and consistently failing to be Höss, Hössler or Mengele.

She wanted those three! Höss, the Auschwitz commandant, an SS man with a bulldog's face, was the one who'd invented the cyanide chambers (as he'd once said to Himmler) "to render service to my Fatherland." Hössler, the commandant of the women's camp and a twin of Vice President Truman, was the one who'd told the Jews, "Good morning! We have some showers," and Mengele, the top doctor and a tall, dark, handsome man, had told them, "Left," or "Right," while whistling a Wagner aria. Lola herself, having mangled her thumb at the Union Factory, had once been "selected" by Mengele, but the girl who wrote down her number later erased it. Höss and Hössler had never themselves hit a Jew, and Mengele had even flirted with one and told her, "Your ass is getting bigger," but the three were the powers that be at Auschwitz and were the logical targets of Lola's wrath.

But alas: the war was still raging eighty miles west. In Berlin, Hitler had shot himself, collapsing, knocking down a vase of daffodils, dying, but Höss was Special Commissioner for the Extermination of Jews, Hössler was at Belsen, and Mengele was an army doctor in Czechoslovakia. They weren't in Gleiwitz, nor were any SS who were known to Lola, and she was soon sitting for hours in her office-apartment, throwing herself at her papers instead of at SS throats. Her adjutant worried about her. *How can I help her?* her adjutant thought.

The adjutant, Moshe Grossman, the boy who saw Lola's brother cry, "Hear, O Israel," on the gallows at Gintergrube, had lost his mother, father, and prosperous business in Lodz when the Germans came, and he'd lost more when the Russians came. On the march to Germany, he had escaped in Gleiwitz by dropping into the snow, crawling into a rabbit hutch, and hiding inside until Gleiwitz fell. He'd then found a horse and wagon, but he hadn't gone far when the Russians said, "What? We're marching and you're riding?" and took them away. He'd then found a bicycle, but the Russians took that away too, and Moshe had walked to Kattowitz, joined the Office, and gone back to Gleiwitz to start again at

square one. A thin, wary, watchful boy, his skill lay in wheeling and dealing or, as Marx called it, in haggling, and in Gleiwitz he fast made friends
with the fat Russian quartermaster. He often went to that bloated man
for potatoes for Lola's Germans, and he brought along vodka to trade for
a barrel of herring, say, to sell to a restaurant manager, to buy gold rings
from a needy woman, to hide till he somehow could get to the West.

Considering there was a war on, Moshe had a good thing going, and he
wanted to stay in Lola's good graces. He often stood at the Kloster Street
Gate to keep an eye out for SS-like faces, and one day in May he spotted
one on a man in a German army uniform. Not following SOP, Moshe
didn't bring him to Interrogation, next door to Lola's office, but to Lola
herself. "I have someone you'll want to see," he said, and he pushed the
German in.

Lola stood up. It was sunny out, and the sun through her two big windows silhouetted her. "Who are you?" she asked in German, using the
you-word the Germans use for children, horses, dogs.

"A soldier. An ordinary soldier."

"Why aren't you in a POW camp?"

"I've lost my Soldier Book."

"What about your ID tag?"

"I've lost that too."

Lola studied him. The man was forty, perhaps, his fat and aristocratic
face had a look of "I'm the high muck-a-muck here," and she couldn't
believe from the stripe on his sleeve that he was merely a PFC. She knew
next to nothing about the German army, but the German didn't know that
Lola didn't know, and she hoped to bluff him. "What unit were you in?"

"The 24th Panzer Reconnaissance Battalion, 24th Panzer Division."
Or some such address.

"What battles were you in?"

"Sevastopol, Stalingrad. . . ." Or some such conductor's call.

"Are you sure you're not an SS?"

"Nein! Ich bin nur ein ordinärer soldat! I'm only an ordinary soldier!"

"Are you really sure?"

"I'm sure! I was drafted for the Fatherland!"

"All right," Lola said to Moshe. "Undress him."

Till then, Moshe had stood aside silently, but at Lola's command he
pulled the old gray jacket off the German, and the white undershirt, too.
Lola's command didn't amaze him, for Moshe, like her, had learned
about the SS at a class in Kattowitz, and the German himself knew what
Lola was looking for. He stood like a court-martialed man as Moshe lifted
his flabby left arm and, in his armpit, discovered a tiny tattoo, an A or B
blood tattoo that all the SS were labeled with. Moshe pointed silently,
and Lola erupted.

"*Du lügner!* You liar!" Lola shouted. Her hand snapped back like a thing on a spring, and she swung it fiercely across the German's face. How long she had waited for this day! "*Du schmutzige SS!*" Lola cried. "How many Jews did you kill?"

"Not any! I wasn't—"

"*Du verfluchtes lügner!*"

"I worked in an office in Kattowitz!"

"*Noch schlimmer!* That's worse!" Lola cried. She hit the German again, exclaiming, "The higher you are, the more of a killer you are!"

"No, I wasn't that big!"

"*Du warst doch!* You were too!"

"Madame Commandant," Moshe said softly. "Look what I found." He was holding a black-and-white photograph from the German's jacket pocket—a photograph of him wearing an SS hat with jolly-roger insignia and Gestapo insignia too. On the German's face was a haughty look, and the scrawl on the back of the photograph said, "*Ein blick.* A certain look."

"*Du verfluchtes Gestapo schwein!*" Lola screamed. Her hand snapped back, but it stayed like a guillotine blade as Moshe started to pummel him. Another guard in Lola's office, a Jew, hit the German too, the blood running from the man's nose till he fell to the floor, where the two men continued to beat him and kick him. "*Du mieses schwein! Du elendes schwein! Du—*" Lola cried.

"*Nein!* No, don't!" the German cried, really cried. He curled to protect himself from the fists and the feet, crawling to Lola and clutching at Lola's smooth leather boots. "No, Madame Commandant! I wasn't a big shot inside the SS!"

"You were! You big pigged-out pig!"

"No, I didn't kill any Jews!"

"It shows all over your bloated face!"

"*Gnade!* Have mercy on me!"

"*Why?*" Lola cried. Oh, how the German enraged her! One day in Auschwitz, Lola had told her Czech barracks boss, "I didn't get any bread," "Yes, you did," "No, I swear I didn't," and the boss had beaten her, kicked her, and pushed her into the pelting rain. Lola had kneeled in the mud, her arms overhead like a drowning woman's, her body a sodden sponge as hour after hour the boss came outside and beat her. Well, where was the fat SS man that day? Why didn't he tell the Czech barracks boss, "*Gnade.* Have mercy," that day? In another world in Będzin, Lola's mother, Rivka, had often quoted the Talmud, the corpus of Jewish laws, "Even as He is merciful, be merciful too," but who was the "He" who had mercy for Lola at Auschwitz? She booted away the SS man's grasping hands, shouting, "Moshe! Take him away!"

"What should I do?"

"Just don't kill him!"

And pummeling him, Moshe and the other guard dragged him to the depths of this place where the last were first, the first were last. *"Bitte nein!* Please don't!" Lola heard him scream, and, as she wrote her report up, she heard his screams expand like a series of organ chords in the prison's enormous nave, till the sounds rose to the highest tier, till the frosted skylight echoed them back. *"Nein!" "Bitte nein!" "Bitte gnade!" "Bitte nein!"* Hath not a Jew eyes? Hath not a Jew passions? If you wrong the Jews, will they not take revenge?

In fact, interrogation was not Lola's job. She theoretically ran the prison as Jews and gentiles from Interrogation did "What did you do in World War II"s. In the one small interrogation room were a desk and two stools, the stool for the German bolted down so he or she couldn't hit the interrogator with it. One room for one thousand suspects wasn't enough, and Interrogation had other rooms in Gleiwitz at the old auto school and the old Gestapo building, as well as other rooms in Kattowitz. There, Germans from Lola's prison met the ice-cold eyes of Pinek's sister's boyfriend—a look so cold, so compassionless, so empty of all human substance but "Oh, what I'll do if you don't confess," that a lot of Germans confessed instantaneously, and one even hanged himself later on. Indeed, Pinek's sister's boyfriend was so upset whenever a German *didn't* confess that Pinek often had to tell him, "Forget it, Chaim! The man might be innocent!"

In Gleiwitz, the chief interrogator was Adam, the philosopher-philanthropist from Auschwitz. Now, Adam knew that a German wouldn't say, "I was SS," "I was a Nazi," or "I was a Nazi collaborator" if he believed that Adam would then beat his brains out. But also Adam knew that the Torah forbade him to hurt an ox or an ass, let alone a thing in God's image, and he ordered his other interrogators in the near words of Leviticus, "Do not take revenge." The trouble was, the Germans would lie, and the lies were like slaps in Adam's own face. It might be two in the morning, he might have had two hours' sleep, and a man might be brought in in German army uniform. "You lost your Soldier Book," Adam might guess.

"Yes, I lost it."

"And your dog-tag too."

"Yes, I lost that too."

"What unit were you in?"

"The 295th Infantry Division."

"You're lying," Adam might say. "It was wiped out at Stalingrad."

"I didn't know that. By then I'd been transferred out."

"When?"

"In 1941."

"Where?"

"In Lublin."

"Why?"

"To, uh, to fight the Polish partisans."

"You're lying! There were no Polish partisans then!" And reflexively, Adam would smack the German's smart-aleck face.

At first, Adam used his bare hands when a German was diddling him. But that would hurt Adam, too, and soon he was using a cane to hit the most obvious liars with. His assistants in Gleiwitz used mopsticks, broomsticks, and sticks as thick as cavemen's clubs, as well as an instrument that the Germans called a *totschläger,* beater-to-death, a two-foot spring with a hard lead ball at the business end. By snapping the beater-to-death like a racket, an interrogator could use his arm, his wrist, and the spring to deliver a triple jolt to a German's arms, legs, body or face while avoiding a sort of tennis elbow himself. The beater-to-death was the favorite tool at Lola's prison, where it was used on Germans like one who Lola didn't recognize but who'd been in the Auschwitz SS. Had the man simply said, "Yes, I worked at the Auschwitz men's camp," he'd have been beaten as badly, perhaps, as the man with the *"Ein blick"* photograph, but he had made impossible claims of *"Nein! Ich hatte die Juden gern!* I liked the Jews!" *"Nein! Ich habe den Juden geholfen!* I helped the Jews!" *"Nein! Ich habe den Juden gutes getan!* I did good deeds for the Jews!" and the outraged interrogators wielded the beater-to-death till the man stopped mocking them. They then dragged him off to the nearest cell, cell 105, but, not indicting him, declared him a sort of full-time suspect, bringing him in each second night until there was no oasis of white on his black-and-blue body, which, if he wasn't moaning, looked like a corpse that was one month dead.

Four blocks away on Teuchert Street, Adam didn't know about this. But the bruises and broken bones he caused, sometimes, simply to get someone with an A or B tattoo and a part of a *uniform,* sometimes, to tell him, "Yes, I was SS," brought pain to Adam himself. He didn't understand why, and one night he pulled a bottle of *bimber,* or moonshine vodka, out of his office cupboard, leaned back in his armchair, put up his feet on his ottoman, sipped the *bimber,* and asked himself, *Why am I feeling rotten?* No one deserved to be thrashed as much as Hitler's henchmen did, and Adam believed that a man shouldn't show a woman's softheartedness, a *muliebris misericordia,* as Spinoza had called it in Latin, by letting them off. But also, Adam remembered, Spinoza had proved by reason alone that a man shouldn't hurt another man—even a very wicked man. Spinoza, a Jew, had lived in the 1600s, when all the philosophers said, as Kepler did, "Geometry is God himself," and Spinoza had summed up the human virtues as neatly as the a^2s, b^2s and c^2s in

Euclid's *Elements.* "Proposition XXVII," Spinoza had written, and Adam, his eyes closed, remembered it. "If we conceive that a thing that is like ourselves is affected with an emotion, we ourselves are affected with a like emotion." Well, Adam thought, an SS man is a man like me. Does that mean—"Proposition XLVII. If we conceive that a thing that is like ourselves is affected with pain, we ourselves feel pain." All right, Adam thought, if I hurt an SS man, then I also hurt myself. But what can I *do* about it? Open up Lola's prison door? Let the war criminals out? Tell them, Go and don't sin? Pretty please?

Every night Adam thought, *What can I do?* He sipped all his *bimber,* tipping the unlabeled bottle till the last drop rolled out. His secretary ordered more, but Adam then downed it like someone with an asbestos throat, and his secretary had to re-order the stone-colored stuff. His boozing was no embarrassment to the other interrogators, who—like the SS at Auschwitz, who got about six shots of schnapps and one quarter-pack of cigarettes every day (and who seemed to need it)—were serious drinkers too. Even some guards at Lola's prison drank a bottle of *bimber* each day and stood on the parapets shooting in Roman-candle trajectories, crying, "To hell with the Germans!" and Adam's intake was par for the Jews in the Office of State Security.

Often, Adam didn't go to interrogations but sat in his office, drinking, listening to distant cries of *"Nein!"* He assumed that one of his boys was slamming a door on a German's arm while driving pins up the German's nails, but he didn't want to go see it. Adam had once been tortured himself, spinning on a spit till he told the Gestapo, "Yes, I'm a Jew!" and going to Auschwitz gratefully, and in Gleiwitz his bones were aching again from the Germans' own screams. He sat in his office wishing, sometimes, that the boys would do something *monstrous,* so a German would just confess and the screams would stop.

One night when a German's pain was a boil in Adam's own ear, Adam had a bright idea. He didn't cry, *"Eureka!"* but jumped up and, not too unsteadily, hurried to where the man was being interrogated, bursting into the noisy room. "What's going on?" Adam cried.

"This man is SS—"

"Stop beating him!"

"Yes, Comrade Captain."

"And take that mask off him!"

"Yes, Comrade Captain."

"I'm sorry about this," Adam said to the German. "What's this man's name?" he asked the Catholic interrogator.

"Müller." Or whatever.

"What crime did he do?"

"He won't tell us."

"Müller," said Adam. "My men shouldn't have hit you. I'm sorry they did. I was at Auschwitz," Adam continued, showing the German his arm and its 104346. "I was beaten. My father and brother died. I'm bitter, but I'm not a beast like you Germans. I don't want to hurt you. I don't want to *kill* you," Adam said, letting the German see his Colt 45. "But what can I do? I can't release you. I can't send you to a court if I don't know your crime. Please," Adam said. "You must help me. Confess. Say, 'I was at this camp, and I did this thing.' You'll go to a court immediately. You'll get a fair trial. You," Adam said, bending forward, letting the German see his three captain's stars, and, in a German's eye, playing his ace—"you have an officer's word for it. Think about it," Adam concluded. "I'll be back in five minutes."

Adam then left. He waited outside, but in his mind's eye he could see the wet smiles on the boys inside, and in his inner ear he could hear the clubs going *slap!* on their palms. He then hurried in, telling the German, "I'm out of patience now. Do you want these people or me?"

"I worked at a camp in Kattowitz," the German began.

"Write that down," Adam said to the much-relieved interrogators. "Sign it," he said to the German eventually. "Send him," he told the inter-rogators, "to Schwientochlowitz," the camp for the Germans waiting for trials in Kattowitz, the camp commanded by Lola's mandolinist lover. "Thank you," he told the German, and went to his office.

And pulled out his *bimber*. All that night, Adam went to the echoing interrogation rooms. He did his "Please help me" bit, but its precondition was pain, the *"Nein"*s still spilled from the bad-guys' room to the good-guy's office, and, as Spinoza had warned, something in Adam also cried, *"Nein."* He hated the Germans for causing this pain, and he sat in his soft stuffed chair, he thought and thought about it, he drank and drank his *bimber,* and at dawn he at last passed out.

Lola, too, was upset by the German screams. A block away from the prison, the German civilians said, "Why are the people screaming so? It's *awful,"* but to Lola the screams were a cat's meow compared to a thou-sand conjectured screams in an Auschwitz cyanide chamber. At night she lay in her office-apartment hearing a German's piercing *"Nein"*s, thinking of Itu, her baby, of Ittel, her brother, of Abramik, Abramik, Abramik, her nephews, or thinking just, *How can I sleep?* Her answer came when an Office associate visited her: the boy who was using his good right arm to punch people's noses in Kattowitz.

The boy's name was Efraim. He was from Lublin, the son of a Jew who did circumcisions. When the Germans came, Efraim had fled to the woods, digging a hole the size of a king-size bed and concealing it under twigs, leaves and dirt, intending to live like a gnome eating mushrooms, rabbits and boars till the end of World War II. But the Germans had hunted him, and, to survive, he'd had to get rifles, establish a partisan unit, cry in Polish, *"Hura!* Hurrah!" meaning "Attack!" and kill the Germans before the Germans killed *him.* Efraim's father, mother, all nine brothers and sisters, and all thirty cousins died, his own left arm was shattered by "friendly fire," and, on his liberation, he joined the Office in Lublin, becoming a very wild officer with an "I don't care if I die" disposition. In early May, he stopped by at Lola's prison and told her, "You mustn't live here. Come," and the two went house-hunting in Gleiwitz.

They walked down Kloster Street. It was loud from trolley cars, but at the corner they saw a quiet street with an arch of red maples over it: Schwerin Street, and Efraim led Lola down it. They came to the old parade ground and a long, lovely, cobblestoned street full of red-tile-gabled homes, each with a plot of tulips as perfect as porcelain. The street's name was Lange Reihe—in English, Long Line—and as Lola watched, Efraim chose the home at 25, whose owner was an old glass-blower in Gleiwitz. Efraim knocked with his good right arm, and a German opened the door saying, *"Ja?"*

"Heraus! Get out!" Efraim shouted. *"Lasst alles hier!* Leave everything here! *Kommt niemals zurück!* Don't ever come back! *Sofort!* At once!"

Saying nothing, the German left, and Efraim politely let Lola in. The vestibule led by some curving stairs to a quaint living room that Lola soon decorated with a baby grand piano that, as a member of State Security, she had picked up at a storehouse for German furniture. She hired a German maid, Gertrude, and, in lieu of a father, mother, brother or sister, sent a car to Będzin to pick up Pinek's pretty sister and to bring her to Lola's new home.

Two hours later, Shoshana arrived. She was three years older than Lola, a girl whose indelible dimples all Będzin had adored. Her sunny spirit hadn't faded in September, 1939, and Lola had often gone to her home to crank up the gramophone, listen to the megaphone end, and dance to,

Tango Milonga,
Tango of Dreams,

with the youths of Będzin. Then came the *Judenrein,* the cleaning-out of the Jews. Lola was sent to Auschwitz, but Shoshana, who had Goldilocks curls and an ID card from Pinek, her partisan brother, passed as a Polish Catholic. She learned the Lord's Prayer, *"Ojcze nasz. . . ,"* and the Hail

Mary, *"Zdrowas Mario. . . ,"* and she found work at a German bomber base. She was doing sabotage there in June, 1944, when the Gestapo discovered, arrested and tortured her. One of her lungs collapsed and she got tuberculosis, and now, the war over, the Germans defeated, the Russians, Americans, British and French in Berlin—now Shoshana was slowly dying in Gleiwitz.

Lola met her and led her upstairs at 25 Lange Reihe. At every step, Shoshana stopped, gasped for air, said, "I'm sorry," and Lola said, "You're doing fine!" Lola helped her to a bedroom, and Shoshana slumped into a bed but, not going to sleep, pulled from her purse a photograph of the cold-eyed interrogator in Kattowitz who she unaccountably loved. "He's beautiful, isn't he?" Shoshana said, and she put the photograph on her table as Lola brought her a drinking glass to prop it up. Then, Shoshana fell back, coughing violently.

Lola brought doctors in all of May. She told them, "Please! No more deaths from the Germans!" At noon she'd climb on her motorcycle, commandeered from a German, and rush from the prison to 25. She'd get off and run upstairs as Gertrude, her maid, more or less tackled her to pull off her boots, telling her, "Madam! One moment!" One boot off and one on, Lola would run to Shoshana's bedroom and lie, "You look better!"

"Did you hear from Chaim?"

"No, he's busy in Kattowitz."

"Do you know when he'll visit?"

"I'm sure very soon." Her eyes wet, Lola wouldn't mention that Chaim, the interrogator, didn't want an invalid girlfriend and was now running around with the fiancée of the Jewish chief of Imprisonment.

"I love him," Shoshana would say, and she'd cry as she kissed his slick picture. Day after day, she lay in her bed, sat in her chair, and walked to her bathroom, gasping for air. Her fever, her cough, and the puffs underneath her eyes were worse than on her first day in Gleiwitz. It broke Lola's heart: Lola's love for this beautiful girl and her hate, hate, hate for the Germans who'd ruined her.

More weary people came to Lola's. The first was a boy from four concentration camps in Germany. After the war, he'd returned to Będzin, where the Poles in his home wouldn't let him in, and he'd then come to Gleiwitz, where Lola hugged him and told him, "You're staying with me." Then more people came from Auschwitz, Buchenwald, up through the whole brutal alphabet, till in the middle of May came the eight hardy girls from near Denmark, dressed like a gypsy tribe in silk, satin, and silver fox, the "gifts" of Germans along their way. Their queen was Zlata, who gasped out, "Lola! It's you!" and had questions about Lola's uniform, Luger, and mission in State Security, as well as about Lola's brothers—

Zlata's and Ada's sturdy husbands—and about Ada herself. Lola hadn't heard from them, and Zlata told her, "I'll wait for them in Będzin."

"No, you're staying with me."

"But there's eight of us."

"So—?"

"We promised we'd stay together."

Lola just shrugged. She called up Moshe, her adjutant, who soon showed up with some prison guards, and Lola and everyone went next door to a German engineer's. Moshe knocked, the German answered, and Lola shouted, *"Heraus! Eine stunde, heraus!* In one hour, get out!" and the German, his wife, and his daughter did. The eight amazed girls moved in as Lola rolled up the rugs to exchange for eggs, explaining, "Well, *they* took from *us.*"

A few days later was Friday, the start of Sabbath. The day was warm, and the chestnut trees on Lola's street were full of cone-shaped ornaments: of clumps of white chestnut flowers. One girl at Lola's, a niece of Zlata's, had gone through the empty shops until, at last, she'd found the two candles needed for Sabbath. She'd set them in silverfoil candlesticks, and at sunset she lit them, saying, *"Baruch ata.* Blessed art Thou, O Lord our God, who has bidden us to kindle the Sabbath lights." It was then Sabbath, and Zlata's niece said, *"Shabbat shalom.* The peace of the Sabbath."

"Shabbat shalom," Lola and everyone answered.

They then ate the herring dinner. They talked of Będzin, of fathers, mothers and loved ones lost, and Lola assured everyone that the dead were being avenged right there in Gleiwitz. "I give the Germans plenty *tsures,"* plenty trouble, said Lola in Yiddish.

"Are you really mean?" said Zlata.

"I'm mean. Do you want to see it?"

"No," Zlata said. She couldn't understand why a Jew would choose to stoke the old embers of hate—on the Sabbath, especially—by seeing an SS man ever again. But also, Zlata remembered the SS man at Auschwitz who'd brought her a bed, blanket, aspirin, a pair of good leather gloves, and a reprieve when her Jewish boss told her, "I'm firing you." How, Zlata wondered, could Lola know that an SS man who was getting the *tsures* deserved it? "No, Lola," Zlata said. "I've seen enough."

"How about you, Gucia?" Lola asked Zlata's niece. "Do you want to see it?"

"No, Lola," Gucia said.

"Moshe? Mania? Pola?" said Lola. "Do you want to see it?"

"No, Lola," Lola's new family said.

7

At that moment, Shlomo, the holy man who'd made *matzo* in Warsaw and who'd found *matzo* in Kattowitz, serving it to Lola for Passover, was observing the Sabbath at his apartment in Kattowitz. With him was Rivka, the girl who was two inches taller and so couldn't romance him, and the two acted as though the words OBSERVE THE SABBATH were written in stone, which indeed they were. All that night and Saturday, Shlomo and Rivka didn't light any fires, put out any fires, turn on any lights, turn off any lights, tie or untie any knots, turn on the radio, pick up the phone, play the piano, water the plants, carry an unfurled umbrella, or walk farther west than Königshütte. Shlomo didn't write any words, erase any words, tear up the paper, paste it together again, shine his shoes, or scrape anything off a page in the Torah, and Rivka didn't do the wash, bake any cakes, braid her hair, put on mascara, sew, or put saffron in chicken soup. Nor were these rules unwelcome, for to Shlomo and Rivka they were reminders that the world was created by God: the world worked, and now they could relish it. On this Sabbath, the two sat and read the Torah, and Shlomo smiled from the gap in his teeth to the tips of his ears and Rivka smiled back. "The Sabbath is God's greatest gift," Shlomo said.

But later in May, Shlomo heard he'd be drafted into the Polish army, and he chose instead to enroll in the Office of State Security. He changed his name to Ignaz, said, *"Zay gezunt.* Stay well," to Rivka, and rode in a truck to Neisse, in Germany, eighty miles west. The road was still full of shell holes that the truck had to navigate like a boat that's avoiding the

Lorelei. On board was a boy, a Jew from Będzin, who'd be the commandant in Neisse, as well as a dozen boys who, like Shlomo, would work with
him. They mostly were Jews, like the boy who'd helped with the *matzo* in
Warsaw, saying to Shlomo, "But hurry," and one who'd once been
"selected," then "de-selected," at Auschwitz, and one who'd been castrated at Auschwitz as part of an SS experiment. In Neisse, all but Shlomo
would work in Intelligence, Interrogation and Imprisonment, and
Shlomo would be the mess officer there.

The trip took four hours. As the truck came to Neisse, Shlomo saw the
old fifteenth-century square: a flatland now, and the fifteenth-century
church of Saint James: a hill of rubble above the portraits of James, Jesus
and Mary. Threading among the ruins were the shoddy people of Neisse.
Few had been in the SS, for Neisse hadn't been near any camps, but, as
elsewhere in Germany, one in ten had presumably been a Nazi, and the
boys' mission in Neisse would be to ferret them out. At 28 Koch Street,
the Jewish commandant said, "Stop," and Shlomo said, "*Czysty dom.* A
nice clean house," in Polish, not Yiddish, and the boys moved into a German's abandoned home. They then went across the street to a gray building full of abandoned apartments that they made offices out of. Shlomo
set up a kitchen, and in the cellar a boy built a prison by bolting an ornate
gate to the door, bolting bars to the windows, and lining up eight double-
decker beds in the boiler room and another eight in the storage room.
One cell would be for sixteen men, the other for sixteen women.

The next day, Shlomo went out for potatoes and the others for Nazi
suspects. They walked down Breslauer Street, the main street of Neisse,
bringing with them some Germans who, for $200 per catch, said, "There!
That man was a Nazi!" or "There! That woman was!" Showing their .38s,
the boys then arrested the suspects and, on foot, brought them to the
cells on Koch Street. Soon there were Germans in every bed, but the
"There!"'s didn't end and the boys kept bringing more Germans in. By the
end of May, there were two, three or four in each straw-covered bed, as
well as more underneath it and in the aisles around it. Shlomo performed
what the Jews call a *mitzvah*, good deed, by sending the Germans plates
of potatoes, carrots and beets, but, after eating this, the Germans had
nothing but pails to put their excrement in. The air in the cells became
dense, the smell of the excrement filled it, the heat was like in Calcutta,
and the flies made the ceiling black. *I'm choking*, the Germans thought,
and one even took the community razor blade and, in despair, cut his
throat open with it. Gasping, the German died, and the boys got a horse
and wagon and carried him to the cemetery across the Neisse River.

D ay after day, the Germans in Shlomo's cellar went to the second and
third-floor offices. As many as eight interrogators, almost all Jews, stood

around any one German saying, "Were you in the Nazi Party?" Sometimes a German said, "Yes," and the boys shouted, *"Du schwein!* You
pig!" and beat him and broke his arm, perhaps, before sending him to his
cell and, from there, to Schwientochlowitz and the Kattowitz courts. But
usually a German said, "No," and the boys, who'd heard otherwise from
the German informants, told him, "You're lying. You were a Nazi."

"No, I never was."

"You're lying! We know about you!"

"No, I really wasn't—"

"Du lügst! You're lying!" they cried, hitting the obstinate man. "You
better admit it! Or you'll get a longer sentence! Now! Were you in the
Nazi Party?"

"No!" the German often said, and the boys had to beat him and beat
him until he was really crying, "I was a Nazi! Yes!"

But sometimes a German wouldn't confess. One such hard case was a
fifty-year-old who was strolling along when a $200 informant said, "You
were in the Party! I know it!" The man was brought to the gray building
and to a third-floor interrogation room, and a boy asked him, "Were you
in the Party?"

"No, I wasn't in it."

"How many people work for you?"

"In the high season, thirty-five."

"You must have been in the Party," the boy deduced. He asked for the
German's wallet, where he found a fishing license with the stamp of the
German Anglers Association. Studying it, he told the German, "It's
stamped by the Party."

"It's not," said the German. He'd lost his left arm in World War I and
was using his right arm to gesture with, and, to the boy, he may have
seemed to be Heiling Hitler. The boy became violent. He grabbed the
man's collar, hit the man's head against the wall, hit it against it ten times
more, threw the man's body onto the floor, and, in his boots, jumped on
the man's cringing chest as though jumping rope. A half dozen other
interrogators, almost all Jews, pushed the man onto a couch, pulled off
his trousers, and hit him with hard rubber clubs and hard rubber hoses
full of stones. The sweat started running down the Jews' arms, and the
blood down the man's naked legs.

"Warst du in der Partei?"

"Nein!"

"Warst du in der Partei?"

"Nein!" the German screamed—*screamed,* till the boys had to go to
Shlomo's kitchen for a wooden spoon and to use it to cram some rags in
the German's mouth. Then they resumed beating him.

But the screams had carried across the Neisse River as well as to

Shlomo's office. *Oh! I hope he's a Nazi!* Shlomo had thought, as had the six interrogators themselves. The more they beat him, the more they had an investment in his reassuring them, "Yes! I was in the Nazi Party! I deserve everything you're doing to me! You're righteous people!" And therefore the more they beat him, till, at last, they paused, pulling the rags from the German's mouth. *"Warst du in der Partei?"*

"Nein! Ich war nicht!"

"Hinunten! Downstairs!" a boy with a drawn revolver screamed, and he chased the German down the stairwell into the cellar into the crowded cell.

All that happened on a Thursday. Two days later, on the Sabbath, the day Shlomo felt that a Jew mustn't hurt the lowliest living thing, the boys brought the German upstairs to validate on Saturday the drastic acts of Thursday. They asked him, "Were you in the Party?" and, when the man said, "No," they resumed beating and whipping him too. The more the man contradicted them, the more they hated him for it. They left him and stared at him ominously through holes in the wall, they shot bullets by his right ear out the open window, they said, "On the double!" and chased him around with a cocked revolver. "No, I was not in the Party!" the German persisted. The days drifted by, May mellowed into June, the boys kept bringing him in, and like cawing crows his *"Nein"*s and *"Nein"*s kept soaring across the Neisse. So did the screams of many other men and women in Shlomo's building.

Shlomo couldn't take it. He wasn't like Lola, who, as the Germans cried, *"Nein,"* had heard the cries of her loved ones at Auschwitz, for Shlomo heard the cries of the Germans themselves. *This isn't right,* Shlomo thought. "Three characteristics do Jews possess," said Shlomo's beloved Talmud, and the first one was "They're merciful." But also Shlomo worried, *What if the man they're beating isn't a Nazi?* Then the Talmud taught that the wicked ones were the Jews. Why, the father of all Jews, Abraham, had reprimanded the Lord himself, saying, "Wilt Thou destroy the righteous along with the wicked? That be far from Thee to do!" Of the 613 duties of Jews, the 545th was "Do not stand by thy neighbor's blood," and Shlomo, at last, went out to confront the Jewish interrogators. He met them in the courtyard, saying, "You must stop doing this."

"No, we must do it," an interrogator said.

"Why?"

"In the name of our murdered parents."

"Are you sure that this individual is one of the ones who murdered them?"

"We must find out."

"No, that isn't right," Shlomo said, but the boys went upstairs, and the German who'd told them, "I wasn't in the Party," was brought in for session number eight. By now, the man was half unconscious due to his many concussions, and he wasn't thinking clearly. The boys worked on him with rubber and oak-wood clubs and said, "Do you still say you weren't in the Party?"

"No! I didn't say I wasn't in the Party!"

"You didn't?"

"No!" said the punch-drunk man. "I never said it!"

"You *were* in the Party?"

"Yes!"

The boys stopped beating him. They practically sighed, as if their ordeal were over now. They lit up cigarettes, and, as the German sat dazed, started to talk of their pre-war days. "I was a big-shot wholesale man," one boy said. "How about you?"

"I owned apartment houses."

"Scram," one said to the German. The man stood up, and he had his hand on the doorknob when one of the boys impulsively hit the back of his head, and he fell to the floor, unconscious. *"Aufstehen, du Deutsches schwein.* Stand up, you German pig," the boys said, kicking him till he stood up and collapsed again. Two boys carried him to his cell and dropped him in a corner, where some of the Germans gave up an upper bunk for him. For days, the man lay on the straw, but Shlomo did *mitzvahs* by sending him down his potatoes, carrots, beets. At times, the Jew who delivered the plate pushed it, instead, in a German's face, and Shlomo sent down another one.

B y now, ninety percent of the German men in Shlomo's cellar—eighty-five of the ninety-four men—had said, "I was in the Party." So had most men and women in the other cellars administered by the Office of State Security. There were many, many cellars, and the Jewish and gentile interrogators weren't there to tell the Germans, "You weren't Nazis. Go home." The boys would ask, "Were you in the Party?" and a German would say in the virtual words of the Ten Commandments, "No. I believe in One God. Not two," yet the boys would beat him or her with whips, clubs, and Toonerville trolley chains, or put his or her fingers into a door jamb, slamming the door, or put wooden wedges under his or her fingernails, driving them in, until the German said, "Yes." The boys sought the truth as others sought olive oil: by crushing the substance around it.

At times, the boys would beat up a German even before his "No, I was not in the Party." In Bielsko-Biała, in Poland, the Jewish commandant asked a Nazi suspect, "What's your name?"

"Mathias Hemschik." The name was a German one, and two other boys from the Office started to slap him. "Sir? Why are they hitting me?" the German asked.

"I lost eighteen relatives," the commandant said. "And now I'm taking revenge." And kicking the German's testicles, the boys locked him in a cellar until, two weeks later, they asked him, "Were you in the Party?"

"No, I was not."

"Yes, you were. Why not admit it?"

"They asked me to join it, but I refused."

"You also were in the Young Farmers."

"How could I have been? I'm sixty-three."

"Lie down." The man did, and a boy with a whip and a boy with a saber belabored him till a girl interrogator told them, "No, stop it."

"No, beat me!" the German screamed. "Beat me to death! And *still* I won't be a Nazi!"

Often the boys wouldn't stop at "Were you in the Party?" At the cellar in Neisse-Neuland, the boys asked a German, "How often did you hit So-and-So?" and when the German said, "Never!" the boys burst the German's eardrums. At the cellar in Bunzlau, the Jewish commandant asked a German woman, "How long were you in Free Germany?" but the woman said, "I never heard of it," and the commandant said, "Confess. Or your parents will hang." At the cellar in Wünschelburg, the boys asked a German, "Where did you hide your gun?" "Who did you shoot with it?" "Why?" and when the German said, "I don't have any gun!" one boy trod on the German's hands, one on the German's feet. Of course, the boys would beat up the Germans for "Yes"es as well as "No"s. In Glatz, the Jewish commandant asked a German policeman, "Were you in the Party?"

"Of course! I was obliged to be!"

"Lie down," the commandant said, and six weeks later the boys were still whipping the German's feet.

It had been Germans who'd fingered the German suspects, and the boys always asked the suspects to finger some more. At another cellar in Glatz, the boys broke a German's ribs till the German wrote, "I promise I'll cooperate with the Office." In the cellar in Ottmachau, the boys stood a German in cold water, naked, until he signed off on "I promise I'll spy for the Office." "Where are the Werewolves?" the boys in Schreiberhau asked, and when a German woman said, "I don't know," a boy hit her twenty-five times with a rubber club. "Where is Herr Klose?" the boys asked at Markt Bohrau, and when a priest said, "I don't know," the boys beat him till he passed out. "Who, besides you, is SS?" the boys asked in Pinek's cellar in Kattowitz, and when a German answered, "I'm not SS!"

the boys beat him and sewed a silk skull-and-bones to his sweater, saying, "You'll never get out."

Upstairs, Pinek didn't know about this. Nor did he know what went on in Neisse or Neisse-Neuland, Bielsko-Biała, Ottmachau, Schreiberhau, Markt Bohrau, Bunzlau, Wünschelburg, Glatz or the many other cellars in Silesia. Pinek was up to his eyeballs in more important matters. At age twenty-three, he wasn't just the Secretary of State Security but now the Secretary to the Governor too. The man who'd been governor in January, who'd often told Pinek, "You people," meaning the Jews, "think you're smarter than I am," had been antisemitic, and Pinek had soon reported him to Warsaw and, to replace him, had recommended a man whose wife was a Będzin Jew. *"Skurwysynie!* You sonofabitch!" the man said to Pinek jovially on coming to Kattowitz, and Pinek—or Paweł, he called himself—was now the number-two man in Silesia. He worked every night until seven or eight, walked home with a Polish bodyguard, and had dinner off Rosenthal gold-bordered china. He often went by Mercedes to Neisse, etcetera, to inspect them, but the cautious interrogators didn't hit the Germans then, and Pinek didn't hear the Germans scream.

If he had, he'd have said, like Shlomo, "You must stop doing this." He'd once been informed against, remember, he'd been arrested at the Silesia Factory, in Będzin, he'd been beaten in this very office in Kattowitz, he'd signed a confession that said, "I did sabotage," and he knew that a man who was beaten enough would confess, "Yes, I was a Nazi." He knew that the Nazis, the real ones, had fled (or been shot by the Russians) in January and that the Germans who'd stayed in Silesia probably weren't Nazis, and, in fact, that a German who was a Nazi wasn't necessarily evil. One day, Pinek was at a Kattowitz prison when he spotted the former director of the Silesia Factory, the man who'd told the Gestapo, "I can't run the factory without him," without Pinek. "Mr. Pitchner!" said Pinek. "What are you doing here?"

"They arrested me," the startled director said. He looked at Pinek and his three captain's stars like a man confronting the Reaper, and Pinek turned to a prison officer crossly.

"Why did you arrest him?"

"He directed a German factory!"

"Did he kill any Jews? Did he kill any Poles?"

"No, he didn't, but—"

"You can't just go and arrest him!"

"—but he's a Nazi!"

"Well, I'm releasing him!" Pinek said, and he brought the German home for a dinner on Rosenthal china. The day after that, Pinek sent out a memo,

In accordance with Regulations, a German must be investigated before he or she is arrested. . . .

and when, for the twentieth time, Pinek's sister's boyfriend came up to Pinek's office moaning, "I've got a German who won't confess," the Secretary exploded. He guessed that the boy had been torturing one of the Germans who were the victims of ill-intentioned informers, and he shouted, "I told you, Chaim! Ninety percent of these people, they're innocent!" A part of Pinek wanted to fire the boy, but Pinek's sister, who'd moved back to Kattowitz, coughing, to be nearer her blue-eyed idol, had said to Pinek, "Be good to Chaim," and Pinek now promoted him to assistant chief of Imprisonment.

The first wedding bells in Kattowitz were for Barek, the boy in Intelligence. He proposed, in his way, to Regina, the girl he'd found in the SS's happy-house at Auschwitz, on a train trip in June. In the car were six Russians, all drunk, all stumbling along the corridor, opening the compartments, roaring, "You're crowding us!" and tossing the Germans off. "*Vy Fritze!* You're Germans!" the Russians roared at Regina and Barek too. "*Vyljezaitje!* Get off!" but Barek showed them his gun and uttered the dreaded words, "I'm with the UB."

"Well, what about her?"

"We're engaged," Barek said, and Regina gasped.

"Oh, then we're sorry."

They were married on Saturday, June 23, in their dusty apartment across from the Kattowitz prison. Regina wore a cream-colored sheath that Barek had found in Kattowitz, and her sister, the maid of honor, wore a white pleated skirt, and her "giver-away" wore a blue pleated skirt with a red painted swastika, a relic of her concentration camp. At the *huppah,* the wedding canopy, the "giver-away" stood still so the pleats would conceal the now-inappropriate swastika, and by the feet of the bride and groom stood iron pails of red gladioluses from the Kattowitz market. "How many?" the black marketeer had asked, and Barek had told him, "All of them, and I'll buy the pails, too."

The last living rabbi in Kattowitz officiated. His *tallit* around him, the rabbi said, "Blessed art Thou, O Lord, who has created love." The groom gave a black-market ring to the bride, and the bride gave the groom a ring inscribed FEBRUARY 25, 1914, that she'd found in a heap of used clothes in Auschwitz. "Now you're married," the rabbi said. He took out his handkerchief, put it around an empty glass, put the glass next to Barek's right foot, and said, "Break it." Barek did, and the rabbi said, "Good luck for 120 years." The thirty guests from Intelligence, Interrogation and Imprisonment said, "Hurrah!" the bride and groom kissed, a boy started slapping a teakwood chair, and the dancing began. The guests did the polka, tango, hora—their boots beat the dusty rugs, the walls were a merry-go-round, and the skirts went up to the girls' naked knees. "Oh!" said Regina's sister. "Remember at Auschwitz? The time that we danced to *In a Persian Market?*"

"Yes!" said Regina. "We held up our skirts like the seven veils!"

"You could see our underwear under them!"

"Yes, you could see our paper bags!" said Regina, whirling around. "They were cement bags! They said CEMENT!"

"And remember?" another girl said. "The barracks boss came? And said, 'Girls—'"

"'—You're being noisy! Do you—'"

"'—Do you want another spanking?'"

"Oh my!" another girl said. "Remember, Regina? You once told the barracks boss, 'I want more soup'?"

"Yes! And she told me, 'No, you ___!'"

"And you threw your soup in her face!"

"And boy, did she ever beat me ___"

"She kept screaming, 'You pig! Y___—'"

"'—Piiig!' But you all applauded ___!"

"Oh! If she could see us right n___"

"She and the SS! Oh, what I'd g___"

The dance ended, and the girls ___ved into the cherries, strawberries, salami. The bride and groom cut t___ sponge cake, and the girls ravished it. They recalled how the SS had sh___ted, "We're marching to Germany!" how the girls had hidden in a pile ___ clothes, and how the SS had said, "You're spies!" and locked them u___ its whorehouse. "And that's where I met my Barek!" Regina said.

"He is so good-looking!"

"I love Barek's chin!"

"Forty-eight countries had Wo___ War II so you could meet him, Regina!"

"How did you do it?"

"With *mazel!* With luck!" Regina said.

It was four in the morning now. The bride, groom and guests made a circle, singing the song from the Zionist camp,

> *Un zol der fayer,*
> *Ferloshen vern,*
> *Shaynt oyf der himel,*
> *Mit zayne shtern,*

And if the fire
At last goes out,
The sky will shine
With all its stars,

and they then went to sleep on the living-room rug. The next day, Regina said, "Why waste the Rabbi?" a boy in Intelligence used the same clergy, flowers and food to marry another girl, a boy in Interrogation married another one, the commandant at Myslowitz married a black-haired guard, and the Office of State Security's Summer of Love began.

One summer day, a Jewish girl smitten by love came to Lola's city of Gleiwitz. She was Ada, praise God, Lola's brother's wife—Ada the girl who'd sung in Będzin, "W żłobie leży. In the manger," who'd sung at Auschwitz, "Sweetheart! Sweetheart!" and whose shoes had fallen apart on the road to Germany. Ada had found a big right shoe and a small left one, and in a barn she'd found potatoes by pushing the irate pigs aside. She'd ridden a coal-car to Germany, had been bombed and been liberated there, and for months had been searching for Lola's brother, Ada's husband, in Czechoslovakia. He wasn't there, but Ada had heard that Lola herself was in Gleiwitz and had come by train, trolley and foot to Lola's home.

Or rather, to Lola's three homes. Ada was dazzled by her old schoolmate's holdings on Lange Reihe. The tulips on Lola's real estate were as soft as an infant's skin, and the houses so full of thin-limbed girls and of yearning boys that to Ada they could be college dorms. Of course Ada recognized Zlata, who cried out, "Ada!" and fell into Ada's arms, but Ada saw sixty other boarders, too. It was noon, when the Jews were putting on weight at Lola's well-endowed tables and, in front of Ada's eyes, were falling in love or were reminiscing of prior romantic encounters at Lola's resort. To listen to, one girl had fallen in love as a boy walked in, and another had met Mr. Right at the corner of Kaiser Wilhelm Street. "He said to me, 'What does that number mean?'" the girl said to Ada. "I said, 'We got it at Auschwitz. Where were you?' He said, 'In the Polish army,' and I said, 'Oh,' and we've been in love ever since." The girl was a former shelf-mate of Ada's at Auschwitz and all but guaranteed her that Gleiwitz was Paradise.

Soon, Ada heard a roar outside, and an officer with a Luger came in. "Lola?" said Ada, thunderstruck, and Lola hugged her and, like a good housemother, sat at the head of the table asking her, "What happened in Germany?" "What camp did you go to?" "What happened then?" and "Where's David?" David was Lola's brother, Ada's husband.

"I'm looking for him."

"You should leave him."

"Lola?" said Ada, amazed.

"He's too old for you."

"But—"

"And his health isn't good."

"I know that," said Ada. One night in Będzin, Lola's mother had said, "If only I had some onions," and David had gone out to get some despite the German curfew. On spotting him, the SS had asked him, "Why are you out?" "To get onions." "You're lying." "I'm not. My mother is making meatballs, and—" "You're lying!" the SS had cried, and it had sent him to Myslowitz prison. For months, David had had to lie on his stomach while the Gestapo asked him, "Why were you out?" "To get onions!" "You're lying!" and while the Gestapo beat on his liver until it was barely functioning. It then sent him back to Będzin, where Ada, who pitied him, married him. "I think I love him," Ada told Lola now.

"No, Ada. Live your life."

"But what about David?"

"Let him live his."

Lola herself lived that way, Lola said. Her movie-matinee husband, Shlomo, had shown up in Gleiwitz, a skinny survivor of Auschwitz, but Lola had been reminded of Itu, their baby, and she had screamed at Shlomo, "Don't touch me!" That night, the bedroom rug was for Shlomo and the bed was for Lola and her Luger, for Lola knew that the most reported (and the least prosecuted) crime in Gleiwitz was rape. At last, Shlomo had left for a refugee center in Germany, and Lola was now romancing the mad Russian colonel from Kattowitz, sitting with him in movies with Fred Astaire or walking with him as, like butterflies, the pods from the maple trees fluttered by in Chopin Park. "You should stay here, Ada," Lola said.

"Oh, I couldn't!" said Ada, but Gleiwitz was tempting her. Lunch ended and Lola strode out, and Ada watched, awed, as Lola straddled her hog, kick-started it, twisted the grip, and roared off, the white exhaust like the train of a gown behind her. At six o'clock, Lola roared back, and Ada now listened as Lola swept upstairs, filled up the four-pawed bathtub, bathed, and cried, "Gertrude!" Gertrude, the maid, said, "Yes, ma'am!" and hurried upstairs, and Ada, intrigued, went too, to watch through the keyhole in Lola's bathroom door. "Oh, what I see!" Ada gasped.

"What's happening, Ada?" another girl from Auschwitz asked.

"Lola's undressed, and Gertrude is *powdering* her!"

"No, I don't believe it!"

"Look!"

"Oh my God! It's true!" the other girl from Auschwitz said. "Does someone even powder the Queen of England?"

"No! But this poor little girl from Będzin! Suddenly she's—"

"*Ayne dame.* A lady," the other girl said in Yiddish.

"*Ayne daaame!*" Ada agreed. And giggling, the two girls ran to their bedroom to sit at their vanity and to powder each other from a big but invisible can. At Auschwitz, the SS commandant, Höss, had lived in a white stucco home, and Jews had cooked, cleaned and gardened for him till his red begonias in his blue boxes were twinkling through the interstices of his white picket fence. "Oh, I could live here till I die," Höss's wife Hedwig once said, and Ada was charmed by Lola's sweet life in Gleiwitz.

"**D**o you want to see it?" Lola asked Ada the next day.

"Yes!" Ada said, and, as Lola motorcycled behind her, Ada walked down the red-maple-shaded street to 10 Kloster Street. The gate guard, saluting, let the two ladies in, and Lola showed Ada the lilac-filled court and the quaint-looking prison, built out of red and lapis-lazuli-colored bricks. At the eaves, the bricks were in diamond designs, and the brick chimneys were old and crooked, just like in Dickens's London. Going inside, Lola and Ada walked down the "cathedral" aisle, and Lola unlocked a cell whose occupants hadn't been in the bloody interrogation room. As Ada peeped in, the Germans jumped up as though to a call of "Attention!" and they stood like a squad of scared soldiers, arms at their sides, till Lola again locked them up.

From there Ada went to Lola's flower-filled office. A well-mannered prisoner clerk, a German, told Ada, "I'll play the violin for you," but Lola said acidly, "No," and the German retreated. A guard with a German prisoner gave Lola the German's jacket—manila file—and Lola glanced at the "Gleiwitz Prison," the German's name, and the "SS" written methodically in the jacket's upper left. "You were SS," Lola told him.

"No, I wasn't."

"You're lying."

"No, ma'am."

"*Du lügst,*" Lola said and, as though it were an old habit, slapped the German's face.

Ada said silently, "No!" She didn't necessarily trust the German, though even his eyes said, "I'm innocent." Back in Będzin, the Gestapo had once said to Ada, "Do you know a man in Switzerland?" and Ada had answered innocently, "Yes!" "Did you once get a parcel from him?" "Yes!" "What was in it?" "Sardines! They were good!" "You ate them?" "Oh, was

I not supposed to?" "You didn't sell them?" "No!" "You didn't buy guns with the money from them?" "Oh no! I was hungry!" "You didn't—" "The next time I get sardines from him, am I supposed to bring them here?" "No. You may go," the Gestapo had told her, and Ada now assumed that an SS man could lie as impressively as she herself had lied in Będzin. But Ada, who'd studied the Torah, could also see the injustice of punishing a German for saying, "I was SS," and a German for saying, "I wasn't." What haven did the German cringing in Lola's office have? Damned for his "Yes" or damned for his "No," he was damned for his having been born a German—just like a Jew at Auschwitz, Ada thought.

But to Lola, the double-damned one was Lola herself. Nothing the German could say could cool the hot lava inside her. If he told her, "I was SS," she would hate him, but now that he'd told her, "I wasn't," she hated him too. How the German enraged her! If only he'd cop to killing a Jew, then Lola could hit him and not become conscience-stricken! If only he'd tell her, "Ja! I was at Auschwitz, and I'm responsible for the murders of Itu, Ittel. . . ," ah, Lola could rip out his heart without enduring the still small voice that told her, *He is accused, that's all.* How dare the man ruin her sweet revenge by declining to tell her, "I did it!" A sort of convulsion struck her now. Her cheeks like a farmer's daughter's turned red. Her lips drew back, exposing her wetted teeth and, to Ada, resembling the ugly grimaces of the SS woman at Auschwitz, the perfumed woman of Lola's age who'd cracked her bead-handled whip on the Jews, including on Lola. And now Lola's body shook like a straining engine as she struck the German again, again, avenging herself for his laying a guilt trip on her by his continuing cries of *"Nein! Ich war nicht in der SS!"*

"*Du lügst!* You're lying!" Lola screamed.

It was too much for Ada. She stayed there till Lola shouted, "Take him away!" and then walked to Lola's home, packed, and left, lest a few months in Gleiwitz make her a Lola-like thing. At the gray-gabled station, she bought a train ticket to Germany, intending to look for David there, but she couldn't forget the red-faced man in Lola's office. *What if he didn't deserve it?* Ada thought as the train went west. *How would Lola ever know?*

8

In June or July, a German at last said to Lola, "I was SS." The man was tall, blue-eyed, blond: an "Aryan" according to Himmler, who had weeded out "Mediterraneans" and "Mongolians" by using his magnifying glass on photos of SS applicants. The man had been trained at an SS camp where the sergeants cried, "Mollycoddle! Mother's little boy!" to men who were wincing as Germans were hanged. By now, the man was as hard as Krupp steel. He was Hitler's ideal, "Imperious, relentless, cruel," and when Lola asked him, "Were you SS?" he didn't grovel and say, *"Ich war nur ein kleiner mann.* I just was a little man," but answered proudly, "Yes."

"Did you kill any Jews?"

"Yes. They deserved it."

"Du schwein! How many?"

"I wish I'd killed them all."

"Du elendes schwein!" Lola then beat him, but his stuff and starch survived and Lola cried, "Take him away!" She hated the Germans more than ever now. To her not unprejudiced ears, the SS man had spoken for *all* her prisoners, who, she was sure, would have told her, "I was SS," or "I was a Nazi," or "I was a Nazi collaborator," if they had had the SS man's insolent honesty. After all, her own hard-working interrogators never said, "So-and-So's innocent," no, sooner or later they said, "Well, So-and-So at last confessed." How blind she'd been in her search for Höss, Hössler and Mengele! By now, the three archetypes were in POW camps: Höss and Hössler in British ones and Mengele in an American

one, but now Lola saw that *all* her one thousand prisoners were Hösses, Hösslers and Mengeles and all must be punished for it.

She didn't tell her Jewish and gentile guards, "Go get 'em." She just didn't enforce the Office's rule that the prisoners couldn't be punished at one's sweet will. She didn't intervene when her guards got drunk, opened the cells, pulled out the Germans, put blankets on them so the welts wouldn't embarrass the Polish courts, said, "Pigs!" and then used their guns like clubs. At Auschwitz, the Jews weren't raped (the SS men could be hanged for it) but at Gleiwitz one ardent interrogator pulled off a German girl's clothes, pulled her onto his lap, and told her, "Let's do it! I've got a Persian lamb coat for you!" but if Lola knew about it, she just ignored it. In time, the Germans' screams seemed an attribute of the prison air, but Lola said nothing, and if any inner voice told the Jewish guards, *You don't know he's guilty,* then the Germans' blond hair, blue eyes, and the Germans' own German language attested that they were Hitler's hatchet men.

One day, a German in pitch-black pants, the SS's color, showed up in Lola's prison. He'd been spotted near the city square by a Pole who'd said, "Fascist! You're wearing black!" At that, the German had bolted off, but the Pole chased him a mile to the Church of Saints Peter and Paul, tackled him by a gold mosaic, hit him, kicked him, and took him to Lola's prison. Some guards, all girls, then seized the incriminating evidence: the man's black pants, pulling them off so aggressively that one of his tendons tore. The man screamed, but the girls said, "Shut up!" and they didn't recognize that the pants were part of a boy scout uniform. The "man" was fourteen years old.

The girls decided to torture him. By now, the Office of State Security had 227 prisons for Germans, and each had its characteristic way of taking revenge for World War II. The boys used sticks in Breslau but splinters in Frankenstein, forcing them up a German's nails. The boys in Wünschelberg whipped a German, poured coffee into the whip-wounds, and told him, "You won't just die! You'll croak!" At the 800-person prison in Myslowitz, whose commandant was a Jew from Auschwitz, twenty years old, the boys dumped excrement on a German's head, told him, "Pick that shit up," and, when the German did, dumped it on his head again. The boys in Glatz played accordions to drown out the *"Nein"*s as they knocked a German's teeth out, and one Jewish boy in Neisse made a German pull out his own gold tooth, yelling, "You did that to me!" The boy was being figurative, for in fact he'd been castrated at Auschwitz as part of an SS experiment, and his Jewish co-workers in Neisse didn't think he had given the German tit for tat.

The girls in Gleiwitz used fire. They held down the German boy, put out their cigarettes on him, and, using gasoline, set his curly black hair

afire. Outside on Kloster Street, the priest from the Church of Saints
Peter and Paul sought, unsuccessfully, to get to Lola's ear and say, "He's
only fourteen." At last released, the German went home, fell into bed,
and, wrapping his arms around his head like a boxer who's on the ropes,
continued screaming, "Don't do it!" His scalp was a moth-eaten rug, and
when, at times, he was sane enough to go out, the other boys in his boy
scout troop collected around him like autograph hounds. They asked
him, "What did they do?"

"I'm sick of it! Go away!"

"How did they do it? Matches?"

"Go away, or I'll beat you up!"

"No, what did the Polish men do?"

"The worst was the women! Beat it!" the German boy said. In time, he
was sent to a mental ward, and he never left it.

It annoyed her, but Lola was expected to feed the Germans. The girl
who at Auschwitz was given a soup full of wood, cotton, buttons, even a
water-logged mouse, was to dish up potato soup to Germans who might
have been on the Auschwitz staff. She grudgingly did, but the Germans
starved on the wet potatoes and the noetic entrees. "Oh God! I want
schnitzel!" one German told another.

"Or schweinebraten!"

"How do you make it?"

"You need some pork—"

"Oh God, I want pork!"

By now, the Germans were skeletons, their orbits black, their eyes like
water in wells. If the guards weren't watching, they ate the wet bread in
the garbage pails and the old seaweed-colored scraps in the halls, scoop-
ing them up as they mopped. To add to the Germans' torment, the
guards at all hours gorged themselves on fried sugar sandwiches. One
day, the guards brought a cow to the prison, shot it, ordered the Germans, "Chop it up," cooked it, and gobbled it down as the Germans
watched. And one day, the guards shot a cow in Gleiwitz, tugged it onto
their truck while calling, "Hou. . . Ruk!" the Polish for "Yo heave. . . Ho!"
and feasted on filet mignon while giving the Germans bones. One guard,
a Jew, who now was two-hundred-and-something pounds, told the others
one day, "My geburtztag's today. My birthday's today," and at six o'clock
served them a platter of ham, bacon, sausage viennois, herring, and carp
marinated in sugar-and-onion sauce. As they chased this down with Russian vodka, the Catholic guards sang, "Tatina, Tatina! My girlfriend!" and
the Jewish guard told them, "Here's how the Jews would sing it." And, his
feet tapping, his elbows high as a scarecrow's, shaking the crows away,

the Jewish guard sang, "Tatina, Tatina! My goilfriend!" as the Catholics roared and the Germans starved.

One morning, a ton of potatoes came to the Gleiwitz railroad station, and Lola's adjutant, Moshe, decided to torment the Germans with them. He ordered a Catholic guard to get the potatoes, telling him, "Don't take the Ford, and don't take Lolek," Lolek being the prison's horse.

"What should I take?"

"Some Germans. Humiliate them."

"How should I do it?"

"Let them pull Lolek's wagon."

"Yes sir." The guard opened one of the cells and let eight gaunt prisoners out, and he put three at each side of Lolek's wagon and two at Lolek's handles. He then told the Germans, "Don't let go, or I'll shoot you," and he led the humans and wagon out the Kloster Street Gate.

The guard had his Mauser with him, and other gun-toting guards came too. The guards called out, *"Hej wio!"* the Polish for "Giddiup!" as the Germans went down Kaiser Wilhelm Street and past the old Gleiwitz Opera House, the site until recently of *Il Trovatore* and *Tannhäuser*. At the corner, the Russians laughed, throwing cigarettes that the Germans couldn't reach, but the German women gave them some bread with oleo. "Do you know So-and-So?" "Is he in the prison?" "How is he?" the German women cried, but the guards said, "No talking!" and the German "horses" didn't answer. The wagon rumbling, the Germans pulled it across the Klodnitz River Bridge, the Klodnitz gray from the Polish mines, and then past the All Saints Church to Gleiwitz's high-windowed station. One hour later, half a ton of potatoes aboard, the Germans dragged it to Lola's prison, where Moshe debriefed the exhausted guards.

"Are there more potatoes?"

"Another half ton."

"Get another eight Germans."

"Nein!" To Moshe's amazement, the Germans he'd been "humiliating" said, "No, we'll do it ourselves!" hoping the German women would give them more precious slices of oleo-covered bread.

No one at Lola's prison had died, but one Jew was putting the fear of death into the Germans there. A girl guard of Lola's age, her maiden name in Będzin had been Jadzia Gutman, but during the war she'd married a Yiddish comedian named Sapirstein. At Auschwitz, the boy had caught typhus, and Jadzia had found a beer barrel, put it through the 6000-volt wire, crawled to his stable, and kissed him before the typhus killed him. She'd then been coal-carred to Germany, but in May, 1945, she'd recovered the mad sense of humor she'd had as a schoolmate of Lola's who'd once played a title role in Grimm's *Snow White and the Seven Dwarfs*. When the GIs rolled into her and Zlata's concentration camp, Jadzia had cried, "Ha-ha-ha!" meaning "Oh, I've a wild idea!" and had led seven girls to the SS's dining room for the SS's wurst and Bulgarian wine. "I won't do the dishes, ha-ha-ha?" Jadzia had cried, meaning, "Well, am I right?" and she'd swept the chinaware and silverware to the center of the tablecloth, rolled them up, and thrown them out the SS's window. She'd then started off to Gleiwitz, the seven girls with her, but she'd stopped at a German's home while the German was cooking a rabbit stew and had told him, *"Probieren!* Try it!" Outnumbered, the German did, and Jadzia said, "Good! He didn't poison it! Ha-ha-ha!" meaning, "Everyone eat!"

She'd come to Lola's in May, shlepping a sewing machine that a German had "given" her and intending to make some money by making hats. "No, you must work with me," Lola told her, and Jadzia, whose mother, horse-dealer father, husband, and baby had died at Auschwitz, eventually said, "Ha-ha-ha!" meaning "Well, I might like it!" and hitched up her skirt, hopped on the back of Lola's cycle, held on to Lola's belt like a Hell's Angelette, and roared into Lola's prison. Once there, she set her mad mind to replicating the Auschwitz experience. A new group of Germans came one day and Jadzia shouted, *"Aufstellen!* Line up! *Alle kleider herunter!* All your clothes off!"

"Our underwear too?"

"Du schwein! You heard me!" Jadzia shouted. "Attention! Right face! Forward march! *Du arschloch!* You asshole!" Jadzia shouted at an eighteen-year-old, his shy body stooped, his hands crossed over his genitals. "You're outta step! *Eins! Zwei! Drei! Vier!* Ha-ha-ha!"

Dead ahead, the Germans could see a room that a row of old pitted faucets implied was a shower room, and in terror they fell to their knees like some Christian penitents. "No, please!" the Germans cried, having heard of the Auschwitz cyanide chambers.

"Hinein! Get in!" Jadzia shouted. She stomped to and fro like some wide-bottomed duck, for her feet had frozen at Auschwitz, her toes had turned black, and, not telling the "doctor," a man who'd commit her to cyanide, she'd pulled off her left little toe and three right ones, and now she teetered and tottered at every step. *"Hinein!"* she cried at the so-called shower room door.

"Bitte nein!"

"Hinein!!!" And suddenly the Germans heard the sound of rusted plumbing, the splash of skin-chilling water, for the "shower room" was just that. *"Einseifen!* Soap up! *Abwaschen!* Rinse off! *Hinaus!* Get out! *Schneller!"* said Jadzia in ten wild seconds, recreating her own arrival at Auschwitz. "Ha!"

Jadzia, in time, perfected her "Soap up!" "Rinse off!" "Faster!" routine, and Lola in June and July often stood at the shower-room door to laugh at the consternation of Jadzia's naked wards. Alas, Lola had quite forgotten what the showers were for and why the Germans needed them. As the signs at Auschwitz had said, EINE LAUS—DEIN TOD, or in English, ONE LOUSE—YOU'RE DEAD.

In the cells, the Germans sat patiently, pulling the lice from their torsos, arms, legs. It was fun for some prisoners, like the German who'd found a rusted pistol, hidden it in his outhouse, and been caught by the Office. Thirteen years old, the German didn't sing his old summer camp song,

> Auf der mauer, auf der lauer,
> Sitzt ne kleine laus,
>
> On the wall, lying in wait,
> Sits a little louse,

but laughing, using his fingernails to tweezer them out, said, "Got it! Another panzer!" meaning another army tank. "How about you?" he said to his cellmate, twenty years old.

"Another panzer kaput."

"I've caught ten."

"Only eight."

But the older prisoners, aware of how three million people died of typhus in World War I, were worried, methodically laying the lice on their tables, grinding them with their thumbnails, brushing them off.

One day in July, a louse bit a German prisoner. The bite itched, and the German scratched it, rupturing it and rubbing some of the louse's feces into it. The *rickettsia* in the feces went into the German's blood, and one week later he wasn't well. His head ached, his back ached too, and his hands, when he held them up, were curiously dirty, as if he'd been reading newsprint. His mouth was dry, its saliva like glue. In the mirror, his teeth had a brown-colored crust and his tongue—which trembled—had a white coat of fur, which turned yellow, then brown, then black as the days passed by, and then cracked off and was superseded by new white fur. By then, the German didn't know what the day was. He lay in his bed, rousing himself just to sit on a hole in a wooden chair and to spill diarrhea into the pail beneath it. The smell was so vile that a cellmate at last pushed a button, and, in the hall, a strip of steel rattled like an old telegraph and a guard pulled the tear-shaped tab in the door aside, asking, "What's wrong?"

"He's sick."

Unlocking the cell, the guard took the foul-smelling man to the prison nurse. A woman of fifty, she had an ether addiction, an addiction to drinking ether. Her hand wasn't steady, but she took the German's temperature, 104, and diagnosed this as a case of famine fever: typhus. She gave him her only available cure: one bed, but the German became delirious and died.

Lola was told, but she wasn't weepy-eyed from the German's misfortune. She felt that the fault was the German's, for the germs he had died of were incubated in German camps like Auschwitz. She didn't phone the priest at the Church of Saints Peter and Paul—did Höss call the rabbi in Auschwitz?—but she did what commandants did if a German died of typhus, amoebic dysentery, whatever. She got a death certificate from a Gleiwitz doctor. She then saved paper by tearing in two a German form ("———Is Hereby Committed to———Concentration Camp") and, on the back, had a prisoner clerk type a letter to Pinek's sister's boyfriend, Chaim, the chief paper-pusher at Imprisonment, and another one-sentence letter to the dead man's wife,

I wish to inform you of your husband's death, and I enclose the death certificate,

and she put these in her out-box. She unlocked the pirate chest, and she took out the German's money, watch, rings to trade for some food for the Jews at her homes on Lange Reihe. She also ordered a guard to bury the German.

The guard put the German's body in Lolek's, the horse's, wagon, and to hide it from peering eyes he covered it with potato peels. He sent for Lolek's groom, a German who always accompanied her, for, to get bread in Gleiwitz, he'd trained her to kick at everyone else. "Good Lolek!" the German exclaimed as he, another prisoner, and the guard climbed aboard and as Lolek clopped out the Kloster Street Gate. They went past the cemetery to a remoter one and, after throwing out the potato peels, went under an arch inscribed in Latin, LIVING TO DIE WELL, DYING TO LIVE WELL, and under another arch of cool linden trees. At the sexton's office, the guard said, "We have a dead body with us," the sexton said, "Go to the morgue," and the hearse continued under the lindens to a stucco-fronted house. The prisoners lifted the German out by his arms and legs, dropped him on a wooden table, left, said, "Good Lolek!" and rumbled back to Lola's prison.

Meanwhile, the German's cellmates, who had inherited his bed, had taken sick too, and soon the smells of typhus suffused much of Lola's domain. One man had red boils, and one had black blisters—one didn't sweat, but one was just sopping, his palms and soles looking water-logged. One man saw and one man heard, hallucinations. In one cell, all the Germans succumbed, but in one they were unaware of the epidemic around them. At dawn every day, the guards who banged on the doors calling in Polish, *"Pobudka!* Get up!" had to use stretchers to get some people to the etherized nurse's room or—again, every day—to Lola's own stopgap morgue. The clerks typed up sets of "I wish to inform you of———'s death," and the guards piled the bodies, four at a time, some-times, onto Lolek's wagon and, to keep the deep secret, covered them up with waste paper or with potato peels. They took the thin bodies to the cemetery, where the sexton shooed off the red-toothed cats and, at night, dumped them into a trench near the linden trees.

Lola didn't close the prison down. She didn't demand, "No more pris-oners," for the Office would just send the suspects to other typhus-filled prisons in Germany. Lola couldn't stay on top of her paperwork, though. Who was still living? Who was deceased? She wasn't really sure.

At last, Lola counted heads. Her guards opened all the cells, shouted, "Get out!" "Line up!" "Move out!" and marched the Germans into the long-unseen sun. Lola was there, dressed in olive clothes, buttoned up to her collar in spite of the sweltering heat. She stood erect, like a girl who's measuring herself on the prison's brick wall or an SS woman at Auschwitz. Twice every day, the SS had counted up Jews there, laying the dead ones out too, but Lola was marshaling only the ambulatories, letting the dead ones lie. She stared around as the prisoners, blinking, lined up on the six-sided-concrete-stoned court. Some hadn't breathed fresh air for months, and they gasped it like sprinters after their race. One man saw another and, not too loudly, cried, "Hans!" or "Horst!" but Lola called to a guard and told him, "That man's talking."

"How many times, Madame Commandant?"

"Twenty."

"You!" the guard roared at the talkative man. "Lie down! Stand up! Lie down! Stand up! Do twenty more!" He flashed all his fingers twice, and the German complied like a Keystone Cop.

"And that man too," Lola said.

"Now you!" the guard roared, and the German did the same waffling dance till the court was as still as Sahara sand. No one even sighed, though one German gestured to one or two others, brushing his ear as though shooing off a mosquito, meaning, "Keep your ears open. The war isn't over. We'll rise again."

"Liczyć! Count them!" Lola then said. Her guards moved among the

Germans, counting, comparing, asking, "Is he on KP?" "Is he sick?" "Is he dead?" and counting again while the master race stayed in rank and file, sweating silently.

How were the mighty fallen! To look at, they could be derelicts, but Lola had seen the inch-thick files from the tireless interrogators, and she knew the Germans' raps. Two men standing in front of her were collaborators, allegedly. The goat-bearded one was accused of writing the Nazis, "Piotr Wons is an enemy of Germany," and the wooden-legged one, who was visibly listing, of telling the Nazis, "Augustyn Kuczera told me, 'I'll come back here on a Polish tank.'" One man in front of Lola allegedly was a Hitler Youth who, prodded by a beater-to-death, had said, "Yes, I was a squad leader there," and who'd acknowledged singing things like *Du Kleiner Tambour (You Little Drummer),*

> *We fight for German soil!*
> *We die for Adolf Hitler!*

According to Lola's manila files, one fat German whose hand had a "P" for "Paul" tattoo was an ex-sergeant from the Storm Section, the Nazis who'd stormed the streets singing,

> *Clear the streets for the Brown Battalions!*
> *Clear the streets for the Storm Section Men!*

and three of the sergeant's reputed troops were also in front of Lola, blond, blue-eyed, dull-looking, scarred. The skull-and-bones set was allegedly there: an SS man who'd burned off his A or B tattoo and an SS man who'd amputated his arm, the scar and the stump still implying the A or B. The worst was an SS woman, forty-four years old, who, the files said, was the former deputy commandant of Gleiwitz's old concentration camp. She—like the other women, who still hadn't gotten typhus—wasn't at Lola's head count but in her cell, knitting sweaters, but the SS man from Auschwitz who'd said, "I liked the Jews," "I helped the Jews," "I did good deeds for the Jews," was standing in front of Lola, his skin still discolored, his Jewish ex-victims staring at him and whispering things in Yiddish.

And these were just ten Germans! In the court and the women's cells were hundreds more! Peering around her, Lola felt blessed among the girls of Będzin, who seldom had someone to hurl their hate at. A cousin in Belsen had been liberated in April, and she'd thrown a rotten potato at an SS man who'd once knocked two of her teeth out. She'd hit him but burst into tears, thinking, *This isn't enough!* The two cousins from

Auschwitz—the ones who'd spoken at Passover—had also sought revenge but had bungled it. One, who worked for the Office, had once clubbed an SS man but had run to the ladies' room, throwing up. "Why are you pale, Adela?" the other workers had asked her, but Adela herself couldn't explain it. The other girl, Rivka, had been ordered by her father in Będzin, "Take revenge." He'd scribbled this in the margin of the *People's Observer*, adding, "Be good. Be gentle. And always believe in God," and had thrown it to her before being taken to Auschwitz. For two years, Rivka had worn these words like a *tefillin*, rolling the scrap of paper up, covering it with cloth, putting a string in, and making a necklace of it: an evil eye for the Germans. She'd recently gone to Neisse and looked up Shlomo, her too-short suitor, but, like him, she couldn't hit the cringing men in the Office's cellar. "You do it," Rivka said to a Jewish guard and, as his punishments fell on a suspect, thought, *That's for my father! That's for my mother! That's for my sister! That's for my brother! That's. . . .* But the power that be in Gleiwitz was Lola.

"*Raport!* Report!" Lola said.

In the court, a guard gave the Polish two-fingered salute. "*Pani Naczelniku!* Madame Commandant!" the guard shouted. "*Sto pięćdziesiąt więźniów!* One hundred and fifty prisoners!" Of close to one thousand who'd been there in May, some were in other prisons now. Lola had taken their photographs, the Office had posted these in Poland's four corners with captions like DO YOU KNOW THIS MAN? and somewhere in Poland a Pole had known them. Some prisoners were on KP, on other crews, in the light-headed nurse's room, in the women's cells, or, like the boy scout, back home in Gleiwitz. But many, many were dead, the victims of typhus as well as of famine, other diseases, diarrhea from fish soup, and an occasional "accident" like a truck running over them.

"*Dziękuję!* Thank you! *Na cele!* To the cells!" Lola said. She wheeled around and, as the Germans shuffled in, went to her cycle, kick-started it, and roared out the Kloster Street Gate. At the corner, she turned from the noisy trolley tracks to the red-maple-shaded street. She had had typhus at Auschwitz and now was immune, but she worried about her Jewish guards. The lice, Lola knew, would as soon bite a Jewish guard's skin as an SS general's. What if the Jews caught the Germans' disease?

The wind in her hair refreshing her, she turned onto Lange Reihe. There, the trees were bouquets of violet flowers, and at her home the tulips were yellow and red. Her new lover, the Russian colonel, the Jew who'd once chased after girls in Kattowitz shouting, "Why won't you sleep with me?" met her and—her hat and goggles coming off—kissed her. Black-eyed, black-haired, black-mustached, the Russian was a fine-looking man who was living with Lola and urging her, "Marry me!" So far Lola hadn't, for she had whole reservoirs of hate that weren't released on the Germans, not yet.

One day in July, Lola motorcycled home, the Russian kissed her, Zlata told her, "My nephew's here!" and Zlata's nephew Pincus, who everyone thought was dead at an Austrian camp, ran up to "Aunt" Lola. At twenty-four, Lola was hardly older than he, but she did her now-normal commandant bit, "Where were you?" "When did you get out?" and Pincus, a very religious boy—in Będzin, he'd studied the Torah from half past seven every morning to seven every night—answered politely. He said he'd gone from Austria to Czechoslovakia to Lola's home.

"Come see the prison," said Lola.

"No, thank you."

"Come! Come with us!" the Russian said.

"No, I'd rather not."

"See if we're treating the Germans right!"

"No, I'm not interested."

"Come see it!" the Russian belabored him.

"No, not after what I saw in Prague."

Pincus explained. A friend in Prague was in Czechoslovakia's own Office of State Security, which—and Pincus didn't know why—Stalin had also packed with Jews. Pincus's friend had said, "Come with me," and had shown him a prison for Germans there. It was five floors high, and the Germans who Pincus saw there weren't in cells but on the five-floor staircase. Boys, girls, men, and old wrinkled women, the Germans were running up the stairs hysterically and, at the top, turning as though playing tag and running down and, at the bottom, turning again and running up. When one German fell, the others didn't stop but, as the man or woman lay moaning, ran up or down over his or her dying body. All the Germans were naked, and the Czechs on all five floors were telling them, "Rychleji! Faster!" "Německe prase! German pigs!" "Nordicka rasa! Master race!" "Heil Hitler!" and rubber-clubbing them if they straggled, egging them on. The runners were shrieking, the floorboards cracking, the Czechs screaming, "Faster!" the noise in the stairwell echoing like in an organ pipe: the music of hell, and Pincus had told his Czech friend, "If I had known this, I wouldn't have come."

"No, I've seen enough," Pincus told Lola and her Russian flame.

"Oh, come on," the Russian insisted.

"Do you know the Jewish teachings?"

"Some."

"Well, once," Pincus said, "there was a bad man in Jerusalem. And the people drowned him, and his body drifted downstream, and Hillel— Do you know who Hillel was?"

"Yes," said the Russian. Hillel was a Jew contemporary with Christ.

"Well, Hillel saw the man's body and said—" and Pincus said six Hebrew words that he then translated as, "'Because you drowned others, they have drowned you, and they who drowned you shall be drowned.'" Or what goes around, comes around.

Just somewhat subdued, the Russian said, "That's how you see it. But Lola and I can't live with this wisdom. Not after what the Germans did."

"Can you live with it, Lola?" Pincus said.

Lola said nothing. Her mother had sometimes quoted the Talmud, "The measure that a man measures with, he shall be measured by," but Lola couldn't see the relevance of the drowned man in Pincus's story. He was a bad man, wasn't he? If guilty Germans in Gleiwitz died, why should *she* die too? And who would kill her? The Allies? The hangman at Nuremburg? The Russians? The Poles? Clearly not God, who'd died at Auschwitz Himself. That night, Lola gave Pincus a welcome-to-Poland dinner, but to her his story was mumbo jumbo: was Hebrew.

9

The weather was in the eighties now. On the chestnut trees, the nuts were little green balls, bobbing in the breeze like the floats on fishing lines. Lola and her Russian went cycling, and Adam, her chief interrogator, who was still hitting the *bimber,* dried out in the daytime by riding a one-horse shay: an upholstered cart. One day, Adam was rolling along when a German in black clothes, white collar, started to run like a thief, and Adam arrested him. The man was a Catholic priest, in his home was an SS man, hiding, and Adam brought them both in.

By now, Adam had polished his black-hat and white-hat bit and often got his confessions completely painlessly. "Please help me," Adam would tell a German suspect. "I don't want to let the interrogators get you. Do you know what they do?" he'd say, and he'd hold a nail to the German's fingernail. "They push this up. Or," and he'd show the German a nail-studded club—"or they beat your feet. Or," and he'd hold his cigarette near the German's eye—"well, it's very unpleasant. I don't want to let them liquidate you as you did to us at Auschwitz. Do you want them or me?" Adam would say, and often the German would sign on the dotted line. But today, Adam was loath to talk of duress with the crew-cut but kindly middle-aged priest. He sent the SS man to his fierce interrogators, but he took the priest to his office, pouring some tea for him. "Please help me," Adam began. "You harbored an SS man, and I need you to admit it."

"My friend, I didn't harbor him. He sought refuge with me."

"Did you give refuge to Jews during the war?"

"If I'd known that Hitler was burning them, yes, I'd have given them refuge."

"You gave an SS man refuge, then, and I need you to admit it."

"But that isn't illegal. It isn't even immoral. Jesus taught us, 'Be merciful.'"

"No, father," Adam said, enjoying his first philosophy since the bishop at Auschwitz. "Jesus didn't originate that. He was repeating a Jewish prayer, 'Elohim rachum. God has mercy.'"

"Jesus taught that a *man* must have mercy too."

"No, a Jew must show mercy even to oxen, asses, birds. If, from a nest, a Jew takes a baby bird, the Torah teaches he can't take the mother bird too."

"I think of myself as a mother bird."

Adam smiled. He felt that the priest could be his good friend in some other life. "Our judges I hope will show mercy," Adam said.

"The Jews in the Bible didn't. The Gibeonites, who were Jews, said to King David, 'We want revenge,' and David gave the Gibeonites seven men, and the Gibeonites hurled them all from the mountaintop."

"And then David said to the Gibeonites, 'You aren't really Jews, for the Jews are merciful people.' And then David banished them."

"Where's that in the Bible?"

"It's in the Talmud," Adam said. "David told the Gibeonites that the Torah says, 'Show mercy,' and David told them they weren't fit to be Jews. And Maimonides, the Jewish teacher, says, 'If a man isn't merciful, maybe he isn't a Jew but a Gibeonite.'"

"Aha. Then you're not a Jew."

Adam sighed. "Father," he told him, "you gave an SS man refuge, and I need you to say so." He handed the priest a document, and the priest took a last sip of tea, then signed it. "You'll go to Schwientochlowitz," Adam said. "Then you'll be tried in Kattowitz. Our judges, I'm sure, will show mercy."

"No, they will kill me."

"You have an officer's word."

Adam believed it. He'd often heard on the radio of SS from Auschwitz getting three years, of SS who'd beaten up Jews, three years, of SS who'd tortured them, life, and he guessed that the priest might get— What? Three months? He didn't calculate that to try ten thousand suspects, the ten busy judges in Kattowitz needed at least ten years. He put the good priest on a jam-packed truck to the coal-mine country, black as Hiroshima, and to a "meadow" made of gray slag near the city of Schwientochlowitz ("Shveen*tokh*lovits"). "Get out!" the guards at the meadow shouted, and, with the other suspects, the priest walked through the double barbed wire and the whine of 6000 volts to an old covered market, the Germans' camp. "Face the wall!" the guards shouted, and the priest turned to a wood barracks wall. Behind him, he couldn't see the giant steel wheels, turning, like in Ezekiel, above the coal-mine shafts, but he heard their dinosaur roars and he smelled a sweet smell that he slowly perceived wasn't of coal but of dead human beings. He wondered, *Who's dead here?* "Don't talk!" the guards shouted, for, like the SS at Auschwitz, the guards didn't want the new arrivals to know they were in a death camp—a death camp for Germans, run by a Jew.

The commandant of Schwientochlowitz and former lover of Lola had her old husband's name: Shlomo. His last name was Morel, and he'd been born in Garbów, a nice little village where the Catholics didn't say, "Dirty Jew." He'd studied the Torah and Talmud, and when he was naughty—when, say, he pulled an onion out of a neighbor's patch to give to his mother saying, "For you"—his handlebar-mustached father didn't cite the Ten Commandments, "You shall not steal," or the comment of Rabbi Samuel in the Talmud, "They will catch you." Shlomo's father knew that Shlomo knew this, and he just spanked him and told him, "Now bring the onion back." His father baked bread in Garbów and lived in Garbów's one brick house, and Shlomo grew up a happy, happy-go-lucky, playful boy, who still put on his *tefillins* and said his *"Baruch ata"*s.

He was twenty when the Germans invaded, but his curse during the war was the Polish collaborators. Poles, not Germans, picked up his father, mother, and one brother in Christmas week, 1942, as Shlomo watched from the top of a haystack, hay in his mouth lest the Poles hear him cry. "Where are your other sons?" said the Poles, but Shlomo's mother wouldn't say, and the Poles, not the Germans, punished her by shooting the father, then brother, then her. That night, Shlomo and another brother hid in a mausoleum, in March, 1943, they joined the Jewish partisans, and Shlomo's brother was on a partisan tank—a horse-drawn sleigh—when some Poles, not Germans, jumped on and killed him. Shlomo didn't hate the Poles for wiping out his whole family, for Poles had also saved *him*, and though he abstractly hated the "Germans," he didn't hate any one German, any Höss, Hössler or Mengele. He went through the war loving laughter, telling the Yiddish jokes he'd heard in Garbów.

He always had his mandolin with him, its strap on his shoulder when he walked, its fingerboard in his fist overhead when the partisans waded across the Wieprz River in March, 1944. In his other fist was his Mauser, on the far bank were the Germans, someone said, "There they are!" and Shlomo emptied his Mauser and shielded his precious mandolin from the German rounds. He then walked thirty miles in his ice-hardened suit-of-armor clothes, the mandolin on his épaulières. He crossed into Russia, fought a battalion of Germans, lifted the C-rations off the German bodies, and at night as the partisans feasted, tuned up the cold mandolin—not too tight, lest he part one of the priceless strings—and as the moon shone down and the birch-barks glowed like fluorescent lights, and as Jewish, Polish and Russian partisans sang along, sang,

> My ze spalonych wsi,
> My ze spalonych miast. . . .
>
> We from burnt villages,
> We from burnt towns,
> Will take revenge for
> The hunger, the blood.
>
> We will point our guns
> At the enemy's heart. . . .

But even as Shlomo sang this (and, having finished, told Yiddish jokes), he had no clear conception of the "enemy's" face.

On his liberation, he was assigned to the Office of State Security and the camp commandant's post at Schwientochlowitz. The camp, during the war, had been run by the SS, and in each of its seven barracks on each of its three-level beds was a card inscribed ABRAMOWICZ, etcetera. Pointedly, Shlomo left all the cards on, and the Germans who started coming in February said, "Oh, they built this for Jews!" Though the Germans were mostly collaborators, allegedly, a hundred had now confessed to Interrogation, "I was SS," or "I was Storm Section," or "I was Hitler Youth," or "I was a Nazi," and Shlomo placed them in the most accessible barracks—the brown barracks, he called it, for brown was the Nazis' color—and at ten that night he visited them. A sergeant smashed the door open, snapped the lights on, and shouted in Polish, "Baczność! Attention!" and, as the Germans climbed from their beds, Shlomo and a dozen guards, some Catholic, some Jewish, walked in. With boots on, Shlomo was six feet tall, in his brown leather coat he had a bear's chest, on his shoulders were three silver captain's stars, and the set of his jaw could drive dowels. All through the war, he'd sung of revenge,

> We will take revenge for
> The hunger, the blood,

his duty, he'd felt, was revenge, revenge, and he clearly could take it tonight. He looked at the Germans sternly, but he really wondered, Who are they? Who do I take revenge against?

"My name is Captain Morel," Shlomo began. A man could lay bricks on his square-shaped brow. "I am twenty-six, and I am a Jew," he continued, proclaiming what all the "Stanisław"s in the Office never acknowledged. "My father, my mother, my brothers, were killed, and I'm the only survivor. I—"

Shlomo paused. The sad sacks standing at half-attention around him had clearly not killed the Morel clan, but Shlomo wondered if some hadn't worked at Majdanek, the closest camp to Garbów. One day in the Jewish partisans, Shlomo had heard of a "harvest festival" there, the SS killing eighteen thousand Jews, and he'd promised himself, *I'll avenge them.* One year later, he'd watched at Majdanek as five former guards stood on top of five cars, nooses around their necks, and as Catholic and Jewish drivers revved up the engines and raced away. And now Shlomo thought, *Maybe these Germans worked at Majdanek too. Maybe they worked at Auschwitz, thirty miles from here. Maybe—*

"I was at Auschwitz," Shlomo proclaimed, lying to the Germans but, even more, to himself, psyching himself like a fighter the night of the championship, filling himself with hate for the Germans around him. "I was at Auschwitz for six long years, and I swore that if I got out, I'd pay all you Nazis back." His eyes sent spears, but the "Nazis" sent him a look of simple bewilderment, and Shlomo now sought to see their true colors by telling them, "Now sing the Horst Wessel Song!" No one did, and Shlomo, who carried a hard rubber club, hit it against a bed like some judge's gavel. "Sing it, I say!"

"The flags held high. . . ," some Germans began.

"Everyone!" Shlomo said.

"The ranks closed tight. . . ."

"I said everyone!"

"Storm Section marches. . . ." The song, composed in the 1920s by Second Lieutenant Horst Wessel, was the anthem of Hitler's bully-boys, the Storm Section, and not everyone in the barracks knew it. "With sure steady steps. . . ."

"Blond!" Shlomo cried to the blondest, bluest-eyed person there. "I said sing!" He swung his rubber club at the man's golden head and hit it. The man staggered back.

"Our comrades, killed by the Reds and Reactionaries. . . ."

"Sonofabitch!" Shlomo cried, enraged that the man was defying him by not singing but staggering back. He hit him again, saying, "Sing!"

"Are marching in spirit with us. . . ."

"Louder!"

"Clear the street for the Brown Battalions. . . ."

"Still louder!" cried Shlomo, hitting another shouting man.

"Clear the street for the Storm Section Men. . . ."

By now, the SS, Storm Section, Hitler Youth and Nazi suspects were like the crowd at a Hitler rally. Their mouths were a row of red circles, as open as megaphone ends. To look at, the men could be singing, marching, stomping over the flopping remains of Shlomo's father, mother, brothers, giving their heils, and Shlomo now hated them. He cried out, "Pigs!"

"Millions of hopeful people. . . ."

"Nazi pigs!"

"Are looking to the swastika. . . ."

"*Schweine!*" Shlomo cried. He threw down his rubber club, grabbed a wooden stool, and, a leg in his fist, started beating a German's head. Without thinking, the man raised his arms, and Shlomo, enraged that the man would try to evade his just punishment, cried, "Sonofawhore!" and slammed the stool against the man's chest. The man dropped his arms, and Shlomo started hitting his now undefended head when *snap!* the leg of the stool split off, and, cursing the German birchwood, he grabbed another stool and hit the German with that. No one was singing now, but Shlomo, shouting, didn't notice. The other guards called out, "Blond!" "Black!" "Short!" "Tall!" and as each of these terrified people came up, they wielded their clubs upon him. The brawl went on till eleven o'clock, when the sweat-drenched invaders cried, "Pigs! We will fix you up!" and left the Germans alone.

Some were quite fixed. A number of Germans lay on the concrete floor, for Shlomo had done what Lola, for all her wild dreams of curling her fingers, scarf, belt on a German's throat, still hadn't done, much as she wanted to. Shlomo and his subordinates had killed them.

T he next night, the sergeant shouted, "Attention!" and Shlomo and the guards went back in. Quickly, the Germans climbed from their beds, Shlomo then told them, "Sing!" and they started the Horst Wessel Song. The sound was now twice as loud, for the choir was now twice as large. The dead had been dumped on stretchers, carried to a wooden-walled morgue, and, to cut the odor, powdered with calcium chloride by a ten-man "ascension" crew, but a trolley car full of Germans had just come to Schwientochlowitz and the SS, Storm Section, Hitler Youth and Nazi suspects among them were in the brown barracks now. As they sang, the hate rose in Shlomo's throat like lava from some long-dormant volcano. "Louder! Still louder!" Shlomo said. "Pigs!" When he found a good target, he grabbed a good wooden stool—the one that he'd split was at the camp carpenter's now, in C-clamps until the hot glue could dry—and he batted the German's head with it. Around him, the guards tried to teach the

Germans to act like men by asking them, "How many blows do you want?"

"None at all!"

"Coward! You're getting fifty!" As the guard's rubber sword came down, the guard told the German, "Count them!"

"Eins!" the German began.

"Count them in Polish! I'm starting again!"

"Raz!" the German began. Soon more Germans were dead, and at dawn the ascension crew transferred them to the ill-smelling morgue and, in horse-drawn carts, to a mass grave near a cemetery by the Rawa River.

Night after night into March, into April, Shlomo fell on the brown barracks, but its population continued to grow as trolleys and trucks full of Germans, mostly from Gleiwitz, arrived. The beds filled up, and soon each bed had two, three or four occupants, lying head-toes, head-toes, at each ABRAMOWICZ, etcetera, card. In each frame were three beds, in each room were twenty-one frames, in the barracks two jam-packed rooms, and on the floor was the overflow, so as many as six hundred people were in the brown barracks now. With the world's best will, the guards couldn't punish more than a tenth on any one night, and Shlomo, to get some help, threw a party—a literal bash—for the Office of State Security.

He invited twenty boys, half Catholics, half Jews. He also invited compliant girls like Beata, who slept with the chief of Imprisonment, Basia, who slept with everyone else, and Lola, who'd just gone to Gleiwitz and said, "I can't come." His guests came to Shlomo's home just outside the barbed wire at sunset on Friday, though that was the start of the Sabbath. Shlomo served sausages and a virtual vat of vodka that the guests guzzled, and Shlomo told Yiddish jokes. *"Siz geven Shabbas.* It was the Sabbath," Shlomo said. "But the Rabbi said, 'We have only nine Jews.' So," Shlomo said, smiling, "the Rabbi's ugly-looking wife went out, and she found a Jewish man. She told him, 'Come inside! *Du zad dayn zente!* You'll be the tenth!' The man told her, 'Lady, I don't even want to be the first!'" Shlomo's mouth opened wide, but no laughter came out. His face was a mask of comedy meaning "Is that or isn't that funny?" and as soon as everyone roared, indicating "Yes!" the mask came alive and Shlomo roared too.

For hours, people drank and Shlomo told Yiddish jokes. "Once, a Jew told another one, 'Our two wives. Do you know the difference between them?' *'Nayn.* No, I don't.' 'Well, I do!'" "Once, a Jew asked the Rabbi, 'May I have sex on the Day of Atonement?' 'Just with your wife.' *'Far vus?* Why so?' 'You can't have fun on the Day of Atonement!'" "Once, the Rabbi told a Jew, 'Your wife said you're sleeping around. Did you sleep

with Anna?' 'No!' 'Did you sleep with Bella?' 'No!' 'Did you sleep with
Channa?' 'No!' 'Very well.' The man then left, and the man's friends said,
'Vus hat der Rebbe gezugt? What did the Rabbi tell you?' 'He gave me
three new names!'" "Once, a Jew—" After that, Shlomo took out his mandolin and sang,

> It's good in the army,
> The girls come all day!
> Once they put out on the sofa,
> Now they put out in the hay!

and the boys and girls sang along.

Still drinking, the guests rolled from Shlomo's house and, in the darkness, past the 6000-volt barbed wire. All had lost loved ones during the
war, and though the Germans in the brown barracks were SS, Storm Section, Hitler Youth and Nazi suspects, to the guests it was quite enough
that they were Germans. They willingly would have shot them dead, but a
club provided a lot more emotional satisfaction, and the boys and girls
brandished some as they marched on the dark brown barracks. At
Auschwitz, the SS had been forbidden to hurt a Jew for emotional satisfaction, and SS men who did this could, sometimes would, be imprisoned, but the guests didn't fear that the Office would punish *them*.
Unlike the SS, the guests had genuine grievances.

They slammed open the brown-barracks door. They switched on the
lights, and the Germans rose so precipitously that a lot of the bedboards
cracked, the men and boards crashing down on the Germans below, the
Germans then screaming, the evening beginning. "Sing the National
Anthem!" Shlomo said for variety's sake. "Sing it!"

"Germany, Germany, over everything. . . ."

"Louder!"

"Over everything in the world. . . ."

"Still louder!"

"Holding together fraternally. . . ."

"Pigs!"

"For defense and defiance. . . ."

"Tall!" Shlomo cried to a tall blond man. "Lie down right here! Tall!"
to another tall man. "Lie down beside him! Tall!" to another one. "Lie
beside *him!*" As soon as the three were lined up, Shlomo cried, "You! Lie
on top of them, crosswise! No!" he said, clubbing the man. "I said crosswise! You!" he continued, and he kept piling up Germans, three this way,
three that, till he had a human cube as high as a hand could reach. "All
right!" Shlomo said, and his guests started swinging the clubs, whacking

away at the cube as if they were hunters and it were a pod of Canadian seals. The air was thick with the grunts of the guests and the *thud!* of the wood upon bones. In the high tiers, the Germans cried, *"Bitte! Please!"* the Germans in the center tiers moaned, but the Germans in the low tiers were mute, for the weight of the two dozen people on top had pushed their viscera out and the Germans were dying. "Pigs!" cried the party guests, pounding away, but Shlomo just leaned on a bed, watching, laughing like a *meshugganer*—a nut, his code name in the Jewish partisans.

At last, the tired guests left, but Shlomo still wasn't satisfied. He had more bashes on Fridays, Saturdays, and Monday, May 7, the day the Germans surrendered—his guests, as they went through the wire, firing their guns at the midnight sky in lieu of Roman candles. On other nights, Shlomo and his guards attacked the brown barracks themselves, asking the Germans, "How many blows?" "I want twenty," "Well, we'll oblige you," and after inflicting the twenty, telling the Germans, "One more! You didn't say, 'Thank you!'" The boys did this every night in May, June and July, until when the crew-cut but kindly priest, the one who'd debated with Adam, came to Schwientochlowitz, the nights were as ritualistic as a "Please tuck me in." At around ten, a sergeant would shout, "Attention!" and the Germans would leap out of bed like volunteers, raise their right arms, say, *"Heil Hitler!"* sing the Horst Wessel Song, and, in answer to "How many blows?" say, "Fifteen," for if a German said, "Ten," the guards would say, "Coward!" and give the German fifty. The guards used clubs, bedboards, crowbars, and the Germans' own crutches to give the Germans their fifteen blows, and at times they blurred the distinction between corporal and capital punishment by seizing a German's arms and legs and swinging his head against the wall like a battering ram. In the center ring, Shlomo used his pet birchwood stools on the Germans, but he was unsatisfied and his guards came back again and again on many marathon nights.

The dead bodies went to the morgue every morning. The broken stools went to the carpenter, a man who sat melting the glue-bars, muttering, "Mary and Joseph! More stools!" and the dead people's names went to Shlomo. He tallied them up—he had twenty, sometimes, from the brown barracks, twenty from the other barracks—and he then mailed a "NOTICE" to all the dead people's wives,

NOTICE. On July——, 1945, the Prisoner——died of a heart attack.

The body count was enormous, but Shlomo was still aware of the six hundred brown-barracks men, the eighteen hundred "collaborator" men, and the six hundred "collaborator" women still alive. He himself didn't touch them (he just touched the brown-barracks men) but the guards started beating them all: if they didn't salute, if they didn't say, "Yes, sir," in Polish, if they didn't pick up their hairs in the barber shop, if they didn't lick up their blood. The guards put the Germans into a doghouse, beating them if they didn't say, "Bow wow." They got the Germans to beat each other: to jump on each other's spines and to punch each other's noses, and if a German pulled his punches, the guards said, "I'll show you how," and hit the Germans so hard that they once knocked a German's glass eye out. The guards raped the German women—one, who was thirteen years old, got pregnant—and trained their dogs to bite off the German men's genitals at the command of "Sic!" And still three thousand remained, and Shlomo hated them more than he had in February, hated them for not dying compliantly. It seemed as though hate were a muscle and the longer he used it, the bigger it got—as though every day he had bench-pressed two hundred pounds and, far from being worn out, now could press 220.

At last, in August, the lice came to Shlomo's aid. A man got typhus, the other men in his bed did too, and the 104-degree fever spread like a flash fire in Shlomo's camp. In their barracks, the Germans lay sprawled in bed, stirring if any urine dripped from the bed overhead, babbling, "Josef!" or "Jacob!" or "Mommy! Please help me!" The rooms were like shell-shock wards, the body count rose to a hundred per day—one day, 138—and the ascension crew was as busy as mailroom boys, chasing from barracks to barracks, from bed to bed. At every dead body, four of the boys took the arms and legs and, saying, *"Hou . . . Ruk!"* swung it onto a stretcher, though once a dead body's arm came off and a legion of half-inch white worms came out. The boys then carried the stretcher (a wake of white worms behind it, once) to the morgue, dumped out the body, chalked it with calcium chloride, and as soon as they could, wearing handkerchiefs, saying the mightiest sort of *"Hou . . . Ruk!"* swung it like something made of straw into a high-sided wagon. They then threw more bodies in, and a horse took the load to the grave by the Rawa River.

In time, three-fourths of the Germans at Shlomo's camp were dead, and Shlomo announced, "What the Germans couldn't do in five years at Auschwitz, I've done in five months at Schwientochlowitz." In fact, the Germans at Auschwitz had killed just as many people in five short hours, and Shlomo still wasn't satisfied with his Schwientochlowitz score. At parties now for the Kattowitz boys, Shlomo told Yiddish jokes but his heart wasn't there. "Before the war, the best-known rabbi was Cadyk of Mount Kalwari," Shlomo might say. "He once went to visit the pope, and the people of Rome said, 'Who is the goy with Cadyk of Mount Kalwari?'"

Some of Shlomo's guests would leave, some would go to Shlomo's bedroom for sex, but others would stay as Shlomo pulled out his mandolin, tuned and retuned it, and, his arms unaccustomedly heavy, began the sad ballad of *Ai Lu Lu Lu.*

> *In the cellar the mother was rocking her son*
> *And was singing this song to put him to sleep,*
> *"Sleep, my son, sleep. My little one, sleep.*
> *Ai lu lu lu, li lu lu lu."*

Then, Shlomo would pause, strumming some A chords. On his face was a look of great sadness, as though the "mother" were his and the "son" were his partisan brother, the one who'd been killed on the horse-drawn sleigh. But then he'd start singing again,

> *She was singing, "I'll get some milk for you,"*
> *And was praying to God that he would grow up.*
> *"Dear God in Heaven. Please let him grow up.*
> *Ai lu lu lu, li lu lu lu."*

Some more chords.

> *And twenty years later her son was grown up*
> *And told her, "The army is calling for me."*
> *"Sleep, my son, sleep. My little hawk, sleep.*
> *Ai lu lu lu, li lu lu lu."*

Verse after verse would go by. The war broke out, and her son was called, and she prayed to God, but her son was killed, and she went to his crowded cemetery, and,

> *She was singing, "Oh, you won't be lonely below,*
> *Because you are buried with all of your friends.*
> *Sleep, my son, sleep. My soldier boy, sleep.*
> *Ai lu lu lu, li lu lu lu."*

Then, Shlomo would stop. His fingers went limp on the mandolin. He hated the Huns more than ever now, for what they'd done was so monstrous that the most drastic measures hadn't made up for it. The two, three or four thousand dead at Schwientochlowitz couldn't compensate him for his sleigh-riding brother, much less for his two other brothers, his father and mother, his uncles and aunts, all but one ailing cousin and six

million more. His revenge wasn't sweet, for Shlomo, like Lola's cousin at
Belsen—like Lola herself—still felt, *It isn't enough.* What had he done to
the Germans, really? He had thrown rotten potatoes.

The Germans at Schwientochlowitz tried to get word out. One man
went to the wire shouting, "This place is hell!" He was killed, one man
who smuggled messages out was tortured, but one Hitler Youth from
Gleiwitz escaped. At three in the morning, he hid in the men's latrine, at
six he escaped with a coal-mine crew, but Shlomo found him in Gleiwitz
and personally drove him to Schwientochlowitz. "Am I allowed to
smoke?" the boy asked in Shlomo's van. "Yes," Shlomo said, but when the
boy pulled out a pouch of Crimean tobacco, Shlomo just laughed and told
him, "You smoke better stuff than I do," and took his tobacco away. Back
at Schwientochlowitz, Shlomo told him, "You swine, you should croak,"
the guards used the iron poles that the soup-tubs were carried with to
beat the boy to a vegetable, and no one tried to escape after that. One
man was released, however: a man who'd once been at Auschwitz and
who said now, "I'd rather be ten years in a German camp than one day in
a Polish one."

Day and night, the civilians of Schwientochlowitz heard the Germans
scream, and one Catholic priest tried to tell the world about them. An
old, soft-spoken, softhearted man, the priest took a train to Berlin to look
up a British officer and to unburden himself upon him. The officer then
put a "melancholy account" in the pouch to London,

> *A priest living in Silesia has been in Berlin. I have known [him] for
> many years, and I consider him absolutely reliable. He is a man who
> was always ready, day or night, to help a victim of the Nazi regime.*

The officer passed along what the Office was doing to Germans,

> *Polish officials have [said], "Why should they not die?" Concentra-
> tion camps have not been abolished but have been taken over by the
> new owners. At Schwientochlowitz, prisoners who are not beaten to
> death stand up to their necks, night after night until they die, in cold
> water—*

a true report, for a cistern of water was Shlomo's punishment cell. His
mission completed, the priest went back to Silesia, but other whistle-
blowers came to Berlin and told the British and Americans of other concentration camps run by the Office of State Security.

The biggest wasn't in Schwientochlowitz but in Potulice, Poland, near
the Baltic Sea. Built for Jews, it now was for thirty thousand suspected

oppressors of Jews. Every night, the commandant went to a barracks there, said, "Attention!" and "Everyone sing *Everything Passes By!*" and the Germans sang,

> *Everything passes by,*
> *Everything passes away,*
> *My husband's in Russia,*
> *And his bed's empty today.*

"You pigs!" the commandant then cried, and he beat the Germans with their stools, often killing them. At dawn many days, a Jewish guard cried, *"Eins! Zwei! Drei! Vier!"* and marched the Germans into the woods outside their camp. "Halt! Get your shovels! Dig!" the guard cried, and, when the Germans had dug a big grave, he put a picture of Hitler in. "Now cry!" the guard said. "And sing *All the Dogs Are Barking!*" and all the Germans moaned,

> *All the dogs are barking,*
> *All the dogs are barking,*
> *Just the little hot-dogs*
> *Aren't barking at all.*

The guard then cried, "Get undressed!" and, when the Germans were naked, he beat them, poured liquid manure on them, or, catching a toad, shoved the fat thing down a German's throat, the German soon dying.

At Potulice, more Germans died than Jews had died there during the war. At the concentration camp at Myslowitz, near Kattowitz, the Jewish survivors of Auschwitz told the Germans, "Sing!" "Sing what?" "Sing anything! Or we'll shoot you!" and the Germans sang the one song they'd all learned in kindergarten:

> *Alle vögel sind schon da!*
> *Alle vögel, alle!*
> *Amsel, drossel, fink und star,*
> *Und die ganze vögelschar!*

> *All the birds are here already!*
> *All the birds!*
> *Blackbirds, thrushes, finches, starlings,*
> *All the flock!*

"You pigs!" the Jews cried, whipping the Germans, and one hundred died at Myslowitz every day. At Grottkau, the Germans were buried in potato sacks, but at Hohensalza they climbed right into the coffins, where the commandant wasted them. At Blechhammer, the Jewish commandant wouldn't even *look* at the Germans, and they died sight unseen. The status of "suspect" wasn't enough to grant any German a pardon in Poland and Poland-administered Germany. In that vast area, the Office of State Security ran 1,255 camps for Germans, and twenty to fifty percent of the Germans died in virtually every one.

But the word got out. Taking trains to Berlin, the whistle-blowers reported this to the British and Americans, who put the reports in fat canvas pouches to London and Washington. Apparently, someone read them, for on Thursday, August 16, 1945, Winston Churchill rose in the House of Commons and said, "Enormous numbers [of Germans] are utterly unaccounted for. It is not impossible that tragedy on a prodigious scale is unfolding itself behind the Iron Curtain." Another member of Commons said, "Is this what our soldiers died for?" and in Washington an American senator put in the *Congressional Record* of Friday, August 2, "One would expect that after the horrors in Nazi concentration camps, nothing like that could ever happen again. Unfortunately. . . ." The senator then told of beatings, shootings, of water tortures, of arteries cut, of "brains splashed on the ceiling" in the Office's concentration camps. The pouches then went to Warsaw, where the British ambassador felt that, like Nelson at Copenhagen, he should hold his telescope to his blind eye, and the American ambassador felt that the Germans were whining. But both ambassadors protested to the Polish government.

The loudest objection was by the Red Cross—not the International one, in Geneva, but the American one. Its people in Warsaw drove down to Kattowitz to speak with the Jewish boy who was Secretary of State Security: Pinek, but Pinek was not his cherubic self. He didn't rise for the three olive-clothed men, and his lips were like tight rubber bands as he asked them in German, "What do you want?"

"To inspect the Silesian camps."

"Good. Go to Auschwitz. Why didn't you go there during the war?"

"We are Americans."

"Why didn't the Red Cross in Geneva go?"

"We don't know."

"If you didn't go to Auschwitz, you won't go anywhere now," said Pinek, who, in the partisans, had once found a German radio, and who'd sent urgent messages out, *"Dot dot dash. . .* Urgent, urgent, hundreds of Jews being murdered," but who'd never gotten messages back. "You didn't help the Jews, and I won't oblige you now."

"We'll have to report that to Warsaw."

"So do it. I don't respect the Red Cross."

"For the record, then. We are asking you—"

"Go to hell!" Pinek shouted in English, and the men in olive hurried out. They then drove to Warsaw and made their complaint to Jacob, the Jew who was chief of the Office of State Security.

Jacob Berman, from Warsaw, was the last person on earth who'd call a German "You pig." In his childhood, he had sipped wine from a silver chalice whenever, on Friday, his father said, "Blessed art Thou, O Lord, who has created the fruit of the vine." His brothers became a surgeon, professor, psychologist, his sister a Ph.D. in Germanic languages, and Jacob himself a Ph.D. in Polish history, writing his dissertation on late-eighteenth-century butlers. In the Communist Party, he became chief of Intelligence but also took care of number one by giving some tips to the Polish police. When the Germans came, Jacob went to Russia, Stalin appointed him to the Polish pro-tem Government, and in January, 1945, he returned to Warsaw the elegant head of the Office of State Security. His tailor made a dummy of him and suits fit for Wall Street, and Jacob wore them to the president's palace, sat on a chair with a deerskin seat and a lyre-like back, made in India, and, with long, graceful fingers, raised his Beaujolais saying, "To the New Poland!"

In Warsaw, Jacob was Stalin's main man. On his desk was a phone that he could pick up and someone would say, "Moscow here." He had no title, however, for he liked being the *éminence grise,* and after he'd heard from Washington, London, Moscow, and the Red Cross, he didn't simply call up Pinek asking, "What's going on?" but drove down to Kattowitz with two Jewish ministers and the Party secretary, Gomulka. The four went to Pinek's plush office, Pinek said, "Comrades! This is an honor!" and Jacob just sat to one side, holding his teacup in ladylike fingers, seldom sipping, seldom speaking, as Gomulka said, "Please brief us," and as Pinek picked up a two-foot pointer, pointed to a map of Poland, and started in.

"Comrades. In Katowice," Pinek said, using the Polish for Kattowitz, pointing, "the Fascists are now rounded up, but the Russians still are committing rapes. Over here," the Czech border, "and here," the German one, "we have patrols, and no one can cross out of Poland illegally. Recently thirty people tried, and the Office brought them to Katowice. They were Jews, and I was told they were trying to smuggle some gold out. Their watches. Their wedding rings. Comrades," said Pinek, tears in his eyes, "these people had been in Hitler's camps. They were alive by the grace of God. If they didn't want to stay in Poland, who was I to obstruct them?"

"What did you do?" Gomulka asked. Gomulka was smoking a cigarette stub in a cheap metal holder, and Jacob was statue still, hanging on Pinek's every word.

"I told the boy who arrested them, 'These watches, these rings, they're garbage. If you jeopardize any Jews again, I won't arrest the Jews but you.'"

"And the Jews?"

"I let them go to Germany."

Gomulka stood up. He walked across to Pinek and patted him. "You did right," said Gomulka. "My wife is a Jew, and I know about them." He sat down again. "Now, what about the camps for Germans?"

"Most of the Germans there don't belong," Pinek said. "They're innocent, and we should free them."

"Why don't we?"

"We need more judges."

"I'll work on it," one of the ministers said.

"But how are the Germans treated?" Gomulka asked.

"As if they're in heaven, compared to how they treated the Jews."

"We mustn't mistreat them," Gomulka said.

"We don't," Pinek said. He really believed this, for he hadn't gone to Shlomo's bashes, and his kid brother, who had, had never described them to Pinek. "We aren't murderers," Pinek said.

"Well, I have a problem with the Red Cross."

"I don't respect the Red Cross."

"But they're worried about the Germans."

"The Germans!" Pinek said angrily. "Who told the Germans to come to Poland? And destroy Polish towns? And kill Polish people? And commit genocide on the Jews? I told the Red Cross it should visit the *Jews* who came out of *German* camps!"

"But comrade!" Gomulka protested. He acted, incredibly, as though he couldn't simply say, "I *order* you, Captain." His fist hit on Pinek's desk, and the skin on his cheekbones stretched like the skin of a warpath-riding indian. "We must observe the Geneva Conventions!"

"If you tell me, 'Let in the Red Cross,' I'll do it."

Gomulka paused. "No, I won't order you."

"Comrade," said Jacob, at last speaking up. "We have your word that the Germans are treated well." Jacob spoke slowly, and, like the greatest actors, he didn't gesture at all. His mother, father, one brother, and sister were dead, and he had little love for the Germans, but he was now forty-four and a power that be in Poland, and he didn't want to derail himself by telling the Red Cross, "Beat it." He was happy to leave that to Pinek and carefully said, "As for the Red Cross—"

Pinek waited.

"Do what seems best."

"Thank you," said Pinek.

Then, Pinek and his four comrades went to Pinek's apartment, where Pinek served vodka in Czechoslovakian crystal and, as hors d'oeuvres, herrings on crackers on Rosenthal gold-bordered china. After dinner, Pinek played Russian songs like *Apples and Pears* on a Steinway piano, and the great men of Poland hopped like the Cossacks, singing along. Pinek called Jacob "Jacob," and Jacob called Pinek "Paweł," his alias in the Office of State Security. He said to Pinek quietly, *"Amcha?"* the Hebrew for "People?" meaning, "Are you our People?" and Pinek answered him, *"Ich bin ayn Yid,"* the Yiddish for "Yes, I'm a Jew." Pinek then said to Gomulka, *"Amcha?"* but Gomulka answered, "What did you say?" and Jacob laughed decorously. One Jewish minister dozed off on Pinek's sofa, but the other was like at a Legion hall, slapping everyone's back. At half past one, the VIPs fell asleep in Pinek's guest rooms, but when Pinek woke up they were gone, as was the Czechoslovakian crystal, the Rosenthal china, and the angel-embellished silver. In their place was a handwritten note,

Dear Paweł,

> *We don't know how to scrounge from the Germans, and we are too prominent to try to. We thank you for your hospitality and for all these beautiful things. We will see you in Warsaw.*

Gomulka and Gang

On reading this, Pinek laughed. At the Office he told all the Jews, "What *gonifs* they are! What thieves they are!" He never let in the Red Cross—the American or International one—nor did the leaders of Poland's other provinces, and the Germans kept singing swan-songs at Schwientochlowitz, etcetera. In the next three years, from sixty thousand to eighty thousand would die in the Office's institutions, much, much less than the number of Jews who'd died at Auschwitz but more than the number who'd died at Belsen or Buchenwald or one thousand places the Jews of the world now proclaim, "We will never forget."

10

At her home in Gleiwitz, Lola remembered the dear departed from Będzin. She lit seven candles on Tuesday night, July 31, the second anniversary of the death of her mother, sister, child, two nephews, two nieces. "May they rest in the Garden of Eden," she said, and she set the candles on a wide dinner table that, with the candles of her boarders, looked like the altar of some mysterious cult. At sunrise on Wednesday, August 1, the flames, like spirits, nodded to Lola as she sat down in this wax museum. She had coffee and drove to her prison, but the flames still played on her retina as a prisoner clerk, a German, gave her the morning list of the German dead. Lola thought of her mother's prayer in Będzin, "Thou shalt cast the abominations off of the earth, amen," and she thought, *I'm doing it, Mama.*

One morning in August, some Jewish guards came to Lola's office. They were survivors of Auschwitz, and they wanted to talk about the German who'd been in the Auschwitz SS. Lola guessed that the Jews had evidence against him. Ever since April, the German, thirty years old, had been telling the outraged boys in Interrogation, "I was anti-war," "I avoided the Army," "I joined the SS instead." The boys had used the beater-to-death, but the German had said that at Auschwitz, "I liked the Jews," "I helped the Jews," "I did good deeds for the Jews," and even when he was whale-blubber-colored, he had moaned that at Auschwitz, "I saved the Jews." He'd become a permanent whipping boy, a German who every second night had been dragged to Interrogation and back to his cell, where he'd knelt at his bed, his elbows on his sack-of-straw mattress, his palms—thick as mittens—pressing on one another like poultry parts. *"Herrgott!* Lord God!" the German had sobbed. "What will become of me?"

He hadn't confessed, so the boys in Interrogation hadn't sent him to Schwientochlowitz. He'd been at the recent head count, and, in the sudden sun, the Jewish guards had seen him and whispered about him, and now Lola guessed that the guards could identify him. The procedure would be, the guards would go to an oak-walled courtroom near Lola's prison. Each guard, wearing a skullcap, would lay his right hand on a Hebrew Bible (a survivor itself of World War II) on the page with the Ninth Commandment, "You shall not bear false witness." The guard would say, "I swear to God that I'll tell the truth," and would testify that he'd seen—or had heard someone say that *he'd* seen—the SS man doing such-and-such at Auschwitz. Three judges in purple-piped robes, in purple cravats, and in gold chains like the ones on sommeliers would say, "Guilty," and they would sentence the SS man to three or more years in Warsaw or Tarnów, in Poland, or in Posen or Gross Strehlitz, in Poland-administered Germany, or to immediate death in Lola's prison, a boy in Implementation lowering the noose, closing the elaborate knot, and kicking the SS man's stool out as Lola looked on.

"Yes," Lola said in her office now. "What about the SS man?"

"He was good to the Jews," said a Jewish guard.

"He was good? In what way?" said Lola, disoriented.

"He didn't beat us at Auschwitz."

"That's all? He didn't beat you?"

"We were on the dirt-digging crew," said the Jew from Auschwitz. "The dirt was like rock, and he didn't force us to dig it. Whenever the SS officers came, he told us, 'Watch out!'" and the Jew shook his hand horizontally to show how the SS man had woken him up. "He told us, 'Start digging!' As soon as the SS officers left, he told us, 'All right. You can rest.'"

"But still," said Lola, resisting. "He did say, 'Start digging.'"

"Sometimes some Poles came by," another guard said. "They brought us some bread, and the SS man looked away."

"He didn't look at the Poles?"

"No."

"He may not have noticed them, then."

"No, he was our lookout."

"Oh," Lola said. She frowned, as though the force of her brow could squeeze an appropriate utterance out. She was upset, though not at the thoughtless boys in Interrogation who, for months, had ravaged a man who evidently didn't deserve it. She was upset at her other prisoners, the

Germans who *did* deserve it. They'd lied at Auschwitz, "We have some showers," they'd lied in Gleiwitz, "I wasn't SS," "I was SS, but I wasn't in a concentration camp," "I was in a concentration camp, but I didn't deal with the Jews." It was the *Germans,* the wolves who'd said, "Baa," who'd taught the honest interrogators never to trust a German's word, and Lola wasn't remorseful now. "Well, what can I do?" Lola said.

"You can let the man out."

"But how?" Lola said. She was just a lieutenant, after all, and even Josef, the chief of the Office in Kattowitz, couldn't get a man out of prison without the imprint of most of Warsaw's rubber stamps. One day a Jew who'd been saying in Kattowitz, "There was a secret resistance at Auschwitz," was arrested, convicted and imprisoned in Kattowitz for telling lies. For months, Josef called up Warsaw saying, "He wasn't lying!" but not till the Polish prime minister said, "Yes, I was in the resistance with him," was the miserable man let out. And that was a *Jewish,* not German, convict! "How can I let him out?" Lola said.

The guards thought about it. At last they remembered, the SS man wasn't a convict, he was a suspect who was still being interrogated, and the guards brought him to Lola. His strange skin was like Job's, and his suffering eyes said, "Why has this happened to me?" Once, Lola's mother had told her how Job was let off, how God had eventually cured him and got him a thousand asses, two thousand cattle, and six thousand camels, and Lola now did as her mother would have wanted her to. She closed the long interrogation by telling the SS man, "You see? We Poles," she was thinking, *We Jews,* "aren't like you Germans at Auschwitz. We'll let you go." The boys in Interrogation approving, the Jews pulled open the Kloster Street Gate, and the SS man tottered out of the prison into the sun.

By now the typhus was like the Plague, and Lola was counting heads every day. One hot afternoon in August, the air like paste around her, she stood in the court as the Germans came shuffling out—shuffling, for the head count at five o'clock was a breath of fresh air and the Germans sought to prolong it. "Faster! Faster! You're walking like cows!" a Jewish guard cried, and a guard who was Catholic started to bawl the Germans out. The guard wore a fresh-pressed olive shirt, but he rolled up his sleeves so his 164996 would show, and he stood sweating in front of Lola yelling, "I was at Auschwitz! I stood twelve hours in a head count once! It was snowing, and I had to stand from six in the evening to six in the morning! Now line up!" The Germans did, and the guard said, "Now *you're* the ones who are standing! You sonofabitches!"

Behind him, Lola felt fidgety. She'd been at head counts at Auschwitz too, and she'd once stood in ten-below-zero cold as the SS conducted one. It had lasted three hours. Some women collapsed, and one Jewish woman from Holland had diarrhea, dumping it onto the snow below her. "You cow!" an SS woman had yelled. "Is that what you did in Holland? Is that what your mother taught you to do in Holland?" the SS woman snapping her whip and Lola silently screaming, *You are the cow, not her!* "Are you going to let it lie there?" the SS woman had yelled, till the Jew from Holland, a doctor, the center of one thousand stares, went in her shame to the wires, killing herself with 6000 volts. And today, the heat in the eighties, the wall behind her a brick oven wall, her jacket hot as a parka, her black collar buttoned up, Lola had an unpleasant sensation of *déjà vu*. In spite of the temperature today, the prison reminded her of Auschwitz. The Germans, like Jews, were in ranks and files, and the fresh-pressed-shirt-wearing boy was moving from German to German, stopping at spitting distance, yelling in the German's language, *"Du!* You! *Du machtest grosse schweinereien!* You did very piggish things!" The Germans were cringing like Auschwitz Jews—like Lola early that year.

She started to pace to and fro, disturbed. Her mother, God bless her, had often told her of Abraham's conversation with God, inscribed in the Book of Genesis. Abraham, father of the Jews, had said, "What if in Sodom there be fifty righteous men? Wilt Thou spare it?" and God had answered, "I will spare it," and Abraham then said, "What if there be only forty? Thirty? Twenty? Ten?" and God had said every time, "I will spare it." Pacing, peering, the Germans sullenly staring back, Lola was satisfied that none of the Germans were righteous men. To be sure, the SS men in this oven weren't from the concentration camps but, now that the Auschwitz man was gone, from the Russian front. The gap-toothed men from the Storm Section were coal miners from Königshütte, men who the Nazis had more or less told, "Sign up or you're shipping out," and who'd never hurt any Jews, and the Hitler Youth were just teenagers all. By now, the war long over, the Germans in front of Lola were mostly brawlers and burglars and men who'd allegedly said, "I don't like the Poles," but compared to Rivka, Lola's mother, they were as guilty as Hitler, and Lola didn't think that her poor, picked-on prisoners were just like Jews. No, Lola saw she was shaky today because her Jewish and Catholic *guards* were like the Auschwitz SS.

"Du bist nicht leute! You aren't people!" the boy with the fresh-pressed shirt cried now. *"Du bist schweine!* You're pigs!" The boy also wore a smart scarf, and his pants were jammed in his high black boots. *"Du!* You!" the boy now cried to a man who was whispering, as Lola winced. *"Halte deine schnauze!* Shut your snout! *Ein schritt vor!* One step forward! *Zwanzige kniebeugen!* Twenty deep knee bends! *Eins!*

Zwei! One! Two—" As the German went down and up, Lola half expected the boy to cold-cock him, just as the head-count-*führer* at Auschwitz had done to a number of Jews. Her nerves were loose wires now, but she didn't censor the shouting boy, for he'd been to Auschwitz and had as much right as she did to blow off the hate inside him. She let the boy bellow on.

"*Zwanzig!* Twenty!" the boy now cried, and the German, gaunt as a ghost from the prison's potato soup, slowly got up. "They're quiet as sheep now," the boy smiled to Lola, and Lola proceeded with the SOP.

"*Liczyć!* Count them!"

The boy and the other guards did.

"*Raport!* Report!"

"One hundred and forty prisoners!"

"*Dziękuję!* Thank you!" Inside of Lola's head, a voice like a migraine headache was pounding on Lola's skull. "You," it was roaring, addressing the Catholic boy—"You sounded like an SS man!" but Lola just smothered it. "*Na cele!* To the cells!" Lola cried, and, wheeling around, she left.

"**D**o *paki!* To the box!" "*Do ciupy!* To the cunt!" "*Do pierdla!* To the fuck!" the guards yelled, and, as the Germans went in, the guards went up to their second-floor rumpus room. At the door, they dipped their hands in a pot of white ointment to ward off the Germans' scabies, and in the room they pulled out the vodka to ward off the Germans' typhus. Every day, the Office allotted them half a pint of that cure-all, but though the guards drank it obediently with a horsemeat hors d'oeuvre, a few had caught typhus and two had died. The others were furious that the Germans were killing them even now, and, not content with the fists, pistols, and six-inch keys they'd used as blackjacks once, they were coming to work with whips to get at the Germans with. In the rumpus room, the guards gulped the Office's vodka as though it were antivenin and, the elixir exhausted, went out for more at the Strzecha Bar.

A few days later, a Jew was whipping a German on Lola's gloomy first floor. In his rage, the Jew's lower jaw jutted out like the claw of a giant ditch-digging machine, and on his teeth the spit almost shone. "*Ty pierdolony skurwysynu!* You fucking sonofawhore!" the Jew screamed, as his six-foot whip went crack! on the German's bare back. His hands on the wall as though being frisked, the German was screaming in bone-chilling counterpoint as Lola passed by. Lola grimaced. She'd seen the Jews beat the Germans before, but on this otherwise normal day she had (or saw that she'd *always* had) the same uncomfortable *déjà vu*, the same recollection of Auschwitz SS. "Why are you whipping him?" she asked the Jewish guard. "What did he do?"

"Well, *they* whipped *me* at Auschwitz!"

Lola half groaned. In her mind were the seven candles, reminding her
of her growing-up in Będzin, and to her ears the Jewish boy sounded like
any of her brothers, ready to punch out the Poles at all calls of *"Parszywy
Żydzie!* You boil-covered Jew!" Her brothers, too, had come on like vigi-
lantes till Rivka, their Solomon mother, said, "No. We live by the Torah."
"Who was it who whipped you at Auschwitz?" Lola asked the Jewish boy.

"The Germans! The beasts!"

"You despise them, then?"

"I do, Madame Commandant!"

"Well, tell me. If you despise them—"

"There is no if!"

"—Why do you want to be *like* them?"

"What?"

"Why do you want to *beat* them if that is what beasts do?" Lola said.
"Why do you hate them if—"

Lola paused. It had struck her, Rivka had said exactly this to the brothers and Lola herself in Będzin. "We hate the Polacks!" the hot-at-the-col-
lar brothers or Lola had often cried, and Rivka had had to remind them,
"Your hate hurts *you*. It eats your heart. It corrodes your soul." One day
in Będzin, Lola, aged twelve, had been walking home in her blue school
clothes when a boy of about eighteen cried, *"Parszywa Żydowa!"* the
feminine form of "You boil-covered Jew!" Lola had stood on her tiptoes
to scratch the boy's sneering face, and she'd run home like a pony before
he could catch her. "Oh, I could kill him!" she'd sobbed, but Rivka had
told her, "Don't say that," and had quoted the Talmud, "Let sins disappear." "It tells us the *sins* should disappear," said Rivka, looking in Lola's
eye. "It doesn't say the sinners should." "Yes, Mama," Lola had dutifully
said, but Rivka's words hadn't pierced like a Biblical prophet's until
today. And today, Lola stood on this gloomy first floor, the light drifting
down from the skylight, the German pressing the concrete wall, the Jew
still holding the whip at his shoulder, cocked, like a man serving a tennis
ball, and Lola wondered what Rivka, if she had been there, would have
thought. Were the sins disappearing in Gleiwitz? Or were they going on
and on? And was Lola casting off the abominations, amen? Or was she
breeding them?

"What should I do, Madame Commandant?" the Jewish boy said.

Lola didn't know. She studied the German. His hands were still on the
wall, but he was now peeping up from under his arm. Lola didn't like this
man—she hated him, really, and didn't really care if he dropped down
dead—but she cared about the Jewish guard. At Auschwitz, the SS had
probably called him a pig, a dog, an inhuman thing, and if Lola did what

the SS couldn't, if she let him become a real beast, well, who would the winner be? The Jewish boy? Or the SS? A year ago, Lola had made anti-aircraft shells to shoot at the men who were trying to liberate her, but then she'd thought, *What am I doing?* and done a full about-face. *What am I doing?* Lola thought now.

Her mother was Rivka, a Jew. The things that made her a Jew had survived since the time of Abraham and been pumped into Lola starting in Rivka's womb. *"L'chaim,"* she often had said in Będzin, meaning "To life," "To survival," "To Jewish existence eternally," and Lola suspected that Rivka wouldn't call it *l'chaim* if the "Jews" survived but the Jewish essentials didn't, if the "Nazis" died but the Nazi spirit infested the Jews. How had her mother once put it? "What does the Lord require," said Rivka, quoting the Bible, "but to do justly and to love mercy and to walk humbly with thy God," the very three rules that the Jew with the twitching whip—that Lola herself—wasn't observing in Gleiwitz.

"Well, what should I do?"

"Put that whip down," Lola said.

"Madame Commandant?"

"And don't ever hurt the Germans."

The boy looked at Lola as if she'd announced, "I'm a Nazi agent," and even the German's red-rimmed eyes rose to Lola astonished. "But what should I *do?*" the boy stammered.

"Where does this German belong?"

"In his cell."

"Put him in. Then come with me."

The boy did, and the two climbed a narrow stairway, bare as an iron fire escape. At the top, Lola called out, and the other guards followed her to her sunless office. On the south it had two giant windows, but the view was the Gleiwitz office of the Office of State Security, and Lola had closed the gray drapes so her nosy associates couldn't look in. She stood at her desk, the guards all around her, and said, "We will do things differently. We will feed the Germans. We'll find them good food, we'll wipe out the typhus, and we won't beat them."

The guards reacted as though she'd said, "We will make this the Gleiwitz Hilton." They interrupted her, "But they beat us at Auschwitz!"

"And Buchenwald!"

"And—"

"Were *these* the Germans at Auschwitz?" Lola asked.

"Maybe they were!"

"Or their brothers were!"

"They're Germans, and the Germans were!"

"And now you hate all the Germans?" Lola asked.

"Don't you, Madame Commandant?" The faces that Lola saw were black. All year, the hate had been seeping from them, and it now caked them like mud-masks, forming scowls. The guards, Lola saw, had been brewing bile, and now they were drowning in it, drowning like the man in Hillel's story. At last Lola saw that what goes around, comes around, that an Auschwitz that's upside down is an Auschwitz nevertheless, and that far from escaping from it, she and her guards had careers inside it.

"Yes, I still hate them," Lola said. She was standing, and in spite of her steel corset she had sciatica pains from the SS beatings at Auschwitz. "My mother was a wise woman, though," Lola continued. "She told me I shouldn't hate. To hate the Germans, what does that get us? It doesn't get us our mothers back. If you and I beat the Germans, how will the world ever know that the beasts at Auschwitz really existed and you and I aren't like them? No," Lola said. "We won't hurt the Germans from now on."

"As you say, Madame Commandant."

The guards filed out. The next day, Lola chose a gentle guard and two women prisoners, and with Lolek, the horse, and Lolek's wagon, the three went to German farms like kids trick-or-treating on Halloween. "We're from the prison," the women said, as, on the wagon, the guard covered them with a shotgun, and the German farmers gave them peas, carrots and cabbages, saying, "Come back tomorrow." For potatoes Lola sent German men, and she then sampled the soup like a chef, making sure that it wasn't just broth. At her orders, the Germans got anti-typhus inoculations, and in place of their ratty blankets they got the dead people's blankets from Schwientochlowitz—but Lola had the blankets steam-cleaned, first.

Once every day, the Germans now strolled round the water tank, and Lola watched lest a Jewish or Catholic guard attempt to torment them. One day she caught one, and she warned that she'd put him in one of her disciplinary cells—a cell just eight inches deep, the cell door crowding the man inside like a waffle iron—if he ever hit, kicked or whipped a German again. Another day, Lola found three German women prisoners who had no jackets—manila files—and she asked them, "Why are you here?"

"The Russians arrested us."

"Why?"

"The Russians didn't say."

Not telling Imprisonment, Lola released them. To do this was daring, for Lola had once known a boy who'd released some SS men (and, said the Office, gotten a few hundred dollars' bribe) and then had to stand with a blindfold on as Implementation shot him and killed him in Kattowitz prison court.

Of course, Lola didn't suddenly love all Germans. But her hate was on a low flame now, and her lid wasn't rattling night and day. As August cooled to September, the flame got lower and lower, and it then went out. The density in the atmosphere like the oily black smoke from a tarpot passed from the prison's interior. The guards didn't even want to abuse the Germans (they even hired them to dust their homes) and Lola became like the girl she'd been in Będzin, humming things from the Hit Parade in the gloom of her Gleiwitz cooler,

> *I'll be seeing you*
> *In all the old. . . .*

The girl who'd needed an outlet for her hot lava suddenly had no more lava left. She wondered, *Why didn't I know it?* Back in Będzin, she'd never believed that if she loved and loved her mother, sooner or later she'd use up the love inside her. So why had she thought that if she hated and hated, someday she'd be rid of her enormous hate? She now understood that she'd only have more of it. Love and hate: the more she expended them, the more she had, and Lola (like everyone everywhere) was a perpetual-motion machine that can be set to generate one or the other, forever. "It's our own choice," said Maimonides.

Well, maybe God wasn't dead. One day the office telephone rang and Zlata told Lola ecstatically, "A letter came from Elijah!" Elijah was Zlata's husband, Lola's gorilla-chested brother, and Lola actually said, *"Baruch Hashem!* Praise the Name!" The bad news wasn't in the letter: that "Elo" had been at the Markstädt camp, been one of the bosses there, used a lead pipe on the Jews, and sent some to cyanide chambers, saying, "They're *dreck."* He now was in France and, not daring to come to Poland, was waiting for Zlata in a chateau near the English Channel. It wasn't easy, but Lola got Zlata a train ticket, an exit visa, and a sort of second dowry: the gold in the Germans' pirate chest. Lola's lover, the Russian colonel, gave a sausage-and-sauerkraut party at Lola's home, and Zlata (her hair unfashionably yellow and red, the effect of louse powder at Auschwitz) left on a train to Paris.

But that wasn't all. A letter came from Lola's brother David, who Ada had found in Germany, and soon letters came like the telegrams-to-a-wedding from four other brothers, miraculously alive. All had escaped from Poland before the Germans had occupied it. One had joined the Polish army in Russia, one the French one in France, and one the Royal

Air Force in England, bombing the Germans and not getting hit by Lola's anti-aircraft shells. The fourth one had landed on D-Day, an American GI. Lola had one living sister, too, the one who'd married the dairy owner in Königshütte and had since married a Jew in France. Lola's brothers and sisters weren't returning to Poland, and Lola's lovestruck boarders told her, "We're leaving," and Lola became the agent who got them the tickets, the visas, the chips from the Germans' pirate chest.

A boy in the Office was leaving too. He was Adam, the chief interrogator, the boy who'd suffered when the Germans did and who'd treated the pain with analgesic alcohol. Adam didn't know, but the SS at Auschwitz had had the same symptoms, same cure. At various times, all but one SS man at Auschwitz had gone to Höss, the commandant, distressed by the last dying cries of the Jews. Höss had had heartaches too, and Himmler, even Himmler, had once conceded that one thousand corpses weren't a joy to look at. He'd told the SS,

> *You must know what it means when a hundred, five hundred, or one thousand corpses are lying side by side. To have stuck it out is a page of glory in our history.*

But the SS hadn't quite stuck it out—it had stunned itself with its Yugoslavian schnapps, as Adam had with his Polish *bimber*.

What saved him, oddly, was Auschwitz. At twilight there, Adam had often stared at the smoke that, as if from volcanoes, had poured from the smokestacks night and day, the enormous embodiment of the SS's hate. He'd often wondered: Why had the SS hated the Jews that extravagantly? and one night in Gleiwitz, the mirror image of Auschwitz, the "Jews" there being the Germans and the "SS" being Adam, he saw in his vodka *veritas:* he saw that to hate, and to act on that hate, was to hate even more later on. To spit out a drop of hate was to stimulate the spitting glands and, in twenty-four hours, to produce a drop-and-a-quarter of it. To spit that out was to then produce a drop-and-a-half, until, in time, there were two drops, three drops, four drops, five, a teaspoon, tablespoon, gallon, a Krakatao. Hate, Adam saw, was a self-replicating thing, like the water in *The Sorcerer's Apprentice,* and the SS, like Lola, like him, had in time become gorged with it. Adam recalled the philosophy of (of all people)— of Nietzsche, who'd said that a man who would go against monsters mustn't become a monster himself, and Adam saw clearly that he must get out of Poland.

He put his vodka down. He thought of his daily prayer in Konin, "May our eyes behold our return to Zion," and he decided to emigrate to the Holy Land. He didn't hop on the train to Piraeus, Greece, for a boy or girl who tried to defect from the Office—from what really was Stalin's secret police—and go to the hated imperialists could end up in prison with the Hitlerites. Instead, Adam got a Czechoslovakian visa and, in his civvies, hopped on the train to Prague early in August. The smoke poured out, the train started off, but August waned to September and no one in Gleiwitz had heard from him. Gleiwitz, as Lola knew, was a rat's nest of spies for the Office's bosses in Kattowitz, and Lola now wondered: Had one of them ratted on Adam?

Saturday, September 8, was the 5,706th anniversary of Creation: was New Year's Day for the Jews. The ones in Będzin had usually blown a ram's-horn trumpet on New Year's Eve, the blast like an "All aboard!" sending shivers down Lola's spine. But this year, the eve was on Friday, the Sabbath: no huffing, no puffing, no playing a musical instrument, and Lola just lit the Sabbath candles saying, *"Baruch ata."* The custom was, Lola would have till Sunday, September 16, the Day of Atonement, to apologize to all Jews and Germans who she had wronged, and, all that week, she apologized to the Germans by bringing bread to her prison and to her German prisoners. She fed them inside their cells, where the guards couldn't see her, for *mitzvahs,* good deeds, were against the Office's rules, and the guards (or the other prisoners) might be spies for her devious boss in Kattowitz, the new Jewish chief of Imprisonment.

But her boss found out. And worse, her new boss was Chaim, the icy-eyed friend of Pinek's sweet sister. All that year, he'd moved up the hier-archy on the power of Pinek's sister's "Be good to Chaim"s. He'd cheated on her in Kattowitz with a Polish writer and a Polish fencing champion and—his fetish—the Polish ex-mistresses of SS men, but Pinek's sister had said, "I love him," and Pinek had now promoted him to chief of Imprisonment. Chaim, whose last name was Studniberg, had set up an office on Seydlitz Street in Kattowitz and sub-offices in Silesia's cities, like Gleiwitz. He had hired numerous spies, and in September they told him of Lola, the German-loving Jew.

Now, Chaim hated all the Germans, *all.* There were good ones at Auschwitz, but Chaim hadn't met one, for during the war he'd lived like a scared rabbit in a hole underneath a barn outside of Będzin. By the light leaking in, he had company-clerked for Pinek, the partisan leader, writing up battle plans with the same careful curlicues that a man might put on some wedding invitations. He'd seldom gone out. To be spotted by anyone, *any-one,* but Pinek or Pinek's sister would have been to be— Chaim didn't know, but he'd shivered to think about it. He'd gotten tuberculosis, and on the train to the doctor's he'd buried himself in a paper, peeping over the top. "Excuse me. Aren't you Chaim Studniberg?" a Polish man had asked him.

"What?"

"Aren't you Chaim Studniberg from Będzin?"

"*What?*" His stomach had turned upside down, but Chaim had taken his glasses off and stared at the man defiantly, as though telling him, "I'm not a Jew!"

"I apologize," the man had said.

At the doctor's, a woman had looked at Chaim curiously. His temperature in the 100s, he'd left at once, forgoing the train, going through the woods, toppling, three hours later, into his little cavity, closing the trap door tightly, thinking that all of Europe was after him. And wasn't it?

He hadn't let his terror show, lest the Germans see it. He'd often looked in a mirror, proud that a man couldn't spot the chaos in him through his dry and straight-staring eyes. He didn't look like a "Jew," for his lips and ears were finer than whittled wood and his nose belonged on a German coin: the Perfect Aryan. When the war ended and he joined the Office, his jitters hadn't cleared up, but his uniform (and, after midnight, pajamas) had helped him to camouflage them. He'd jammed his pants into German boots, and he'd kept a trim silhouette by wearing his .25, his dainty little five-shot pistol, in a pocket instead of a fat black holster, though to his annoyance it often fell out. To romantics like Pinek's sister, Chaim had looked like a Hollywood hero, like Fairbanks or Flynn.

At the Office, he had attacked his dragons, the Germans, and he'd often told the Kattowitz prison guards, "Kill this man." "Chaim!" a German had cried out in Beuthen prison once. "I was your teacher in Będzin! You must help me!" "Why?" answered Chaim, and from his eyes came a glacier that must have crushed the man, who killed himself right after that. In his way, Chaim was the SS's victim as much as the Jews at Auschwitz were, for he'd consciously copied the SS's evil eye, the SS's twisted lip, and the SS's other tried-and-true ways with the Jews, and his body and soul had rebuilt themselves in the SS's image. Not heeding Nietzsche, he had become a monster, and he'd even changed his nickname from Yiddish to Polish to German: from Heniek to Henryk to Heinrich, as in Himmler.

At twenty-six, he'd become chief of Imprisonment. But still the rats clawed at him, clawed even more, and to quell them he longed for the same solution that Hitler had had for the Jews. When, in September, he heard how Lola was coddling the Goths in Gleiwitz, he was quite panic-stricken. He paced in his office in Kattowitz, his fingers intertwining behind him, his eyes darting around him, as if Lola's protégés might lie in the shadows under his table or teacart. His mouth was a cud-chewing creature's: it went left, it went right, it muttered to its own components, vowing to God to put the screws to Saint Lola, the Office's heretic, the "Be good to Germans" apostate.

11

"Be good to Germans" was not, repeat, not, the policy of Chaim's superiors. The President of Poland had decreed on Wednesday, February 28,

> In the territory of the Polish Republic and the former free city of Danzig, the possessions of (a) Citizens of the German Empire, and (b) Germans regardless of citizenship, will be subject to registration and confiscation.

Germans were people whose fathers were German, and possessions were the Germans' farms, homes, tables, tablecloths, teapots, even the shirts on the Germans' backs. On Friday, March 2, the Poles had also decreed this for the Germans in Poland-administered Germany, eight million people, some of whom hastened to hide their clothes in their milk-cans and to bury these cans in their pastures.

To no avail. With the Polish officials like Lola came an army of Poles (often from Eastern Poland, now Russia) who knocked on the Germans' doors and said, "Alles mein. Everything's mine." On Lange Reihe, Lola had thrown out a German glass-blower, tax-collector and engineer, and the Catholic across the street had thrown out a German mailman, the Catholic saying, "Thirty minutes!" "Twenty!" "Ten!" the mailman and his three daughters scramming, taking a bag of beans to a German friend's attic. Quite typically for 1945, the mailman died, one daughter jumped under a train, one daughter escaped to Germany, and one daughter stayed in the German friend's attic. By summer, the name of Lola's street was Lange Reihe in Polish: Ulica Długa. The signs by Neptune's statue were CAFE, RESTAURACJA and APTEKA, and Gleiwitz itself was Gliwice. Breslau, Stettin and Stolp were Wrocław, Szczecin and Słupsk, the currency was the Polish złoty, and a German who spoke in German or, as happened in Gleiwitz, who sang the German ragman's song,

> *Lumpen, knochen, eisen und papier,*
> *Ausgeschlagene zähne sammeln wir,*
>
> *Rags, bones, iron and paper,*
> *We collect knocked-out teeth,*

had his own teeth knocked about in Lola's prison.

In command of the Germans now was the Minister of "Repossessed" Territories, for Poland had "possessed" some of them in 1772 and the others in 1335 and had now "repossessed" them, and on every street were Polish policemen: *boys,* some Catholic, some Jewish, many of them still teenagers. The policemen arrested the Germans indiscriminately. Once, they heard that a German in Gleiwitz was stealing coal, but at the German's home they searched in some corners where even a lump wouldn't fit. "I don't keep coal in my sugar bowl! I don't keep coal in my tea kettle!" the German, another mailman, cried. "You want to steal from me!" but the Poles said, "Enough!" and sent him to Lola's prison for mocking the Polish police. At other homes in Gleiwitz, the cops told the Germans, "You're Nazis," and packed them off to Chaim's concentration camps while the Poles moved in. Often the "Nazis" were well below the minimum membership age. At one of Chaim's camps in Silesia was a German who'd just been born, and at a camp near the Baltic Sea was a whole barracks of white-striped cribs and of eight-pound prisoners. They didn't have milk, for the red-headed doctor, a Jew from Auschwitz, didn't let the mothers in, telling the Polish inspectors, "It's enough if my papers say I did." Of the fifty babies there, forty-eight died.

By summer the Poles were pouring into Silesia, and the Silesian police chief, a Jew so small that, to show that he was a colonel, he wore his three colonel's stars on his shoulders and *collars,* directed his boys to clean out the Germans and to relocate them in Chaim's crowded camps. The roles were completely reversed now for Jews and Germans. Early on Friday, July 27, the Catholic and Jewish policemen swooped down on Bielitz, a village near Neisse, a couple of hundred homes surrounded by wheat, rye and barley fields peppered with red-petaled poppies. To the best of anyone's knowledge, none of the German farmers there were Nazis, but they were Germans and, at the H-hour, six in the morning, the cops started pounding on their doors, shouting, *"Wohnen hier Deutsche? Do Germans live here?"*

"Ja, ich bin Deutscher."

"Get out!"

The Germans got out.

"Climb on!"

And prodded by rifle butts, the one thousand men, women and children of Bielitz, many still barefoot, got on some trucks, and as the Poles moved in, the one thousand people rode off. In their caps and kerchiefs, the Germans looked quite like the Jews of Będzin as the Germans rode south to Chaim's very final solution. Oh, Chaim really hated them!

F̲ive minutes later, the Germans got off, and the police delivered them to Chaim's new concentration camp in the village of Lamsdorf. During the war, the camp had been for British officers, but Chaim had just reopened it and appointed some boys with Polish-sounding names to run it. The commandant, Czesław, was twenty years old, and, when the Germans lined up, he called to a school-teacher's son, *"Du dort komm runter!* You there come here!" The boy did, and Czesław took him to a room with an upright piano and told him, *"Spiel!* Play!" The boy sat down and started the Czechoslovakian tune that Americans know as

> *Roll out the barrel!*
> *We'll have a barrel—*

and Czesław and his ten drunken guards began to polka, circling like at a wedding, doing it wilder, wilder, dancing on benches, dancing on tables, leaping off and shouting, *"Hej!"* The pianist stopped, and Czesław, now sweat-drenched, told him, "You are our organist now," and called a retired mailman in. The pianist started up,

> *Roll out the barrel!*
> *We'll—*

and Czesław and his ten guards kept time by clubbing, whipping, stomping and killing the German mailman, seventy years old.

Chaim had chosen these boys for the heat of their hatred of Germans. His commandant, Czesław, had lost his mother, father, sisters and brothers, and Czesław himself had tuberculosis from Auschwitz. The deputy commandant was a Hitler-mustached boy who once said, "As many hairs as I have, I must kill that many Germans," the guards were a gap-toothed and nine-fingered lot, and the German prisoner "boss" was a former policeman, a man who'd tortured a number of Germans during the war. The staff didn't kill the one thousand people of Bielitz that very day. One by one, it called them to the piano parlor, taking their bread, butter, cheese, their spare pants, shirts, skirts, their babies' diapers, tossing these in the corner, telling the Germans, *"Heraus!"* "Please," one German woman said, "may I keep the baby's clothes?" but Czesław pointed his gun at the baby shouting, *"Ich geschuss!"* meaning "I'll shoot!" the deputy booted the woman out, and Czesław tossed the bawling baby after her.

That night, the Germans lay in their barracks, sewing the W's for *więzień,* prisoner, and for *więźniarka,* prisoneress, to their clothes, and the next day the staff began killing them. And what inventive ways it had to do it! Czesław would stomp on a German's throat, but he once told a German to climb up a tree crying, "I am a monkey!" and as the German did, Czesław took out his gun and shot him. The deputy shot the Germans too ("I shot fourteen today") but he once asked a German, "Do you know what my name is?" "No, Herr Deputy Commandant." "It's Ignaz!" the deputy said, and crack! he cracked his saber across the German's head. One day, the deputy started a fire in one of the German barracks, cried, "Sabotage!" and as the German women scooped up the sand, carried it in their skirts, and dumped it on the ferocious flames, he pushed the hysterical women in. As for the guards, they once put a German's black beard in a vise, locked the vise solidly, and set the German afire.

Every day, the names of the Germans who'd died went to Czesław, who always said, "Why so few?" In time, almost all of Bielitz was dead, but the trains full of Poles kept coming, and the police had to clean out Arnsdorf, Bauersdorf, and three dozen other villages and to deliver the Germans to Czesław's camp. The wretchedest Germans there were the women of Grüben. During the war, the SS had buried some Poles, five hundred bodies, in a wide meadow near Lamsdorf, but Czesław had heard there were ninety thousand, and he ordered the women of Grüben to dig them up. The women did, and they started to suffer nausea as the bodies, black as the stuff in a gutter, appeared. The faces were rotten, the flesh was glue, but the guards—who had often seemed psychopathic, making a German woman drink urine, drink blood, and eat a man's excrement, inserting an oily five-mark bill in a woman's vagina, putting a match to it—shouted at the women of Grüben, "Lie down with them!" The women did, and the guards shouted, "Hug them!" "Kiss them!" "Make love with them!" and, with their rifles, pushed on the backs of the women's heads until their eyes, noses and mouths were deep in the Polish faces' slime. The women who clamped their lips couldn't scream, and the women who screamed had to taste something vile. Spitting, retching, the women at last stood up, the wet tendrils still on their chins, fingers, clothes, the wet seeping into the fibers, the stink like a mist around them as they marched back to Lamsdorf. There were no showers there, and the corpses had all had typhus, apparently, and sixty-four women of Grüben died.

All this was known to Chaim. He did inspections at Lamsdorf, and he often spoke to Czesław at his own office in Kattowitz. Then, Chaim was always driven home, but Czesław went to the Jewish Club, two second-floor rooms on Rüppel Street, for his friends were all Jews although he insisted (and all the Jews accepted) that *he* was a Polish Catholic. At the Club, Czesław sat and related all the weird ways that he'd killed the Germans that week. "They did it to us," he announced, often incorrectly, "and I did it to them," and the Jews at his table nodded, eating their borscht. The Jews wouldn't have wept if every farmer at Lamsdorf died, but in fact almost twenty percent of the Germans there—1,576 of the 8,064 men, women, boys, girls and babies—somehow survived.

And now the month was September, and Chaim was brooding on Lola, the "Be good to Germans" girl. He paced like a man in a crazy-house around his office in Kattowitz, afraid that the suspects in Lola's prison might be more comfortable than the Germans outside it. Lola, he felt, was commanding a German castle, and Chaim now resolved to defeat her. He snapped on his visored hat and, going outside, stepping into his big Mercedes, telling his Polish driver, "Gliwice," meaning Gleiwitz, and cursing at every red light, he raced past the steel, lead and zinc mills to Lola's prison. The day before, he'd driven to a prison in Sosnowiec, cried, "Open up!" and, when the gate guard did, cried, "Why did you let me in?"

"You're the Chief of Imprisonment."

"How do you know that I am?"

"Well—"

"You didn't ask for my ID!"

"Well, I recognize you."

"I may have been *fired!*" Chaim had cried, and he'd clapped the poor guard in a Sosnowiec prison cell. At other times, Chaim had even imprisoned a commandant, a Jew. Soon he would visit the new commandant in Neisse—Efraim, the one-armed boy—and would stare at Efraim's three German motorcycles, saying, "I want one."

"You can have that one."

"No, I want *that* one," Chaim would say, and he'd point to the newest and shiniest one.

"Well, that one's mine, but you can have *that* one."

"I said I want *that* one."

"Hey, Captain! I commandeered that one for me! But you can have *that* one!"

"No, I want *that* one," Chaim would say, but Efraim wouldn't budge and Chaim would arrest him and lock him in Kattowitz prison. And today, Chaim headed west to look for some grounds to lock up Lieutenant Lola.

His car sped into Gleiwitz. It went up Mühl Street and pulled up at Lola's back door, the driver tormenting the horn and Chaim shouting, just like in Sosnowiec, "Open up!" In the door was a wooden window, and one of Lola's guards opened it.

"Who are you?" the boy said to Chaim.

"The chief of Imprisonment!"

"Have you any ID?"

"Dammit!" Chaim cried. "I'm Captain Studencki!" his new Polish name. "Open this door up! Or," and he pulled his gun out—"or I'll *shoot* you!"

And slam! The boy closed the window in Chaim's raging face. "I'll need your ID!" the boy cried, for Lola had spies in Sosnowiec too, and she had alerted the Mühl Street Horatius.

"All right!"

The boy peeped out. Still boiling, Chaim was holding his Office ID, and, two-finger-saluting him, the boy now opened the door and Chaim, so far unsuccessful, shot by.

He descended on Lola's office. His strict rule was "No jobs for Germans," so Lola had hidden her two impermissible clerks in a perfect place: their cells, and at their desks she'd stationed a Jewish girl, Jadzia, the "Ha-ha-ha!" humorist. "Good morning, Lieutenant!" said Chaim, coming in, to the Lola he'd known in the 1930s when he had scruffy sideburns and she had braids, and he started to go methodically through the papers on Lola's desk. He pretended he was after something specific, and he even frowned at one or two items, casting his icicle eyes at Lola, smiling his ten-below-zero smile, signaling her, *Well, I've caught you*—but Lola was smart and didn't stutter, "I can explain it." Still unsuccessful, Chaim went to Lola's prison and to her cells, shower, cookroom, hospital, morgue, but he couldn't get the goods on Lola and saw that he'd have to entrap her. He stole away, whispered to a German prisoner spy, returned, said, "Thank you, Lieutenant," and headed to his Mercedes.

Lola was onto him. Suspicious, neurotic, sick, this Chaim was a boy she hadn't liked in Będzin, and she'd made a face whenever she'd told her Będzin friends, "He's a *macher* now. He's a big shot now." Precisely what he was up to, Lola couldn't figure out, but she was aware he was dangerous, was full of demons he had to destroy, come what may. By now his cells, cellars, camps were a universe both of Germans and of German-loving Poles. No one could soften him: Gleiwitz would be an Auschwitz of Chaim's creation, and Lola could be its perpetrator or prisoner, at one or the other end of the whip, in pain in her spirit or flesh: those were her choices in Gleiwitz. "Give my love to Shoshana," to Pinek's sister, Lola said, and "I will," said Chaim, driving off, but Lola now wanted out.

For months, her mad Russian lover, a man who had often barreled into the prison telling her, "Marry me!" had also been telling her, "Come with me!" to Vienna, Venice, anywhere, but Lola had been afraid of jumping out of Silesia into what might be Siberia. That was the rumor in Gleiwitz: that Adam, the chief interrogator, still was in Czechoslovakia, that Shlomo, the holy man, and Rivka, his too-tall friend, were also in Czechoslovakia, that hundreds of Jews who'd escaped from the Office (*escaped*, for the Office didn't say, "They deserted," or "They defected," but "They escaped") were now in a Czechoslovakia full of the Office's WANTED posters and Russian posses. "We'll live in the West!" the Russian had often blurted, but Lola had been afraid that a colonel in Stalin's army and a lieutenant in Stalin's secret police wouldn't end up on the Côte d'Azur but north of the Arctic Circle. And today, she was still scared as she motorcycled to Lange Reihe—Ulica Długa—and told the Russian, "Let's get out."

"Get packed," the Russian said.

His plan was to drive to Vienna, for the Nazis had stolen some Polish art and sent it to Austria, and, with official documents, the two would go get it. But then they would drive to Paris and *sell* it and, now bankrolled, would say, "I do," and would re-create the flesh and blood that Lola had lost during the war. All this, the Russian explained to Lola in Yiddish, a language like German, and Gertrude, her powder-packing maid, over-heard him. "Merciful lady! Please help me!" Gertrude cried.

Gertrude was scared and Lola knew why. Her family, friends, were now in the Office's concentration camps, the Office renting them out to coal, lead and zinc mines just as the SS had rented out Lola for twelve cents an hour to the Union Factory, at Auschwitz. Gertrude, as Lola's maid, was still exempt from the slave-labor camps, but if Lola left Poland, Gertrude would go to the camp in Gleiwitz or to the camp at Schwien-tochlowitz. Looking at Gertrude's saucer eyes, Lola recalled what Rivka, her ever-present mother, once said in Będzin. God, Rivka said, had cre-ated one man, not one million as God surely could. "He taught us to trea-sure every man," said Rivka, quoting the Talmud. "If we destroy one, we destroy the whole world, but if we *save* one, we save the whole world." It now was the week of the Day of Atonement, of Sunday, September 16, and Lola, who longed to atone for her time in Gleiwitz, seized on Gertrude's predicament. "Truda! You're coming with us!" Lola said, and she phoned for her Jewish driver.

The next day was almost autumn. The chestnuts were falling off, and the children of Gleiwitz, mostly Poles, were whittling them into tiny baskets and putting in Polish coins. At the prison on Kloster—Józefa Wieczorka—Street, the roses were drooping but Lola, the rose-growing commandant, didn't show up. A guard drove to Lola's home, but Lola wasn't there. The guard called up Chaim, in Kattowitz, and soon some machine-gun-brandishing boys were in Lola's office, shouting, "Where did she go?" In her desk, they found a carbon copy of a letter to Chaim,

> In accordance with the circular letter of July 30, 1945, I report that I'm
> due a vacation and I now request it,

and in her pirate chest, her safe for the Germans' money, watches, rings, the boys found nothing at all, the chest was as empty as Old Mother Hubbard's Cupboard. "You!" a gun-wielding boy said to Jadzia, whose "Ha-ha-ha!"s now rattled like hollow gourds. "Where did she go?"

"I don't know!"

"You were friends!"

"Ha-ha-ha, I don't know!" said Jadzia, who then stole away, got the first train to Kattowitz, went to a Jew's apartment, locked it, and slept on his bedroom floor as Lola's adjutant Moshe scrammed out of Gleiwitz too.

The prison was different immediately. A series of commandants, all of them males, showed up in Lola's place. The first was a Jew from Warsaw who was tiny, oily, lubricious, rubbing his hands unattractively like a caricature of a Jew. He spoke with a Yiddish accent, telling his girl guards, "Oh, miss! My house is so nice! You must come and see it!" the girls saying, "Thank you, sir, but my mother is waiting for me," the boy then hitting on German women prisoners.

He didn't last long in Gleiwitz. One night, he took a German prisoner home to "clean" it, the fat and 40-ish woman coming back to her cell hysterical.

"What's wrong?" a girl guard asked her.

"He tried to rape me!"

The girl guard reported this to Chaim, who fired the Jew but who now mistrusted the German-loving guard (Our Angel, the Germans called her) and who resolved to entrap her. One day, a German prisoner gave her a letter and told her, "Please mail it." The guard hid the letter in one of her boots, but the German was spying for Chaim, and the Office arrested the kindhearted guard, tried her, and sent her to Kattowitz prison. And *then* the Office swooped down on Chaim, for he had a brother, a black marketeer, who he had once loaned his Mercedes to. "Confess!" cried the boys in Interrogation in Kattowitz. "Read this! Finish it! Sign it!" they cried to the former chief of Imprisonment, and they sent him to Kattowitz prison. The Office was eating its own.

A lot of Lola's old guards wanted out. Day after day, her successors would tell the Germans, "Get undressed!" "To the showers!" "Get out!" and *"Run!"* and the Germans, still naked, would run the length of the nave as, with belts, whips and clubs, the guards would beat them and, at times, kill them, and a lot of Jewish and Catholic guards didn't like it. One let a German climb out the window, climb off the roof, and escape, the guard getting sort of a dishonorable discharge, and one took the portrait of Stalin down, telling a Jewish interrogator, "I was at Auschwitz, I'm crazy," getting a week in Kattowitz prison, getting a DD after that. Unlike everyone in the Auschwitz SS, who had had the right to resign but who rarely did, the Jews in Gleiwitz *couldn't* resign but all got out—and sought to get out of Poland too. Even at Schwientochlowitz, Shlomo was dreaming of Israel and telling his new Yiddish joke, "Once a Jew asked another one, 'What's happening?' 'MF.' 'What does that mean?' *'Me furt!* I'm outta here!'"

As for Lola, she never was seen in Gleiwitz again. The word was, the Russian had double-crossed her, had tipped off his Russian friends at the Czechoslovakian border town, Ostrava. He, Gertrude and Lola, the word was, had driven up, and in Lola's suitcase the Russians had found $60,000 in German money, watches and rings that the Russians had then disappeared with. Gertrude, the rumor was, had disappeared too, and Lola had been indicted as an American spy, had been tried and convicted in Kattowitz, had been sentenced to ten, or perhaps fifteen, years in Gross Strehlitz, twenty miles west of Gleiwitz, and was now wasting away in Germany's Sing Sing. Hearing this, Lola's old guards in Gleiwitz discussed it over their six o'clock *bimber*. The guards were of three minds about it:

"She deserves it. She was too tough on us."
"I'm sorry about it. She was quite nice."
"I don't believe it. I bet she escaped."

The Poles were trying the Germans, too, in courtrooms from Warsaw down. Of their 200,000 prisoners, the Poles in time convicted about one thousand, so Pinek had been mistaken when he said to Chaim, "Ninety percent of the Germans, they're innocent." Pinek should have said, "Ninety-nine percent."

The major trials in Silesia were in Kattowitz, but one cold day in October ten Polish judges in suits, winter coats, and hats climbed onto an open-sided truck in Kattowitz and, saying, *"Sakramencko zimno!* It's sacramentally cold!" drove out to Shlomo's camp at Schwientochlowitz. In the guardroom, they set up ten tables, twenty chairs, in the form of a U, and, sitting down, they called in ten residents of the brown barracks, the site of Shlomo's bloody community sings. The first was a German who weighed ninety pounds. He was limping, his left hand was misshapen, his nose like an old beaten boxer's. He sat down in front of a mild-eyed judge, a man who looked at a one-and-one-half-page document and said, "You are Heinz Becker?"

"Yes." The German had turned his left ear to the judge, for he couldn't hear with his right one.

"You were born on January 30, 1930?"

"Yes." The German was fifteen years old.

"And you were arrested in February?"

"Yes, Mister Judge," the German said.

He was shaking, and the judge told him, "Be calm." The judge took a silver cigarette case and lit himself one, but the German didn't smoke. "The document says, 'He admitted being in Hitler Youth.' Hm-hm-hm-hm," the judge said, rocking his head from side to side, meaning, *Well, what German wasn't?* "Were you in Hitler Youth?"

"Yes, Mister Judge."

"'In his pocket was a swastika, so he must have been a Nazi.' Hm-hm-hm-hm. Did you have a swastika?"

"Yes, Mister Judge. I won it at the school track meet."

"'In his pocket was a cartridge case, so he must have owned a gun.' Hm-hm-hm-hm. Did you have a cartridge case?"

"Yes, Mister Judge. It was on the road and I picked it up."

"'We can conclude that he killed some Poles.' Hm-hm-hm-*hm.* 'I certify that this statement is true, signed, Heinz Becker.' Did you really sign this?"

"Yes, Mister Judge. I had to."

"Why?"

"They were beating me. *And,"* the German suddenly cried—"and they still are!" He burst into tears, showing the judge his nose and ears, arms and hands, legs and ankles, lifting up his gray shirt, showing the judge his chest. The judge stared at the crisscross wounds, and he used his ash tray to put his cigarette out.

"I believe you," the judge decided. He wrote up a second document, and the German nervously signed it. A guard handed him a half-pound of bread, a Toonerville trolley ticket to Schwientochlowitz city, and a train ticket to Bielsko-Biała, the German's home town, and, his body still shaking, his hands in prayer, his lips whispering, "Thank you, God," the German lurched out of Shlomo's camp. In the camp were other survivors, and the judges released almost all.

The Germans in Gleiwitz had trials too. The judges took the train there and put on purple-piped robes, while the Jew who was prosecutor put on a red-piped one and the defense attorneys green-piped ones. The witnesses swore on the Ninth Commandment if they were Jews, while the Catholics held up two fingers in front of a small silver cross. At one trial, a witness testified that a German in Lola's old prison once said,

> *Cici, cici,*
> *Polska w życi,*
>
> *Laddies, lasses,*
> *The Poles are asses.*

At one trial, a witness testified that a German had written the Nazis, "Piotr Wons is an enemy of Germany," but Piotr testified that the Nazis had never hassled him, and at another trial a witness testified that a German had told the Nazis, "Augustyn Kuczera told me, 'I'll come back here on a Polish tank,'" but Augustyn testified for the German, saying, "He was anti-Hitler." A lot of Germans at Lola's old prison turned out to be the Good Guys. One had helped the Jehovah's Witnesses, and one had even helped the Jews, crouching outside a camp in Gleiwitz, waiting till the SS men couldn't see him, and then throwing potatoes, carrots and beets to the Jews inside.

In the end, about twenty of Lola's old prisoners were convicted of very minor war crimes, and for one, two, or three more years they stayed in the prison if they didn't die of a "heart attack" first. One, only one, of Lola's old prisoners was convicted of something major. She was the woman who'd knitted sweaters for Lola's guards, the woman who'd once been a deputy commandant in Gleiwitz, beating up Jewish women, sending some to die at Auschwitz. For these crimes, she was ushered out of her cell at half past five one September morning. She had last rites, a Polish priest putting oil on her brow and the woman kissing his stole, saying in Polish, "Thank you, Father." She then strode like a commandant into the prison court, went to a stool, stepped onto it. The prosecutor, a Jew, wore a pair of white gloves while holding the woman's sentence. He read it, then pulled off the gloves, threw them to the ground, and told her, "Not I but the Law has condemned you."

"*Ich bin unschuldig.* I'm innocent."

The boy who was executioner was in Batman black, a costume he sometimes wore to the women's prison, saying, "Let me in!" then peeping at the women inside their cells. He had soaped the noose, and he now lowered it over the German, tightened it, and kicked out the stool from under her. Her body dropped, then spun like a ballerina's, and then stayed still for the fifteen minutes decreed by Polish law. "She's dead," the doctor reported, then Lolek, the horse, brought her to the LIVING TO DIE WELL, DYING TO LIVE WELL, cemetery, where the sexton put her in the wide mass grave for Lola's old German prisoners. Her name was Małgorzata Zapora.

On Wednesday, October 17, the President of Poland decreed that the Germans who weren't in prisons be thrown out of Poland and Poland-administered Germany, and, to the pealing of bells, the Polish police now rounded them up and herded them—ten million people—onto the trains, enforcing the biggest migration in all human history. In Kattowitz, as in Kielce, Breslau, Stettin, and some other cities, the chief of police was a Jew. Many were former partisans who, in August, 1944, had been celebrating in Lublin when the police chief of Poland, a Catholic, went to their rowdy quarters on Ogrodowa Street. "What should I do?" the chief asked the Jews. "Let you sit here? Say you're all heroes? Do portraits of you and hang you up? No," he said, smiling, "you'll have to *work*," and he made a Jew the police chief of Lublin and Jews all the precinct chiefs there. The next year, 1945, these people became the chiefs in some of Poland and Poland-administered Germany.

In Breslau, the biggest city in Poland-administered Germany, with 300,000 inhabitants, the chief of police, the chief of the Office's section for Germans, the chief of the Polish army's own Office (its Corps of Internal Security) and even the mayor of Breslau were Jews. Starting in August, their troops went to German homes, said, "*Wyjść*. Get out," and sometimes put their machine guns on German chests, said, "Just as the Germans did. You have seven minutes. Six minutes. Five minutes. Four...," and chased them to Breslau's railroad station. In the hot cattle cars, the forty-four pounds of food, water and clothes that a German could bring (a German couldn't bring jewels) were robbed by the Polish police, and a lot of the Germans died. Many were wrapped in brown wrapping paper, to be eventually buried.

Most of the Germans got off at the Office's camps on the German border. For food, they begged from the German civilians—from Germans who, every day, had only four ounces of bread themselves—and begged from the Russians, tore up the grass, cooked it, and ate it. At last they crossed into Germany, weeping, singing in German *Holy Lord, We Praise*

Thee, and, alas, ending up at jam-packed stations like one in Berlin that, in a pouch to Washington, an American described like this,

> *The mind reverts to Buchenwald,*

and a Britisher like this,

> *Children had running sores. Old men, unshaven, red-eyed, looked like drug addicts, who neither felt, nor heard, nor saw. They sat on the platform looking like a lot of duffel bags,*

and ten Germans died on that platform every day. In time, the rest of the Germans settled in Germany, East and West, and then, like the Jews, they counted heads, and of the ten million who'd lived in Poland and Poland-administered Germany after the war, one-and-one-half million were dead. "What happened to the Jews was sad," a mother from Gleiwitz said. "But there was *another* holocaust too."

In time, all of Poland and 44,000 square miles of Germany were rid of Germans, were *Deutscherein,* and the Office's institutions were full of Poles, 150,000 Poles from the antecedents to Solidarity. In places like Gleiwitz, the Poles stood against the prison wall as Implementation tied them to big iron rings, said, "Ready!" "Aim!" "Fire!" shot them, and told the Polish guards, "Don't talk about this." The guards, being Poles, weren't pleased, but the Jacobs, Josefs and Pineks, the Office's brass, stayed loyal to Stalin, for they thought of themselves as Jews, not as Polish patriots. And *that's* why the Good Fairy Stalin, the man who didn't hate the Germans but who abhorred the Enemies of the People, the Agents of Reactionary Elements, the Oppressors, Imperialists and Counterrevolutionaries, be they the Germans, Russians or Poles, had hired all the Jews on Christmas Eve, 1943, and had packed them into his Office of State Security, his instrument in the People's Republic of Poland.

And now, 1945, the Poles went to war with the Office, shooting at Jews in Intelligence, Interrogation and Imprisonment, the Jews concluding that the Poles were antisemitic, the Poles contending that no, they were only anti the Office. One night in October in Kattowitz, the Poles tossed a couple of hand grenades into Barek's, the middleweight's, apartment, the grenades going off in his kitchen, the air filling up with smoke and the walls with shrapnel. At the time, Barek and Regina, his bride, and Regina's mother were out at a Russian movie, but on their return they saw the black smoke, a shroud over all the tables and chairs, and Regina cried, "We must leave Poland!"

"No, we must take revenge!" Barek said.

"Haven't we had enough revenge?" said Regina's mother.

"No, my blood is boiling again!"

"It's enough! We must leave!" cried Regina's mother. "Or this will go on, and on, and *on*," and in front of Barek, she and Regina burst into tears.

Soon after that, at seven on a Sabbath evening, Barek, carrying no Office ID, only Polish money, and Regina, carrying her toothbrush, stood in the dark on Andreas Place as the twice-weekly courier truck to Czechoslovakia pulled up. The two hurried into the van and sat down on the fat canvas pouches, and the driver, a Russian, drove off. Barek said, "Should we trust him?" and Regina said, "We have no choice," and the truck turned south on Beate Street. By November, the word in Kattowitz was that they'd gotten to Plzeň, Czechoslovakia, on the border of Germany, and been turned back by Americans. "Your papers are forged," the MPs reportedly told them.

One boy contented in Poland was Pinek. At twenty-four, he was a very important person, but in December he needed to pass through the Iron Curtain for Shoshana's, his sister's, sake. She was dreadfully ill, she needed to go to some magic mountain in the Alps, and Pinek arranged to bring her to one in Merano, Italy, and to then scurry back to his desk in Kattowitz. Compared to the other boys from the Office, he would be traveling like a king, for he had a potent diplomatic passport, a visa to Czechoslovakia, Austria and Italy, and a generous gift of $500, more than enough, from the Office's bosses in Warsaw. He imagined he'd have a red carpet all the way.

He and Shoshana, coughing blood, got on a train in Kattowitz early in December, and he held her hand as they rode by the skeletal trees to Bratislava, Czechoslovakia, on the Austrian border. But there the red carpet unraveled, for the tracks were in ruins, and the two passengers had to get off and, like refugees, hitch a ride on a Russian truck. They were just past the Danube when the Russian driver stopped, pulled out a gun, and leveled it at Shoshana, apparently planning to murder her and Pinek and sell their luggage in Vienna, and Pinek had to pull his own Mauser out and cry to the Russian, *"Ruki v verch!* Hands up!"

"Nye strelyay! Don't shoot!"

"Stoy! Just stay there!" Pinek cried, and he covered the double-crosser till he and Shoshana, now swooning, could catch a real ride to Vienna.

Pinek lived just for Shoshana now. In Vienna, he put her into a hospital, run, quite ironically, by the Red Cross, and ten days later he took her by train to Innsbruck, in the Austrian Alps, and to another hospital of the Red Cross. By now Shoshana couldn't walk, and Pinek had to lift her onto a train that huffed and puffed toward the tunnel under the Brenner Pass. But there his heart broke again, for the tracks were in ruins there too, and he had to hire a horse-drawn sleigh, to put his shivering sister on, and, as the horse labored up the snow-covered road, to push from behind like one of Hannibal's elephants. "How are you?" said Pinek, panting for air.

"I'm such trouble for you!"

"No, you aren't!" said Pinek, his shoes slipping under him.

By mid-afternoon, they were at 4,500 feet and the border of Italy. On guard in long olive coats were Americans, British, French and Italians, even some Poles from the anticommunist government in London. Pinek went straight to the Poles, who asked for his passport, kept it, and told him, "You're under arrest."

"What for?"

"We don't recognize the government in Warsaw."

Pinek's serenity left him. He cried, "We're desperate!" first to the Poles, then to the Allies, who didn't understand his Polish. "*Wir sind verzweifelt!*" he tried in German.

"*Was ist los?*" a German-speaking American said.

"*Meine schwester!* My sister! *Sie ist sehr krank!* She's very sick!"

"*Warten Sie.* Wait." The American spoke to the Poles, the Poles gave Pinek his passport, and Pinek and his sister soon were staggering down into Italy. But still their alarms weren't over. They took a train to Merano, Pinek took her to a clean-smelling sanatorium room, he collapsed on a bed in the attic, then bang! he awoke to a sound like a gun going off. And bang! he sat up in bed thinking, *It must be Germans,* and, not grabbing his Mauser, he looked out the attic window. On the street was a mob of Italians, surging, shouting, throwing things that went bang! and one man looked up at Pinek and cried, "*Ti auguro buon anno!*"

"What what?" Pinek said.

"*Buon anno! Buon anno!*" the Italian shouted, and Pinek caught on: the words were Italian for "good" and "year" and tonight must be New Year's Eve. "*Viene giù!*" the Italian shouted to Pinek, his gesture translated this to "Come on down," and Pinek pulled on his clothes and ran downstairs, into the boisterous street.

Hundreds of happy people swept him up. The boys wore feathered hats, and the girls wore flowered skirts with a whirling and swirling life of their own, like enormous tops. All the Italians had pots that they pounded with spoons, as if they were driving the dibbuks off the whole planet earth. "*Chi sei?*" they shouted to Pinek.

"I don't speak Italian!"

"*Da dove sei?*" they shouted, pointing over the snow-topped mountains to Austria and Switzerland, indicating that the Italian words meant "Where are you from?"

"*Polonia!*" said Pinek, hoping that that was Italian for Poland.

"*O! Un straniero!* A foreigner!"

"*Si!*"

"*Que bello straniero!* A good-looking foreigner!" the Italians shouted. The boys with the feathers gave him a guzzle of Merlot wine, and the pretty girls kissed him. "*Buon anno! Buon anno!*" they cried.

"*Buon anno!*" cried Pinek, feeling like someone who'd stumbled onto the Big Rock-Candy Mountain.

The people led him to one of their homes. At the celebration inside it, Pinek had hot Merlot wine full of sugar, cinnamon and cloves and a cake full of candied cherries and candied quince, and he clapped as the happy people yodeled for him, "*Yodeli yadi yo!*" He was surprised, then amazed, that no one cared if he was or wasn't a Jew, and in a few minutes his memory of Jews against Germans, Jews against Poles, seemed as remote as something from the Dark Ages. He partied all night, and at seven there came the most dazzling dawn in Pinek's life. To the west, the orange on one of the snow-topped mountains was as if God had awakened there, then, like a shroud, the shadows slid off and all Pinek's world shone white. For six years, his days and nights had been wrapped in a vast super-night, like a bulb that went on and off in a bat-crowded cave, and now the night and the super-night were gone. Pinek hugged the Italians goodbye. He cried, "*Buon anno!*" then walked to the heart of Merano, the Promenade. The day was now porcelain bright. It was winter, but Pinek saw crowds of red flowers, and he smelled the calycanthus, the jasmine, the *air*. . . .

He'd been born again. He rented a home in Merano, and after he got his brothers out, he never went back to Poland and Poland's long-lasting night.

12

Forty-four years later, I went to Gleiwitz, now Gliwice, Poland, to learn what I could about Lola. The air was peppered with soot from the mines and mills nearby, the houses were gray and I often couldn't read the street-signs under the melancholy soot. But the people were wonderful, and the new warmhearted warden gave me a tour of Lola's old red-and-lapis-lazuli prison. It now was for three hundred men, all Poles, who I saw walking, talking, playing ping-pong, and watching the one TV. One man (I later found out) had dug a tunnel to the old auto school and, in time, would escape through it, and one man on a hard-labor crew had dug up two human skeletons in Lola's old concrete-stoned court. The arms had been broken, a jaw had been cracked, a skull had been dented by something sharp, but no one knew who the people were or if they'd been beaten and buried in Lola's time.

On duty were none of Lola's old guards, but I found three retired ones in Gleiwitz/Gliwice. All were Catholics and men, and they lived in dim walk-ups where, for hour after hour, we sat as they reminisced about 1945. One man told me he'd beaten the Germans, and another said Lola had told him, "We aren't like them." All three had heard the rumor that Lola, her maid, and the Russian had fled to Vienna in September, 1945, and that Lola had been locked up in Gross Strehlitz, Germany, but I said that that hadn't happened. I didn't know about the Russian, but I said I'd done research and Lola and Gertrude had boarded a train in Gleiwitz, had gone due west, and, getting off, had crept through a German forest into the American occupation zone, and all three retired guards said, "I'm glad." I told them that Lola hadn't brought a chestful of money, watches and rings into the German forest, I told them everything else I'd learned about her, I gave them gifts from America, and I went twenty miles east to Kattowitz, now Katowice, Poland.

I am a Jew, and I went to the Sabbath service in Kattowitz/Katowice. The temple was no longer there, for the Germans had dynamited it in September, 1939, and turned it to red-and-green rubble, but on Saturday morning some Jews, just enough for a ten-man minyan, met on a drab second floor above the Zodiak Bar. At sixty, I was the youngest there, but the others graciously let me say the *"Baruch ata"* over the Torah, and, as I did, they hovered around me solicitously, as if I were doing some difficult surgery on it. One man present was Shlomo, the former commandant at Schwientochlowitz, who, as the service ended, went to an old acquaintance saying, *"Shabbat shalom.* The peace of the Sabbath." Shlomo said this with a wide-open mouth, a mask of comedy meaning, "Well? Do you recognize me?" and when his old friend said, "Shlomo! *Shabbat shalom!"* the mask came alive and Shlomo roared. He had a heart condition now, but he still was a big, burly, happy-go-lucky man.

By now, I'd heard of Shlomo's old camp at Schwientochlowitz, and I'd even seen the locale—a lot of small gardens now, full of roses—in Świętochłowice, Poland, and I wanted to talk to Shlomo about it. We met many times in Katowice at the Jewish Club, two rooms as empty as pool rooms now, and while we ate borscht from the United Jewish Appeal, Shlomo told me he'd been in the Office twenty-four years, first as the commandant at Schwientochlowitz, then at the prison in Oppeln, then at Kattowitz prison, where one of his unhappy prisoners was Chaim, then at a camp for Poles—the subject, he said uncomfortably, of a recent exposé in a Polish paper—then he'd been chief of Imprisonment in Kattowitz, then, in 1968, the Party secretary, Gomulka, who'd spent three years in an Office prison, fired all the Jews in the Office. Shlomo still thought of going to Israel but, his smile widening, told me, "Once, a Jew was going to Israel and a Jew was *coming* from it. And the two met in the Suez Canal, and they both went like this," and Shlomo put a finger to his head and twirled it, meaning "You're nuts!" "Don't write about Schwientochlowitz," he told me one day at the Jewish Club, but I said that I might and Shlomo turned black, like the sky in a sudden thunderstorm. The light in his eyes disappeared, and a black cloud of terror replaced it. He asked me for my address in California and my mother's address in New York and said, "If you write about it, I'll move heaven and earth against you." I changed the subject sadly.

I met many people in Kattowitz/Katowice, but one person there who I didn't see was Czesław, the former commandant at Lamsdorf, the camp

where the guards said, "Hug them," "Kiss them," "Make love with them."
In 1965, I learned, a group of Germans had asked the Poles to try him for
mass murder, the Poles had answered that Czesław—a police major in
Katowice—had never murdered anyone, and Czesław was now in Katowice lying low. I also learned that no one, no Jew or Catholic, had ever
been tried in Poland for crimes against the Germans, though the deputy
commandant of a camp for Germans in Czechoslovakia had once been
given eight years by an American judge in the American occupation zone.
Höss, for the record, was hanged in Auschwitz, Hössler was hanged in
Hameln, Germany, the pied-piper place, and Mengele, who'd been a
POW in an American camp in July and August, 1945, was carelessly let
go, escaped to Brazil, and drowned like the bad man in Hillel's story, first
in an ocean of loneliness, then in the Atlantic.

One day I went up to Warsaw, but I learned that Jacob was dead. For
twelve years he'd run the Office, dining on salmon and lobster in Warsaw
and roast brown bear in Moscow and even waltzing with Molotov (who'd
wanted to whisper something) as Stalin wound the Victrola and put on a
series of Georgian 78s. Then, Jacob had been fired, cast out of the Party,
and erased from the *General Encyclopedia*—a series of disasters that
Jacob, wearing an old gray sweater, sipping tea, gracefully slicing an
orange from Israel, and chatting with a Polish writer, a member of Solidarity, had, in 1983, attributed to Polish antisemitism. "Polish society,"
said Jacob, sipping and slicing, his fingers like wands, "is very antisemitic."

"You can say that? You?" the Solidarity woman said.

"It's the truth. My daughter was often called a *śledziara*," a smelly herring, a dirty word for a Jew.

"And you—" said the Solidarity woman, who, for hours, had had to
remind him how the Office had tortured the Poles, had torn their nails
out, cut their tongues out, and burnt their eyes out, let alone executed
them, and who'd listened to Jacob's bland explanation, "A revolution's a
revolution"—"and you don't see why?"

"No," Jacob said. He died of testicle cancer in April, 1984.

All added up, I was two months in Poland and two months elsewhere in
Europe. In Germany, I went to immense reunions of Germans from
Gleiwitz and stopped like a girl selling roses at each of their beer-laden
tables, saying, "*Verzeihen Sie mir.* Excuse me," and asking the partying
people if they'd been in Lola's prison. I found five, of whom four had
been beaten, one with the beater-to-death, as well as some scarce survivors of Schwientochlowitz, still jumpy, jittery, retired. One, who I found
in a village full of contented cows and of Germans who constantly said,

"Guten tag!" was just fifty days older than me, and I felt an affinity with him. During the war, I'd been in Larchmont, north of New York, and I'd been learning my German, *"Ich bin. Du bist. Er ist,"* as, in Bielsko-Biała, near Czechoslovakia, he was learning in English,

> *Little Tommy Tittelmouse,*
> *Lived in a little house,*

and conjugating the verb *to be*. At his new village in Germany, we calculated in German and English that I'd been a boy scout when he was being impressed into Hitler Youth, and that I'd been at my summer camp, earning my rowing, canoeing and lifesaving merit badges, when he was at Schwientochlowitz in Shlomo's wild brown barracks. He now had heart, lung and liver troubles and a 240 blood pressure, and as I gadded about in Europe, he lived on his old-age pension in his quiet and clean-as-china village near Düsseldorf.

In Koblenz, on the Rhine, I spent several days at the national archives of Germany, scanning a thousand statements by Germans who once were the Office's prisoners. Characteristically, a man or woman might begin,

> *Everything that I write below, I can bear witness to. I am prepared to*
> *answer for every sentence and every word,*

then he or she might grind out a horror story of Lola's or Shlomo's institution. Often the Germans had typed this up, but often they'd written it in a pretty but very cryptic script that I had to peer at before concluding that "*Gefängnis Gleiwitz*" was *"Gefängnis Gleiwitz,"* was Gleiwitz Prison, and that the commandant there was a "*Polin*" a *"Polin,"* a Polish woman. Puzzling over this Gothic hand, I often felt like a man decoding a treasure map, but the most mysterious words were the "1960"s, "1961"s and "1962"s that were stamped at the top of these statements in black bureaucratic ink. They meant, for example, that the Germans had known for thirty years that a Jew had committed murder at Schwientochlowitz, but that the Germans hadn't cared (or hadn't dared) to tell the world about him.

I was surprised, but I found lots of Jews from the Office living in Germany. In Munich, I learned, was the former chief of police of Kattowitz, but I may have missed him, for the man with that name in Munich insisted, "I'm not a Jew," and "I wasn't in Kattowitz." In another city in Germany was Adela, of "Why are you pale, Adela?" who was now selling television sets, and Efraim, the one-armed boy, who was now serving beer. Having slipped out of Poland, the two were happy in Germany, but they used aliases and told me, "Please don't say we are in—" and they named the German city I'd found them in. Lola, too, had once lived in Germany, for in 1945 she'd gone through the forest to Schwandorf, had stayed there, had run into Shlomo, her husband, and had divorced him, and had then met and married a Jewish doctor, Michal. But then, in 1946, she'd gone with him and Gertrude, her *femme de chambre*, to Paris.

In Europe, I also went to Denmark and looked up Josef, the old lingo-talking communist, who I found in a Copenhagen flat. Josef had been the Office's chief for Silesia—I'd even seen the documents saying so—but he told me in Copenhagen, "They're fairy tales," the communist term for "They're lies," and said he'd just been a Polish army officer. In 1948, he said, he'd gone to Warsaw as an economist at the Institute of Comparative Development, but twenty years later the Institute had fired its Jews and he'd emigrated to Denmark. I asked him, "Do you still not believe in God?" and Josef said, "I still don't." I asked him, "Do you still believe in communism?" and Josef began, "Well, Marxism is the product of French philosophy, German sociology and English economics and—" but Josef's wife simply said, "No. We don't believe in it."

My one other stop in Europe was France. Lola, very pregnant, and Michal, her Jewish doctor (but not her Gertrude), had left by December, 1948, but in the Alps, in Annecy, a place as pretty as a postcard—a stream, a stone embankment, above it a row of ocher-painted homes—was Zlata, Lola's brother's wife. Still jolly, Zlata now rocked like a roly-poly doll while telling me, laughing, about her one year in Auschwitz and her four months in Gleiwitz, as if she were recollecting a day at a House of Fun. She said that in September, 1945, she'd taken the train from Gleiwitz to Paris to Pas-de-Calais, to Lola's wide-open-armed brother and Lola's dissenting sister, who'd said, "You look like a crazy-woman," and who'd sent her to a *coiffeuse* to get a more stylish tint in her louse-powder-discolored hair. Zlata and "Elo" had had one son, one daughter, then "Elo" had died, the son had had one daughter, and I calculated sadly that the Potok name will die out in approximately 2020, the slow but sure consummation of the cyanide chambers at Auschwitz.

I went to Israel and saw Ada there. She said that in 1945 she'd taken the train to Germany and met David, her husband and Lola's brother, in Schwandorf, and later met Lola there. Ada and David had had one child, who promptly had died, and the two had soon gotten divorced. In 1953, Ada had sailed to Israel, the land she'd sung of at Auschwitz and, at the bow, was still singing of,

> The land of the palm
> And the almond tree,

and her voice had bewitched a Canadian Jew, a veteran of World War II. He had soon married her and they'd settled in—and, healthy and happy, were still living in—the seaside city of Ashkelon, where Samson killed thirty men in the Book of Judges.

For two weeks I was in Israel, and I of course went to Jerusalem and, on a hot little hillside, to the archives of Yad Vashem, the government of Israel's agency for the Holocaust. The mission of Yad Vashem is "Never forget," and, to that end, it had collected documents on what happened during the war to practically all of Europe's Jews. By then, Yad Vashem had fifty million pages, five, on the average, per man, woman and child, a mile-long tunnel of pages, pages, all indexed, all cataloged, so I was surprised it had nothing at all on the Office of State Security or the Jews who had run it. It had nothing on Lola, and when I mentioned her, the Chairman of Yad Vashem said, "The story sounds rather imaginary," and the Director of Archives said, "It sounds made up."

"Why so?" I asked.

"A commandant who was a Jew? That wasn't the way the Poles were," the Director of Archives said. He himself was a Jew and a Pole, a man who now sat in his shirt sleeves at his piled-up-with-papers desk. "I'd advise you to check it."

"I did," I said. "I've met about forty people, mostly Jews, who remember her, and I've seen the letter appointing her."

"But who would appoint her?"

"Her bosses were Jews."

"Impossible!" the Director said. He practically made a fanfare out of the "Im," pronouncing it, "Im-mm-mm," and ending with "Possible!" and glowering at me as though he would choke me, a man who might someday write that the Jews sometimes killed the Germans when all the fifty million pages said it was always the other way round.

Yad Vashem, an Israeli agency, had an international arm, the International Society for Yad Vashem, and I tried hard to meet its vice chairman, a man who'd once served in the Office, I'd heard. Unhappily, he was in Tokyo, not letting the Japanese forget what the Germans, their allies, had done, and selling the Japanese his made-in-Switzerland watches, but I kept trying. I'm jumping ahead, but after my trip to Israel, I phoned him again and again, arranging to meet him in Auschwitz (he wanted to tell me about it) or Venice, or Geneva, or New York City, but always he had to cancel out. One dizzy day, I was back in Poland, and from a Vietnamese restaurant I phoned him in Switzerland, and a Portuguese woman told me in Spanish that he was in Chile. Much as I wanted to, I never met him, but on the phone he confirmed what I'd heard: that he had been one of the heavy-handed interrogators in Neisse. "I was terrible," said the vice chairman of the International Society for Yad Vashem. "But better not to speak about this."

But back to my trip to Israel. Without the assistance of Yad Vashem, I found another interrogator from Neisse living in Haifa and the chief interrogator from Gleiwitz, Adam, in Tel Aviv. Adam was very frank, telling me and *showing* me, by holding a nail to his fingernail and by closing a door on his arm, how the Office had tortured the Germans. In August, 1945, he'd taken the train to Plzeň, Czechoslovakia, and gone on foot through the forest—through the green curtain, the Jews had called it—to Schwandorf, Germany. The last he'd seen of Lola was there, for he'd sailed to Israel, married a Jew from Warsaw, had one son, one daughter, run the Red Star-of-David (the equivalent of the Red Cross) in Tel Aviv, and was now reading the Torah devotedly. Wise, witty, intense, he told me he'd gone off the *bimber* before he'd come to the Holy Land. Listening to Adam, I felt that if I'd been in Poland in World War II, and if I'd been older, I'd have reacted just like him, and when he asked me to write about him as Adam "K," I told him I'd rather call him Adam "Krawecki," the name of my mother's mother, from Cracow, and I've done exactly that on page 28.

I couldn't find Chaim, the cold-eyed chief of Imprisonment, in any of the files at Yad Vashem, but he was listed as Heinrich in the Tel Aviv Telephone Directory. In 1948, I learned, he'd been let out of Kattowitz prison and, for ten years, had managed all of Silesia's hotels, then gone to Israel. He'd been a software salesman there, a man who was often on the road, speeding to Jaffa, Jerusalem, cursing the slower (and faster) drivers, shouting in Hebrew, "You sonofabitch!" Having run out of Germans, Chaim had then picked on Krystyna, his blindingly beautiful wife, a Jew who'd once been a German colonel's mistress, giving her the silent treatment, putting her in Coventry. Often, he used his old officer's belt, on its buckle the Polish eagle, to wallop his son, and once when his daughter, then seventeen, came home at midnight, he slapped her and shouted in Hebrew, "You whore! You were whoring around!" Ever suspicious, he often tiptoed up to his daughter's door, then wham! he burst through it shouting, *"What are you doing?"* his daughter displaying her Hebrew or English textbook, silently saying, "I'm reading," staring at Chaim very sadly.

He hated the Arabs. "A dead one's the only good one," he often declared. In 1982, when Israel invaded Lebanon, he told his son, then thirty-five, "Well, we've found the final solution to the Arab problem."

"Dad! Do you hear what you're saying?"

"What?"

"The final solution! That's what the Germans said about *us!*"

"I haven't forgotten the Germans, believe me."

"No, you've forgotten everything, Dad! We keep saying, 'We'll never forget,'" said Chaim's passionate son, "but if we hadn't forgotten, we Jews wouldn't do it ourselves."

"No, you're wrong," said Chaim.

"We say we're the chosen people," his son persevered. "Well, what are we chosen for? To oppress other people, or to teach other people that no one must ever do what the Nazis did?"

"No, you're totally wrong," said Chaim. He hurried away, and in August, 1987, just before I went to Israel, he sped into a parking lot, stopped, had a stroke, and died, his body slumped over his steering wheel. He and I never met, but I talked to his daughter, his adopted daughter, his one good friend and his girlfriend in Tel Aviv, by phone to his brother in Sydney, Australia, and, in person again, to his sun-tanned, high-diving, wind-surfing son, now a hypnotherapist in Miami, Florida.

Most of the Jews from the Office went to America. As early as June, 1945, the commandant at Ziegenhals, near Neisse, went through the green curtain to Germany with the gold he'd taken from the Germans and sailed to New York, and Lola and her Jewish doctor, Michal, flew to New York by December, 1948, teamed as a doctor and doctor's assistant, and had four daughters there. Lola then moved on, but a Neisse interrogator now was a Baltimore coat manufacturer, a Kielce boy in Intelligence was a Queens contractor, a boy who'd been to the bashes at Schwientochlowitz was a salesman in Paramus, New Jersey, and a Kattowitz boy in Intelligence was a Chicago gynecologist. Barek, the middleweight, and his Regina, who'd both despaired when the MPs said, "Your papers are forged," but who'd bought bread from a Czech and, hiking all day, had crossed the green curtain, were now in Toronto, retired, and I went up for their joyous forty-fourth anniversary, their son, two daughters, and four grandchildren coming or phoning too. Shlomo, the holy man, and Rivka, his too-tall friend, who'd suddenly felt, *So I'm taller. So what?* and who'd crossed the curtain with him and, in Regensburg, married him, now were in Brooklyn, and I went there and had Rivka's delicious gefilte fish. At Shlomo's suggestion, I started the prayer over food, *"Baruch ata, Adonoy elohenu,"* but I got hopelessly lost and Shlomo, smiling, led me at once through the Hebrew lest I'd have said *"Adonoy,"* the name of God, in a less-than-immaculate prayer. Shlomo and Rivka now had one son and two daughters, and had their eleventh grandchild while we were eating the awesome gefilte fish.

For weeks I was in the east hunting up Jews from the Office, but many of them wouldn't talk to me or, if they talked, only lied to me. An interrogator from Neisse said, "I can't help you," a guard from a Kattowitz cellar said, "I'm not going to talk about myself," and the former commandant at Myslowitz said, "I was no commandant," "I didn't work in Myslowitz," and "I don't know what you're talking about." Moshe, Lola's adjutant, who'd made a killing wheeling-and-dealing in Gleiwitz and now did construction in Linden, New Jersey, said nothing at all, and on the phone his wife told me sternly, "We don't give you the permission to write this."

"I— You— One—" I stammered.

"You don't understand that?"

"One doesn't *need* permission," I said, but Moshe's wife hung up. Jadzia, the girl guard in Gleiwitz, said on the phone, "I was never in Gleiwitz!" and later said, "I was in Gleiwitz, but I'll never talk about it!" and still later talked for an hour, insisting, "I don't know nothing! Nothing! Nothing! Nothing! Nothing! Nothing!"

One day, I ran into Jadzia and others from the Office at a vast cemetery in Woodbridge, New Jersey. It was a special day, for hundreds of Jews from Będzin had gathered among the graves to remember the mothers and fathers, sisters and brothers, who'd died at the SS's hands. The day was cold, the sky was leaden, and Jadzia was wearing a slick black trenchcoat against the imminent rain. As soon as she saw me, she screamed in Yiddish, "I don't want to talk to him!" and as she stomped off, the man who was president of the Fraternal Order of Będzin came up and, red-faced, shouted at me, "If you write about her, I'll sue you!" I hadn't come for Jadzia but for the ceremony, and I sat down on one of the cold folding chairs.

The principal speaker was Pinek, the man who'd once been the Secretary of State Security. "How appropriate the weather is," he began, standing at a loud microphone. "It is as if the heavens are trying to cry with us." Pinek had the same full-moon face that I'd heard he'd had in Będzin, and though he spoke in English, his vowels were slightly off center and his "It-is-as-if" sounded closer to "It-is-ez-if." In September, 1946, Shoshana, his sister, had passed away in Merano, the Germans' delayed-action victim, and Pinek had come to America and to New Jersey. He'd married a Jew who, during the war, had hidden in the woods in Russia, and they'd had a daughter, two sons, and four frisky grandchildren. An alumnus of Warsaw Polytechnic, Pinek had founded a firm that cut the rectangular holes in the plastic plates on the tops of ten-button telephones, but, like others from the Office, he'd also become a *macher* as a vice president of United Synagogues of America and a chairman of United Jewish Appeal. Once every year, he was the principal speaker here in Woodbridge, reminding the Jews of Będzin how the "animals" or the "barbarians" or "the Nazis *yimach sh'mom*," meaning the Cursed Nazis, had, one terrible night in July, 1943, destroyed the world the Jews of Będzin had grown up in. This year, Pinek said earnestly, "It will be our children's, and their children's, responsibility, to carry the torch of remembrance until the world realizes that never again," he stressed the words *never again*, "will such atrocities occur to any human being."

Then, Pinek's wife lit the six candles for the six million dead. It started to drizzle, the candles stayed lit, the Jews of Będzin departed, and Pinek took me to his two-story home in Montrose. He ushered me into it. He still was a warm, compassionate, and old-world-courteous man—he always was, and I'd be dismayed if I thought that I haven't communicated that. We sat down in Pinek's den, and I told him about his old friends who I'd found in Poland, elsewhere in Europe, and Israel. But also I felt I'd be tricking him if I didn't tell him about his old German prisoners, and I handed him my photocopies of statements in the German national archives. He picked up one by a woman from Bunzlau, near Breslau, who'd written that the Office had interrogated her from three in the afternoon to eight in the evening on Sunday, June 3, 1945, and he started to read it.

> *My cell door opened. The guard, who, because of the foul smell, held a handkerchief to his nose, cried, "Reimann Eva! Come!" I was led to a first-floor room.*

Outside of Pinek's window, the rain came in torrents now. It was chilly, and Pinek wore a gray sweater with a jazzy black, blue, green and red geometric design.

> *He shouted at me, "Take off your shoes!" I took them off. "Lie down!" I lay down. He took a thick bamboo stick, and he beat the soles of my feet. I screamed, since the pain was very great.*

Pinek frowned. "But this is exactly what the Germans did to the Jews," Pinek said. On his desk was a pre-war photograph of Shoshana, looking lovely.

> *The stick whistled down on me. A blow on my mouth tore my lower lip, and my teeth started bleeding violently. He beat my feet again. The pain was unbearable. Why didn't I lose my senses?*

"No, this is what the *Germans* did. Not *us*," Pinek said. "It must have been an SS man who wrote this."

The door opened suddenly, and, smiling obligingly, a cigarette in his mouth, in came the chief of the Office, named Sternnagel. In faultless German he asked me, "What's wrong here? Why do you let yourself be beaten? You just have to sign this document. Or should we jam your finger in the door, until the bones are broad?"

"I can't believe this," Pinek said. "It's fabricated."

A man picked me up by the ankles, raised me eight inches above the floor, and let me fall. My hands were tied, and my head hit hard.

"Or if certain people did this, it's understandable," Pinek said. "They copied it from the Germans."

I lay in a bloody puddle. Someone cried, "Stand up!" I tried to, and, with unspeakable pain, I succeeded. A man with a pistol came, held it to my left temple, and said, "Will you now confess?" I told him, "Please shoot me." Yes, I hoped to be freed from all his tortures. I begged him, "Please pull the trigger."

Pinek finished reading. He still hadn't seen the statements from the other cells, cellars and camps of Silesia or the statistics that said that from twenty to fifty percent of the people in these institutions—*his* institutions—had died, but he told me, "I promise I'll read them."

I thanked him and left. He did indeed read the statements, but he didn't know whether to believe them. He showed them to the president of the Fraternal Order of Będzin, who put out an all-points bulletin that no one in the Order should talk to me—but Pinek, God bless him, has never complied with it, we talk on the phone very often, and we are still friends.

I was living then in Los Angeles. One chilly day, I drove along the Pacific and into the bird-loud mountains of Topanga Canyon. By a quiet stream was the Inn of the Seventh Ray, a terrace where each of the tables had a vase of violets and baby's breath and each of the wrought-iron chairs had a violet cushion, violet being the seventh ray. It was chillier here, and a wide-skirted waitress stood on a chair, raising a match as long as a taper, attempting like an old lamplighter to light the heater above her. A customer close to seventy, a woman in leopard pants and a black silk blouse and, on a wide gold chain, a Lion of Judah medallion, sat at a table holding the waitress's violet-flowered skirt, lest, in a gust of wind, the chair should tip and the waitress plummet to earth like a sky diver whose chute doesn't open. "Be careful, honey," the woman said.

"I'm okay," said the waitress, smiling.

"The chair won't fall?" the woman continued. She rolled her *r*. The chairrr.

"I'm all right."

"It's not windy up there?" Up derrr.

"No, I'm doing fine."

It was close to noon, and I had a lunch appointment—my twentieth, probably—with the firm-fisted woman. "Good morning, Lola," I said.

"Good morning. I'm worried about her," said Lola. Her cheeks were as red as they'd probably been in her farmer's-daughter days in Będzin. The red precluded the need for any blush, but she had coral lipstick and black eyeliner, stretched to the sides like on femmes fatales, and her perfume was Opium, by Yves St. Laurent. "She could fall into the creek," said Lola, still clutching the girl's wide skirt. "The poor little thing."

English was Lola's fifth language. She'd learned it in New York City by listening to authors (among them, me) on the radio programs of Mary Margaret McBride. She'd worked for her doctor husband, but in time she'd heard of a firm that made parts for DC-3s, DC-4s and DC-6s but, with a $1,000,000 debt, was then in Chapter Eleven, and she'd decided to buy it. She'd borrowed $25,000 from Jewish friends, made a down payment, told her unhappy lawyer, "Chapter Eleven? What's that? A book?" washed all the windows, scrubbed all the floors, fired the crooked accountant, a Jew from Auschwitz, signed a thick contract with the air force, and used her first aid to stanch the firm's red ink. She was soon grossing $10,000,000 a year, and she moved to California. Her first husband, Shlomo, was living in Encino but Lola didn't know it, Michal, divorced, was still in New York, and Lola went west to be near her four daughters: a prosecutor and a housewife in Sacramento, a stock broker and a secretary in Los Angeles. Lola had kept her place in New York (and another in Rio), and today, once the heater was lit, and the food was served, and the bill was paid, she intended to fly there, to sign with the eager air force of Indonesia and, the ink dry, to take in Verdi's *Luisa Miller* at the Met.

By now I'd known Lola for one-and-one-half years. One day in April, 1986, I'd had business at Paramount Pictures, and I'd met her secretary daughter, who, in the course of conversation, had told me of Lola's two lives, first under the Germans, then over them. I'd been amazed, and I'd wanted to write about her, and Lola soon told me she wanted this too. I'd then done some research in Europe: her story was true, and Lola and I had met since then at a dozen locations: cafes on the Champs d'Elysée, wet cemeteries in Woodbridge, her condo in West Hollywood, and many others, and she'd poured out her memories of Poland, down to the words on the back of the SS man's photo, *"Ein blick."* In forty years she'd forgotten a lot, but she'd sent me to Pinek, the man who'd appointed her, to Moshe and Jadzia, her guards, to Ada and Zlata, her stable-and-house-mates, and to others who'd often had the right puzzle-parts. I'd known that as a reporter—and as a Jew, who must bear honest witness, the Torah says—I'd have to write whatever the truth might be, but I'd hoped that the truth might be one of Jewish revenge and *also* of Jewish redemption.

I was still doing research today. By now, the heater was orange, above it the hot air jiggled, the pine needles were a mini-mirage, and Lola was sitting and eating a spinach and mushroom omelet, her knife lightly slicing the snippets off, scraping the cheese sauce up, and then buttering it on. "Here. Try the omelet," Lola directed me. "It's what we dreamt of at Auschwitz."

"You told me you dreamt of getting revenge," I said, helping myself to some of Lola's goodies.

"We dreamt that too. We dreamt that we'd— *Uh-uh!*" said Lola, rapping her fork peremptorily. Her thumb on her fork was still deformed from the anti-aircraft machine at Auschwitz. "That isn't trying! Here!" said Lola, and passed me the hub of her omelet, a big bronze mushroom dripping with cheddar and gruyère, spinach and egg.

"Thank you, Lola. You dreamt—?" I said.

"We dreamt that what the Germans did, we'd do to them someday," said Lola, her memories of Auschwitz suffusing her. "We'd force them to stand in the cold, twenty below, half-naked, naked, force them to stand there humiliated like us. We'd force them to lift up rocks, impossible rocks, to break their backs carrying them to and fro. We'd beat them all to a bloody pulp, we'd. . . ." Lola paused. She stirred her omelet silently. The brook pitter-pattered along, and a tree frog like an old wagon wheel went, "Ark. Ark."

"Lola, I understand," I said. "You did it, and you aren't proud of it."

"It's nothing I'd want to put a star on my shoulder for," Lola said.

I brushed a small insect from Lola's hair. At the end of the terrace, a harpist was nudging the notes of a Debussy arabesque, fifty or sixty people were sitting silently, and a man in a tux was standing next to a woman in a white wedding gown. A minister was telling them, "May you laugh often, and may—"

"She's cold, poor thing," said Lola, and, once again, her memories overwhelmed her. "My mother said life's like a wedding," said Lola. "She said that we're born, and the orchestra's playing, and everyone's eating and drinking and singing and dancing. But eventually there is some garbage on the floor where the wedding is, and we get tireder and tireder of singing and dancing there. We walk to the door, and we look back at what we're leaving and ask, Did we laugh? Did we cry? Did we have a good time? Did we do good things? Then slowly we walk through the door that closes behind us. That's what my mother said."

Lola looked pensive. At the end of the terrace, the man and the woman kissed, and the rest of the party toasted them with white organic wine. I passed Lola a hornbook with a pile of fresh-baked honey bread, and Lola took off a slice, slowly buttering it. The harpist caressed the chords of *The Little Fountain,* by Samuel Platt.

"We look back," Lola said. "And we ask, Did we live a good life?"

For six more months, the memories flowed out of Lola's soul. One day she even remembered a scandalous song that Rivka, her mother, had sung in Będzin,

> *Kasha the maid said,*
> *"It's very erect!"*
> *I said, "What's erect?"*
> *"Your starched collar!"*

She remembered the red-headed freckle-faced prostitute boss at Auschwitz who'd cried, *"Schweinehunde Juden!"* and the wide-bottomed-duck-walking guard at Gleiwitz, *"Du schwein!* You're outta step!" She didn't remember (or didn't remember that she remembered) that any Germans in Gleiwitz had starved, had been tortured, had come down with typhus, or had died dreadfully, and I didn't know it myself, for I had much more research to do in Poland and Germany. But now, I wrote up an outline for *An Eye for an Eye,* this book, and, with a letter from Lola declaring, "I want to tell my life story," I sent the outline to New York City, and one day a publisher there said yes, that I should proceed. I phoned the good news to Lola, who said, "Listen, John. I really don't want you to do it."

I was stunned. We had now worked together for two-and-one-quarter years. I couldn't understand: Why had Lola had second thoughts? Was she afraid that the things she'd done to the Germans were somehow unspeakable? Had other people from Poland, perhaps from the Office, told her to drop it? "Lola, this is the first time you've said this," I said.

"I really don't want to discuss it," said Lola, but then she invited me to her condo in West Hollywood, and I hurried there. Lola sat on a sectional sofa, her two local daughters, both about thirty, sat on the carpet and I did too, and Lola said, "Lookit, John. We don't like the way you write. You write like a *reporter,*" frowning, stressing the word *reporter,* "but I don't want that book, and if you start writing it, I'll stop you."

"I hear you," I said, still stunned by this sudden U-turn.

"I—will—*stop* you," said Lola, dealing the words out like trumps. "I don't know how long I have to live on this earth, but I'm not going to leave with this book on my *tuchis*," her *derrière*. "You understand?"

"Lola," I said. "Did you ever say *anything*—"

Her two daughters interrupted me. And maybe I was over-obsessed with Auschwitz and Gleiwitz, for I suddenly felt like a Jew or a German in a 1940s interrogation room. One daughter told me, "Give it up. Just give it up. Please give it up. I'm *begging* you." She sounded sincere, but she may have been playing good cop, for the other daughter suddenly screamed, "This isn't a matter we are willing to even discuss!" The two daughters took out a one-and-one-half-page document, telling me, "John, please sign the release, please, please," but also telling me, "John!!! Sign the release!!!"

"Look," I stammered, "I'm not going to sign a paper without—without—without—*looking* at it!" I felt I was drowning in *déjà vu*.

"Are you saying, 'No, I just want to wait an indefinite period?'"

"No, I'm saying that if you know anything about me—"

One daughter sighed, as though she'd rather know nothing about me.

"—and you've known me," I said, "for two-and-a-half years, I keep my commitments. I keep my promises. They know in New York that when I give my word, that I'm going to do it."

"So fuck me! You gave your word!" one daughter suddenly shouted.

"Who gives a shit that Lola doesn't want it?" the other daughter shouted.

"How *dare* you, John!" the first daughter shouted. "John," she said sweetly. "Sign this."

"John! Just leave! Just leave!" the second daughter shouted.

"Get out of our lives," said Lola, and I left the condo without a clue to the cause of Lola's sudden recantation—I left it glad to be out but sorry for the tormented people inside it. I've had no contact with Lola since then. I've phoned her but she hasn't answered, I've written but she's sent the letters back, unopened, inscribed REFUSED.

I did more research in Europe and wrote this book. When it comes out, I'll send a copy to Lola, and I'd like to think she'll accept it. I do believe it's a story of Jewish redemption. All but a scattering of Jews returned to the Torah and Talmud and, at great peril, fled from the Office by December, 1945. Tragically, that was too late for all the Germans who'd died, but the SS had killed one hundred times what the Office had, and the SS had staffed the cyanide chambers until the end. In the days when the world said that Hitler was bad and Stalin was good, the

SS had listened to Hitler but the Jews, as Lola's mother might say, had eventually listened to God. If Lola won't do it, I now pin a star on Lola's black-silked shoulder. Her life, I say, was exemplary. She learned, in the nick of time, what the SS never did: that to hate your neighbors may or may not destroy them but it surely destroys yourself, and she teaches this to a world running wild with Jews and Arabs, Sunnis and Shiites, Serbs and Bosnians, Crips and Bloods. As, at age seventy-two, she stands at the flower-decorated door, I hope that Lola will look back and say, "Yes, I'm proud," and I hope that maybe, just maybe, the rest of the world will look back at Lola.

That is my prayer today, and may the Name grant it. Praise the Name.

Aftermath:
The Interrogation of Shlomo Morel

Notes

Sources

Acknowledgments

Query

Index

AFTERMATH

The Interrogation of Shlomo Morel

On Monday, December 11, 1989, while I was writing this book, I was scooped by an unlettered woman in Radlin, in Poland. Her spelling was bad (she spelled the word *rządzić, żądzić*) and her data was sometimes wrong (she referred to Świętochłowice as Siemianowice) but her letter to the Minister of Justice, in Warsaw, was straight from her Polish heart. She began,

> *Dear Minister,*
>
> *Please forgive me for daring to write you. I meant to write a long time ago, but,*

but Poland had been under communism till June that year. The woman wrote that in May, 1945, a man had pointed at her father saying, mistakenly, "He is a German," and the Office of State Security had seized him and sent him to Świętochłowice/Siemianowice: to Shlomo's new concentration camp. Four months later, in September,

> *my mother got a letter from this same camp that my father was dead. My mother said he'd been polished off in a very short time. I can't understand why this was done by Poles to a Pole,*

and the woman double-underlined the *Poles* and the *Pole*,

> *and you, Mr. Minister? What do you think about it?*

On getting this in December, 1989, the Minister of Justice sent it downstairs to what would become the Commission for the Investigation of Crimes Against the Polish Nation, and the Commission passed it along to its prosecutor in Katowice. The man, whose name was Piotr Bryś, was almost as old as Shlomo was. For forty years, he'd worked in the communist apparatus, and he started slowly—*slowly*—to collect evidence on Shlomo's institution. He got documents from the clerk and the priest in Świętochłowice city. He got documents from the Red Cross, in Geneva, stating that in August, 1945, a certain person had died at Świętochłowice. He met the unlettered woman from Radlin, near Katowice, and got the dingy mimeoed notice telling her, "NOTICE. On September 8, 1945, the Prisoner Benczek, Paweł, died." The notice was signed by Shlomo, and Bryś summoned him to his clothes-closet office on Wolności Place, and Shlomo (the Poles called him Salomon, he spelled it Salamon) lumbered in on Wednesday, February 27, 1991.

I wasn't there, but I now know what happened there. It was cold that day, and Shlomo wore an old overcoat, and Shlomo's wife—who'd met him, not too romantically, when she was one of his guards at Świętochłowice—did too. "Sit down, please. Do you want some tea?" the old gray-haired secretary said.

"No, thank you," said Shlomo, and Bryś then walked in.

"Good day," Bryś began. "I'm going to interrogate you in the case concerning the camp at Świętochłowice. You can be prosecuted for perjury on the basis of Article 172 of the Penal Code, but you have the right not to answer me on the basis of Article 166, Paragraph 1."

"All right," said Shlomo calmly.

"Did you work at Świętochłowice?" said Bryś.

"Yes. I was the commandant there."

"You were the commandant starting when?"

"The first days of February, 1945."

"As commandant what did you do?"

"I commanded that camp."

"And when did—"

In no way was Bryś inflicting the third degree. He wasn't inflicting even the one-and-one-halfth, and Shlomo sat there serenely, his hands on his overcoated lap. It was Bryś who was nervous, for he had never interrogated anyone from the Office, the focus of all of his fears since 1945. Bryś may have felt that Shlomo might say, "Off with this meddler's head!" and not till the end of his courtly interrogation did Bryś tell him, "Some people died at Świętochłowice. What of?"

"Typhus," said Shlomo.

"And where were they buried?"

"At the cemetery in Świętochłowice."

"Thank you," Bryś said. He was scribbling notes, and he now turned to the secretary, saying, "In the first days of February, 1945, I was sent to work in Świętochłowice. When I came to Świętochłowice," and as Bryś continued, the woman minded her *e*'s and *ę*'s while typing the statement up. Then, Shlomo read it, signed it, and said goodbye, and he and his wife rumbled off in a Toonerville trolley to Bryś's relief.

But somehow, the Polish press found out. The story of Bryś's slow, steady investigation and a series of second-coming headlines like HELL STARTED AFTER THE WAR commenced on the front page, top, of a Cracow paper, *Wieści*, on November 24, 1991, but the story apparently wasn't fit for the *New York Times* or *Los Angeles Times*, and I, back in California writing of Świętochłowice, didn't know about it. Neither did you.

Two weeks later, Bryś called in Shlomo again. By then Bryś had moved to Warszawska Street, and his office was much, much bigger and much, much colder, but in the anteroom was an electric heater and Bryś, his gray-haired secretary, and an elegant gray-haired woman were near it as Shlomo entered. "Good day," Bryś said. He handed a couple of *Wieści*s to Shlomo, saying, "There's things there that I didn't ask you. Can you please read them?"

"Of course I can," Shlomo said. "I'll take them home, and I'll write you." He started to go, but Bryś then turned to the second woman, who, in a black mink coat with a diamond brooch, still sat at the heater, warming herself.

"Do you know this man?" said Bryś.

"No, I don't," said the woman, surprised.

"This man is Mr. Morel," said Bryś.

The woman gasped. Her hands and her fifteen diamonds started shaking. In 1945, she'd been in Świętochłowice, a prisoner of Shlomo's, she had observed him for one-half year, and if Bryś were to accuse him of assault, battery, murder, or complicity in any or all of those crimes, she'd be one of Bryś's witnesses.

Her name was Dorota Boreczek, and she'd grown up a mile from here on Dombrowskiego Street. In 1945 she'd been fourteen, going to Catholic school, taking history, geography and German (the Germans required it) and, at the grand piano, playing the Beethoven song *For Elise* and stretching, stretching her fingers to the G flat in Liszt's *Dream of Love*. Her parents were Poles in the Polish resistance, but someone must have been telling lies, for on Wednesday, February 28, 1945, two men from the Office came to Dorota's home and said, "Come with us." Dorota's father disappeared, and she and her mother went to Świętochłowice. As they stood against a wall there, their hands on their heads, the Catholic and Jewish guards started shooting, and as Dorota turned around, thinking,

What's happening, Mama? a guard said, "Don't worry. No one will shoot you. You're going to die very slowly." She and her mother were sent to the women's barracks, to a "bed" on the concrete floor and to rations of boiled beetroot, and Dorota soon wasted away to eighty pounds. "Oh, Mama!" she often said. "Let's run to the gate and they'll shoot us! *Please!*" but her mother didn't do it.

Often, Dorota saw Shlomo at the morning and afternoon head counts. He stood in his captain's stars as the guards whipped the women and men, and one day he came to Dorota's barracks and said, "All the sick people, out!" Among all the typhus victims was Dorota's mother, and as a crew of prisoners seized her, she tried to cheer up Dorota by singing a Schubert song,

> *In a bright brook,*
> *A capricious trout*
> *Shot in happy haste*
> *Like an arrow.*
>
> *I stood on the bank—*

but the prisoners said, "She's dying, she's crazy," and carried her out. Against regulations, Dorota crept to the barracks for dying prisoners, and she crawled through a window into it. Her mother lay amid urine and feces, and as Dorota washed her, the "doctor" at Świętochłowice strode in and shouted, "I'm going to punish you! You're getting three days in the Bunker," the cistern, the pool of cold water higher than Dorota's head. "It will be your end," the doctor shouted, but Dorota came down with typhus before he could execute her. All month she lay delirious, the rats crawling over her and Dorota too feeble to shoo them away, but one day a man in a suit appeared at her bed and asked her, "How old are you?"

"Fourteen."

"What are you doing in Świętochłowice?"

"I don't know." Her fever was near 104, and Dorota thought she was dreaming, but she wasn't and she (with her mother, who still hadn't died) was released in October, 1945.

Three years later, Dorota saw Shlomo again. She'd been swimming, and as she climbed from the pool, he was standing above her in his black bathing suit. Frightened, Dorota fell back in—in the 50s she went to medical school, in the 70s she became wealthy, but in the 90s she was still having nightmares of Świętochłowice, and now Bryś was telling her, "This man is Mr. Morel."

Her hands started shaking. The ring with the diamonds clicked on the

one with the sapphire as she stared at Shlomo, terrified. But then a great
weight fell from her, and she said to Shlomo, "I've always hated you, but I
don't hate you now. I look and I see this ragged old man, and I feel terri-
bly sorry for you. I know that you've had a hard life," for Dorota (like
everyone else from Świętochłowice) knew that Shlomo was a Jew, "but
you did the same thing the Fascists did."

"I don't know what you're talking about," said Shlomo.

"Well, that's what the Fascists say," Dorota continued. "They don't
know what we're talking about, about Auschwitz. You *murdered* people,"
Dorota explained, getting louder. "Why did you do it? Why?"

"You're lying," said Shlomo. Near him was Bryś, who was listening
carefully, and Shlomo stayed as serene as a Buddha. "The prisoners at
Świętochłowice loved me. A guard even married me."

"No, think about it!" Dorota implored, getting louder. "If you do what
the Fascists do, you're as bad as the Fascists are!"

"No, *you* are the Fascist," Shlomo snapped. "It's people like you who
killed my mother and father!" He then said goodbye to Bryś and left, but
a few days later he came back with a four-page answer to *Wieści*. It said
that the prisoners at Świętochłowice were always treated well. It said that
the guards didn't shoot except on Monday, May 7, 1945, to celebrate the
Allies' victory over the Germans. It said ("I recall with pity") that the prisoners had died of typhus, but it said that the prisoners had brought the
typhus to Świętochłowice. It said,

> I'm very sorry that I, an old man, am being investigated now, but one
> can conclude this is Drejfosjada,

is Dreyfusism. Bryś slowly read this, then Shlomo started to go but Bryś
stopped him.

"I'm sorry," said Bryś, who was less daunted by Shlomo now, "but you
and *Wieści* disagree, and I must interrogate you. You may sit down. You
can be prosecuted for perjury on the basis of Article 172, but you have
the right not to answer me on the basis of Article 166. Was there a torture
cell at Świętochłowice?"

"No, not that I know of," Shlomo said.

"Miss Truda," said Bryś, and the old secretary turned to her Polish
typewriter. "There was no torture cell at Świętochłowice. Did," Bryś continued to Shlomo—"did the doctor commit any crimes at
Świętochłowice?"

"No, not that I know of."

"Miss Truda. The doctor didn't commit any crimes at Świętochłowice.
But," Bryś continued to Shlomo, commencing the two-and-three-fourths

degree, "if you were the commandant there, you'd have to have known that crimes were committed, wouldn't you?"

"No, I know nothing about them."

"Miss Truda," said Bryś.

Still hitting her *o*'s and *ó*'s, the secretary scowled at Shlomo. By now she'd heard a dozen witnesses from Shlomo's camp, and at their dozen stories she'd wept. She herself had been born in Brazil, been foster-mothered in Poland, been sent, at age nine, to a camp close to Świętochłowice, and been very scared as, day after day, the men around her were killed, and she blurted now to Shlomo, "You *must* have known about crimes, since *everyone* knew about crimes!"

"Miss Truda," said Bryś, "I know nothing about them." At last, Bryś said to Shlomo, "Now you may go," and Shlomo vanished into a Toonerville trolley. Bryś didn't know, but Shlomo went home, wrote a cousin in Israel, asked him for $490, and, the next month, in January, 1992, took the first plane that he could to Tel Aviv.

The story of Shlomo's exodus hit the Katowice papers but not the *New York Times* or *Los Angeles Times*, and I still didn't know about it. But later, I spoke to people in Israel, and I learned that he'd had an apartment on Hevron Street, near the Mediterranean Sea. His wife, who was Catholic, hadn't come with him, and Shlomo was often alone at the TV: *The Cosby Show* and *The Simpsons* and the European soccer games. On Saturdays, he went to the Sabbath services across the street, and on Friday, April 17, he and his daughter went to a Passover dinner, repeating in Hebrew, "We were the slaves of Pharaoh in Egypt," thinking of Hitler in Poland. Often, Shlomo contacted the old Jewish partisans, telling them, "I need some money." At seventy-two, he was unemployed, his pension from Poland couldn't go to him in Israel, and, for that matter, he hadn't escaped to the Promised Land, for if the Poles accused him of crimes in a concentration camp, the Israelis might have to prosecute him, like Eichmann, under the Hague and Geneva conventions.

Nor was Israel good for Shlomo's health. In its winter rain, he got thrombosis, in the hot summer his blood pressure rose to 200, and in June, 1992, he flew back to Poland. By then, Bryś, age seventy, had retired, and the Commission for the Investigation of Crimes Against the Polish Nation had appointed a Polish major, thirty-seven, to replace him. The major, Leszek Nasiadko, now had the big corner office on Warszawska Street. Unlike Bryś, who'd worn suits, Nasiadko wore T-shirts, like one with a black skull-and-crossbones like on an iodine bottle and, underneath it, a Polish inscription, NIEPALĄCY ŻYJA DŁUŻEJ—in English, NON-SMOKERS LIVE LONGER, for the shirt was a gift from Nasiadko's mother-in-law. All week and Saturday, too, Nasiadko sat in his office, dragged on his Camels, thought, *I should quit,* and assembled the documents from the German Federal Archives, in Koblenz, the Commission's office in Ludwigsburg, and the criminal court in Essen, where, in 1961, the "doctor" at Świętochłowice had been tried for murder, getting two years.

The documents were in German, and, to turn them to Polish, Nasiadko gave them to the head of the German community in Katowice, Dietmar Brehmer. Brehmer had curly black hair, blazing eyes, and a Merchant of Venice nose: the Poles at his grade school had called him the Little Jew, and, indeed, he'd often supposed that he was descended from Jews. In 1945, at age two, he'd watched as a Pole hit his German mother, tore all her hair out, and told her, "You Nazi!" and he still grieved when he heard of a German, of *anyone,* who'd been mistreated. He practically wept as he read the German documents from Nasiadko,

The commandant was Morel, a Hun in human form. . . .

The commandant was Morel, a schweinehund *without equal. . . .*

The commandant, Morel, appeared. The clubs and the dog whips rained down on us. My nose was broken, and my ten nails were beaten blue. They later fell off. . . .

The commandant, Morel, arrived. I saw him with my own eyes kill many of my fellow prisoners. . . .

but Brehmer wept too for Shlomo Morel. He guessed that Morel, a Jew, had suffered in World War II and had taken revenge on the Germans. He saw that he, Brehmer, a German, could now take revenge on Morel, but he saw that the wheel of revenge, revenge, could roll on for one thousand years, just as in Yugoslavia, three hundred miles away, and he saw that he now could stop it. He gave the documents back to Nasiadko saying, "There's nothing important here," and he told the German survivors of Świętochłowice—he knew 235—that if Nasiadko asked them, they should say, "No, I know nothing about Morel."

Nasiadko, in his corner office, didn't catch on. He, too, was aware that Shlomo was a Jew (the story in *Wieści* had mentioned it in the 102nd paragraph) and he had sympathy for the Jews, who'd suffered so much in the Holocaust, but he knew that a prosecutor shouldn't think about this. If somehow he got some evidence, he figured he'd ask the police to dig at the Rawa River, in Świętochłowice, and he didn't let himself think that the TV cameras absent at Auschwitz (and even the *Times* and the *Times*) might gather at Świętochłowice to capture the mind-numbing sight: the bones of thousands of Germans who'd died in the custody of a Jew. How many thousands of Germans were there? Nasiadko didn't know, but he knew that on Thursday, November 1, 1945, the night of All Saints' Day, the bereaved of Świętochłowice had gone to the Rawa carrying candles, and the Rawa had looked like Woodstock. If the Germans were ever dug up, Nasiadko figured he'd send them to a forensic pathologist to add up the broken heads, ribs, arms and legs, then, if he got some evidence, and if the Commission in Warsaw approved, he'd give all his documents to Jerzy Hop, the district attorney for Katowice, who'd wear a black robe with red piping and be the real prosecutor at Shlomo's trial. Shlomo's jury would be three judges, who, if their verdict was guilty, would sentence him too. The penalty for murder in Poland was eight years minimum, hanging max.

By now, I'd read in a German paper about the Polish investigation (the Germans didn't write that Shlomo was a Jew) and in September, 1992, I went back to Katowice. I ran into Shlomo at a Sabbath service above the Zodiac Bar, as jolly as I remembered him from the Sabbath three years earlier. He was using an all-Hebrew prayer book, and a Jew who'd once been in the Office said, "You read Hebrew?" and Shlomo laughed and said, "I was six months in Israel." I saw Shlomo again on New Year's Day and the Second Day, in September, and Shlomo said, "Can you come to my house tomorrow? You'll have good food, and I can speak freely," and I told him yes.

The next night, I went to his little apartment on Wita Stwosza Street. In the light of one forty-watt bulb was a bed-living-dining room, the walls were purple and on the few shelves were a teddy bear, teddy panda, and a blue book in Hebrew. Shlomo's wife was away, and Shlomo, in his old slacks and an old plaid shirt, was in the kitchen using a small black frying pan. "I'm cooking something good!" he called to me in Yiddish. "Zetzen zee!" I seated myself at a table in the all-purpose room, and Shlomo brought in some dark scrambled eggs and said, "Eat!" and, as soon as I'd started, said, "It tastes good?"

"It tastes good," I repeated in Yiddish. In the eggs were some onions, mushrooms and sausages.

"Eat! Or it'll get cold!" Shlomo said, and as I did, he ate his own eggs and said, "Listen. There is much antisemitism in Poland. In December, a German woman from Stuttgart came—" He suddenly stopped and said, "Do you have a tape recorder?"

"Yes."

"Let me see it." I opened a leather carrying case and took my Sony out, and Shlomo said, "Is it on?"

"No, it's off."

"How do I know?" I turned the Sony on, and the tape went around and a red light went on. "Okay," Shlomo said, and I turned the Sony off. "Eat some more food. In December," Shlomo said, "a German woman from Stuttgart came here to Katowice," and I guessed that Shlomo meant Dorota, the survivor of Świętochłowice, who was a Pole but who usually lived near Stuttgart and who was interviewed by *Wieści*, the paper in Cracow, "and she told stories about me. She didn't say the Germans killed Jews, she said that the Jews killed Germans."

"But didn't they?" I said. "Even some Jews have told me, 'Yes, I killed Germans.'"

Shlomo looked alarmed. "No no! That's a Jewish fantasy!" Shlomo said. "The woman from Stuttgart said that Morel, a Jew, did things at Świętochłowice, and the story ran in *Der Stürmer*, an antisemitic paper in Germany. You," he continued earnestly, and he leaned toward me—"you mustn't write about me. There is much antisemitism in Poland, and you will increase it."

"I haven't seen it," I said.

"But there is! I have two children in Poland, and I have—" Shlomo paused, forgetting the Yiddish word.

"*Grosskinder?*" I attempted.

"Grandchildren, yes, and if you write about me, there will be antisemitism against them."

"Salamon," I said gently, using his present name. "The German woman from Stuttgart. What did she say you did at Świętochłowice?"

"It isn't true," said Shlomo.

"But what did she *say* that isn't true?"

"It just isn't true!" Then suddenly, Shlomo lunged at me. He seized my hand, shook it, and said, "All right? You won't write about me? All right. Have some Holland cheese. It's good!" He then turned the TV on: the Lodz versus Frankfurt soccer game, but Lodz let the balls by like cannonballs and Shlomo gestured in disgust at the Lodz goalie, saying, "*Gai avek*. Go away." At eight-thirty I left, but I often watched the TV in Katowice and, the next day, I saw some ominous news: the Commission had had its first score, arresting a man in Warsaw who, in the 1940s, had been the Office's Deputy Director of Intelligence. I learned that Shlomo, soon after seeing this, had gotten thrombosis again, and on the Day of Atonement, in October, he couldn't stand up and I went to the service alone. In the drizzle, the soot on the sidewalk was like the sand on a ballroom floor, and I kept slipping on it. Above the Zodiak Bar, the Jews were sitting, then standing, then facing east to Wawelska Street and Jerusalem, then unscrolling the Torah as if they were rolling a rolling pin, then saying in Hebrew, "Blessed art Thou, O Lord our God, the Giver of the Torah," the Law. In Shlomo's absence, I sat by a Jew who'd once been an Office inspector, and I prayed all day,

> For the sin we've committed in Thy sight
> By oppressing our fellow man,
> O God of Forgiveness,
> Forgive us,

then the sun set, the Day of Atonement ended, the Jews of Katowice took their canes off the wooden railing around the Torah, we went to another room, and we all had some good sardines and tea.

I then flew back to America. One day, there was a memorial service for Jews who'd died in the Holocaust, it was held at the Jewish cemetery in Woodbridge, New Jersey, and two hundred mourners and I attended it. The day was hot, and the Jews who didn't wander among the tombstones, sobbing, looking lost, sat on chairs under black umbrellas. The rabbi prayed for the Jews who'd been killed, cremated, slaughtered, and buried alive by the Germans, and the speaker said, "Never again." As they spoke, they stood at a black marble stone that said,

> TO OUR BELOVED BRETHREN
> WHO FELL VICTIM TO BRUTAL PERSECUTION
> 1939–1945
> MAY THEIR SOULS BE BOUND
> IN ETERNAL PEACE.

The stone was (and certainly *should* be) a good deal larger than the one I had seen in Świętochłowice, by the Rawa River,

> TO THE VICTIMS
> OF THE CAMP
> IN ŚWIĘTOCHŁOWICE.

As the service went on, I looked around and I saw some half-dozen people who, after the Holocaust, had stayed awhile in Poland to work in the Office of State Security. One woman had been a guard in Myslowitz, and another had been the guard in Gleiwitz who'd told me, "I was never in Gleiwitz!" and later had told me, "I was in Gleiwitz, but I'll never talk about it!" and later had talked for an hour, telling me, "I don't know nothing! Nothing! Nothing! Nothing! Nothing! Nothing!" One man, I'd once been told, had been in the Office in Reichenbach, but the man had told me, "I wasn't, but my cousin was the commandant in Myslowitz," but the cousin had told me, "I don't know from nothing." One man was Pinek, the Secretary of State Security for all Silesia, who'd told me he'd often confronted the Jews in the Office, saying, "I tell you! Ninety percent of the Germans, they're innocent!" but who'd confessed that the Jews wouldn't listen.

One man who'd been in the Office had told me he'd been to some parties—some bashes—at Shlomo's camp, killing the Germans there. He'd told me, "They deserved it," and, when the service ended, I sought him out. His original name was Moshe, or Moses, he'd just put a bunch of orange and yellow marigolds on a gray granite stone for his father, who, the stone said, had died in May, 1944, he was walking away and I greeted him, and I told him the Poles might prosecute his Świętochłowice comrade Shlomo Morel. Moshe was just incredulous.

"For killing some Germans? For that?" Moshe said. "For that he should get a medal!" The man had the rough, rugged features of Spencer Tracy and was wearing a blue shirt, a loosened blue tie, and, in his thick, curly hair, a blue skullcap.

"But Moshe," I said, except that I used his American name. "Do you really know that the Germans at Świętochłowice were Nazis? Or—"

"How should I know?"

"Or were they just Germans who got picked up?"

"Too bad for them."

"But some of the Germans—"

"For that they would prosecute someone?"

"But some were just fourteen, fifteen years old."

"We could talk about that," said Moshe. "The fourteen, fifteen-year-olds used to go with big dogs, used to rip apart people, so that's no excuse to be fourteen, fifteen years old. Let them drop dead," said Moshe. "We should have dropped an atom bomb on Germany and killed everyone, innocent and guilty, and I bet that ninety-nine percent of the people here feel that way. Ask *him*," said Moshe, and he turned to a man whose original name was Mendel and who'd been in the concentration camp at Płaszów. "Should have the Germans survived?" said Moshe.

"Absolutely not!" Mendel said.

I thanked Moshe and Mendel, and I left feeling infinitely sad. What the Germans—some Germans—did to the Jews was monstrous, but the first people to do it again were the ones who were telling me, "Never again." In Europe, I'd met some survivors of Świętochłowice, such as Dorota, and I had great sympathy for them all. But also I had great sympathy for the Jews at the service in Woodbridge, New Jersey, and yes, for the SS men in Poland, who didn't have the antidote of the Torah and Talmud or, in their vicious environment, of the New Testament, and I had great sympathy for Shlomo, too. Dorota had told him in Katowice, "You should repent. You should beg all the people of Świętochłowice, 'Forgive me,'" but Shlomo hadn't done it. In his letter to Bryś, he'd blustered,

> Mrs. Boreczek says that I should repent, but I don't know why. Maybe
> I should repent because the Hitlerites killed my father, my mother, my
> brothers. . . .

Well, I know Shlomo pretty well, and as I read this, I hear him say, "Understand me! Have mercy on me! Forgive me!" and I have compassion for him. Whatever men do, I must hold them responsible for, but as Adam (the chief interrogator) said to the German priest, a man without mercy isn't a Jew, and I am a Jew.

I went back to Katowice in June, 1993. It was summer, but the rain was cold, and the Poles who I met were still wearing sensible sweaters. Nasiadko, the Camel-addicted prosecutor, was a Polish major again. By day, he was an army judge, and at night, as president of the Polish Association of Breeders of Exotic Birds, he sat in his laundry room, greeted his twenty-nine screeching parrots, said in English, "Hello," and in Polish, *"Co słychać?* What's up?" and fed them all oat, millet and sunflower seeds. At the Commission for the Investigation of Crimes Against the Polish Nation, the new prosecutor was a Polish captain, Marek Grodzki, and the head of the German community still was Brehmer, the man who'd looked at the "Hun" and *"schweinehund"* documents and said, "No, there's nothing important." By now, Brehmer had many more documents, like one from a man who, at age fourteen, had been in Shlomo's brown barracks though he was a Dutchman, an ally of Poland's in World War II,

> I said I was a Dutch citizen. A man said, "You're lying. You're German,
> for the Dutch speak French."

One night in the barracks, the boy had been beaten calamitously,

> I'd no sensation left in me. The guards said, "How is he doing?" and my
> buddies said, "He's dying."

His buddies took him to Shlomo's infirmary,

> My body was green, but my legs were fire red. My wounds were bound
> with toilet paper, and I had to change the toilet paper every day. I was
> in the perfect place to watch what went on at Świętochłowice. All the
> patients were beaten people, and they died everywhere: at their beds, in

*the washroom, on the toilet. At night, I had to step over the dead as if
that were normal to do.*

On healing, he'd joined the ascension crew, and, at the Rawa, he'd buried
at least fifty people every day.

*One day, Morel and his Audi appeared. He stood at the edge of the
mass graves. He and I looked at each other, and he said, smiling, "So,
comrade? Are you still alive?"*

On reading this, Brehmer had practically wept, but to stop the great
wheel of revenge, revenge, he hadn't told the Commission: he'd said that
the people at Shlomo's camp had died of typhus, that's all, and when I
was in Katowice, Grodzki, the prosecutor, hadn't caught on. At the city
clerk's office in Świętochłowice, Grodzki had found from 1,800 to 2,000
death certificates from Shlomo's camp, but, at his office, he told me help-
lessly, "We still have no evidence on Morel," on Shlomo himself.

Still, Grodzki had sent him a letter, summoning him on Thursday,
June 24. He'd learned that Shlomo was in Israel again, living in his peach-
colored place on Hevron Street and on Saturdays (panting as if he'd been
jogging) walking across the street to the Sabbath services. His heart was
bad, he went to the hospital often, but he'd sent word to Grodzki that
he'd be in Katowice on Monday, November 15. He said he'd come then
for his third interrogation.

NOTES

Preface

"My mother's mother. . . ."

My grandmother from Cracow was Bessie Krawecki Levy, and I was at Auschwitz on May 4, 1989. Hundreds of Jews joined the organization that ran the prisons and camps for German civilians in Poland and Poland-administered Germany. According to Pinek Mąka, the Jew who was Secretary of State Security for Silesia, the number of Jewish *officers* was 150 to 225 in Silesia alone, and I learned of others in Cracow, Kielce, Lublin, Warsaw, and other cities in Poland and Poland-administered Germany. According to American estimates, the Germans lost 35,000 civilians in Dresden in February, 1945, and the Japanese lost 66,000 to 78,000 in Hiroshima in August, 1945. The Americans lost 2,400 servicemen and civilians at Pearl Harbor, and the British lost 70,000 civilians in the Battle of Britain. No one knows how many people the Jews lost in Poland's pogroms, but the number was much less than 60,000. "Thou shalt not bear false witness" is, of course, in the Ten Commandments in Exodus 20:16, and "If he do not utter it, then he shall bear his iniquity" is in Leviticus 5:1. The story of Abraham is in Genesis 12:1–10, and Nachmanides, a much revered rabbi in the twelfth century in Spain, specifically said that Abraham sinned. The story of Judah is in Genesis 38:15–26, and the story of Moses in Deuteronomy 32:48–52. The three-volume work was *Die Vertreibung der Deutschen Bevölkerung aus den Gebieten Östlich der Oder-Neisse*, edited by Theodor Schieder. "Eye for eye" is in Exodus 21:24, but the Talmud rejects it, and it's never been part of Jewish law.

Sources. On Dresden, Hiroshima and Pearl Harbor: *The Simon and*

Schuster Encyclopedia of World War II. On the Battle of Britain: *The World Almanac*. On the Polish pogroms: Aaron Brightbart.

1

"At five o'clock. . . ."

In Southern Poland, the Russian offensive began on Friday, January 12, and in Northern Poland on Sunday, January 14. The letters SS are short for Schutzstaffel or (Hitler's) Protective Force. The SS woman with the bead-encrusted whip was Irma Grese. SS sergeants were called *hauptscharführer*, or chief group leaders, lieutenants were *untersturmführer* and *obersturm-führer*, or lower and upper storm-leaders, and captains were *hauptsturm-führer*, or chief storm-leaders.

Lola's Hebrew name was Leah and her Polish name was Laja. Some people in this book had as many as five names and nicknames in Yiddish, Hebrew, Polish and English, and I use the Hebrew name unless I'm asked otherwise. Auschwitz was Oświęcim before 1939 and after 1945. Some cities in this book had as many as six consecutive names, and, except for Auschwitz, I use the name they had at Lola's birth, in 1921. For clarity's sake, I capitalize German nouns according to English rules. I call the Soviets "Russians," because they were called that in 1945.

Sources. On the Russian offensive: Georgi Graff, Yuri Shaligin, *The Road to Berlin* by John Erickson, *The Last Hundred Days* by John Toland, *Newsweek*, January 12, 1945. On Auschwitz and the SS: Lola Potok Acker-feld Blatt, *The Diary of Johann Kremer* by Johann Kremer, *Five Chimneys* by Olga Lengyel, *Auschwitz* by Sara Nomberg-Przytyk, *I Was a Doctor in Auschwitz* by Gisella Perl, *Smoke over Birkenau* by Seweryna Szmaglewska.

"It was ten below. . . ."

In this book, almost everything in quotation marks is a true quotation. The source of the Russian words *"Sabachi holod!"* was Georgi Graff, a Russian veteran. The source of the German order *"Schmutzige Juden! Her-aus!"* was Lola. The sources of Lola's exchanges with Ada and Zlata, "Eat it," "I can't," "Swallow it!" were Ada, Zlata, and Genia Rosenzweig Tigel. The source of Ada's exclamations, "I see some meat!" "No, it was human," was Ada, who was saying this to Genia Rosenzweig. The source of the SS commands, *"Stehen bleiben!" "Weiter gehen,"* was Olga Lengyel in *Five Chimneys*. The source of Lola's request, "We need some bread," was Lola. The source of Zlata's order, "Put your shoes on! Or you'll never be able to!" was Zlata. The source of Lola's words, "I'm not walking another step," "I've had it, I'm walking away," "If that's what my destiny is, it will happen right here," "Whatever will be will be," and of Zlata's replies was Lola. Of course, Lola couldn't swear the quotations occurred in that exact order, so the conversation is "reconstructed" to that extent. The source of the SS man's question to Lola *"Sie, gehören Sie dazu?"* was Lola, who also reported it in 1945 to Moniek Rappaport and to Zlata. On rare occasions, something in this book in quotation marks is deduced from the circumstances around it, and I acknowledge this in the Notes.

I put all temperatures in Fahrenheit. Gleiwitz now is Gliwice, Poland.

Sources. On the Russian offensive: Georgi Graff, Yuri Shaligin, *War on the Eastern Front* by James Lucas. On the death march from Auschwitz: Lola Potok Ackerfeld Blatt, Ada Neufeld Potok Halperin, Zlata Martyn Potok, Moniek Rappaport, Gucia Martyn Schickman, Genia Rosenzweig Tigel, *None of Us Will Return* by Charlotte Delbo, *Anus Mundi* by Wiesław Kielar, *Five Chimneys* by Olga Lengyel, *Auschwitz* by Sara Nomberg-Przytyk, *I Was a Doctor in Auschwitz* by Gisella Perl, *Night* by Elie Wiesel.

"That night, Zlata. . . ."

Zlata's concentration camp was Neustadt-Glewe, in Mecklenburg, Germany. The other girls who went to Gleiwitz were Jadzia Rappaport Ackerfeld, Helen Eisenman, Lusha Frischman, Gucia Martyn, Mania Rappaport, Jadzia Gutman Sapirstein and Pola Wollander. They first walked, then commandeered a German's horse and wagon, then took the train to Silesia. Lange Reihe now is Ulica Długa or, on the maps of Gliwice, Ulica Iwana Koniewa. Some conversation at Lola's home may have taken place later on.

Sources. On the death train to Germany: Zlata Martyn Potok, Paul Steinberg, *Night* by Elie Wiesel. On the trip to Gleiwitz: Jadzia Gutman Sapirstein "Banker," Helen Eisenman Fortgang, Jadzia Rappaport Ackerfeld Jacobs, Mania Rappaport Novak, Zlata Martyn Potok, Gucia Martyn Schickman. On Lola's home in 1945: Lucjan Zenderowski, Archives of the Department of Criminal Institutions in Katowice. On Zlata's meeting with Lola: Lola Potok Ackerfeld Blatt, Jadzia Rappaport Ackerfeld Jacobs, Zlata Martyn Potok. On Lola's uniform: Jadzia Gutman Sapirstein "Banker," Efraim Blaichman, Lola Potok Ackerfeld Blatt, Barek Eisenstein, Zlata Martyn Potok, Lucjan Zenderowski.

2

"Lola was born in Będzin. . . ."

Kattowitz now is Katowice, Poland. I convert złotys to dollars at the prewar exchange rate of 5 to 1. Lola's sisters at Lola's birth were Basia, 21, and Cyrla, 16. Her brothers were Mordka or Motcha, 17, David, 16, Judka, Juleck or Ittel, 14, Eljasz, Elijah or Elo, 12, Daniel, 10, Chaim, 9, Jacob, 6, and Barek, 4. I number floors the American way, the first floor being the ground floor.

Sources. On Będzin: Lola Potok Ackerfeld Blatt, Pinek Mąka, *A Vanished World* by Roman Vishniac, Museum of the Diaspora. On Lola's family: Lola Potok Ackerfeld Blatt, Pinek Mąka, Rózia Ickowicz Rechnic, Archives of Będzin.

"In March, 1933, Hitler. . . ."

Lola's sister Basia's husband was Adolf Steinhardt, and Cyrla's husband was Alfred Hermstein. I use the English spelling of Cracow, Warsaw, Lodz and Lvov. Ada's neighbors in Będzin were the Olszenkos, and the Catholic priest was Father Anton Zimniak.

Sources. On Lola: Lola Potok Ackerfeld Blatt, Ada Neufeld Potok Halperin, Pinek Mąka, Batia Martyn, Rózia Ickowicz Rechnic. On the Church of the Holy Trinity in Będzin: Father Kazimierz Szwarlik.

"In 1939, Kattowitz. . . ."

In 1939, there were 27,500 Jews in Będzin. The law that a Pole who harbored a Jew would die was later published in the German daily gazette on October 15, 1941, page 595. The new priest in Będzin was Father Mieczysław Zawadzki. I convert deutschmarks to dollars at the pre-war exchange rate of 2.5 to 1.

Sources. On Gleiwitz: *The Last Polka* by Horst Bienek, *History of the SS* by G. S. Graber, *Uns Geht die Sonne Nicht Unter* by the Hitler Youth, *Gleiwitz* by Richard Pawelitzki, Archives of Gliwice. On Będzin: Eva Studencki Landau, Pinek Mąka, Zizi Stoppler, Father Kazimierz Szwarlik, Moshe Szwarz, *The Jews and the Poles in World War II* by Stefan Korbonski, *Gleiwitz* by Richard Pawelitzki, Museum of the Diaspora.

"Now, this was early in World War II. . . ."

The girl who said, "We're going to a chocolate factory," was Fredka Bramowicz, from Sosnowiec, and the one who dreamt of her mother's noodles was Edzia Gutman, from Sosnowiec. The camp commandant in Gleiwitz was Bernhard Becker, and the Senior Jew was Sonia Baumgarten, from Będzin. Lola's sister Basia lived in Włocławek, near Cracow, and Cyrla lived in Paris, married to Michel Frydman. Lola's friend, Shlomo's brother's bride, was Jadzia Rappaport. Another Jadzia married Ittel Potok, Ada married David Potok, and Zlata married Elo Potok.

Sources. On the soot factory in Gleiwitz: Edzia Gutman Ackerfeld, Affidavits of Dora Kalb, Fela Kolatacz, Fela Turner and Ryfka Weisbrod in the Archives of Yad Vashem. On Lola's brothers: Lola Potok Ackerfeld Blatt, Mendel Blatt. On Lola's marriage: Shlomo Ackerfeld, Archives of Będzin.

"She gave birth to Itusha. . . ."

Pinek's Hebrew name was Pincus. The bats, for the Polish game *palant*, were thinner than baseball bats. The chief of the Jewish police was Julek Furstenfeld, the director of the knife factory was Duksztulski, and the director of the nut-and-bolt factory was Pitchner. Two antisemitic German engineers falsely informed on Pinek.

Sources. On Lola and Itu: Shlomo Ackerfeld, Lola Potok Ackerfeld Blatt, Pinek Mąka, *Encyclopaedia Judaica*, Archives of Będzin. On Pinek: Julek Furstenfeld, Pinek Mąka.

·"Itu was fifteen months old. . . ."

The director of the uniform factory was Roszner, who learned about the *Judenrein* from the Gestapo chief in Będzin, Alfred Dreier, and who revealed it to several people, including his Jewish accountant, Pincus Groncki. The girl who put her newborn boy by the statue of the Virgin Mary was Jadzia Rappaport Ackerfeld.

Sources. On the deportation from Będzin: Shlomo Ackerfeld, Lola Potok Ackerfeld Blatt, Ada Neufeld Potok Halperin, Genia Rosenzweig Tigel, Museum of the Diaspora.

3

"That same day, the Jews. . . ."

Roszner, the director of the uniform factory, recounted his conversation with Dreier, the Gestapo commandant in Będzin, to Pincus Groncki, Roszner's accountant, who then relayed it to Genia Rosenzweig. Ada's husband David, and Zlata's husband Elo, were Lola's two brothers at the uniform factory. Both went to far-off concentration camps, but Ittel and Basia went to Auschwitz. Motcha, Daniel, Chaim, Barek and Cyrla were outside of Poland but Lola didn't know where, and Jacob had died before the war. Auschwitz consisted of Auschwitz I and, two miles northwest, of Auschwitz II or Birkenau, and Ada and Zlata went to Auschwitz II. I use the words "boys" and "girls" for the prisoners at Auschwitz because they themselves did.

Sources. On the German uniform factory: Ada Neufeld Potok Halperin, Genia Rosenzweig Tigel, Museum of the Diaspora. On Ada and Zlata's trip to Auschwitz: Ada Neufeld Potok Halperin, Zlata Martyn Potok, Genia Rosenzweig Tigel, *The Last Polka* by Horst Bienek, Auschwitz Museum.

"But they stopped. . . ."

The man who said, "Give them something good to eat," was Sergeant Moll, the man who said, "No! You can't have these people gassed!" was Berliner, from Berlin, and the woman who said, "Don't tell them you're with me," was Neuman. The girl who swallowed the poison survived in Auschwitz and was liberated in 1945. At Zlata's window, Lola really said, "Zosia," the Polish for Zlata, but I keep names consistent.

Sources. On Ada and Zlata in Auschwitz: Ada Neufeld Potok Halperin, Zlata Martyn Potok, Genia Rosenzweig Tigel, *The Last Nazi* by Gerald Astor, *Reminiscences of Pery Broad* in *KL Auschwitz Seen by the SS*, *The Drowned and the Saved* by Primo Levi, *Five Chimneys* by Olga Lengyel, *Auschwitz* by Sara Nomberg-Przytyk, *Mengele: The Complete Story* by Gerald L. Posner and John Ware, Auschwitz Museum. Ada, who lives in Israel, Zlata, who lives in France, and Genia Rosenzweig Tigel, who lives in Australia, gave compatible accounts of their first night at Auschwitz.

"Soon after that, Ada, Zlata. . . ."

The people who Lola lost were Lola's mother Rivka, Lola's sister Basia, Basia's husband Adolf Steinhardt, Basia and Adolf's daughters Edzia and Roma, Lola's brother Ittel's wife Jadzia, Ittel and Jadzia's children Abramik and Edzia, Lola's brother Elo and Zlata's son Abramik, Lola's brother Daniel's wife Ida, Daniel and Ida's son Abramik, Lola's brother Jacob's wife Hannah, and Lola and Shlomo's daughter Itusha. The barracks boss, who was the *stubenälteste*, not the *blockälteste*, was Rashka.

Sources. On Ada, Zlata and Lola in Auschwitz: Shlomo Ackerfeld, Lola Potok Ackerfeld Blatt, Ada Neufeld Potok Halperin, Zlata Martyn Potok, Rózia Ickowicz Rechnic, Genia Rosenzweig Tigel, *Return to Auschwitz* by Kitty Hart, *Five Chimneys* by Olga Lengyel, *Values and Violence in Auschwitz* by Anna Pawełczyńska, *I Was a Doctor in Auschwitz* by Gisella Perl, *Smoke over Birkenau* by Seweryna Szmaglewska, Auschwitz Museum.

"The quarantine ended. . . ."

A boss at Auschwitz was called a *kapo*, from either the Italian *capo*, chief, or the German *kamerad polizei*, comrade police, and the red-headed prostitute boss was Maria. The letter "My Dear Heniek" was written by Genia Rosenzweig, from Będzin, to Heniek Kopito, from Italy, and the story of "She pulled her underpants off" was told by Pavelik, from Sosnowiec. Lola's cousin was Regina Sapirstein, from Będzin.

Sources. On the Krupp Factory: *The Arms of Krupp* by William Manchester, *SS: Alibi of a Nation* by Gerald Reitlinger, *United States vs. Alfred Krupp von Bohlen und Halbach et al.* at the United States Military Tribunals in Nurnberg. On the Union Factory: Lola Potok Ackerfeld Blatt, Barek Eisenstein, Regina Ochsenhendler Eisenstein, Ada Neufeld Potok Halperin, Adam "Krawecki," Zlata Martyn Potok, Genia Rosenzweig Tigel, Adela "Glickman," *Fighting Auschwitz* by Józef Garliński, *Anthology on Armed Jewish Resistance* by Isaac Kowalski, *Technical Manual TM9-1985-3: German Explosive Ordnance* by the U.S. Department of the Army, Center of Military History for the U.S. Department of the Army, Military History Research Office for the Federal Republic of Germany, Federal Office for Weapon Technology and Procurement for the Federal Republic of Germany.

"The eight hundred oven-crew boys. . . ."

At his request, I've changed Adam's last name. Adam gave the shears to Adela, from Nifka, who gave them to Cyla, from Białystok.

Sources. On the oven crew: *Fighting Auschwitz* by Józef Garliński, *Anthology on Armed Jewish Resistance* by Isaac Kowalski, *Eyewitness Auschwitz* by Filip Müller. On the smoke: Regina Ochsenhendler Eisenstein, *Five Chimneys* by Olga Lengyel, *They Fought Back* by Yuri Suhl, *Smoke over Birkenau* by Seweryna Szmaglewska. On Adam: Adam "Krawecki." On the gunpowder plot: Adela "Glickman," Adam "Krawecki," Genia Rosenzweig Tigel, Archives of the Department of Criminal Institutions in Katowice.

"In October, Adam still worked. . . "

The lyrics to Ada's song are by the Hebrew poet Hayyim Nahman Bialik. Ada's bread came from Genia Rosenzweig, her buttercups from a Czech named Yuri, and her kiss from a Pole named Adam. Her one-eyed murderer boss was Willi. The SS woman was Liehr, and the girl next to Ada was Sonja, from Wilno. The leader of the rebellion was Josef Dorebus, whose alias was Josef Warszawski. The SS men who were killed were Senior Corporals Jozef Purke, Rudolf Erler and Willi Preeze. The girl with the shears was Cyla, from Białystok. The girls who were hanged with Regina Sapirstein were Rosa Robota, from Czechanów, Rachel Baum, from Lodz, Ella Gartner, from Lodz, and possibly also an Esther and a Toshka. Rachel Baum said, "Avenge me!" and either her or Ella Gartner's sister started screaming. At the time, Lola was living in Auschwitz I. The man who said, "Let's celebrate without Leon," was Hans Mayer, from Vienna. Leon, whose last name was Schultz, was killed in Block Sixteen in Auschwitz I on December 24, 1944. Lola was back in Auschwitz II, or Birkenau, for the death march on January 18, 1945.

Sources. On the Union Factory: Lola Potok Ackerfeld Blatt, Regina Ochsenhendler Eisenstein, Adela "Glickman," Ada Neufeld Potok Halperin, Adam "Krawecki," Genia Rosenzweig Tigel. On the SS concerts: Janina Bleiberg Lieberman. On the Auschwitz rebellion: *Fighting Auschwitz* by Józef Garliński, *Return to Auschwitz* by Kitty Hart, *Anthology on Armed Jewish Resistance* by Isaac Kowalski, *Eyewitness Auschwitz* by Filip Müller, *Auschwitz* by Sara Nomberg-Przytyk, *They Fought Back* by Yuri Suhl, Auschwitz Museum. On the shears: Adela "Glickman," Adam "Krawecki," Genia Rosenzweig Tigel. On the hanging of Regina Sapirstein: Lola Potok Ackerfeld Blatt, Zlata Martyn Potok, *Fighting Auschwitz* by Józef Garliński, *Return to Auschwitz* by Kitty Hart, *Anthology on Armed Jewish Resistance* by Isaac Kowalski, *They Fought Back by Yuri Suhl.* On Little Leon: Barek Eisenstein, Adam "Krawecki." On the death march: Lola Potok Ackerfeld Blatt, Zlata Martyn Potok.

"Was, sind Sie verrückt?. . . "

Lola, most likely, was in a village near Rybnik, and the day was Saturday, January 20, 1945.

Sources. On Lola's escape: Lola Potok Ackerfeld Blatt, Zlata Martyn Potok, Moniek Rappaport. Lola told the story to Zlata and Moniek Rappaport in 1945, and they remembered it almost exactly as Lola did.

"I've one place to go. . . ."

The tower was a *trangulacyja* for surveying, too. Königshütte and Kattowitz were closer to Lola than Myslowitz, but there were no signs to those cities, apparently. Myslowitz now is Mysłowice, Poland, and Königshütte is Chorzów, Poland.

Sources. On Lola's trip to Königshütte: Lola Potok Ackerfeld Blatt, Zlata Martyn Potok, Moniek Rappaport, *Gleiwitz* by Richard Pawelitzki.

4

"She came to a few hours later. . . ."
Adam and Barek were at Auschwitz I. There was a third person with them,
Simon, from Belgium. The commentator on Esther was Moses Alshekh, a
sixteenth-century rabbi in Safed, Israel. Barek's Hebrew name was Dov.
Sources. On Lola in Königshütte: Lola Potok Ackerfeld Blatt, Zlata Martyn Potok. On the liberation of Auschwitz: Barek Eisenstein, Regina Ochsenhendler Eisenstein, Adam "Krawecki."

"On Saturday, January 27. . . ."
The boy with the Russian flag was Samek, from Warsaw. The girl who fell
on her bed, sobbing, and who Barek told, "My blood is boiling," was Regina
Oksenhendler, from Będzin. The man who shouted, "Friends! The war will
soon end!" was Hans Mayer, from Vienna. Barek went east to Cracow, west
to Auschwitz, north to Będzin, and south to Kattowitz. Kattowitz was the
capital of Silesia, and the Office of State Security was recruiting there for
Silesia. The name of the Office in Polish was Urząd Bezpieczeństwa Pub-
licznego. Beatestrasse now is Ulica Kościuszko.
Sources. On the liberation of Auschwitz: Barek Eisenstein, Regina
Ochsenhendler Eisenstein, Adam "Krawecki," Jacob Lewin. On the Office of
State Security: Efraim Blaichman, Lola Potok Ackerfeld Blatt, Krystyna
Zielinska Dudzinska, Barek Eisenstein, Regina Ochsenhendler Eisenstein,
Stanisław Eweik, David Feuerstein, Israel Figa, Stanisław Gazda, Adela
"Glickman," Moshe "Grossman," Rose "Grossman," Josef Jurkowski, Hanka
Tinkpulver Kalfus, Hela Kleinhaut, Colonel Wacław Kożera, Adam
"Krawecki," Efraim Lewin, Moshe Mąka, Pinek Mąka, Gaby Mamu, Shlomo
Morel, Shimon Nunberg, Józef Pijarczyk, Stanisław Poszado, Ze'ev Sharone,
Rivka "Glickman Singer," Shlomo "Singer," Zizi Stoppler, Eva Stundecki,
Ilana Studencki, Max Studniberg, Major Bogdan Szczepurek, Wilhelm Szew-
czyk, Ruth Wilder, Lieutenant Edward Witek, Leo Zelkin, Lucjan Zen-
derowski, Sara "Zucker," Salek "Zucker," *The Jews and the Poles in World
War II* by Stefan Korbonski. On Barek in Kattowitz: Barek Eisenstein, State
Archives in Kattowitz.

"Will the New York City Police. . . ."
Of the Jews in the Office, Itzak Klein had been liberated at Auschwitz.
Adela "Glickman" had escaped by hiding in a forester's house near Pless,
Moshe "Grossman" and Shimon Nunberg by diving into the snow in Glei-
witz, and Salek "Zucker" by running into the woods near Gleiwitz. Leo
Zelkin had escaped after an all-night ride in a coal car. David Feuerstein had
come from the camp at Gęsia, Ayzer Mąka from Markstädt, Jadzia Gutman
Sapirstein from Neustadt-Glewe, and Shlomo "Singer" from Gęsia. Aaron
Lehrman had hidden during the war in Grójec and Chaim Studniberg in
Badkowice. Josef Jurkowski and Hanka Tinkpulver were from the Polish
army, and Efraim Lewin, Moshe Mąka, Pinek Mąka and Shlomo Morel from

the Polish partisans. Some other Jews in the Office in the Kattowitz area were Yurik Chołomski, Barek Eisenstein, Major Frydman, Jacobowitz, Mordechai Kac, Leon Kaliski, Moshe Kalmewicki, Herman Klausner, Shmuel Kleinhaut, Josef Kluger, Heniek Kowalski, Adam "Krawecki," Laudon, Lieutenant Malkowski, Nachum "Salowicz," Captain Stilberg, Moshe Szajnwald, Vogel, Hela Wilder and Leo Zolkewicz. At their requests, I've changed the last names of Glickman, Singer and Zucker.

Barek Eisenstein estimated that 90 percent of the Jews in the Office in Kattowitz changed their names to Polish ones. Barek said one was even buried in a Catholic cemetery. Pinek Mąka, the Secretary of State Security for Silesia in 1945, estimated that 70 or 75 percent of the officers in Silesia were Jews. Barek Eisenstein estimated that 75 or more percent were, Stanisław Gazda that "most" were, Adam "Krawecki" that 70 to 80 percent were, and Moshe Mąka that 70 or 75 percent "maybe" were. Józef Musiał, the Vice Minister of Justice for Poland in 1990, said, "I don't like to talk about it," but most officers in the Office in all of Poland were Jews. The only gentile officers in Kattowitz who I was told of were Captain Zdzisiek Kupczyński, the chief of Personnel; Kowalski and Zawicki, two deputies in Imprisonment; and a Ukrainian lieutenant who, in fact, was executed. Pinek estimated that two or three hundred officers worked for the Office in Silesia, and three-fourths of that would be 150 to 225.

Stanisław Gazda, who was secretary to Chaim Studniberg, the Director of Prisons and Camps for Silesia, said there were twenty to thirty prisons in Silesia, as did Efraim Lewin, the commandant at Neisse. Among them, Pinek, Stanisław Gazda, Shlomo Morel and Colonel Wacław Kożera, the Director of the Department of Criminal Institutions in Katowice in 1989, remembered prisons in Będzin, Beuthen, Bielsko-Biała, Breslau, Częstochowa, Hindenburg, Jastrzębic, Kattowitz, Königshütte, Nikolai, Myslowitz, Neisse, Oppeln, Schwientochlowitz, Sosnowiec (three prisons), Tarnowitz and Zawiercie. Among the Jewish commandants in Silesia were Major Frydman at Beuthen, Jacobowitz at an unidentified camp, Shmuel Kleinhaut at Myslowitz, Efraim Lewin at Neisse, Shlomo Morel at Schwientochlowitz, Oppeln and Kattowitz, and Lola Potok Ackerfeld at Gleiwitz. Czesław Gęborski, the commandant at Lamsdorf, was probably a Catholic, but I was told of no other gentile commandants.

Moshe was Moshe "Moniek" Szajnwald, from Miechów, who used the name of Max Savitski, and the Miechów butcher was Tomasz Jurkowski. Regina was Regina Oksenhendler, from Będzin. The boy with the mandolin was Shlomo Morel, from Lublin, the boy who was Stanisław Niegosławski was Shimon Nunberg, from Będzin, and the boy with the mangled left arm was Efraim Lewin, from Lublin. Schwientochlowitz now is Świętochłowice, Poland. Barek's apartment in Kattowitz was at Andreasplatz 23, now Ulica Andrzeja 23.

Sources. On Barek at the Office of State Security: Barek Eisenstein. On the parties in Kattowitz: Shlomo Morel, Soviet communiqué for February 6, 1945. On the Jews in the Office of State Security: Efraim Blaichman, Leon

"Chaimowicz," Lusia Feiner, David Feuerstein, Adela "Glickman," Rivka "Glickman," Shmuel "Gross," Moshe "Grossman," Rose "Grossman," Shmuel Kleinhaut, Adam "Krawecki," Efraim Lewin, Pinek Mąka, Shlomo Morel, Shimon Nunberg, Shlomo "Singer," Hela Wilder, Leo Zelkin, Salek "Zucker," Statements of Mathias Hemschik (Ost-Dok. 2/236B/106), Josef Mosler (Ost-Dok. 2/236C/354) and Eva Reimann (Ost-Dok. 2/236C/288) in the German Federal Archives.

"Some girls were smooching. . . ."
The boy who saw Ittel hanged was Moshe "Grossman," from Lodz. Four other boys—Heniek Aaronfud, Motek Bakalash, Moniek Buchweis and Karmo "Pipek" Furstenfeld—were hanged with Ittel. Lola met "Grossman" in Kattowitz but couldn't remember where, and "Grossman," if he remembered, wouldn't tell me. I have assumed they met at a party, as Lola met many other boys. Bernhardstrasse now is Ulica Powstańców.
Sources. On the party in Kattowitz: Shlomo Morel. On Lola's brother Ittel: Lola Potok Ackerfeld Blatt, Shimon Nunberg, *Hitler's SS* by Richard Grunberger. On Lola's application form: Colonel Wacław Kożera, Stanisław Poszado, Archives of the Department of Criminal Institutions in Katowice. On Lola's visit to Pinek: Lola Potok Ackerfeld Blatt, Pinek Mąka, State Archives in Kattowitz.

"In 1942 he'd been saved. . . ."
The director of the Silesia Factory was Pitchner, who later met Pinek in Kattowitz and told him what he'd told the Gestapo. Pinek's sister was Shoshana, and her boyfriend was Chaim "Heniek" Studniberg, both from Będzin. The patient in Kattowitz was Yasiek, the partisans north of Będzin were in Zombkowice, and Pinek's name in the partisans was Antek Zeziskowski. The major in Kattowitz was Josef Jurkowski, from Lublin. The home that Pinek found was in Badkowice, his brother in the partisans was Moshe, and his brother at Markstädt was Ayzer, or Olek in Yiddish. Pinek's proper title in the government of Silesia was Deputy Director of the First Department, and his assumed name was Paweł Mąka, "Mąka" being a Polish as well as Jewish name. In the Archives of the Provincial Police in Katowice, I found his personnel file as Deputy Director, and on September 27, 1992, Edmund Kwarta, the Deputy Director of Archives, signed a certificate saying, "I hereby certify that Paweł Mąka, born September 23, 1920, worked at the Department of State Security from February 15, 1945, to April 17, 1946, in the capacity of Deputy Director of the First Department of Office of State Security in Katowice." Twelve people—Jadzia Gutman Sapirstein "Banker," Lola Potok Ackerfeld Blatt, Barek Eisenstein, Regina Ochsenhendler Eisenstein, David Feuerstein, Julek Furstenfeld, Adela "Glickman," Josef Jurkowski, Moshe Mąka, Pincus Schickman, Rivka "Glickman Singer" and Shlomo "Singer"—also confirmed that Pinek had an important job in the Silesian government.
Sources. On Pinek: Pinek Mąka.

"'I want revenge,' Lola told him. . . ."

Pinek's mother's mother was Hannah Solewicz, and Lola's brother Elo jumped into bed with her. The girl who said, "I'm going crazy," was Hanka Tinkpulver, and her insane asylum was at Tworki, near Warsaw. There were about ten sections in the Office of State Security, including Commercial, Industrial and Administrative. "Lola" and "Potok" are Polish names, and Lola didn't change them.

Pinek appointed Lola as Commandant, but her actual titles were Deputy Commandant and Acting Commandant. In 1945, the Poles often appointed a nominal "commandant" who was a Catholic and a real "deputy commandant" who was a Jew, and in Gleiwitz the nominal "commandant" was a sergeant, twenty years old, who Lola in fact outranked. The boy had been appointed on January 2, 1945, when the Germans still were in Gleiwitz, but broke his leg in May, was still in the hospital in August, and was still on crutches in May, 1946. No one I spoke to in Gleiwitz remembered his name, but I got it in confidence from the Provincial Court in Katowice. I tried, but I couldn't find him or anyone who knew him in Poland.

I've interviewed thirty-five people who say that Lola was commandant in Gleiwitz. In addition to Lola, they are: Officers of the Department of Criminal Institutions in Katowice in 1989: Colonel Wacław Kożera, Director; Stanisław Poszado, Manager of the Department of Law and Organization; Major Bogdan Szczepurek, Commandant of the prison at Gliwice. Officers of the government of Silesia in 1945: Pinek Mąka. Officers of the Office of State Security in Silesia in 1945: Adela "Glickman," Moshe "Grossman," Shmuel Kleinhaut (through Hela Kleinhaut), Efraim Lewin, Moshe Mąka, Shlomo Morel, Rivka "Glickman Singer," Shlomo "Singer," Leo Zelkin. Guards at the prison in Gleiwitz in 1945: Jadzia Gutman Sapirstein "Banker," Krystyna Zielinska Dudzinska, Stanisław Eweik, Józef Pijarczyk, Lucjan Zenderowski. Lola's husbands: Shlomo Ackerfeld and Dr. Michal Blatt. Lola's family in Gleiwitz in 1945: Jadzia Rappaport Ackerfeld Jacobs, Ada Neufeld Potok Halperin, Josef Martyn (through Basia Martyn), Pincus Martyn, Zlata Martyn Potok, Mania Rappaport, Moniek Rappaport, Gucia Martyn Schickman. Lola's acquaintances in Gleiwitz in 1945: Helen Fortgang, Rose "Grossman," Leibish Jacobs, Pincus Schickman, Sam Schickman, Genia Rosenzweig Tigel. I also spoke to Salek "Zucker," who remembered that Lola worked in the Office of State Security, and to three people who remembered that a woman was commandant in Gleiwitz in 1945: Günther Ciesla, a prisoner in Gleiwitz in 1945; Major Josef Jurkowski, Director of the Office of State Security in Silesia in 1945; and Lieutenant Edward Witek of the Kattowitz police in 1945. At the German Federal Archives, I found a letter from a former prisoner in Gleiwitz, Elfriede Gawlik, saying, "The overseer was a Polish woman," and, most importantly, in the Archives of the Department of Criminal Institutions, in Katowice, I found a document in Polish saying, "Polish Republic. Ministry of State Security. Department of Prisons and Camps. May 10, 1945. To the Ministry of State Security. Personnel Department. On the premises. Please

admit and employ Citizen Potok Lola to the post of deputy prison commandant dealing with political and educational matters in Gliwice from 14 February 1945." The letter was signed and sealed by the Manager of the Personnel Department and by the Director of the Department of Prisons and
Camps. I also found a letter from Lola saying, "To the Provincial Office of
State Security. Department of Prisons and Camps. In Katowice. Request
for vacation for the Deputy Commandant. Report. In accordance with the
circular letter of July 30, 1945, I report that I'm due a vacation, and I now
request it, as I need a rest and my health is not good. I ask you to kindly
approve this report and grant me a vacation. Deputy commandant. Lola
Potok. Katowice, September 7, 1945."

Sources. On Pinek and Lola: Lola Potok Ackerfeld Blatt, Hanka Tinkpulver Kalfus, Pinek Mąka. *Sources for the Notes.* On nominal commandants:
Shmuel "Gross."

5

"Gleiwitz was occupied now. . . ."

The Yalta Conference ran from Sunday, February 4, to Sunday, February
11, 1945. Lola went to Pinek's office on Tuesday, February 13, and started
work on Wednesday, February 14. That was the day the Russians put up the
"All male Germans" poster.

Sources. On the Russians in Gleiwitz: Horst Bienek, Erwin Klose, Engelbert Liszok, Josef Wiescholek, Statements Number 4, 12, 17, 49 and others
in *The Tragedy of Silesia* by Dr. Johannes Kaps, Introductory Description
and Statements of A. B. (187), Hermann Balzer (171), I. F. (224), O. M.
(208) and others in *Die Vertreibung der Deutschen Bevölkerung aus den
Gebieten Östlich der Oder-Neisse* by Theodor Schieder, Statements of Maria
Behrens, N., Margarete Sack, M. Wallura and one anonymous man in *Die
Flucht und Vertreibung Oberschlesien 1945/46* by Wolfgang Schwarz, State-
ments of D. Häusler (Ost-Dok. 1/251/3) and Doctor von T. (Ost-Dok.
2/235/128) in the German Federal Archives, *Earth and Fire* by Horst
Bienek, *From the Ruins of the Reich* by Douglas Botting. On the Tehran and
Yalta Conferences: *Speaking Frankly* by James F. Byrnes, *Closing the Ring*
by Winston Churchill, *Nemesis at Potsdam* by Alfred de Zayas, *Stalin: The
Man and His Era* by Adam B. Ulam. On the train to Russia: Introductory
Description and Statements of F. K. (140) and others in *Die Vertreibung der
Deutschen Bevölkerung aus den Gebieten Östlich der Oder-Neisse* by
Theodor Schieder. On the camps in Russia: Statements of Gertrude Schulz
(166), Anna Schwartz (169), Gerlinde Winkler (143) and others in *Die
Vertreibung der Deutschen Bevölkerung aus den Gebieten Östlich der Oder-
Neisse* by Theodor Schieder. On the camp in Auschwitz: Statement Number
12 in *The Tragedy of Silesia* by Dr. Johannes Kaps.

"Auschwitz by now was a tourist town. . . ."

Adam and Major Jurkowski met in Auschwitz and went to Kattowitz on

Sunday, March 18. The SS woman at Auschwitz was Irma Grese.

Sources. On Adam in Auschwitz: Josef Jurkowski, Adam "Krawecki," *Reminiscences of Pery Broad* in *KL Auschwitz Seen by the SS, Eyewitness Auschwitz* by Filip Müller. On Adam in Kattowitz: Lola Potok Ackerfeld Blatt, Adam "Krawecki," Shlomo Morel, Lucjan Zenderowski.

"Later that day, Adam saw Barek. . . ."

Thirteen people—Barek Eisenstein, Israel Figa, Stanisław Gazda, Adela "Glickman," Mordechai Kac, Adam "Krawecki," Efraim Lewin, Moshe Mąka, Pinek Mąka, Shlomo Morel, Nachum "Salowicz," Zizi Stoppler and Salek "Zucker"—said that Josef was the Office's chief for Silesia, as do the files of the Office of State Security in the Archives of the Provincial Police in Katowice. Josef himself denied it, claiming that he did liaison for the Polish army. Josef was bar-mitzvahed at twelve, not thirteen, because his father wasn't alive. Marx's quotation was in *On the Jewish Question,* which Josef found at the Lopacinskis Library in Lublin. Josef escaped from the prison in Tarnów on Wednesday or Thursday, September 13 or 14, 1939. Stalin's statement on antisemitism was to a correspondent of the Jewish Telegraph Agency on January 12, 1931. In Kattowitz, the Jewish chief of Intelligence was Major Koplinski and of Imprisonment, Wassersturm. Stalin lived in Vienna in January and February, 1913, and his statement on Hitler and the German people was in his Order of the Day for February 23, 1942. The Polish absentee government was called the Polish National Committee. Jacob Berman, from Warsaw, was the real chief of the Office, though the nominal chief was Stanisław Radkiewicz, whose wife, Ruta Teisch, was a Jew, but who probably was a Catholic himself. Some Jewish department chiefs were David Schwartz, who was known as General Julius Hibner; Natan Grunsapau-Kikiel, who was known as General Roman Romkowski; Josef Goldberg, who was known as Colonel Józef Różanski; Josef Licht, who was known as Colonel Józef Światło; three Jews who were known as Colonel Anatol Fejgin, Colonel Czaplicki and Zygmunt Okręt; and a Jewish woman, Luna Brystygier. The real names of the department chiefs ran in Polish and Russian newspapers in the 1950s. Adam was the head administrator at the Auschwitz hospital, and the head doctor was Dr. Wollman. Adam's girlfriend was Pola Davner, from Będzin, and his instructor was Lieutenant Malkowski. Another of the top six students was Barek Eisenstein.

Sources. On Adam at Josef's office: Adam "Krawecki." On Josef: Josef Jurkowski, Bronisława Jurkowska, *Anthology on Armed Jewish Resistance* by Isaac Kowalski. On Stalin: Statement of Anna Schwartz (169) in *Die Vertreibung der Deutschen Bevölkerung aus den Gebieten Östlich der Oder-Neisse* by Theodor Schieder, *Closing the Ring* by Winston Churchill, *Stalin: The History of a Dictator* by H. Montgomery Hyde, *Them* by Teresa Torańska, *Stalin: The Man and His Era* by Adam B. Ulam. On Hitler: *Hitler: A Study in Tyranny* by Adam Bullock. On Berman and the section chiefs in Warsaw: Istvan Deak, Andre Korbonski, Zofia Korbonski, Artur Kowalski, Georg Lerski, Efraim Lewin, Pinek Mąka, Andrew Pomian, Tadeusz Zawadzki, *The*

Jews and the Poles in World War II by Stefan Korbonski, *Them* by Teresa
Torańska. On the course in Kattowitz: Barek Eisenstein, Adam "Krawecki."
On Adam's trip to Gleiwitz: Wilhelm Szewczyk.

"Gleiwitz was the Wild West. . . ."
Gleiwitz's and Hindenburg's populations were both close to 125,000.
Since the Russians seized thirty thousand men in Hindenburg, I've assumed
there were as many as thirty thousand eligibles in Gleiwitz. Adam's office was
at the corner of Teuchertstrasse and Friedrichstrasse (now Ulica Zygmunta
Starego and Ulica Pogodna) in Gleiwitz, and the deserted street was Kaiser
Wilhelmstrasse (now Ulica Zwycięstwa). After the war, the Polish police were
called the Militia.
   Sources. On the Russians in Gleiwitz: Adam "Krawecki," Engelbert Liszok, Zlata Martyn Potok, Lucjan Zenderowski, Statement Numbers 7, 14 and
82 in *The Tragedy of Silesia* by Dr. Johannes Kaps, Statement of M. Wallura
in *Die Flucht und Vertreibung Oberschlesien 1945/46* by Wolfgang Schwarz,
From the Ruins of the Reich by Douglas Botting. On Adam in Gleiwitz:
Adam "Krawecki." On the "Polish SS" and "Polish Gestapo": *Die Vertreibung
der Deutschen Bevölkerung aus den Gebieten Östlich der Oder-Neisse* by
Theodor Schieder, Statement Number 110 in *The Tragedy of Silesia*, Statements of H. Aschmann (Ost-Dok. 2/236E/950), Elli Bech (Ost-Dok.
2/233/3), Johannes Bech (Ost-Dok. 2/233/11), Emil Gawoll (Ost-Dok.
2/236D/667), Pawil Hesse (Ost-Dok. 2/227/64) and an anonymous person
from Heinersdorf (Ost-Dok. 2/227/7D) in the German Federal Archives.

"Lola had lost her patience. . . ."
The Jewish police chief was Julek Furstenfeld, from Będzin. The boy who
said, "Vodka!" was Daniel. At Shlomo's request, I've changed Shlomo's last
name. At Gęsia, Shlomo was cleaning up the Jewish ghetto, and the boy who
made *matzo* with him was David Feuerstein, from Będzin. The Russian
colonel was Colonel Zacharow, and one girl he chased was Gucia Wiener.
The Jewish organization was the Joint Distribution Committee of the United
Jewish Appeal. Shlomo's apartment was at Mühlstrasse 16, and Mühlstrasse
now is Ulica Młyńska, though 16 is no longer there. Some other guests at his
seder were Josef Feuerstein, Adela "Glickman," Rivka "Glickman," Gucia
Mandelbaum, David Reif and Pola Reif.
   Sources. On Lola in Kattowitz: Julek Furstenfeld, Adela "Glickman,"
Marek Katz, Pinek Mąka, Shlomo Morel, Genia Rosensweig Tigel, Leo
Zelkin, Statement of Max Kroll (Ost-Dok. 2/236B/52) in the German Federal
Archives, *Soviet War News Bulletin,* April 4, 1945. On Shlomo Singer: David
Feuerstein, Shlomo "Singer." On the Passover dinner: David Feuerstein,
Adela "Glickman," Pola Reif, Rivka "Glickman Singer," Shlomo "Singer,"
State Archives in Kattowitz.

"Shlomo put down his prayer book. . . ."
In Hebrew, "Praise the Name" is *"Baruch Hashem."* Rivka was Rivka

"Glickman," from Dombrowa, near Będzin, who escaped between Auschwitz and Pless. Adela was Adela "Glickman," from Nifka, near Będzin, who escaped in Pless, and the man who bicycled her to the station was Kloc. At their requests, I've changed Adela's and Rivka's last name. The two Jews who were killed were Stasiek and Lieutenant Malkowski. In all, the Russians sent 20,000 people from Gleiwitz to Russia. Lola was in Gleiwitz by April 23, 1945, and Klosterstrasse now is Ulica Józefa Wieczorka. The Russians left Lola's prison, but Poland was a Russian satellite and the Russians kept an eye on Lola throughout 1945.

Sources. On the Passover dinner: David Feuerstein, Adela "Glickman," Pola Reif, Rivka "Glickman Singer," Shlomo "Singer." On the dangers of Kattowitz: Barek Eisenstein, Pinek Mąka. On Lola in Gleiwitz: Lola Potok Ackerfeld Blatt, Efraim Lewin, Lucjan Zenderowski, Statement by Dr. N. N. (Ost-Dok. 2/213D/173) in the German Federal Archives, Archives of the Provincial Court in Katowice, *Die Vertreibung der Deutschen Bevölkerung aus den Gebieten Östlich der Oder-Neisse* by Theodor Schieder.

O

"The next day, the Germans came. . . ."

Some incidents at the Germans' arrival may have taken place later on. I don't know how many of Lola's fifty guards were Jews. Lola said that all fifty were, but I know of three who were Jews—Moshe "Grossman," Heniek Kowalski and Jadzia Gutman Sapirstein—and of five who were Catholics—Stanisław Eweik, Klapcia, Józef Pijarczyk, Szczęsny, and Lucjan Zenderowski. According to the Suchdienst, or Search Service, of the German Red Cross, from five hundred to one thousand prisoners were in the Gleiwitz prison, but one guard believes there were fewer than five hundred, and Lola and two German prisoners believe there were more than one thousand. In the men's prison, the Germans got potato soup, but in the women's prison, at least one German got kasha three times per day. Höss's statement to Himmler was overheard by Sophie Stipel, of Mannheim-Ludwigshafen, Germany, and reported to Stanisław Dubiel. The girl who Mengele flirted with was Mala. Hitler shot himself and, at the same time, bit a cyanide capsule on April 30, 1945, but the German city of Breslau, eighty miles west of Gleiwitz, was still holding out when the Germans surrendered on May 7.

This book first appeared in June, 1988, as an article in *California* magazine. I wrote there what Pinek, Lola, and a half-dozen other sources told me, "Pinek offered her a job as the commandant of a POW prison for German soldiers, Gestapo police and SS." In fact, as I learned when I went to Gleiwitz in May, 1989, the prison was used for (1) About twenty German soldiers, working as car mechanics, carpenters and painters, (2) Hundreds of Gestapo and SS *suspects* and Nazi and Nazi collaborator *suspects,* some of whom *claimed* to be German soldiers, (3) Forty-two war-crime *convicts,* almost all of whom were convicted after Lola left, and (4) Hundreds of suspects and convicts for common crimes.

Sources. On the German arrival: Lola Potok Ackerfeld Blatt, Günther Ciesla, Günter Plasczyk, Pincus Schickman, Josef Wiescholek, Lucjan Zenderowski, *Zur Geschichte der Deutschen Kriegsgefangenen des Zweiten Weltkrieges* by Erich Maschke. On Höss, Hössler and Mengele: Lola Potok Ackerfeld Blatt, Regina Ochsenhendler Eisenstein, Janina Bleiberg Lieberman, Statement of Stanisław Dubiel at Auschwitz, August 7, 1946, *Five Chimneys* by Olga Lengyel, *Eyewitness Auschwitz* by Filip Müller, *Mengele* by Gerald Posner. On Hitler: *From the Ruins of the Reich* by Douglas Botting.

"The adjutant, Moshe Grossman. . . ."

At his request, I've changed Grossman's last name. "Even as He is merciful, be merciful too" is in Shabbat 133b.

German prisoners of war were also beaten in American camps. In 1945, George Orwell saw a Jewish interrogator at an American camp for Germans kicking an SS general, shouting, "Get up, you swine!" Orwell wrote in the *Tribune* of November 9, 1945,

> *I concluded that he [the Jew] wasn't really enjoying it, and that he was merely—like a man in a brothel, or a boy smoking his first cigar, or a tourist traipsing round a picture gallery—telling himself that he was enjoying it.*

I don't agree with Orwell, for even the SS had never claimed to "enjoy" it. More likely, the Jew was doing some heavy-handed status-seeking, as though he were saying to Orwell, the SS general, and particularly himself, "I'm doing what the SS did, so I'm as good as the SS."

Sources. On Moshe: Lola Potok Ackerfeld Blatt, Moshe "Grossman," Rose "Grossman," Simon Nunberg, Lucjan Zenderowski. On the fat SS man: Lola Potok Ackerfeld Blatt, Günther Ciesla, Eva Woitinek Lischevski. *Sources for the Notes.* On the SS general: *The Collected Essays, Journalism and Letters of George Orwell, Volume 4: In Front of Your Nose, 1945–1950.*

"In fact, interrogation was not. . . ."

The auto school was next door to the prison, also at Klosterstrasse 10. Kindness to oxen and asses is in Deuteronomy 5:14, 22:10 and 25:4, and "Do not take revenge" is in Leviticus 19:18. The man from the Auschwitz SS was Georg.

The interrogators also beat the women at Lola's prison. One whose name was Ogórek used clubs and a brass-buckled belt to beat a Kattowitz girl, Elfryda "Uracz," age twenty, every night in April, May and June. He asked her, "Are you a German?" "What is your name?" "Where were you born?" and "When were you born?" but he never let her answer him. She lost her left teeth, her body became bloody, black and blue, and a part of the belt buckle lodged in her hip. One day, one of her cellmates told her, "I thought you were wearing something blue. But it's your skin."

Sources. On the interrogations in Kattowitz: Eva Studencki Landau, Pinek Mąka, Gaby Mamu, Ze'ev Sharone, Ilana Studencki, Max Studniberg, Zizi Stoppler. On the interrogations in Gleiwitz: Dorota Niessporek Boreczek, Günther Ciesla, Josef Gorka, Adam "Krawecki," Renate Zurek Misior, Shimon Nunberg, Günter Plasczyk, Elfryda "Uracz," Lucjan Zenderowski, *Martyrdom of Silesian Priests* by Dr. Johannes Kaps. On Adam: Adam "Krawecki." *Sources for the Notes.* On the Kattowitz girl: Dorota Boreczek, Elfryda "Uracz."

"Every night Adam thought. . . ."
Adam, who was passing as a Catholic, was arrested on November 18, 1942, was tortured in Breslau in November and December and in January, 1943, and was sent to Auschwitz on February 23, 1943. Some of the conversation at the interrogation may have happened at later interrogations.
Sources. On Adam: Adam "Krawecki." On *bimber:* Barek Eisenstein. On drinking at Auschwitz: *The Diary of Johann Kremer* by Johann Kremer. On drinking at Lola's prison: Józef Pijarczyk, Lucjan Zenderowski.

"Lola, too, was upset. . . ."
The girl who heard screams was Eva Woitinek Lischevski, of Klosterstrasse 18 in Gleiwitz, and Efraim was Efraim Lewin, from Lublin. Schwerinstrasse now is Ulica Jana Sobieskiego, and Lange Reihe now is Ulica Długa or, on the maps of Gleiwitz, Ulica Iwana Koniewa. The glass-blower was Robert Sindermann, who had fled from Gleiwitz in October or November, 1944. The Imprisonment chief was Wassersturm, and his fiancée was Beata, from France. Lola called Shoshana "Róśka," her Polish name.
Sources. On the screams in Lola's prison: Günther Ciesla, Eva Woitinek Lischevski. On the boy with the good right arm: Efraim Blaichman, Efraim Lewin, Shlomo Morel. On house-hunting in Gleiwitz: Efraim Lewin. On Lola's home: Lola Potok Ackerfeld Blatt, Lucjan Zenderowski, Archives of the Department of Criminal Institutions in Katowice. On Lola and Shoshana: Lola Potok Ackerfeld Blatt, Pinek Mąka.

"More weary people came. . . ."
The boy who'd been to four concentration camps—Bergen-Belsen, Buchenwald, Gross Rosen and Markstädt—was Pincus Schickman, from Będzin, and the girl with the silver fox was Jadzia Rappaport Ackerfeld, from Będzin. The house next door was 27 Lange Reihe, the engineer there was Julius Koloch, and his daughter was Majza. Zlata's niece was Gucia Martyn, from Będzin. Some conversation on the Sabbath eve may have taken place later on.
Sources. On the people in Lola's homes: Jadzia Gutman Sapirstein "Banker," Lola Potok Ackerfeld Blatt, Helen Eisenman Fortgang, Jadzia Rappaport Ackerfeld Jacobs, Mania Rappaport Novak, Zlata Martyn Potok,

Gucia Martyn Schickman, Pincus Schickman. On *"Eine stunde, heraus"*: Lola
Potok Ackerfeld Blatt, Jadzia Rappaport Ackerfeld Jacobs, Zlata Martyn
Potok, Moniek Rappaport, Archives of Gliwice. On Zlata: Zlata Martyn
Potok.

7

"At that moment, Shlomo. . . ."

Shlomo's name Ignaz has been changed at Shlomo's request. The com-
mandant in Neisse was Captain Stilberg, from Będzin. The boy who helped
with the *matzo* was David Feuerstein, the boy who was "selected" and "de-
selected" was Shimon Nunberg, and the boy who was castrated was Salek
"Zucker," all from Będzin. The gray building was at Kochstrasse 13, now
Ulica Armii Czerwonej 11 and 13. The man who cut his throat was Juppe, of
Gross Neundorf, who was buried near the Jerusalem Cathedral. The Neisse
River was the Eastern, not Western, Neisse—not the Neisse of the Oder-
Neisse Line.

Sources. On Shlomo: Rivka "Glickman Singer," Shlomo "Singer." On the
prison at Neisse: Barek Eisenstein, David Feuerstein, Shimon Nunberg,
Shlomo "Singer," Statements of Max Cyrus (Ost-Dok. 2/227/20), Maria
Rother Halke (Ost-Dok. 2/227/48), Pavil Hesse (Ost-Dok. 2/227/62), Hubert
Jaeschke (Ost-Dok. 2/227/88) and Wilhelm Neuber (Ost-Dok. 2/236B/132)
in the German Federal Archives.

"Day after day, the Germans. . . ."

A man whose arm was broken was Mahl, the mayor of Ziegenhals. The
"hard case" was Hubert Jaeschke, from Neisse, who was arrested on Thursday, May 24, 1945. The informant was Seidel, from Neisse, who got one
thousand złotys, or $200 at the pre-war exchange rate. In 1945 he could buy
one hundred pounds of bread, twenty gallons of milk, ten pounds of sugar,
six pounds of pork, or one shoe with it. The boy who said, "It's stamped by
the Party!" was Lieutenant Kolano, who Jaeschke believed was a Jew but
Shlomo believes wasn't. "Three characteristics do Jews possess" is in
Yebamoth 79a, and the suggestion that the wicked ones were the Jews is in
Aboth IV, Mishnah 7. "Wilt thou destroy the righteous along with the
wicked?" is in Genesis 18:23, and "Thou shalt not stand by thy neighbor's
blood" is in Leviticus 19:16. According to Moses Maimonides, a twelfth-
century rabbi in Spain, Jews have 365 negative and 248 positive duties, or
613 duties in all. I have "reconstructed" the conversation "Do you still say
you weren't in the Party?" "No! I didn't say I wasn't in the Party!" "You
didn't?" "No! I never said it!" "You *were* in the Party?" "Yes!" In his statement at the German Federal Archives, Jaeschke simply says, "At my eighth
interrogation, the thought came to me to declare that I wasn't in the Party,
but I declared that I was in the Party."

My major source for this scene is a statement by Hubert Jaeschke in the German Federal Archives, and I have accepted what Jaeschke says. He begins,

Everything that I write below, I can bear witness to. I am prepared to answer for every sentence and every word,

and he continues in this precise and almost pedantic tone, as most statements in the Archives do. His story is consistent with many other statements in the Archives and in *The Tragedy of Silesia,* by Dr. Johannes Kaps, and with my own interviews with Jews who'd been at Neisse—with Barek Eisenstein, David Feuerstein, Moshe Mąka, Shimon Nunberg and Shlomo "Singer"—and with my own inspection of Jaeschke's former prison. One man I interviewed, Israel Figa, a Jew who'd been in Silesia in 1945 and who now reports for the Jewish *Workmen's Circle,* in New York City, told me, "Whatever the Germans say, it's true," and I'd no sooner write that Jaeschke was beaten *allegedly* than I, or any other author, would write that the Jews were allegedly beaten at Auschwitz.

I accept most of the statements in the German Federal Archives, and I've used them throughout this book. The few that I'm unsure of, I haven't used.

Sources. On the prison at Neisse: Barek Eisenstein, David Feuerstein, Moshe Mąka, Shimon Nunberg, Shlomo "Singer," Statement Number 194 in *The Tragedy of Silesia* by Dr. Johannes Kaps, Statements of Max Cyrus (Ost-Dok. 2/227/20), Maria Rother Halke (Ost-Dok. 2/227/48), Pavil Hesse (Ost-Dok. 2/227/62), Hubert Jaeschke (Ost-Dok. 2/227/88) and Wilhelm Neuber (Ost-Dok. 2/236B/132) in the German Federal Archives.

"By now, ninety percent. . . ."

The man who said, "I believe in One God! Not two!" was Pavil Blacha, from Trockenberg, who was then in the camp at Myslowitz, and the chains, jambs and wedges were used in Falkenburg, among other places. The commandant at Bielsko-Biała was Herman Klausner, from Alexanderfeld. The man at Neisse-Neuland was W. M., an architect from Neisse-Neuland, the policeman at Glatz was Paul Seifert, from Bad Reinerz, the man at Ottmachau was Bernhard N., from Eichenau, the woman at Schreiberhau was from Petersdorf, and the man in Kattowitz was Max Kroll, from Dombrowa. The cellar in Falkenburg was in the former district administrator's villa, the one in Bielsko-Biała in the Polish Bank, the one in Neisse-Neuland in the former villa of Dr. Tschoetschel, the one in Wünschelburg in the Wünschelburg town hall, the ones in Glatz on Grünenstrasse, in the Office's building on Wagnerstrasse, and in the old garrison on Zimmerstrasse, and the ones in Ottmachau and Markt Bohrau at the Polish government headquarters. The previous governor of Silesia was Colonel Jerzy Ziętek, the new governor was General Aleksander Zawadzki, and his wife was Gloria Furstenberg, from Będzin.

Another man who Pinek released was Julek Furstenfeld, the former chief of the Jewish police in Będzin. Julek was in a concentration camp and was working in a coal mine when Mania, his wife, went to Pinek's home in Kattowitz. She knelt on Pinek's rug, saying, "Help me. Most of my family didn't survive, and I need to build another one." Pinek released Julek, brought him to Pinek's own home, fed him, and got him and Mania exit visas from Poland.

Sources. On eighty-five out of ninety-four men in Neisse: Statement of Hubert Jaeschke (Ost-Dok. 2/227/88) in the German Federal Archives. Independently, Shimon Nunberg, a Jewish interrogator, estimated that ninety percent of the Germans at Neisse eventually confessed. On the cellars in Silesia: Heinz "Becker," Karl Frank, Statements Number 33, 47, 62, 101, 192 and 196 in *The Tragedy of Silesia* by Dr. Johannes Kaps, Statement of Doctor I. R. (223) and Paul Seifert (229) in *Die Vertreibung der Deutschen Bevölkerung aus den Gebieten Östlich der Oder-Neisse* by Theodor Schieder, Statements of Pavil Blacha (Ost-Dok. 2/236C/318), Mathias Hemschik (Ost-Dok. 2/236B/106), Max Kroll (Ost-Dok. 2/236B/52) and Eva Reimann (Ost-Dok. 2/236C/288) in the German Federal Archives. On Pinek: Barek Eisenstein, Pinek Mąka. On the big Nazis: Introductory Description in *Die Vertreibung der Deutschen Bevölkerung aus den Gebieten Östlich der Oder-Neisse* by Theodor Schieder. *Sources for the Notes.* On Julek Furstenfeld: Julek Furstenfeld, Pinek Mąka.

"The first wedding bells. . . ."
The train that Barek and Regina were on was going from Neisse to Kattowitz. Regina's sister was Jadzia Ochsenhendler, the "giver-away" was Blima Grosberg, and the rabbi was Rabbi Lieberman, all from Będzin. "Blessed art Thou, O Lord, who has created love" is part of the Seven Benedictions, and the ring that Regina had found at the "Kanada" was also inscribed BJ. The "drummer" was Wolf Grauer, from Cracow, and the girl who said, "Forty-eight countries," was Rachel Fontanck. Some other wedding guests were Jacob Eisenstein, Josef Eisenstein, Sala Garfinkel, Luba Młynarski, Bluma Nunberg, Machela Ochsenhendler, Mania Ochsenhendler, Lola Plasznick, Heniek Raber, Fela Zelkowicz, and one sister and two brothers whose names were Halina, Tadeusz and Władek. The Kattowitz boy in Intelligence was Itzak Klein, and the girl he married was Tesia. Another couple, Jacob Eisenstein and Luba Młynarski, were also married on Sunday. Shimon Nunberg, an interrogator in Neisse, married Rachel; Leo Zelkin, a guard in Kattowitz, married Regina Skoczezylas, from Będzin; and Shmuel Kleinhaut, the commandant in Myslowitz, married Hela Wilder, a guard in Myslowitz.

Sources. On Barek and Regina's wedding: Barek Eisenstein, Jacob Eisenstein, Jadzia Ochsenhendler Eisenstein, Regina Ochsenhendler Eisenstein, Blima Grosberg Golenser, Machela Ochsenhendler. On the other weddings: Barek Eisenstein, Regina Ochsenhendler Eisenstein, Ruth Wilder, Leo Zelkin.

"One summer day, a Jewish girl. . . ."

Ada went to Malchów concentration camp, was bombed in Magdeburg railroad station, and was liberated in Leipzig. Gucia Martyn and Shmuel Schickman had fallen in love as Shmuel walked into Lola's house, and Jadzia Rappaport Ackerfeld and Leibisch Jacobs had met on Kaiser Wilhelmstrasse. Some other people at Lola's three homes were Helen Eisenman, Zlata Martyn Potok, Mania Rappaport, Moshe Rappaport, Jadzia Gutman Sapirstein and Pincus Schickman. The girl who said, "What's happening, Ada?" was Genia Rosenzweig, who had traveled to Gleiwitz with Ada.

Sources. On Ada: Ada Neufeld Potok Halperin. On Ada in Lola's home: Jadzia Gutman Sapirstein "Banker," Lola Potok Ackerfeld Blatt, Helen Eisenman Fortgang, Ada Neufeld Potok Halperin, Jadzia Rappaport Ackerfeld Jacobs, Mania Rappaport Novak, Zlata Martyn Potok, Moshe Rappaport, Gucia Martyn Schickman, Genia Rosenzweig Tigel. On David: Lola Potok Ackerfeld Blatt, Ada Neufeld Potok Halperin. On Shlomo: Shlomo Ackerfeld, Jadzia Gutman Sapirstein "Banker," Ada Neufeld Potok Halperin, Zlata Martyn Potok, Archives of the District Attorney's Office in Gliwice. On Höss: Statements of Stanisław Dubiel at Auschwitz, August 7, 1946, and of Janina Przybyła Szczurek at Auschwitz, January 13, 1963, *Commandant at Auschwitz* by Rudolf Höss.

"'Do you want to see it?'. . . ."

With Ada at Lola's prison was Genia Rosenzweig, who believes that the visit took place in August on Ada's first day in Gleiwitz. Ada, Genia and Lola didn't remember what Lola accused the German of, and I have supplied the "You were SS." Around 1941, Ada had been arrested in Będzin and interrogated in Sosnowiec, near it. The SS woman at Auschwitz was Irma Grese.

Sources. On Ada in Lola's prison: Ada Neufeld Potok Halperin, Efraim Lewin, Pincus Schickman, Genia Rosenzweig Tigel. On Ada in Sosnowiec: Ada Neufeld Potok Halperin. On the SS woman at Auschwitz: *Five Chimneys* by Olga Lengyel, *I Was a Doctor in Auschwitz* by Gisella Perl.

8

"In June or July, a German. . . ."

Höss was in a POW camp near Flensburg, Germany; Hössler near Hameln, Germany; and Mengele near Weiden, Germany. The ardent interrogator was Ogórek, and the German girl was Elfryda "Uracz." The boy with black pants was apparently in Lola's prison as early as April. The commandant in Myslowitz was Shmuel Kleinhaut, from Będzin. He was humane, apparently, for one German wrote in a statement in the German Federal Archives, "There also were several reasonable guards, among them a Jew who never did anything to any of us. The prison director, too, had the fullest understanding of our situation." The boy in Neisse was Salek "Zucker," from Będzin, who was castrated by Dr. Horst Schumann at Auschwitz. The priest

from the Church of Saints Peter and Paul was Father Jagła. While still in the
mental ward, the boy died in the mid-1950s.

Sources. On the SS man: Lola Potok Ackerfeld Blatt, *Licensed Mass
Murder* by Henry V. Dicks, *Commandant at Auschwitz* by Rudolf Höss,
Anatomy of the SS State by Helmut Krausnick et al., Auschwitz Museum.
On Höss, Hössler and Mengele: *Commandant at Auschwitz* by Rudolf
Höss, *Mengele: The Complete Story* by Gerald L. Posner and John Ware,
New York Times, December 15, 1945. On beatings in Gleiwitz: Lola Potok
Ackerfeld Blatt, Günther Ciesla, Józef Pijarczyk, Horst Planelt, Günter
Plasczyk, Lucjan Zenderowski. On the ardent interrogator: Elfryda
"Uracz." On the boy with black pants: Jakob "Schultz." On 227 prisons:
Zivilverschollenenliste des Suchdienstes des Deutschen Roten Kreuzes by
the German Red Cross, *Vertreibung und Vertreibungsverbrechen 1945–
1948* by the German Federal Archives. On punishments in Polish prisons:
Barek Eisenstein, Jadzia Ochsenhendler Eisenstein, Ze'ev Fryszman, Hela
Kleinhaut, Ruth Wilder, Sara "Zucker," Salek "Zucker," Statements Num-
ber 105, 191, 192 and 196 in *The Tragedy of Silesia* by Dr. Johannes Kaps,
Statements by Max Kroll (Ost-Dok. 2/236B/52) and Georg Paff (Ost-Dok.
2/236B/162) in the German Federal Archives. On castration at Auschwitz:
Five Chimneys by Olga Lengyel, *Mengele: The Complete Story* by Gerald
L. Posner and John Ware. *Sources for the Notes.* On "The prison director,
too": Statement by Max Kroll (Ost-Dok. 2/236B/52) in the German Federal
Archives.

"It annoyed her, but Lola. . . ."
The man who said, "I want schnitzel," was Horst Planelt, from Gleiwitz.
One man who ate from garbage pails was Günther Ciesla, from Gleiwitz, and
one man who ate from corridor floors was Horst Planelt. The guard who said,
"My *geburtztag*'s today," used the Polish name Heniek Kowalski, and the
guard who Moshe told, "Let's humiliate them," was Lucjan Zenderowski,
from Sosnowiec.

Sources. On food in Auschwitz: Lola Potok Ackerfeld Blatt, *Five Chim-
neys* by Olga Lengyel, *I Was a Doctor in Auschwitz* by Gisella Perl. On food
in Lola's prison: Günther Ciesla, Horst Planelt, Günter Plasczyk. On food for
Lola's guards: Jadzia Gutman Sapirstein "Banker," Rose "Grossman," Lucjan
Zenderowski. On the potato trip: Moshe "Grossman," Józef Pijarczyk, Lucjan
Zenderowski.

"No one at Lola's prison. . . ."
Jadzia's husband was David Sapirstein, Lola's mother's sister's son and the
brother of Regina Sapirstein, the girl who was hanged at Auschwitz. Jadzia's
concentration camp was at Neustadt-Glewe, in Mecklenburg, Germany, and
she was still there in April, when the girl guards in Gleiwitz apparently
burned the German's hair. She was liberated on Wednesday, May 2, 1945.

Sources. On Jadzia: Jadzia Gutman Sapirstein "Banker," Lola Potok Ackerfeld Blatt, Henry Cook, Gertie Gutman Cook, Regina Ochsenhendler

Eisenstein, Zlata Martyn Potok, Leibish Rechnic, Rózia Ickowicz Rechnic, Gucia Martyn Schickman, Bella Kaplan Zborowski. On Jadzia in Lola's prison: Lola Potok Ackerfeld Blatt, Zlata Martyn Potok, Gucia Martyn Schickman, Pincus Schickman, Lucjan Zenderowski.

"In the cells, the Germans. . . ."

The German who said, "Another panzer!" was Günter Plasczyk, from Gleiwitz, and the one who said, "Another panzer kaput!" was a German private who'd been caught at his parents' home in Gleiwitz. The three million victims of typhus from 1917 to 1925 were in Russia and Serbia. I don't know who the first typhus victim in Lola's prison was, but the symptoms are the classic ones and the nurse was Janinska. The cemetery was on the north side of Coselerstrasse, now Ulica Kozielska. Günther Ciesla, a German prisoner, said that the typhus became epidemic in August, the month it also became epidemic in Schwientochlowitz, nearby, and the prison sent a letter about it to the District Attorney's Office in Gleiwitz on September 29, 1945. The letter itself is lost, but the log of incoming letters at the District Attorney's Office says, "This refers to the outbreak of the epidemic of typhus in the prison." A letter from Shlomo Morel to the Commission for the Investigation of Crimes Against the Polish Nation, written in December, 1992, says, "Typhus was present in the prison in Gliwice." Among the Germans who died there were Josef Grzyb, Kibitz and Kalinke, all from Königshütte. The stopgap morgue was in the north corner of the women's prison, where the lower serif of the crossbar of the "T" would be. One guard who went to the cemetery was Józef Pijarczyk, and two prisoners who did were Georg Kowalski and Karl Urbanke.

Sources. On typhus in Lola's prison: Günther Ciesla, Stanisław Eweik, Józef Pijarczyk, Horst Planelt, Günter Plasczyk, Josef Wiescholek, Lucjan Zenderowski, Statements of Georg Kowalski (Ost-Dok. 2/236C/467) and Karl Urbanke (Ost-Dok. 2/236D/721) in the German Federal Archives, Archives of the District Attorney's Office in Gliwice. On form letters: Archives of the Provincial Court in Katowice. On the pirate chest: Jadzia Gutman Sapirstein "Banker," Lola Potok Ackerfeld Blatt, Zlata Martyn Potok. On the cemetery trip: Józef Pijarczyk, Statements of Georg Kowalski (Ost-Dok. 2/236C/467) and Karl Urbanke (Ost-Dok. 2/236D/721) in the German Federal Archives.

"At last, Lola counted heads. . . ."

Some conversation at the head count may have taken place at later ones. The goat-bearded man was Emanuel Stein, from Königshütte, and the wooden-legged man was Tomasz Kopółka, from Schwientochlowitz. The boy in the Hitler Youth was Günther Ciesla, from Gleiwitz. The platoon sergeant in the Storm Section—the Sturmabteilung or SA—was Paweł Mróz, from Königshütte, and his three troops were Josef Krawczyk, Jan Manka and Piotr Szydłowski, all from Königshütte. The SS man who'd burned off his tattoo was Josef Gorka, from Gleiwitz, the SS woman was Małgorzata Gröner Zapora, from Gleiwitz, and the SS man from Auschwitz was Georg. Lola's cousin at Belsen was Rózia Ickowicz, from Będzin, and the two cousins were

Adela "Glickman," from Nifka, who worked for the Office in Kattowitz but beat the SS man in Dziedzice, and Rivka "Glickman," from Dombrowa. Rivka's necklace was taken away at Auschwitz. The Jew who hit the German at Neisse was David Feuerstein, from Będzin. One man killed by a truck in Gleiwitz was Ferdinand Perenerstorfer, from Gleiwitz.

I don't know how many people died in Lola's prison. If there were a thousand prisoners, and if they died at the rate of the guards, there would have been twenty-five to fifty deaths, but if they died at the rate of other prisoners in Poland and Poland-administered Germany, there would have been two hundred to five hundred deaths. Of three Jewish prison officials in Gleiwitz, Lola didn't remember that Germans died, Jadzia said, "I don't know," and Moshe refused to talk about it. Of three Polish guards, Lucjan Zenderowski said, "I remember two," Józef Pijarczyk said, "I remember six," and Stanisław Eweik said, "Only Lola knew." Of six German prisoners, Günther Ciesla, in whose cell eight of ten prisoners died, said, "Certainly more than half died," Karl Urbanke wrote, "Cases of death occurred everywhere daily," Georg Kowalski wrote, "Many died. I once had to carry four corpses," Josef Wiescholek said, "I don't know anyone who died," and Horst Planelt and Günter Plasczyk apparently left before the epidemic began.

German prisoners of war also died of hunger, dysentery and typhus in American camps in the American occupation zone. According to James Bacque, an author, there were 217,223 deaths attributable to treatment in U.S. army camps, but I don't accept this. Dr. Alfred de Zayas, a human rights officer with the United Nations, told me the number was 70,000, and the American army in February, 1946, said it was 15,225.

On coming to Gleiwitz, Zlata had said to Lola, "What do you do?" and Lola had told her, "The same things the Germans did to us," meaning the same things the Germans did to the Jews. Lola, of course, and the rest of the Office, hadn't done the same things at all. They hadn't planned the extermination of the German people. They hadn't mobilized all the Jews and the Jewish state: there *was* no Jewish state. They hadn't acted without any provocation, hadn't sent any Germans to cyanide chambers and crematoriums, and, in the end, didn't kill even two percent of what the Germans did. Less creditably, the Jews in the Office had acted willfully, but the Germans had mostly had orders, and the Jews—who'd studied the Torah—had known they were doing wrong, but the Germans had mostly thought that *they* were doing right. Myself, I would never contend that Lola or anyone else in the Office did just what the Germans did, and I would never contend that they and the Germans were equivalent, even morally.

Sources. On Lola's head count: Günther Ciesla, Lucjan Zenderowski. On the head count at Auschwitz: *Five Chimneys* by Olga Lengyel, *Smoke over Birkenau* by Seweryna Szmaglewska. On Lola's prisoners: Günther Ciesla, Krystyna Zielinska Dudzinska, Hatko Ewald, Horst Planelt, Günter Plasczyk, Josef Wiescholek, Lucjan Zenderowski, Statements of Elfriede Gawlik (Ost-Dok. 2/236C/503) and Angela Schymitzek (Ost-Dok. 2/236D/652) in the German Federal Archives, Archives of the Provincial Commission (for

Katowice) for the Investigation of Crimes Against the Polish Nation, Archives of the Provincial Court in Katowice, *Uns Geht die Sonne Nicht Unter* by the Hitler Youth. On the Będzin girls: Adela "Glickman," Rózia Ickowicz Rechnic, Rivka "Glickman Singer." On other deaths in Lola's prison: Heinz "Becker," Jakob "Schultz," Josef Wiescholek. On Lola: Lola Potok Ackerfeld Blatt, Genia Rosenzweig Tigel. *Sources for the Notes.* On the death estimates: Günther Ciesla, Stanisław Eweik, Józef Pijarczyk, Lucjan Zenderowski, *Vertreibung und Vertreibungsverbrechen 1945–1948* by the German Federal Archives. On German POWs: Alfred de Zayas, *Other Losses* by James Bacque.

"The wind in her hair. . . ."
The Russian colonel was Colonel Zacharow. Pincus, whose last name was Martyn and who'd been in the concentration camp at Mauthausen, in Austria, came to Gleiwitz late in July. In Czechoslovakia, the counterpart of the Office of State Security was the Committee for National Security, the Sbor Národni Bezpecnosti, the SNB. Pincus's friend in Prague wasn't a Jew. Pincus had read his Hillel story in *Pirkei Arot (Ethics of the Fathers)* II:7, and Lola's mother got her Talmud quotation from Sotah 8b and Megillah 12b.
Sources. On the Russian colonel: Lola Potok Ackerfeld Blatt, Stanisław Eweik, David Feuerstein, Jadzia Rappaport Ackerfeld Jacobs, Pincus Martyn, Zlata Martyn Potok, Pola Reif, Gucia Martyn Schickman, Shlomo "Singer." On Pincus: Pincus Martyn. On Jews in Czechoslovakia: Istvan Deak, Andre Korbonski.

9

"The weather was in. . . ."
Adam arrested the priest in June. "Be ye therefore merciful" is in Luke 6:36. Mercy to oxen and asses is in Deuteronomy 5:14, 22:10 and 25:4 and to birds in Deuteronomy 22:67. David and the Gibeonites are in II Samuel 21:1–9 and, in the Talmud, in Yebamoth 79a. "And show mercy" is in Deuteronomy 13:18, and Maimonides' words are in *Isurai Biah* 19:17. The mines at Schwientochlowitz had belonged to Deutschlandgrube, or Germany Mines. Inmates of Schwientochlowitz called it a death camp, death mill, and extermination camp.
Adam was stricter with Germans than with Jews and Poles. Once, a Jewish boy played with a Polish policeman's gun and accidentally killed him, but Adam just put the boy on a Toonerville trolley and told him, "Get out of Gleiwitz." Adam also released some Poles whose "crimes" were to be anticommunists.
Sources. On Adam and the Catholic priest: Adam "Krawecki." On sentences for the SS: Adam "Krawecki," Judge Adam Panek. On ten judges in Kattowitz: Heinz "Becker," Pinek Mąka. On Schwientochlowitz: Heinz "Becker," Statements of Albert Cyprian (Ost-Dok. 2/236C/258), Helena

Hoinkes (Ost-Dok. 2/236C/456) and Max Witkowski (Ost-Dok. 2/235/178, 2/235/183 and 2/235/185) in the German Federal Archives, *Die Arbeitslager in Myslowitz, Schwientochlowitz und Eintrachthütte* (in *Vermächtnis der Lebenden*) by Konrad Anders. On the words *death camp:* Statements of G. Arbansky (Ost-Dok. 2/236B/100), Martha Helisch Kempny (Ost-Dok. 2/237/162), Max Witkowski (Ost-Dok. 2/235/178, 2/235/183 and 2/235/185) and Günther Wollny (Ost-Dok. 2/236C/297) in the German Federal Archives.

"The commandant of Schwientochlowitz. . . ."
Shlomo, like Lola, was nominally the deputy commandant till he was named commandant on June 6, 1945. Shlomo's father was Chaim, his mother was Hannah, his brothers were Itzak, Josef and Israel. "You shall not steal" is, of course, the Eighth Commandment, in Exodus 20:15, and "They will catch you" is in Sanhedrin 7a. Shlomo's father and mother and Shlomo's brother Israel were in Garbów, in the barn of Stanisław Gąsik, when the Poles, led by Bronisław Lalak, picked them up on December 21, 1942, and they were shot by Władysław Mazurczak, a Polish policeman. Shlomo and Itzak were hidden by Józef and Genowefa Filipek, two Poles, and Itzak was killed on a sleigh in Ługów in December, 1943, while Shlomo was in Starościn. Shlomo's brother Josef disappeared in Russia. Shlomo's unit of Jewish partisans became part of the Holod Battalion under Captain Aleksander Skotnicki, known as Zemsta. Shlomo crossed the Wieprz on March 15, 1944, was liberated by Russians on July 22, 1944, and, with one or two hundred other Jewish partisans, lived in quarters on Ulica Ogrodowa in Lublin till August. Then, Juzwak, known as General Witold, who was the police chief for Poland, came to Lublin and told Shlomo's superiors, Yechiel Grynspan and Shmuel "Gross," "You can't just sit and do nothing," and he assigned the Jews to the Office and to the Militia, the Polish police. Shlomo was assigned to Lublin and, on February 2, 1945, when the Russians liberated it, to Kattowitz.
Shlomo's camp at Schwientochlowitz, which under the SS had been a sub-camp of Auschwitz, opened for Germans early in February, 1945. I don't know how many of Shlomo's guards were Jews. The commandant of the camp at the Polska mines, also in Schwientochlowitz, told the Commission for the Investigation of Crimes Against the Polish Nation that Shlomo's guards were Jews *exclusively;* Elfryda "Uracz," a prisoner at Shlomo's camp, overheard that the deputy commandant was a Jew; and the clerk at Shlomo's camp, Wacław Łochocki, said that some of the Jewish guards were Jasny, Sachs and Skibinski. But Łochocki himself wasn't a Jew, nor was the woman guard who Shlomo later married, and the former prisoners at Shlomo's camp confirm that the guards were both Catholics and Jews. The *erntedankfest* or harvest festival at Majdanek was on November 3, 1943, and Shlomo was told about it by Smolak, a Polish courier, in Woła Przemysławska. Six managers, guards and kapos from Majdanek—Wilhelm Gerstenmeier, Edmund Pohlmann, Theodor Scholen, Heinrich Stalp, Antoni Thernas and Herman

Vögel—were sentenced to death on December 2, 1944. One hanged himself, and the other five were hanged at Majdanek. One person who didn't know the second and third verses of the Horst Wessel Song was Gerhard Gruschka, age fourteen, who learned them the following morning so Shlomo wouldn't hit him and tell him, "Sing it, I say!"

Sources. On Shlomo in Garbów: Shlomo Morel. On Shlomo in the Jewish partisans: Efraim Blaichman, Shmuel "Gross," Efraim Lewin, Shlomo Morel, *The War of the Doomed: Jewish Armed Resistance in Poland 1942–1944* by Shmuel Krakowski. On Catholic and Jewish guards: Piotr Bryś, Eric van Calsteren, Archives of the Provincial Commission (for Katowice) for the Investigation of Crimes Against the Polish Nation, *Dziennik Zachodni*, July 20, 1992. On Shlomo at Schwientochlowitz: Heinz "Becker," Shlomo Morel, Statements of G. Arbansky (Ost-Dok. 2/236B/100) and Paul Cyl (Ost-Dok. 2/236D/726) in the German Federal Archives, Protocol signed by Shlomo for the Provincial Commission (for Katowice) for the Investigation of Crimes Against the Polish Nation, on February 27, 1991. On Majdanek: Efraim Lewin, Shlomo Morel, *Obóz Koncentracyjny* by Czesław Rajca and Anna Wiśniewska. *Sources for the Notes*. On Shlomo in Lublin: Shmuel "Gross," Shlomo Morel. On Gruschka: Gerhard Gruschka.

"The next night, the sergeant. . . ."

"Ascension crew" is *himmelfahrtkommando* in German. At the mass grave, at the edge of the old cemetery in Schwientochlowitz, there now is a stone that says, TO THE VICTIMS OF THE CAMP AT ŚWIĘTOCHŁOWICE/ZGODA, and, though the guards fired to scare them away, the neighbors remember seeing the victims buried. Some incidents at Shlomo's party in Schwientochlowitz may have happened at Shlomo's parties later. Himmler ordered on August 16, 1935, "Any independent individual action against the Jews by any member of the SS is most strictly forbidden," and, among others, an SS second lieutenant who had killed them in Alexandria, Egypt, was convicted of "gross dereliction of duty" on June 9, 1943.

Sources. On nights at Schwientochlowitz: Heinz "Becker," Günther Wollny, Statements of Heinz Biernot (Ost-Dok. 2/236C/431), Paul Cyl (Ost-Dok. 2/236D/726), Albert Cyprian (Ost-Dok. 2/236C/258), Erich Kischel (Ost-Dok. 2/236B/3 and 2/236B/5), Viktor Kubitza (Ost-Dok. 2/236B/227), Max Ogorek (Ost-Dok. 2/236C/362), Leo Schwierzok (Ost-Dok. 2/236D/635), Josef Sczakiel (Ost-Dok. 2/236B/130), Max Witkowski (Ost-Dok. 2/235/178, 2/235/183 and 2/235/185) and Günther Wollny (Ost-Dok. 2/236C/297) in the German Federal Archives. On the mass grave: Józef Blaza, Adelajd Małota, Jan Michen, Eric van Calsteren. On the Germans mostly from Gleiwitz: Adam "Krawecki," Johanna Frystatzki (Ost-Dok. 2/230/2, also published as Number 215 in *Die Vertreibung der Deutschen Bevölkerung aus den Gebieten Östlich der Oder-Neisse* by Theodor Schieder) in the German Federal Archives. On Shlomo's party: Heinz "Becker," Efraim Blaichman, Moshe Mąka, Shlomo Morel, Günther Wollny. On the SS at Auschwitz: *Anatomy of the SS State* by Helmut Krausnick et al. On the human cube: Moshe Mąka, Günther Wollny, Statements of Heinz Biernot (Ost-Dok. 2/236C/431), Max Witkowski (Ost-Dok. 2/235/178, 2/235/183 and 2/235/185) and Günther Wollny (Ost-Dok. 2/236C/297) in the German Federal Archives. *Sources for the Notes.* On the SS in Alexandria: *Anatomy of the SS State* by Helmut Krausnick et al.

"At last, the tired guests. . . ."

Estimates of the camp population were from 1,500 to 6,000 people. At night, the guards went to the women's barracks, chose half a dozen women, took them to their quarters outside the barbed wire, and gang-raped them. Some estimates of the body count during the typhus epidemic were sixty to eighty, eighty to one hundred, and more than one hundred people per day. Some estimates of the total body count were as high as nine-tenths of the German prisoners. One prisoner saw the head-count report in September or October: it said there were 345 Germans left. At the city clerk's office in Świętochłowice are the death certificates for 1,800 to 2,000 prisoners at Shlomo's camp, but Shlomo didn't report every death. According to Dietmar Brehmer, the head of the German community in Katowice, half of the Germans whose relatives died in Shlomo's camp didn't get any death certificates, so Brehmer estimates that as many as four thousand died. I don't know if Adam's priest was among them. In 1945, at least 131 Catholic priests died in Silesia, and at least three died at Schwientochlowitz: Eggert, from Kanth; Heidenreich (who may have been a Lutheran pastor) from Beuthen; and Edgar Wolf, from Schönwald. I know of no Catholic priest at Schwientochlowitz who survived.

Sources. On Monday, May 7: Heinz "Becker," Moshe Mąka, Günther Wollny, Statement of Heinz Biernot (Ost-Dok. 2/236C/431) in the German Federal Archives, Letter from Shlomo to the Commission for the Investigation of Crimes Against the Polish Nation, December, 1992. On Shlomo's visits: Heinz "Becker," Günther Wollny, Statements of Heinz Biernot (Ost-Dok. 2/236C/431), Paul Cyl (Ost-Dok. 2/236D/726), Albert Cyprian (Ost-Dok. 2/236C/258), Erich Kischel (Ost-Dok. 2/236B/3 and 2/236B/5), Viktor Kubitza (Ost-Dok. 2/236B/227), Max Ogorek (Ost-Dok. 2/236C/362), Leo Schwierzok (Ost-Dok. 2/236D/635), Josef Sczakiel (Ost-Dok. 2/236B/130), Max Witkowski (Ost-Dok. 2/235/178, 2/235/183 and 2/235/185) and Günther Wollny (Ost-Dok. 2/236C/297) in the German Federal Archives. On the body count: Statements of Johanna Frystatzki (Ost-Dok. 2/230/2, also published as Number 215 in *Die Vertreibung der Deutschen Bevölkerung aus den Gebieten Östlich der Oder-Neisse* by Theodor Schieder), Paul Cyl (Ost-Dok. 2/236D/726), Max Ogorek (Ost-Dok. 2/236C/362), Georg Samol (Ost-Dok. 2/236C/330), Max Witkowski (Ost-Dok. 2/235/178, 2/235/183 and 2/235/185) in the German Federal Archives. On "NOTICE": Heinz "Becker." On beating the Germans: Heinz "Becker," Elfryda "Uracz," Statements of Paul Cyl (Ost-Dok. 2/236D/726), Martha Helisch Kempny (Ost-Dok. 2/237/162), Max Witkowski (Ost-Dok. 2/235/178, 2/235/183 and 2/235/185) and Günther Wollny (Ost-Dok. 2/236C/297) in the German Federal Archives, Letter from Roman Ladenberger to Albert de Zayas, *Die Arbeitslager in Myslowitz, Schwientochlowitz und Eintrachthütte* (in *Vermächtnis der Lebenden*) by Konrad Anders. On typhus: Heinz "Becker," Statements of G. Arbansky (Ost-Dok. 2/236B/100), Kunigunde Arondarczyk (Ost-Dok. 2/236D/724), Heinz Biernot (Ost-Dok. 2/236C/431), Johanna Frystatzki (Ost-Dok. 2/230/2, also published as Number 215 in *Die Vertreibung der Deutschen Bevölkerung aus den Gebieten Östlich der Oder-Neisse* by Theodor Schieder), Helena Hoinkes (Ost-Dok. 2/236C/456), Walter Freund (Ost-Dok. 2/236C/351, also published as Number 216 in *Die Vertreibung der Deutschen Bevölkerung aus den Gebieten Östlich der Oder-Neisse* by Theodor Schieder) and Günther Wollny (Ost-Dok. 2/236C/297) in the German Federal Archives, Statement Number 16 in *The Tragedy of Silesia* by Dr. Johannes Kaps. On the ascension command: Heinz "Becker," Statement of Helena Hoinkes (Ost-Dok. 2/236C/456) in the German Federal Archives. On the body count: Heinz "Becker," Statements of Drabik (Ost-Dok. 2/236D/680), D. Häusler (Ost-Dok. 1/251/3) and Max Ogorek (Ost-Dok. 2/236C/362) in the German Federal Archives. On "What the Germans couldn't do : Heinz "Becker," Statement of Gertrud Schyma (Ost-Dok. 2/236D/704) in the German Federal Archives. On Shlomo's party: Ephraim Blaichman, Moshe Maka, Shlomo Morel. On two, three or four thousand dead: Dietmar Brehmer, Michael Gavshon, Marek Grodzki. *Sources for the Notes.* On rape: Dorota Niessporek Boreczek, Elfryda "Uracz." On 345 Germans: Gerhard Gruschka. On priests dying: Statements of D. Häusler (Ost-Dok. 1/251/3), Max Ogorek (Ost-Dok. 2/236C/362), Günther Wollny (Ost-Dok. 2/236C/297) in the German Federal Archives, *Schönwald* by Pieter Bielke, *Martyrdom of Silesian Priests* by Dr. Johannes Kaps.

Other corroboratory statements on Schwientochlowitz are by Erich Kischel (Ost-Dok. 2/236B/3 and 2/236B/5), Karl Kukla (Ost-Dok. 2/236C/372), Johann Kworka (Ost-Dok. 2/236C/388), Hedwig Lücke (Ost-Dok. 2/236C/512), Hedwig Respondek (Ost-Dok. 2/236C/462), Inge Rotter (Ost-Dok. 2/236C/391), Gertrud Furgol Schnapka (Ost-Dok. 2/236C/369), Anneliese Thiele (Ost-Dok. 2/236D/692), and others in the German Federal Archives.

"The Germans at Schwientochlowitz. . . ."
The man who said, "This place is hell," was Franz Ciupka, from Beuthen, and one man who smuggled messages out was Heinz "Becker." The Hitler Youth from Gleiwitz was Eric van Calsteren, who wasn't a German but a Dutchman and who was fourteen years old, and who died of a heart attack on February 16, 1993, in Ryswyk, Holland. A man who escaped with him and wasn't caught was Bartfeld, an SS soldier, who probably died in the 1980s in Germany. The boy's tobacco was Russian, but Shlomo's was Polish, so coarse that he had to roll it in newspaper paper. The man who said, "I'd rather be ten years in Auschwitz" was Professor Morawietz, a Pole. Another prisoner who'd been at Auschwitz, a German, said, "The methods used by the Ger-

mans at Auschwitz were horrible, but the methods of the Poles are even more horrible." One civilian in Schwientochlowitz who heard the German screams and saw the German bodies called the process a "special action," the word that the SS had used for the cyanide-and-cremation process at Auschwitz. "For safety's sake," the British didn't identify the Catholic priest, but he spoke to R. W. F. Bashford, a Public Relations Officer for the Advanced Headquarters of the Control Commission for Germany (British Element). Bashford wrote the "melancholy report," using the Polish name of Schwientochlowitz, Świętochłowice, and Sir William Strang, the Political Adviser to the Commander in Chief, sent it to Oliver C. Harvey at the Foreign Office in London on September 25, 1945. The commandants of Potulice were Czajka, Dzieczół and Stolarski, and the Jewish guard was Isidor. The song that I've translated as "All the dogs" is not, in fact, about dogs and hot dogs but about *möpse* and *rollmöpse*—pugs and herrings. The commandant of Hohensalza was Władysław Dopierała. The senator was William Langer of North Dakota, the British ambassador was Victor Cavendish Bentinck, and the American one was Arthur Lane. Pinek didn't remember that the Red Cross was the American one, but (except for the Polish one) the American one was the only one in Poland, having arrived in February, 1945. The International Committee of the Red Cross, in Geneva, in fact sent delegates to Auschwitz in September, 1944, but the Germans restricted them. "A rumor," a delegate wrote, "was going round that the camp was equipped with a very modern shower room where groups of detainees were being gassed." The delegates in Pinek's office said they'd report to Warsaw, and I have assumed that they did.

Sources. On getting word out: Heinz "Becker," Hedwig Rogier. On the Hitler Youth from Gleiwitz: Eric van Calsteren, Gerhard Gruschka, Günther Wollny, Statements of Heinz Biernot (Ost-Dok. 2/236C/431), Max Ogorek (Ost-Dok. 2/236C/362) and Günther Wollny (Ost-Dok. 2/236C/297) in the German Federal Archives. On the man who'd once been at Auschwitz: Günther Wollny, Statement of Günther Wollny (Ost-Dok. 2/236C/297) in the German Federal Archives. On the priest and the British: Statement of R. W. F. Bashford, *FO371/46990*, Public Records Office in Kew, Richmond, Surrey, England. On the water treatment: Dorota Niessporek Boreczek, Elfryda "Uracz," Statement of Martha Helisch Kempny (Ost-Dok. 2/237/162) in the German Federal Archives. On Potulice: Statement of P. L. (268) in *Die Vertreibung der Deutschen Bevölkerung aus den Gebieten Östlich der Oder-Neisse* by Theodor Schieder, Statements of Christa-Helene Gause von Shirach (Ost-Dok. 2/148/103) and E. Zindler (Ost-Dok. 2/64/18) in the German Federal Archives. On Myslowitz: Kurt Hellebrandt, Statements of Hugo Dohn (Ost-Dok. 2/236D/735) and Mathias Hemschik (Ost-Dok. 2/236B/106) in the German Federal Archives, *Die Arbeitslager in Myslowitz, Schwientochlowitz und Eintrachthütte* (in *Vermächtnis der Lebenden*) by Konrad Anders. On Grottkau: Statement of Joseph Buhl (343) in *Die Vertreibung der Deutschen Bevölkerung aus den Gebieten Östlich der Oder-Neisse* by Theodor Schieder. On Hohensalza:

Statement of R. S. (267) in *Die Vertreibung der Deutschen Bevölkerung aus den Gebieten Östlich der Oder-Neisse* by Theodor Schieder. On Blechhammer: Statement of Ernst Leistritz (Ost-Dok. 2/198/47) in the German Federal Archives. On 1,255 camps: *Zivilverschollenenliste des Suchdienstes des Deutschen Roten Kreuzes* by the German Red Cross, *Vertreibung und Vertreibungsverbrechen 1945–1948* by the German Federal Archives. On twenty to fifty percent of the Germans: *Vertreibung und Vertreibungsverbrechen 1945–1948* by the German Federal Archives. On Churchill: *Parliamentary Debates, House of Commons, Fifth Series, Volume 413.* On another member of Commons: *From the Ruins of the Reich* by Douglas Botting. On the American senator: *Appendix to the Congressional Record, Volume 92, Part 12, Page A4778, August 2, 1946.* On the British and American ambassadors: *Nemesis at Potsdam* by Alfred de Zayas. On the Red Cross: Pinek Mąka. *Sources for the Notes.* On the special action: *Dziennik Zachodni,* July 20, 1992. On "The methods used by the Germans": Statement by Max Ogorek (Ost-Dok. 2/236C/362) in the German Federal Archives. On the American Red Cross: Donald Castleberry, Patrick Gilbo, Harry Grady, Archives of the International Committee of the Red Cross, Archives of the Swedish Red Cross, Letter from G. R. More, Deputy Director, Civilian Relief, Insular and Foreign Operations, American Red Cross, to the Honorable Arthur Bliss Lane, Department of State, July 3, 1945, in the U.S. National Archives, *Foreign War Relief Operations, World War II, July 1, 1940–June 30, 1946* by the American Red Cross, *The Red Cross Courier,* October, 1946. On the Red Cross in Auschwitz: *The Work of the International Committee of the Red Cross for Civilian Detainees in German Concentration Camps* by the International Committee of the Red Cross.

Other corroboratory statements on Potulice are Statements of K. E. (269), E. K. (266), Sister M. (270) and R. S. (267) in *Die Vertreibung der Deutschen Bevölkerung aus den Gebieten Östlich der Oder-Neisse* by Theodor Schieder, Statements by Marta Büller (Ost-Dok. 2/60/11), Heinrich Dinkelmann (Ost-Dok. 2/73/32), Margarete Fischer (Ost-Dok. 2/137/45), Ella Gierszowski (Ost-Dok. 2/55/7), Sister Erna Kelm (Ost-Dok. 2/51/99), Anna George (Ost-Dok. 2/52/29), Ingeborg Spandera (Ost-Dok. 2/131/55) and others in the German Federal Archives. Other corroboratory statements on Myslowitz are by Pavil Blacha (Ost-Dok. 2/236C/318), Raimund Bronder (Ost-Dok. 2/236C/270), Konrad Filippek (Ost-Dok. 2/236D/641), Florian Kernbach (Ost-Dok. 2/236D/622 and 2/236D/633), Paul Klaus (Ost-Dok. 2/236D/746), Franz Mainka (Ost-Dok. 2/236B/208), Hedwig Michalik (Ost-Dok. 2/236B/48), Cäcilie Muschalik (Ost-Dok. 2/236C/309), Georg Paff (Ost-Dok. 2/236B/162), Georg Pielka (Ost-Dok. 2/236D/637), and others in the German Federal Archives.

"Jacob Berman, from Warsaw. . . ."

The "Polish pro-tem Government" was first the Polish National Committee and then the Polish Committee of National Liberation. The palace in Warsaw was the Belwedr Palace, the office of Bolesław Bierut, the President of Poland. In 1945, Jacob was technically the Undersecretary of State, but he had no title in the Office of State Security. The two Jewish ministers were Jacob Sawicki and Hilary Minc. It was Sawicki who said, "I'll work on it," and Minc who dozed off on Pinek's sofa. Pinek's brother was Moshe Mąka, from Będzin. Gomulka's word for *scrounge* was *szabrować* and for *gang* was *grupa*. According to the International Committee of the Red Cross, in Geneva, it wasn't allowed to visit the camps for German POWs in Poland until the summer of 1946, and it was never allowed to visit the camps for German civilians. At the order of the German Parliament, a secret study was made by the German Federal Archives and was delivered to Parliament on May 28, 1974. The report concluded, "In the Polish camps and prisons, there were probably 200,000 or more people, with a death rate of twenty to fifty percent. This would mean that 40,000 to 100,000 but certainly more than 60,000 people perished there." Since at some camps the death rate was fifty percent, 40,000 would be too low, and since at some camps the death rate was twenty percent, 100,000 would be too high, and I've estimated that 60,000 to 80,000 died. The number, in fact, may be higher, for though the report doesn't say so, the death rate at some camps was eighty percent. From 50,000 to 60,000 Jews died at Bergen-Belsen, and 43,045 people, both Jews and gentiles, at Buchenwald.

Sources. On Jacob: Paula Oleska, Teresa Torańska, Interviews with William Tonesk in *Nowy Dziennik (Polish American Daily News)* on June 9, 1987, and with Józef Światło on Radio Free Europe, June 11, 1954, *Mówi Józef Światło* by Zbigniew Błażyński, *Them* by Teresa Torańska. On Gomulka: *Gomulka* by Nicholas Bethell. On Pinek's meeting with Jacob and Gomulka: Pinek Mąka. On the Red Cross: Heinz "Becker," Alfred de Zayas, International Committee of the Red Cross, Swedish Red Cross. On sixty thousand to eighty thousand deaths: *Vertreibung und Vertreibungsverbrechen 1945–1948* by the German Federal Archives. On Belsen and Buchenwald: Aaron Brightbart.

10

"At her home. . . ."

The SS man from Auschwitz was Georg. The guards told Lola about him, and I've "reconstructed" some of that conversation from the facts of Georg's case. On another occasion, Lola indeed released some innocent prisoners saying, "You see? We Poles aren't like you Germans." The Jew in Kattowitz prison was Stasiak, and Josef phoned Kliszko in Warsaw.

Sources. On Lola's home: Gucia Martyn Schickman. On the German from the Auschwitz SS: Günther Ciesla. On trials in Gleiwitz: Robert Geilke, Adam Panek. On Lola, the Jewish guards, and the German: Günther Ciesla, Stanisław Eweik. On the Jew in Kattowitz prison: Josef Jurkowski. *Sources for the Notes.* On "You see?": Stanisław Eweik.

"By now the typhus. . . ."

The guard who said, "I was at Auschwitz!" was Lucjan Zenderowski, from

Sosnowiec, and the SS woman who'd said, "You pig!" was Irma Grese. She had railed at length at the Jew from Holland, but I've just guessed what the words would have been. The story of Abraham and God is in Genesis 18:23–32. The head-count-*führer*, or *rapportführer*, at Auschwitz was Taube.

Sources. On Lola's head count: Lucjan Zenderowski. On the head count at Auschwitz: Lola Potok Ackerfeld Blatt. On the Germans in Gleiwitz: Archives of the Provincial Court in Katowice. On the head-count-*führer* at Auschwitz: *Return to Auschwitz* by Kitty Hart, *Auschwitz* by Sara Nomberg-Przytyk.

"'*Do paki!*' 'To the box!'. . . ."

The two guards who died were from Warsaw. Some of Lola's conversation with the Jewish boy may have happened later. "Let sins disappear" is in Psalms 104:35 as translated in the Talmud in Berakoth 10a. It says there that the wife of Rabbi Meir, Beruria, told him, "Is it written the *sinners?* It is written the *sins.*" "What does the Lord require" is in Micah 6:8.

Sources. On the guards: Lola Potok Ackerfeld Blatt, Józef Pijarczyk, Lucjan Zenderowski. On the Jew whipping the German: Lola Potok Ackerfeld Blatt, Horst Planelt. On Lola in Będzin: Lola Potok Ackerfeld Blatt.

"The boy looked at Lola. . . ."

The Gleiwitz office of the Office of State Security was in the old auto school at Klosterstrasse 10. The Kattowitz boy who was executed was a Ukrainian lieutenant in Implementation who wasn't a Jew. "It's our own choice," or, more literally, "Man's actions are in man's own hands," is in *Yad*, Chapter 5, by Moses Maimonides.

Sources. On Lola's meeting: Lola Potok Ackerfeld Blatt, Lucjan Zenderowski. On the changes in Lola's prison: Stanisław Eweik, Józef Pijarczyk, Lucjan Zenderowski. On the Kattowitz boy: Pinek Mąka.

"Well, maybe God. . . ."

One Jew from Będzin who Elijah "selected" was Moshe Blatt, the second husband of Hannah Potok, the widowed wife of Lola's and Elijah's brother Jacob. Moshe's friend Hille Hollander, from Będzin, interceded for him, but Elijah said, "Let him go. He's *dreck.*" Elijah was waiting for Zlata at Lola's sister Cyrla's home in Pas-de-Calais, and David and Ada were in Schwandorf, Germany. Of the four brothers, the one in the Polish cavalry was Barek, the one in the French army was Daniel, the one in a Polish squadron of the Royal Air Force was Chaim, and the one in the American Army—in the Air Corps—was Mordka. The sister, Cyrla, had also gotten out of Poland and was married to Michel Frydman. Some love-struck boarders were Shmuel Schickman and Gucia Martyn, and Leibisch Jacobs and Jadzia Rappaport Ackerfeld, who all left to Germany. One boarder who got the Germans' money was Zlata's nephew Josef Martyn. Himmler's speech was at Posen on October 4, 1943. "A man who would go against monsters" is in *Beyond Good and Evil* by Friedrich Nietzsche.

Sources. On Elijah: Edzia Gutman Ackerfeld, Lola Potok Ackerfeld Blatt, Mendel Blatt, Zlata Martyn Potok. On David: Lola Potok Ackerfeld Blatt, Ada Potok Halperin. On Lola's other brothers and sisters: Lola Potok Acker- feld Blatt. On the pirate chest: Jadzia Gutman Sapirstein "Banker," Lola Potok Ackerfeld Blatt, Zlata Martyn Potok. On Adam: Adam "Krawecki." On the SS at Auschwitz: *Commandant at Auschwitz,* by Rudolf Höss. According to *Injustice Armed,* a doctoral dissertation on Höss by Mark Steven Clinton at Claremont Graduate School, "Scholars generally agree" that Höss was telling the truth in *Commandant at Auschwitz,* though Clinton himself dis- putes it. On Himmler: *SS: Alibi of a Nation* by Gerald Reitlinger.

"Saturday, September 8. . . ."
One ex-mistress of an SS man was Beata. The first Jewish chief of Impris- onment, Wassersturm, emigrated with her to France, leaving the job to Chaim. Seydlitzstrasse now is Ulica Poniatowskiego, and Chaim's hole was in Badkowice. Chaim said, "Kill this man," of Kuczynski, an SS man in Będzin, among others. The .25 (or 6.35 millimeter) automatic was a Mauser vest- pocket pistol, a WTP. Chaim changed his last name too, to Studencki. His proper title was Director of the Department of Prisons and Camps for Sile- sia.
Sources. On Lola bringing bread: Stanisław Eweik. On Chaim: Lola Potok Ackerfeld Blatt, Stanisław Gazda, Ada Neufeld Potok Halperin, Ilana Stu- dencki Hammer, Josef Jurkowski, Eva Studencki Landau, Efraim Lewin, Pinek Mąka, Gaby Mamu, Shlomo Morel, Józef Pijarczyk, Ze'ev Sharone, Zizi Stoppler, Max Studniberg, Genia Rosenzweig Tigel, Edward Witek, Lucjan Zenderowski, *Tel Aviv Telephone Directory.*

11

"'Be good to Germans'. . . ."
The President of Poland was Bolesław Bierut. His decree of February 28 was Dziennik Ustaw Pos. 30, Chapter III, Article 18, and the decree of March 2 was Dziennik Ustaw Pos. 45. The tax-collector (a cask-gager) was Konrad Reck, who was the owner of 29 Lange Reihe, Lola's most plausible third home. The Catholic across the street was Sławska, from Kielce, the mailman was Józef Strzysz, his home was at 36 Lange Reihe, and his daugh- ters were Helene, Klara and Elisabeth. Gerhardt Ronskowski, of Gleiwitz, sang *"Lumpen, knochen,"* in 1952 and was imprisoned for it. The Minister of Repossessed Territories after November 9, 1945, was Gomulka. Poland pos- sessed Danzig until 1772, East Prussia until 1660, Pomerania, including Stet- tin, until 1637, and Silesia, including Breslau, until 1335. After the war, the Polish police were called the Militia. In some cities, like Kattowitz and Bres- lau, almost all the police were Catholic but the police chief was Jewish: Pinek Pakanowski in Kattowitz and Shmuel "Gross" in Breslau. In other cities, like Ziębice and Żabkowice, about twenty-five percent of the police themselves

were Jewish. The German who said, "I don't keep coal!" was Josef Wiescholek, who lived at Am Bergraben 28, now Przewózowa 28, in Gleiwitz. The law against mocking the Polish People's Republic (and Polish police) was Number 152 of the Criminal Code, and Wiescholek was in Lola's prison from May to October, 1945. In July, 1945, a German baby four days old was in Lassowitz concentration camp, near Tarnowitz, in Silesia. The northern camp was Potulice, near Nagel, and the Jewish doctor was Cedrowski. The police chief for Silesia was Colonel Kratko, from Lublin, the governor for the Neisse area was Władyslaw Wędzicha, and the police chief in Neisse was Lieutenant Bugajski, Bugalski or Bukalski. Just west of Neisse, twenty-five percent of the Ziębice and Żabkowice police were Jews, and I have assumed that some of the Neisse police were too. Bielitz, or Bielitzfelde, north of Neisse, isn't Bielsko-Biała but Bielice, Poland. On the trucks were 897 men and women and probably about a hundred children.

   Sources. On the Polish decrees: Introductory Description and Volume III of *Die Vertreibung der Deutschen Bevölkerung aus den Gebieten Östlich der Oder-Neisse* by Theodor Schieder. On milk-cans: Statement Number 53 in *The Tragedy of Silesia* by Dr. Johannes Kaps. On Poles throwing out Germans: Lola Potok Ackerfeld Blatt, Elisabeth Strzysz, Statement by I. F. (Number 224) in *Die Vertreibung der Deutschen Bevölkerung aus den Gebieten Östlich der Oder-Neisse* by Theodor Schieder, Archives of Gliwice. On singing in German: Gerhardt Ronskowski. On police: Josef Wiescholek, Statement Number 163 in *The Tragedy of Silesia* by Dr. Johannes Kaps, Archives of the District Attorney's Office in Gliwice. On the baby in Silesia: Statement of Maria Zimmermann (Ost-Dok. 2/215/40) in the German Federal Archives. On the babies near the Baltic Sea: Statements of E. K. (266) and P. L. (268) in *Die Vertreibung der Deutschen Bevölkerung aus den Gebieten Östlich der Oder-Neisse* by Theodor Schieder, Statements of Emil Finkgruber (Ost-Dok. 2/146/98), Anna George (Ost-Dok. 2/52/29), Sister Erna Kelm (Ost-Dok. 2/51/99), Ingeborg Spandera (Ost-Dok. 2/131/55), Christa-Helene Gause von Shirach (Ost-Dok. 2/148/103), E. Zindler (Ost-Dok. 2/64/18) and others in the German Federal Archives. On the police chief for Silesia: Jacob Alfiszer, Shmuel "Gross," Mordechai Kac. On Catholic and Jewish policemen: Mordechai Domb, Shmuel "Gross." On Bielitz: Israel Figa, Krzysztof Swierkosz, Statements of Paul Erbrich (Ost-Dok. 2/236E/890), Ottilie Artelt Hoffmann (Ost-Dok. 2/236E/910), Karl König (Ost-Dok. 2/236E/994), Erna Lyga (Ost-Dok. 2/223/2), Erzpriester Obst (Ost-Dok. 2/218/79) and Magda Walke (Ost-Dok. 2/236E/884) in the German Federal Archives, Statement Number 34 (by A. Schm., Ost-Dok. 2/236E/941) in *The Tragedy of Silesia* by Dr. Johannes Kaps, *Die Hölle von Lamsdorf* by Dr. Heinz Esser (Esser's sources are in Ost-Dok. 2/236E/747-1012 in the German Federal Archives). *Sources for the Notes.* On Gomulka: *Gomulka,* by Nicholas Bethell. On the police chief in Kattowitz: Lusia Feiner, Pinek Mąka. On the police chief in Breslau: Shmuel "Gross," Nachum "Salowicz." On the police in Ziębice and Żabkowice: Mordechai Domb. On the governor and the police chief in Neisse: Barbara Zaliwska.

"Five minutes later. . . ."

Lamsdorf now is Łambinowice, Poland. Czesław was Czesław Gęborski, the pianist was Erzpriester Obst, who knew the Czechoslovakian tune as *Rosamunde,* its German name, and the mailman was Richard Schmolke. The deputy commandant was Ignaz Szypulla, the nine-fingered boy was Antek, and the German "boss" was Herbert Pawlik, from Kattowitz. I don't know if any guards at Lamsdorf were Jews. The man who said, "No, Herr Deputy Commandant," and who didn't die, was J. Th., from Grüben, and the black-bearded man was Johann Langer, from Weidengut, or Johann Laqua, from Lippen. The number of Germans from Arnsdorf was 195, from Bauersdorf 76. The other villages and their populations were Bauerngrund 82, Buchengrund 88, Ellguthammer 335, Falkenberg 420, Fischbach 41, Floste 22, Friedland 180, Freudendorf 18, Fuchsberg 36, Geppersdorf 47, Goldmoor 595, Groditz 84, Gross Mahlendorf 23, Gross Mangersdorf 482, Gross Schnellendorf 46, Grüben apparently 606, Heidersdorf 39, Hilbersdorf 340, Jacobsdorf 285, Jatzdorf 172, Kleine Mangersdorf 91, Kleuschnitz 283, Lamsdorf 310, Lippen 160, Neuleipe 320, Neustadt 260, Oppeln 130, Oppeln area 23, Schurgast 88, Steinaugrund 332, Tillowitz 70, Villa Wackerzapp 40, Weidendorf 12, Weidengut 8. Not counted are 828 children. Rüppelstrasse now is Ulica Wawelska, and the Jewish Club—the Social and Cultural Club of the Jewish People of Poland—is at Number 6. Among others, Czesław spoke to Shlomo Morel and Israel Figa, who now writes for the Jewish *Workmen's Circle* in New York City. They both believe that Czesław was a Polish Catholic, as do Mordechai Kac and Paweł Lisiewicz. Dr. Heinz Esser, the Germans' doctor at Lamsdorf, counted 8,064 prisoners and 6,488 who died, and he listed the names, home towns, and occupations of 1,462 in *Die Hölle von Lamsdorf.* Edmund Nowak of the Łambinowice Museum has written that Esser's count of 6,488 is "somewhat" too high, but the count was reported in the Bundestag on September 16, 1974.

Sources. On Lamsdorf: Statement of J. Th. (233) in *Die Vertreibung der Deutschen Bevölkerung aus den Gebieten Östlich der Oder-Neisse* by Theodor Schieder, Statements Number 5, 27, 32, 34 (by A. Schm., Ost-Dok. 2/236E/941 in the German Federal Archives), 35, 36 and 193 in *The Tragedy of Silesia* by Dr. Johannes Kaps, Statements in *Die Hölle von Lamsdorf* by Dr. Heinz Esser (Esser's sources are Ost-Dok. 2/236E/747-1012 in the German Federal Archives), Statements of H. Aschmann (Ost-Dok. 2/236E/950), Johannes Bech (Ost-Dok. 2/233/9), Karl Donitza (Ost-Dok. 2/236E/773), Paul Erbrich (Ost-Dok. 2/236E/890), Dr. Heinz Esser (2/236E/946), Ottilie Artelt Hoffmann (Ost-Dok. 2/236E/910), Rudolf Hübner (Ost-Dok. 2/228/64), Karl König (Ost-Dok. 2/236E/994), Gustav Krell (Ost-Dok. 2/236E/802), Erna Lyga (Ost-Dok. 2/223/2), Erzpriester Obst (Ost-Dok. 2/218/79), Wilhelm Schneider (Ost-Dok. 2/236D/713), Paul Schon (Ost-Dok. 2/236E/979), Magda Walke (Ost-Dok. 2/236E/884) and Paul Willner (Ost-Dok. 2/236E/407) in the German Federal Archives, *Der Schlesier,* December, 1989. These sources are Germans, but Israel Figa, a Jew who often spoke with

Czesław Gęborski, the commandant, and who now writes for the Jewish
Workmen's Circle, told me, "Whatever they say, it's true." On Czesław in Kat-
towitz: Israel Figa, Shlomo Morel. On Czesław as a Polish Catholic: Israel
Figa, Mordechai Kac, Paweł Lisiewicz, Shlomo Morel, Thomas Urban. On
twenty percent of the Germans: *Die Hölle von Lamsdorf* by Dr. Heinz Esser.
Sources for the Notes. On Ignaz: *Bild Zeitung*, May 19, 1990. On Esser:
Stuttgarter Zeitung, December 12, 1991, *Bundestag Drucksache 7/2642, 7
Wahlperiode.*

"And now the month. . . ."
Chaim, who went to Neisse in August or September, 1946, didn't lock up
Efraim for saying, "That one's mine." Efraim also owned a car, and when he
sold it, Chaim said the car belonged to the Office and locked up Efraim for
that, and Efraim spent three months in Kattowitz prison. Mühlstrasse now is
Ulica Młyńska. The gate guard in Gleiwitz was Józef Pijarczyk, and one Ger-
man prisoner clerk was Mika. Some incidents at Chaim's inspection may
have happened at other inspections of Chaim's. It was Ada who Lola told,
"He's a *macher* now." The Polish word for *escape* was *ucieczka.*
Sources. On Chaim in Sosnowiec: Stanisław Gazda, Józef Pijarczyk. On
Chaim in Neisse: Efraim Lewin. On Chaim in Gleiwitz: Jadzia Gutman
Sapirstein "Banker," Krystyna Zielinska Dudzinska, Ada Neufeld Potok
Halperin, Eva Studencki Landau, Józef Pijarczyk, Ze'ev Sharone, Lucjan
Zenderowski. On Lola's impression of Chaim: Ada Neufeld Potok Halperin.
On Lola and the Russian: Lola Potok Ackerfeld Blatt, Pola Reif, Lucjan Zen-
derowski. On Jews in Czechoslovakia: Adam "Krawecki," Rivka "Glickman
Singer," Shlomo "Singer," Ruth Wilder, Leo Zelkin.

"His plan was. . . ."
The plan was for Lola's adjutant, Moshe, and one of Lola's guards, Lucjan
Zenderowski, to go to Vienna too. Rivka was quoting the Talmud, Sanhedrin
37a. Lola's driver was Heniek Kowalski, and the guard who went to her home
was Szczęsny. The boy said to Jadzia, "Where did she go?" at Jadzia's home
in Gleiwitz, and Jadzia stole away to Bernard Fontak's in Kattowitz. The
immediate commandant after Lola was a Catholic sergeant, but Chaim then
appointed a Jew, Moshe Kalmewicki, from Falenica, near Warsaw, who, like
Lola, had the title of Deputy Commandant. The girl who said, "Thank you,
sir," and "What's wrong?" was Krystyna Zielinska. In 1946, she was sentenced
to two years in Kattowitz prison. In 1948, Chaim, whose brother was Marek
Studniberg, was sentenced to six months in Kattowitz prison. Two more successors to Lola were Młynczak and Wróblewski. The German who escaped
was Hartz, the guard who let him escape was Józef Pijarczyk, and the guard
who took down the portrait of Stalin was Lucjan Zenderowski. On April 1,
1937, Theodor Eicke, the Inspector of Concentration Camps, announced,
"Any man in the death's-head units who cannot obey must go," and that year
eighty-eight men resigned. It was harder to resign at Auschwitz. Höss asked

twice to transfer to the Armed SS on the Russian Front but "I was not allowed to," but Dr. Wilhelm Hans Münch, who had been assigned to make selections with Mengele, did indeed resign.

Sources. On the escape plan: Lucjan Zenderowski. On Lola and Gertrude: Lola Potok Ackerfeld Blatt. On plow, harrow, sower pullers: *Die Hölle von Lamsdorf* by Dr. Heinz Esser. On twelve cents at Auschwitz: *The Arms of Krupp* by William Manchester. On Lola's disappearance: Jadzia Gutman Sapirstein "Banker," Lola Potok Ackerfeld Blatt, Gertie Gutman Cook, Henry Cook, Józef Pijarczyk, Pincus Schickman, Lucjan Zenderowski, Archives of the Department of Criminal Institutions in Katowice. On missing money, watches, rings: Jadzia Gutman Sapirstein "Banker," Lola Potok Ackerfeld Blatt, Gertie Gutman Cook, Henry Cook, Lucjan Zenderowski. On Jadzia: Jadzia Gutman Sapirstein "Banker," Gertie Gutman Cook, Henry Cook. On the new Jewish commandant: Krystyna Zielinska Dudzinska, Zofia Kalmewicki, Paweł Lisiewicz, Józef Pijarczyk, Rudek Schmer, Jerzy Szok, Lucjan Zenderowski. On "Please mail it": Krystyna Zielinska Dudzinska. On Chaim in Kattowitz prison: Stanisław Gazda, Ilana Studencki Hammer, Eva Studencki Landau, Zizi Stoppler. On "Get undressed": Josef Gorka, Erhard Wierschin, Lucjan Zenderowski. On dishonorable discharges: Józef Pijarczyk, Lucjan Zenderowski. On quitting the SS: *The Last Nazi* by Gerald Astor, *Licensed Mass Murder* by Henry V. Dicks, *Commandant at Auschwitz* by Rudolf Höss, *Anatomy of the SS State* by Helmut Krausnick. On Shlomo: Shlomo Morel. On rumors on Lola: Edzia Gutman Ackerfeld, Shlomo Ackerfeld, Jadzia Gutman Sapirstein "Banker," Stanisław Eweik, Józef Pijarczyk, Lucjan Zenderowski. On the guards' three minds: Stanisław Eweik. *Sources for the Notes.* On Lola's successors: Stanisław Gazda, Lucjan Zenderowski.

"The Poles were trying the Germans. . . ."

Of the approximately 200,000 prisoners in Office institutions, approximately 60,000 to 80,000 died. Of the approximately 120,000 to 140,000 remaining, about 1,000 or about .8 percent were convicted of war crimes and about 99.2 percent were presumably innocent. Of the 119 war-crime convicts sentenced to death in Silesia, fifty were tried in Kattowitz. In October, a Polish commission headed by Rybakiewicz also came to Schwientochlowitz. It turned out, the "Germans" at Schwientochlowitz included some Poles, Dutch, Swiss, and, the prisoners say, an American. At his request, I've changed Becker's last name. On February 27, 1991, Shlomo told the Provincial Commission (for Katowice) for the Investigation of Crimes Against the Polish Nation, "Almost all of the prisoners who survived were released." One who wasn't, and who was sent to Jaworzno, then prison in Cracow, was Gerhard Gruschka, a fourteen-year-old from Gleiwitz who, when the judges told him, "We can release you in Gliwice, Poland," was puzzled and answered that he was from Gleiwitz, Germany. When I was in Katowice, I went through several hundred dossiers, but I didn't find any prisoners who were SS, Storm Section or Nazis, or who were tried, convicted and sentenced to Polish prisons, but I've been told that one man, Schneider, was a Nazi, and one man, Bartfeld, was an SS soldier from the Russian front. Schneider, who had only one leg, was beaten to death with his crutch, and Bartfeld escaped. Schwientochlowitz was closed in November, 1945, and Shlomo was made commandant of Oppeln prison. The Jewish prosecutor in Gleiwitz was Rosenkranc. Paweł Pijowczak, a Storm Section man from Königshütte, said, "*Cici, cici,*" Emanuel Stein, from Gleiwitz, said, "Piotr Wons is an enemy of Germany," and Tomasz Kopółka, from Schwientochlowitz, said, "Augustyn Kuczera told me." The man who helped the Jehovah's Witnesses was Gottschalk, a school principal in Gleiwitz, and the Witness he helped was Brigitte "Petermann," a student in Gottschalk's school. The man who helped the Jews was Josef Wiescholek, from Gleiwitz, and the camp was on Am Bergraben, now Ulica Przewózowa, in Gleiwitz.

According to the Provincial Commission (for Katowice) for the Investigation of Crimes Against the Polish Nation, there were thirty-eight war-crimes convicts in Gleiwitz prison: Antoni Badura, Jan Bebek, Maks Brzeczek, Adolf Czapla, Konrad Danczyk, Maksymilian Działas, Karol Eiserman, Josef Gorka, Elżbieta Grzybek, Tadeusz Gzurko, Emil Janiczek, Franciszek Jarząbek, Jan Jenel, Jan Karmański, Franciszek Kiełkowski, Gerard Klimek, Tomasz Kopółka, Wilhelm Kozieł, Józef Krawczyk, Jan Manka, Wilhelm Manzel, Henryk Matusiak, Bruno Michalik, Paweł Mróz, Wilhelm Müller, Władysław Pietrzak, Rudolf Poloczek, Ryszard Sobota, Franciszek Stas, Emanuel Stein, Franciszek Stus, Wincenty Sudlik, Piotr Szydłowski, Emanuel Tiszbirek, Rufin Trzcionka, Melchior Witek, Małgorzata Zapora and Henryk Zydek. In the Archives of the Provincial Court in Katowice, I found the names of four other war-crime convicts in Gleiwitz prison: Gerhard Janicki, Hubert Kokoc, Josef Lefniok and Paweł Pijowczak. Of these forty-two people, I interviewed one, Gorka, and, in the Archives of the Provincial Court in Katowice, I found the files of twenty-one others: Eiserman, Grzybek, Janicki, Janiczek, Jarząbek, Karmański, Klimek, Kokoc, Kopółka, Kozieł, Krawczyk, Lefniok, Manka, Matusiak, Mróz, Pietrzak, Pijowczak, Stein, Szydłowski, Zapora and Zydek. To my mind, Matusiak, who strangled his girlfriend, and Pietrzak, who gave flour, potatoes, cigarettes and a cow to the anticommunists, weren't really war-crime convicts. Of the rest, only nine or ten were in Lola's prison while Lola was there: Kopółka, Krawczyk, Manka, Mróz, Pijowczak, Stein, Szydłowski, Zapora, Zydek and possibly Karmański. At that ratio, about eight of the nineteen convicts whose files I didn't find would have been in Lola's prison while Lola was there. That means that a total of about twenty people in Lola's prison while Lola was there were later convicted of war crimes by the court in Gleiwitz. Among those convicted were the Germans who'd said, "Laddies, lasses, the Poles are asses," "Piotr Wons is an enemy of Germany," and "Augustyn Kuczera told me, 'I'll come back here on a Polish tank.'" More may have been convicted in other cities, and hundreds were convicted of common crimes by the court in Gleiwitz.

Emanuel Stein, from Gleiwitz, died of a "heart attack" in Gleiwitz prison on July 7, 1946, and Małgorzata Gröner Zapora, born in Beuthen, living in Gleiwitz, was hanged in Gleiwitz prison on September 28, 1948. Matusiak and Stus were also hanged in Gleiwitz, but Matusiak wasn't really a war-crime convict, and Stus, convicted of strong-arm robbery, probably wasn't one. Elfryda "Uracz," the girl who was beaten every night in April, May and June and whose clothes were once pulled off, was never indicted for any crime. At her arrest, she was on vacation from medical school in Vienna, in June she went from Gleiwitz to Schwientochlowitz, then Kattowitz prison, then Jaworzno, and she now lives in Katowice.

    Sources. On 200,000 prisoners: *Vertreibung und Vertreibungsverbrechen 1945–1948* by the German Federal Archives. On one thousand convictions: Jerzy Jaruzelski. On the judges in Schwientochlowitz: Heinz "Becker," Dorota Niessporek Boreczek, Gerhard Gruschka, Statement of Günther Wollny (Ost-Dok. 2/236C/297) in the German Federal Archives. On the trials in Gleiwitz: Robert Geilke, Gerard Jankowiak, Adam Panek, Stanisława Świątnicka, Zygmunt Urbisz, Maurice Zak, Files of Tomasz Kopółka, Paweł Pijowczak and Emanuel Stein in the Archives of the Provincial Police in Katowice. On the Jewish prosecutor: Lucjan Zenderowski. On the two Good Guys: Brigitte "Petermann," Josef Wiescholek. On twenty convictions: Archives of the Commission for the Investigation of Crimes Against the Polish Nation, Archives of the Provincial Court in Katowice. On the hanging of Małgorzata Zapora: Krystyna Zielinska Dudzinska, Józef Pijarczyk, Lucjan Zenderowski, Statements of Elfriede Gawlik (Ost-Dok. 2/236C/503) and Angela Schymitzek (Ost-Dok. 2/236D/652) in the German Federal Archives, Archives of the Commission for the Investigation of Crimes Against the Polish Nation, File of Małgorzata Zapora in the Archives of the Provincial Court in Katowice. On the executioner: Krystyna Zielinska Dudzinska. *Sources for the Notes.* On the Polish commission: Shlomo Morel. On Gruschka: Gerhard Gruschka. On Schneider and Bartfeld: Eric van Calsteren. On the closing of Schwientochlowitz: Statements of Johanna Frystatzki (Ost-Dok. 2/230/2, also published as Number 215 in *Die Vertreibung der Deutschen Bevölkerung aus den Gebieten Östlich der Oder-Neisse* by Theodor Schieder), Martha Helisch Kempny (Ost-Dok. 2/237/162) and Erich Kischel (Ost-Dok. 2/236B/3, 2/236B/5) in the German Federal Archives, Protocol signed by Shlomo for the Provincial Commission (for Katowice) for the Investigation of Crimes Against the Polish Nation, on February 27, 1991. On Shlomo in Kattowitz prison: Efraim Lewin, Shlomo Morel, Lucjan Zenderowski.

    "On Wednesday, October 17. . . ."

    Roosevelt, Stalin and Atlee, meeting in Potsdam from July 17 to August 2, 1945, agreed in Article XIII of the Potsdam Protocol, "The Three Governments . . . recognize that the transfer to Germany of German populations, or elements thereof, remaining in Poland, Czechoslovakia and Hungary, will have to be undertaken. They agree that any transfers that take place should be effected in an orderly and humane manner." This Article cleared the way for the Polish decree of October 17. When the Russians came in 1945, the number of Germans living in Poland was 1,293,000, in Danzig 373,000, and in Poland-administered Germany 8,182,100, a total of 9,848,100. Germans were also thrown out of Czechoslovakia, Hungary, Romania and Yugoslavia, making a grand total of 16,600,000. After the war, the Polish police were called the Militia. The police chief in Kattowitz was Pinek Pakanowski, and the police chief in Breslau was Shmuel "Gross," who used the Polish name Mieczysław "Gross." Some other Jewish police chiefs in Poland and Poland-administered Germany were Yechiel Grynspan in Hrubieszów, Ayzer Mąka in Bielsko-Biała, and an unidentified man in Żabkowice. The partisans in Lublin—two hundred men, all Jews—were in the "Chiel Group" of the Holod Battalion: the group commander was Captain Yechiel "Chiel" Grynspan and the battalion commander, who was killed in 1944, was Captain Aleksander Skotnicki, known as Zemsta. The police chief of Poland was Juzwak, known as General Witold, who spoke in Lublin to Captain Grynspan and Grynspan's executive officer, Captain Shmuel "Gross." "Gross" became the police chief of Lublin (and was transferred to Breslau in May, 1945) and one of his eight precinct chiefs was Sever Rubinstein. According to "Gross," eighty percent of the police officers in Lublin and fifty percent of the policemen in Lublin were Jews. Some more Jewish partisans who got assignments in 1944 and 1945 were Jacob Alfiszer as a policeman in Kattowitz, Chanina and Shimon Barbanel as policemen somewhere in Poland, Efraim Blaichman as an Intelligence officer in Lubartów and Kielce, Yurik Chołomski as an officer in Kattowitz, Stefan Finkel as chief of Imprisonment in Cracow, Yechiel Grynspan as the police chief in Hrubieszów, Efraim Lewin as an Imprisonment officer in Lublin and Kattowitz and as the prison commandant in Neisse, Shlomo Morel as an Imprisonment officer in Lublin and Kattowitz and as the camp commandant in Schwientochlowitz, Oppeln, Kattowitz and Jaworzno, David Rubinstein as a policeman in Hrubieszów, and Adam Winder as a policeman in Hrubieszów. In Breslau, the chief of the Office's section for Germans was Kleks, the chief of the Polish army's Corps of Internal Security was Colonel Rubinstein, from Lodz, and the mayor was Drobner, from Cracow, who in mid-1945 became the Minister of Labor for Poland. Some other Jews in Breslau were Nachum "Salowicz," who was known as Tadeusz Zalewski and who was the chief of the Office's section for Germans for Breslau county, and Schumacher, who was the chief of Imprisonment for all of Lower Silesia. The station in Berlin was the Lehrter station. The American was Robert Murphy, the political adviser of the American Military Government in Berlin, who memoed the State Department on October 12, 1945, and the Britisher was Lieutenant Colonel W. Byford-Jones, who wrote in *Berlin Twilight*. The Gleiwitz woman was Eva Woitinek Lischevski, who spoke to me at a Gleiwitz reunion in Bottrop, Germany, on April 15, 1989. Similarly, Anne O'Hare McCormick, in her column in the *New York Times* of February 4, 1946, compared what the Poles were doing to the Germans to Nazi cruelties, and Congressman B. Carroll Reece, of Tennessee, in the House of Representatives on May 16, 1957, called it genocide.

Of the Germans who'd lived in Poland and Poland-administered Germany after the war, I calculate that by 1950 approximately 1,467,700 died. According to the German Federal Statistical Office, the number of Germans from

Poland who died was 185,000, the number from Danzig was 83,200, and the number from the German territory east of the Oder-Neisse Line was 1,338,700. The total comes to 1,606,900. But the northern part of East Prussia was taken by Russia, and I've subtracted the 139,200 people who (by prorating the 1939 population) probably died in the Russian part. The eastern part of Poland was also taken by Russia, but practically all the Germans there had left, and I haven't subtracted them. That leaves 1,467,700. Other sources have made higher estimates: that of the German Federal Ministry of Expellees was 18 percent higher, and that of Chancellor Konrad Adenauer (at a Silesian reunion in Hanover in June, 1961) was 48 percent higher. At the other extreme, the Western Press Agency in Poland estimated in 1966 that no Germans died at all.

The main anticommunist organization in Poland was the Home Army: the Armia Krajowa, or AK. Among the Poles in Lola's old prison was a woman who'd let the anticommunists into her hut and a man who'd given them half a ton of flour, a bag of potatoes, a carton of cigarettes, and a cow. The woman got fifteen years, and the man, whose name was Władysław Pietrzak, got the gallows, commuted to life imprisonment. Barek and Regina's apartment was at Andreasplatz 23, now Ulica Andrzeja 23.

Sources. On the decree of October 17: Introductory Description in *Die Vertreibung der Deutschen Bevölkerung aus den Gebieten Östlich der Oder-Neisse* by Theodor Schieder. On ten million people: *Die Deutschen Vertriebungsverluste* by the German Federal Statistical Office. On the Jewish police chiefs: Mordechai Domb, Lusia Feiner, Shmuel "Gross," Pinek Mąka. On the Jewish partisans in Lublin: Shmuel "Gross." On 300,000 people in Breslau: *The Tragedy of Silesia* by Dr. Johannes Kaps. On the Jews in Breslau: Shmuel "Gross," Nachum "Salowicz." On the German expulsion: Introduction and Statements Number 11 and 16 in *The Tragedy of Silesia* by Dr. Johannes Kaps, Introductory Description and Statements of B. F. (218), Georg Fritsch (219) and Adolf Walda (220) in *Die Vertreibung der Deutschen Bevölkerung aus den Gebieten Östlich der Oder-Neisse* by Theodor Schieder. On the station in Berlin: *From the Ruins of the Reich* by Douglas Botting, *The German Expellees: Victims in War and Peace* by Alfred de Zayas. On one-and-one-half million dead: *Die Deutschen Vertriebungsverluste* by the German Federal Statistical Office. On 150,000 Poles: Teresa Torańska. On executions in Gleiwitz: Lucjan Zenderowski. On Barek: Barek Eisenstein, Regina Ochsenhendler Eisenstein, Machela Ochsenhendler. *Sources for the Notes.* On Jews in the Office and Polish police: Jacob Alfiszer, Ephraim Blaichman, Yurik Chołomski, Mordechai Domb, Lusia Feiner, Shmuel "Gross," Ephraim Lewin, Pinek Mąka, Shlomo Morel. On estimates of German dead: *Die Vertreibung der Deutschen Bevölkerung aus den Gebieten Östlich der Oder-Neisse* by Theodor Schieder, *Truth or Conjecture?* by Stanisław Schimitzek, *Bulletin des Presse-und Informations-amtes der Bundesregierung*, June 13, 1961. On the Poles in Lola's prison: Krystyna Zielinska Dudzinska, Archives of the Provincial Police in Katowice.

"One boy contented in Poland. . . ."
With Pinek and Shoshana were Pinek's mother, Hannah, and, to the Italian border, Pinek's brother Ayzer.
Sources. On Pinek and Shoshana: Pinek Mąka.

12

"Forty-four years later. . . ."
This chapter is organized geographically and not chronologically. To research this book, I was in Poland from May 2 to May 24, 1989, from May 11 to June 16, 1990, from September 23 to October 10, 1992, and from June 15 to June 22, 1993. East Germany on June 7, 1950, and West Germany on December 7, 1970, recognized Gleiwitz, Kattowitz, and the rest of Poland-administered Germany as part of Poland. In the province of Katowice, including Gliwice, are seventy-two coal, lead and zinc mines and twenty-four steel, lead and zinc mills. The man who dug the tunnel in Gliwice escaped late in 1989, and the other man dug up the bones on October 11, 1984. The three retired guards were Stanisław Eweik, Józef Pijarczyk and Lucjan Zenderowski. Pijarczyk said that he briefly beat the Germans, and Zenderowski said that Lola said, "We aren't like them. We must be humane." The Jewish services in Katowice were at the Gmina Wyznaniowa Żydowska Kongregacja, or the Congregation of the Jewish Religious Community, at Ulica Młyńska 13, and the Social and Cultural Club of the Jewish People of Poland is at Ulica Wawelska 6. Shlomo was commandant at Jaworzno, a camp for Poles, from 1949 to 1951, and *Komendant S. M.,* an exposé by Grażyna Kuźnik, ran in *Tak i Nie* in the issue of May 18–20, 1990. Gomulka had been behind bars in one of the Office's villas, Międzyszyn, in Warsaw, from July, 1951, to September or December, 1954, or to April, 1955. The Landsmannschaft der Oberschlesier, in Bonn, wrote to the Polish government about Czesław on April 13, 1965, and the Poles replied in *Kierunki* on June 6, 1965. In October, 1992, the Provincial Commission (in Opole) for the Investigation of Crimes Against the Polish Nation was investigating the camp at Lamsdorf, and Tadeusz Imielski, my researcher-interpreter, called up Czesław in Katowice. Czesław screamed at Imielski, "Who are you?" "Where do you live?" "Where do you work?" and when Imielski didn't tell him, hung up. Vaclav Hrnecek, the deputy commandant of the camp for Germans at Budweis, Czechoslovakia, was tried in May, 1954, by the United States Court, Allied High Commission for Germany, Fifth District, President Leo M. Goodman. A man who was tried by the Germans for crimes against the Germans was Głombica, the doctor at Schwientochlowitz, who was tried for murder in Essen in 1961 and who got two years in a German prison. In 1979, Mengele apparently died of a stroke while swimming off the coast of Brazil. In addition to Höss and Hössler, Irma Grese, the SS woman of Lola's age at Auschwitz, was hanged in Germany. Jacob Berman was fired as Deputy Pre-

mier, Member of Parliament, Member of the Politburo, and untitled chief of the Office in May, 1956, and in 1957 he was cast out of the Communist Party. The Polish writer was Teresa Torańska, and her interview appears in *Them,* by Teresa Torańska. She also said to Jacob, "In 1948–49, you arrested members of the Home Army Council of Aid to Jews." Jacob said, "Yes," and Torańska said, "Mr. Berman! The security services, where all or nearly all the directors were Jewish, arrested Poles because they had saved Jews during the Occupation, and you say that Poles are antisemitic. That's not nice." Jacob said, "We later released them all," and Torańska said, "Władysław Bartoszewski was in prison almost seven years."

Sources. On the tunnel: Bogdan Szczepurek, Polish National Television. On the bones: Krystyna Kraska, Bogdan Szczepurek, Archives of the District Attorney's Office in Gliwice. On Lola and Gertrude: Lola Potok Ackerfeld Blatt, Pincus Schickman. On Shlomo's old camp at Schwientochlowitz: Edmund Chanak, Heinz Koizekwa, Rafał Syska. On Gomulka: *Gomulka* by Nicholas Bethell. On Czesław: Shlomo Morel, *Die Hölle von Lamsdorf* by Dr. Heinz Esser. On the Czech deputy commandant: *Nemesis at Potsdam* by Alfred de Zayas. The case is *In re Hrnecek,* Matter Number Crim 52-A-5-486, of 26 May 1954. On Höss, Hössler and Mengele: *Commandant at Auschwitz* by Rudolf Höss, *Mengele,* by Gerald L. Posner and John Ware, *New York Times,* December 15, 1945. On Jacob: Teresa Torańska, *Mówi Józef Światło* by Zbigniew Błażyński, *Them* by Teresa Torańska. *Sources for the Notes.* On Głombica: Piotr Bryś, Leszek Nasiadko, *Wieści* of December 1, 1991.

"All added up. . . ."

I was in Germany from April 12 to April 28, 1989, from April 30 to May 2, 1989, from May 24 to May 27, 1989, from June 10 to June 12, 1989, from May 4 to May 10, 1990, from June 22 to June 25, 1990, on October 10 and 11, 1992, on June 15, 1993, and on June 22 and 23, 1993, in Denmark from April 28 to April 30, 1989, in France (only partly for research) from September 9 to October 22, 1986, and from March 12 to March 14, 1991, and in Austria from June 17 to June 21, 1990. One reunion, for one thousand people from Gleiwitz, was in Bochum from April 14 to April 16, 1989, and one, for 100,000 people from all of Silesia, was in Essen from June 22 to June 24, 1990. The five Germans from Lola's prison were Günther Ciesla, Horst Planelt, Günter Plasczyk, Elfryda "Uracz" and Josef Wiescholek. All but Wiescholek had been beaten, and Ciesla had been beaten with the beater-to-death. The Germans from Schwientochlowitz were Heinz "Becker," Dorota Niessporek Boreczek, Elfryda "Uracz," Eric van Calsteren and Günther Wollny, and the one in the village was "Becker."

Just as thousands of Jews made oral and written statements about their experiences in the Holocaust, so did thousands of Germans write statements about their experiences after the war. Forty thousand of these are stored at the Bundesarchiv, the German Federal Archives, in Koblenz. Of these, 748 are published in eight volumes in *Dokumentation der Vertreibung der*

Deutschen aus Ost-Mitteleuropa, edited by Theodor Schieder. In volumes 1 and 2, *Die Vertreibung der Deutschen Bevölkerung aus den Gebieten Östlich der Oder-Neisse,* are 382 reports by Germans from what now is Poland and, in the Königsberg area, Russia. Of these, 45 are translated into English and published in *The Expulsion of the German Population from the Territories East of the Oder-Neisse-Line,* edited by Theodor Schieder. In the Bundesarchiv, I read about a thousand statements by Germans who'd once been the Office's prisoners. "Everything that I write below" is from the statement by Hubert Jaeschke, the man in Neisse who'd said, "I was not in the Party" (Ost-Dok. 2/227/88), and *"Gefängnis Gleiwitz,"* is from the statement by Elfriede Gawlik (Ost-Dok. 2/236C/503). In the Bundesarchiv, I also found twenty-seven reports on Schwientochlowitz. Six mentioned Shlomo's last name, and two mentioned that he was a Jew.

Another Jew in Munich was Sonia Baumgarten, the Senior Jew at the German concentration camp in Gleiwitz, and another in Frankfurt was Pincus Martyn, the man who'd told the Hillel story in Gleiwitz. Lola met Dr. Michal Blatt in Zeilsheim, Germany. Zlata was at an Annecy spa, but she usually lives in Albertville, nearby. Zlata and Elo's son was Simon, and their daughter was Monique. An earlier son was killed at Auschwitz, and Lola's other brothers had two sons, both of whom died at Auschwitz, and seven daughters. Simon will be seventy-five in the year 2020.

Sources. On Lola: Lola Potok Ackerfeld Blatt. *Sources for the Notes.* On the Senior Jew: Edzia Gutman Ackerfeld.

"I went to Israel. . . ."

I was in Israel from May 27 to June 10, 1989. Ada's song was by Hayyim Nahman Bialik, the Hebrew poet, and her second husband was Sid Halperin. "Yad Vashem" is Hebrew for "Place and Name," a reference to Isaiah 56:5, "A place and a name. . . an everlasting name, that shall not be cut off." One of the documents there is by Shlomo Morel, the former commandant of Schwientochlowitz, but Shlomo just writes of the Jewish partisans, not of Schwientochlowitz or the Office. The Chairman of Yad Vashem, Dr. Yitzhak Arad, wrote me on June 6, 1988, and I spoke with the Director of Archives, Dr. Shmuel Krakowski, on June 6, 1989. My mother's mother was Bessie Krawecki Levy. There are four vice chairmen of the International Society for Yad Vashem, and the one I wanted was David Feuerstein, who normally lives in Geneva. My call from the Vietnamese restaurant in Warsaw was on Friday, June 15, 1991, and Feuerstein said, "I was terrible," when I called from Brilon, Germany, on Saturday, May 5, 1991. The man in Haifa was Shimon Nunberg. Chaim's son was Ze'ev, and his daughter was Eva. In 1982, Ze'ev was in Miami and spoke by phone with Chaim. The words "chosen people" come from Deuteronomy 7:6, "For thou art an holy people unto the Lord thy God: the Lord thy God hath chosen thee," and similarly from Deuteronomy 14:2. Chaim's adopted daughter was Ilana, his good friend was Gaby Mamu, his girlfriend (after the death of Krystyna, his wife, in 1978) was Zizi Stoppler, his brother was Max Studniberg, and his son was Ze'ev Sharone.

Sources. On Ada: Lola Potok Ackerfeld Blatt, Ada Neufeld Potok Halperin. On Chaim: Gaby Mamu, Ze'ev Sharone, Zizi Stoppler, Ilana Studencki Hammer, Eva Studencki Landau, Max Studniberg.

"Most of the Jews. . . ."

The commandant at Ziegenhals was Leo Zolkewicz, from Kattowitz. The Neisse interrogator was Salek "Zucker," the Kielce boy was Efraim Blaichman, the boy who'd been at Schwientochlowitz was Moshe Mąka, and the Kattowitz boy was Itzak Klein, who died in the early 1980s. Blaichman lives in Queens, but his construction and management company is in West New York, New Jersey. I was at Barek's and Regina's home in Toronto from June 23 to June 25, 1989, and I must report with sadness that Barek, who was expecting his fifth and sixth grandchildren, died of pancreatic cancer on May 21, 1991. I was at Shlomo and Rivka's home in Brooklyn on April 9, 1989, and September 7, 1992, in Miami from April 4 to April 7, 1989, and, for research, in New York and New Jersey on September 20, 1987, from April 7 to April 11, 1989, from June 12 to June 23, 1989, on November 30, 1990, and from September 20 to 22, 1992. The Neisse interrogator was Salek "Zucker," the Kattowitz guard was Leo Zelkin, and the Myslowitz commandant was Shmuel Kleinhaut, whose wife, among others, confirmed that he was the commandant, and who one German prisoner praised, saying, in a statement in the German Federal Archives, "The prison director, too, had the fullest understanding of our situation." Moshe's wife Rose said that she was writing a book about him and that he would talk to *her* not me, but Moshe eventually called me. He told me, "I wasn't aware nothing," but said that there were no women in Lola's prison and that no one died in Lola's prison. I was at the Beth Israel Memorial Cemetery on September 20, 1987. Pinek married Hanalah Stolawicki, from Lida, Poland, his firm was the Livingston Circle Tool Company, and he'd been the vice president of United Synagogues of America, the Chairman of United Jewish Appeal, and the Honorary Chairman of Bonds for Israel in his part of New Jersey. Pinek called the Germans "animals" and "barbarians" in September, 1985, and "Nazis *yimach sh'mom*," in September, 1988. The president of the Fraternal Order of Będzin (or, more properly, of Bendin-Sosnowicer) was Henry Cook. The statement Pinek read was by Eva Reimann. By then, the president of the Order was Henry Major.

Another man in New York was Julek Furstenfeld, the former chief of the Jewish police in Będzin, who lived in a nursing home in Queens and told people that Pinek was *dreck*, saying, "He sent me to prison!" He died on October 22, 1991.

Sources. On the commandant at Ziegenhals: Statement of Joseph Langer (Ost-Dok. 2/232/18) in the German Federal Archives. On Lola: Lola Potok Ackerfeld Blatt, Dr. Michal Blatt. On twenty to fifty percent: *Vertreibung und Vertreibungsverbrechen 1945–1948* by the German Federal Archives. On the all-points bulletin: Henry Major. *Sources for the Notes.* On the com-

mandant in Myslowitz: Statement by Max Kroll (Ost-Dok. 2/236/52) in the
German Federal Archives.

"I was living then. . . ."

My lunch at the Inn of the Seventh Ray was on January 16, 1988, the wait-
ress was Anna, and Lola's daughter Cynthia was also with us. The firm was
Aircraft Supplies, of Clifton, New Jersey. Lola moved to California in 1986.
Lola's first husband, Shlomo, was married to Edzia Gutman, from Będzin, a
survivor of the Gleiwitz concentration camp, who Shlomo had met in
Schwandorf, Germany. They have since moved to Tamarac, Florida. Lola's
daughters were Estelle, an assistant district attorney in Sacramento County,
Evelyn, a housewife, Arlene, a national manager for E. F. Hutton, and Cynthia, a secretary at Paramount Pictures. My business at Paramount was at the
office of Lynda Obst, of Hill-Obst Productions, on April 22, 1986, and Lola
and I first met for dinner early in May at the Moustache Cafe. I went to
France on a working vacation from September 9 to October 22, 1986, and I
spoke to Michel, Basia's son, and to Monique, Zlata's daughter, in Paris, and
to Zlata in Annecy, as well as to Lola in Paris. Among other things, Lola had
forgotten that the prison was in Gleiwitz, thinking that it was in Breslau.
She'd forgotten that the Germans were mostly civilians, were mostly suspects, were partly women, and that many Germans died. Of what I've written
of Lola's life in Będzin and Auschwitz, about fifty percent is from other
sources than Lola. Of her life in Kattowitz and Gleiwitz, about ninety percent
is from other sources than Lola. The parts that Lola told me, I've mostly confirmed through other sources. It was elsewhere, not at the Inn, that Lola
said, "It's nothing," and elsewhere that same day that Lola said, "My mother
said." The couple was Maré Payne and Jason Sakurai, and they were married
by Robert Ringler of Bel-Air Wedding Ceremonies and Service.

Sources. On Lola's life: Lola Potok Ackerfeld Blatt, Dr. Michal Blatt, *New
Jersey Business,* May, 1981.

"For six more months. . . ."

My first publisher was Don Hutter Books, an imprint of Henry Holt. We
signed a contract on September 9, 1988, but Don, my editor, publisher, and
new good friend, suddenly and tragically died on February 23, 1990, and I
contracted with Basic Books in June, 1993. My telephone call to Lola was on
August 25, 1988, and my meeting with Lola, Cynthia, Arlene and a man who
identified himself as Bud Richardson was at 8:45 that evening at a condo
owned by Lola but occupied by Cynthia. The document, which I read later,
said that I was confirming that Lola's letter was void. Cynthia claimed that if
I didn't sign it, Cynthia couldn't produce a TV movie on Lola's life, but Lola
never mentioned this. I never signed it.

Again, this chapter is not chronological, and on August 25, 1988, the day
of the meeting at Lola's condo, I'd been to France but not to Poland, Germany, Denmark, Austria or Israel, and I'd spoken to Jews but not to Polish

guards or German prisoners. I still didn't know that the Germans in Gleiwitz were mostly civilians, were mostly suspects, were partly women, and that the Germans often died. I didn't know that the Office ran 227 prisons and 1,255 concentration camps for Germans, and I didn't know that the Office was run by Jews. I still hadn't been to the German Federal Archives, I hadn't shown the photocopies to Pinek, and the president of the Fraternal Order of Będzin hadn't told the Order not to speak to me.

Sources. On the meeting at Lola's condo: Lola's daughter Cynthia and I tape-recorded this.

Aftermath

"On Monday, December 11. . . ."

The woman in Radlin was Edna Kołodziejczyk, and her word for *polished off* was *wykończyć.* In December, 1989, the Commission for the Investigation of Crimes Against the Polish Nation was the Commission for the Investigation of Hitlerite Crimes in Poland. Its name and its duties were changed by the Polish parliament on April 4, 1991. A letter from the Geneva Central Agency for Prisoners of War, of the International Committee of the Red Cross, stated that Wanda Lagler had died in Schwientochlowitz on August 1, 1945. Bryś's office was at the Provincial Commission (for Katowice) for the Investigation of Hitlerite Crimes in Poland, at Plac Wolności 10, Katowice. The secretary was Gertruda Sawer. The articles in *Wieści,* by Jakub Ciećkiewicz, ran on November 24, December 1, and December 8, 1991.

Sources. On the investigation of Świętochłowice: Piotr Bryś, Leszek Nasiadko, Urszula Watoła, Archives of the Provincial Commission (for Katowice) for the Investigation of Crimes Against the Polish Nation. On Bryś: Piotr Bryś. On Bryś and Shlomo: Piotr Bryś, Paweł Lisiewicz, Gertruda Sawer, Archives of the Provincial Commission (for Katowice) for the Investigation of Crimes Against the Polish Nation.

"Two weeks later, Bryś. . . ."

Bryś's new office was at the Provincial Commission (for Katowice) for the Investigation of Crimes Against the Polish Nation, at Ulica Warszawska 19, Katowice. Dorota's maiden name was Niessporek. The Schubert song was *Die Forelle,* the "doctor" was Głombica, and Truda's camp was at Wujek.

Sources. On Bryś and Shlomo: Dorota Boreczek, Piotr Bryś, Paweł Lisiewicz, Shlomo Morel, Gertruda Sawer, Archives of the Provincial Commission (for Katowice) for the Investigation of Crimes Against the Polish Nation. On Dorota: Dorota Niessporek Boreczek. On Dorota and Shlomo: Dorota Niessporek Boreczek, Piotr Bryś, Shlomo Morel, Archives of the Provincial Commission (for Katowice) for the Investigation of Crimes Against the Polish Nation. On Bryś, Shlomo and Truda: Piotr Bryś, Shlomo

Morel, Gertruda Sawer, Archives of the Provincial Commission (for Kato-wice) for the Investigation of Crimes Against the Polish Nation. On Truda: Gertruda Sawer. On Shlomo's going to Israel: Shlomo Morel.

"The story of Shlomo's exodus. . . ."

Among the old Jewish partisans who Shlomo approached was Ephraim, his former prisoner in Kattowitz. Nasiadko was a military judge in the Polish army. The German community in Katowice was the Deutsche Arbeitsge-meinschaft, with offices at Ulica Młyńska 2. Brehmer had an ancestor who, in 1727, changed the family name from Bremer to Brehmer, somewhat as Abram changed his name to Abraham in the Torah, and Brehmer suspects that this ancestor was a Jew. Brehmer saw his mother beaten in their home on Ulica Ligocka. The four documents were from the German Federal Archives and were by Günther Wollny, Walter Freund, Max Ogorek, and Heinz Biernot. Jerzy Hop is a judge now, and the new district attorney in Katowice is Olko.

Sources. On Shlomo in Israel: Efraim Blaichman, Ben Caspit, Michael Gavshon, Efraim Lewin, Shlomo Morel. On the Hague and Geneva Con-ventions: Alfred de Zayas. On Nasiadko: Leszek Nasiadko. On Brehmer: Dietmar Brehmer, Thomas Kleine-Brockhoff. On All-Saints Day: Josef Blaza. On the Commission's routine: Stanisław Biernacki, Piotr Bryś, Sena-tor Ryszard Juszkiewicz, Waldemar Kaim, Stanisław Kaniewski, Paweł Lisiewicz, Mieczysław Motas, Leszek Nasiadko, Mieczysław Sosinski, Urszula Watoła.

"By now, I'd read. . . ."

The man who said, "You read Hebrew?" and who was the Office inspector was Mordechai Kac, and the Deputy Director of Intelligence was Adam Humer, who was probably a Jew. Another investigation, this by the Provincial Commission (in Opole) for the Investigation of Crimes Against the Polish Nation, is of the former camp at Lamsdorf, now Lambinowice, commanded by Czesław Gęborski.

Sources. On the Deputy Director of Intelligence: Stanisław Biernacki, Senator Ryszard Juszkiewicz, Waldemar Kaim, Stanisław Kaniewski, Zofia Korbonski, Paweł Lisiewicz, Mieczysław Motas, Mieczysław Sosinski.

"I then flew back. . . ."

The service was at the Beth Israel Memorial Cemetery, on the plot of the Fraternal Order of Bendin-Sosnowicer, on September 20, 1992. The rabbi was Stuart W. Klammer, and the speaker was Toby Reiner. The woman guard in Mysłowice was Hela Wilder Kleinhaut, the woman guard in Gliwice was Jadzia Gutman Sapirstein "Banker," the man who told me, "My cousin was the commandant in Mysłowice," was Ze'ev Fryszman, and the man who told me, "I don't know from nothing," was Shmuel Kleinhaut. Moshe was Moshe Mąka, and Mendel was Mendel Goldman.

Sources. On Shlomo's letter to Bryś: Piotr Bryś, Shlomo Morel, Archives of the Provincial Commission (for Katowice) for the Investigation of Crimes Against the Polish Nation.

"I went back to Katowice. . . ."

After six months at the Commission, Nasiadko, under Polish law, had to return to the Polish army, and he returned on November 2, 1992. He was replaced temporarily by Jerzy Ruciński, then, for six months, ending on December 31, 1993, by Grodzki, a Polish army prosecutor. The Dutchman was Eric van Calsteren, who was the Hitler Youth from Gleiwitz who once escaped from Shlomo's camp. In 1945, an Audi was called a DKW. According to Shlomo's wife, Shlomo went to Israel for his heart, then for a vacation.

Sources. On Nasiadko: Leszek Nasiadko. On Brehmer: Dietmar Brehmer. On the Dutchman: Eric van Calsteren, Statement by Eric van Calsteren. On Grodzki: Michael Gavshon, Marek Grodzki. On Shlomo: Ben Caspit, Michael Gavshon, Marek Grodzki, *60 Minutes.*

SOURCES

Interviews

Almost all of these interviews were tape-recorded. The tapes, more than three hundred hours, will eventually go to the John Sack Collection at Boston University and will be accessible there.

Jewish officers in the Office of State Security, 1945:

Ackerfeld, Lola Potok. Now Blatt. Prison commandant in Gleiwitz.

Blaichman, Efraim. Intelligence officer in Kielce.

Chołomski, Yurik. Officer in Kattowitz.

Eisenstein, Barek. Intelligence officer in Kattowitz.

Feuerstein, David. Interrogator in Neisse.

"Glickman," Adela. Secretary in Kattowitz. Interpreter: Erika Nottebohm.

"Grossman," Moshe. Prison adjutant in Gleiwitz.

Jurkowski, Josef. Chief of the Office for Silesia. Interpreter: Hanna Lehrmann.

Kac, Mordechai. Inspector in Kattowitz.

Kleinhaut, Shmuel. Prison commandant in Myslowitz.

"Krawecki," Adam. Chief interrogator in Gleiwitz. Interpreter: Josef Kowalski.

Lewin, Efraim. Prison commandant in Neisse. Interpreters: Madzia Kukulska, Jerzy Lewinski.

Mąka, Moshe. Personnel officer in Kattowitz.

Mąka, Pinek. Secretary of State Security for Silesia.

Morel, Shlomo. Camp commandant in Schwientochlowitz. Interpreters: Mordechai Kac, Ewa Nowakowska.

Nunberg, Shimon. Interrogator in Neisse.

"Salowicz," Nachum. Chief of the German section in Cracow and, later, in Breslau county.

Sapirstein, Jadzia Gutman. Now "Banker." Prison guard in Gleiwitz.

"Singer," Shlomo. Mess officer in Neisse.

Tinkpulver, Hanka. Now Kalfus. Secretary in Kattowitz.

Wilder, Hela. Now Kleinhaut. Prison guard in Myslowitz.

Zelkin, Leo. Prison guard in Kattowitz.

"Zucker," Salek. Interrogator in Neisse.

Family, friends of Jewish officers in the Office of State Security, 1945:

Ackerfeld, Jadzia Rappaport. Now Jacobs. Boarder at Lola's home in Gleiwitz.

Ackerfeld, Shlomo. Lola's first husband.

Blatt, Dr. Michal. Lola's second husband.

"Chaimowicz," Leon. Friend of Yurik Chołomski.

Cook, Henry. Husband of Gertie Gutman Cook.

Eisenman, Helen. Now Fortgang. Boarder at Lola's home in Gleiwitz.

Eisenstein, Jacob. Brother of Barek Eisenstein.

Feiner, Lusia. Cousin of Pinek Pakanowski, Chief of Police in Kattowitz, 1945.

Figa, Israel. Member of the Jewish Committee in Kattowitz.

Finkelstein, Chaim. Friend of Jacob Berman, Chief of the Office of State Security.

Fontak, Bernard. Friend of Jadzia Gutman Sapirstein.

Fryszman, Ze'ev. Cousin of Hela Wilder.

"Glickman," Rivka. Now "Singer." Wife of Shlomo "Singer."

Grosberg, Blima. Now Golenser. Friend of Regina Ochsenhendler.

"Grossman," Rose. Wife of Moshe "Grossman," Lola's adjutant.

Gutman, Gertie. Now Cook. Sister of Jadzia Gutman Sapirstein.

Ickowicz, Rózia. Now Rechnic. Cousin of Lola.

Jacobs, Leibish. Second husband of Jadzia Rappaport Ackerfeld Jacobs.

Jurkowska, Bronisława. Wife of Josef Jurkowski. Interpreter: Hanna Lehrmann.

Kalmewicki, Andre. Son of Moshe Kalmewicki, Commandant in Gleiwitz after Lola, 1945–46.

Kalmewicki, Zofia. Wife of Moshe Kalmewicki, Commandant in Gleiwitz after Lola, 1945–46.

Kaplan, Bella. Now Zborowski. Schoolmate of Jadzia Gutman Sapirstein.

Lewin, Kazimera. Wife of Efraim Lewin.

Mamu, Gaby. Neighbor (in the 1980s) of Chaim Studniberg, Director of the Department of Prisons and Camps for Silesia, 1945.

Martyn, Batia. Wife of Josef Martyn, a boarder at Lola's home in Gleiwitz.

Martyn, Gucia. Now Schickman. Boarder at Lola's home in Gleiwitz.

Martyn, Pincus. Nephew of Zlata Potok. Interpreter: Andrea Seppi.

Ochsenhendler, Jadzia. Now Eisenstein. Wife of Jacob Eisenstein.

Ochsenhendler, Machela. Mother of Regina Ochsenhendler.

Ochsenhendler, Regina. Now Eisenstein. Wife of Barek Eisenstein.

Oleska, Paula. Niece of Jacob Berman.

Potok, Ada Neufeld. Now Halperin. Wife of Lola's brother David.

Potok, Monique. Daughter of Lola's brother Elo.

Potok, Zlata Martyn. Wife of Lola's brother Elo. Interpreter: Mary Gantet.

Rappaport, Anna. Wife of Moniek Rappaport.

Rappaport, Mania. Now Novak. Boarder at Lola's home in Gleiwitz.

Rappaport, Moniek. Boarder at Lola's home in Gleiwitz.

Rechnic, Leibish. Husband of Rózia Ickowicz Rechnic.

Reif, Pola. Wife of David Reif, the adjutant to Colonel Zacharow, Lola's lover.

Rosenzweig, Genia. Now Tigel. Friend of Ada Neufeld Potok.

"Salowicz," Mania. Wife of Nachum "Salowicz."

Schickman, Pincus. Boarder at Lola's home in Gleiwitz.

Schickman, Shmuel. Boarder at Lola's home in Gleiwitz.

Schmer, Rudek. Member of the Jewish Committee in Gleiwitz, 1945.

Sharone, Ze'ev. Son of Chaim Studniberg, Director of the Department of Prisons and Camps for Silesia, 1945.

Stenard, Jacqueline. Wife of Michel Stenard.

Stenard, Michel. Son of Lola's sister Basia.

Stoppler, Zizi. Friend (in the 1980s) of Chaim Studniberg, Director of the Department of Prisons and Camps for Silesia, 1945. Interpreters: Stewart Lyndh, Danny Stoppler.

Studencki, Eva. Now Landau. Daughter of Chaim Studniberg, Director of the Department of Prisons and Camps for Silesia, 1945.

Studencki, Ilana. Now Hammer. Adopted daughter of Chaim Studniberg, Director of the Department of Prisons and Camps for Silesia, 1945.

Studniberg, Max. Brother of Chaim Studniberg, Director of the Department of Prisons and Camps for Silesia, 1945.

Szok, Jerzy. Friend of Moshe Kalmewicki, Commandant in Gleiwitz after Lola, 1945–46.

Wilder, Ruth. Sister of Hela Wilder.

Zelkin, Regina. Wife of Leo Zelkin.

"Zucker," Sara. Wife of Salek "Zucker."

Prisoners of the Office of State Security, 1945:

"Becker," Heinz. Prisoner in Schwientochlowitz. Interpreters: Karl Dietz, Karl G. Frank, Jody Melamed.

Bienek, Walter. Prisoner in Gleiwitz (1950). Interpreter: Doris Diana Dame.

Ciesla, Günther. Prisoner in Lola's prison. Interpreters: Doris Diana Dame, Thomas Jarosch, Andrea Seppi.

Foitzik, Ursula. Prisoner in Beuthen. Interpreter: Doris Diana Dame.

Gorka, Josef. Prisoner in Gleiwitz (1946).

Gruschka, Gerhard. Prisoner in Schwientochlowitz.

Hellebrandt, Kurt. Prisoner in Myslowitz camp. Interpreter: Stefanie von Heygendorff-Hoffken.
Niessporek, Dorota. Now Boreczek. Prisoner in Schwientochlowitz.
Planelt, Horst. Prisoner in Lola's prison. Interpreter: Stefanie von Heygendorff-Hoffken.
Plasczyk, Günter. Prisoner in Lola's prison. Interpreters: Doris Diana Dame, Stefanie von Heygendorff-Hoffken.
Ronskowski, Gerhardt. Prisoner in Gleiwitz (1952). Interpreter: Doris Diana Dame.
"Uracz," Elfryda. Prisoner in Lola's prison and in Schwientochlowitz. Interpreters: Dorota Niessporek Boreczek, Marilyn Jeanne Odell.
van Calsteren, Eric. Prisoner in Schwientochlowitz. Interpreter: Annelies van Calsteren-Lek.
Wiescholek, Josef. Prisoner in Lola's prison. Interpreters: Doris Diana Dame, Andrea Seppi.
Wollny, Günther. Prisoner in Schwientochlowitz. Interpreters: Stefanie von Heygendorff-Hoffken, Jody Melamed, Maximillian Vrecer.

Family, friends of prisoners of the Office of State Security, 1945:

Ewald, Hatko. Friend of Josef Gorka. Interpreter: Stefanie von Heygendorff-Hoffken.
Jendryschik, Sepp. Son of Josef Jendryschik, a prisoner in Schwientochlowitz.
Knabe, Elisabeth. Mother of Johanne Knabe, a four-year-old prisoner in Gleiwitz camp. Interpreter: Doris Diana Dame.
Liszok, Engelbert. Son of Josef Liszok, a prisoner of the Russians in Gleiwitz. Interpreter: Doris Diana Dame.
Palmer, Engelbert. Cousin of Rudolf Palmer, a prisoner in Lola's prison. Interpreter: Stefanie von Heygendorff-Hoffken.
Palmer, Gertrude. Now Junge. Sister of Rudolf Palmer, a prisoner at Lola's prison. Interpreter: Stefanie von Heygendorff-Hoffken.
Rogier, Hedwig. Cousin of Franz Ciupka, a prisoner at Schwientochlowitz.
"Schultz," Jakob. Friend of a prisoner in Lola's prison. Interpreter: Ewa Nowakowska.
Wierschin, Erhard. Son of Karl Wierschin, a prisoner in Lola's prison. Interpreter: Stefanie von Heygendorff-Hoffken.
Zellner, Bruno. Cousin of Rudolf Palmer, a prisoner in Lola's prison. Interpreter: Stefanie von Heygendorff-Hoffken.
Zurek, Renate. Daughter of Johann Zurek, a prisoner in Lola's prison. Interpreter: Stefanie von Heygendorff-Hoffken.

Gentiles in the Office of State Security, 1945:

Eweik, Stanisław. Guard at Lola's prison. Interpreter: Ewa Nowakowska.
Gazda, Stanisław. Secretary to Chaim Studniberg, Director of the Department of Prisons and Camps for Silesia, 1945. Interpreter: Ewa Nowakowska.

Jaruzel, Władysław. Prison guard in Kattowitz. Interpreter: Ewa Nowakowska.

Pijarczyk, Józef. Guard at Lola's prison. Interpreters: Tadeusz Imielski, Ewa Nowakowska.

Skowyra, Tadeusz. Prison guard in Kattowitz. Interpreter: Ewa Nowakowska.

Zenderowski, Lucjan. Guard at Lola's prison. Interpreters: Tadeusz Imielski, Ewa Nowakowska.

Zielinska, Krystyna. Now Dudzinska. Guard at Lola's prison. Interpreter: Ewa Nowakowska.

Jews in the Polish Police, 1945:

Alfiszer, Jacob. Policeman in Kattowitz.
Domb, Mordechai. Policeman in Ziębice.
"Gross," Shmuel. Chief of Police in Lublin and later in Breslau.

Other persons, 1945:

Bienek, Horst. German author from Gleiwitz. Interpreter: Erica Nottebohm.
Blatt, Mendel. Jewish survivor from Będzin.
Blaza, Józef. Civilian in Schwientochlowitz. Interpreter: Tadeusz Imielski.
Bleiberg, Janina. Now Lieberman. Jewish survivor of Auschwitz.
Bugayski, Renate. Friend of Zlata Potok. Interpreter: Mary Gantet.
Castleberry, Donald. Worker, American Red Cross in Poland.
Chanak, Edmund. Civilian in Schwientochlowitz. Interpreter: Wojciech Mrożek.
Frank, Karl. Civilian in Bielsko-Biała.
Furstenfeld, Julek. Chief of the Jewish Police in Będzin.
Geilke, Robert. Legal apprentice in Silesia.
Geller, David. Jewish survivor in Kattowitz.
Goldman, Mendel. Jewish survivor of Płaszów.
Grady, Harry. Worker, American Red Cross in Poland.
Graff, Georgi. Russian soldier.
Gutman, Edzia. Now Ackerfeld. Jewish survivor from Będzin.
Klose, Erwin. German commandant at Gleiwitz. Interpreter: Doris Diana Dame.
Koizekwa, Heinz. Civilian in Schwientochlowitz. Interpreter: Iwona Karewicz.
Lewin, Jacob. Jewish survivor of Auschwitz.
Lewkowitz, Stanisław. Jewish survivor in Sosnowiec.
Lipman, Feliks. Jewish survivor in Kattowitz.
Małota, Adelajd. Civilian in Schwientochlowitz. Interpreter: Iwona Karewicz.
Michen, Jan. Civilian in Schwientochlowitz. Interpreter: Iwona Karewicz.
Panek, Adam. Legal apprentice in Silesia. Interpreter: Ewa Nowakowska.
"Petermann," Brigitte. Neighbor of Lola's prison.
Romankiewicz, Michal. Jewish survivor in Kattowitz.

Rozenzvajg, Dov. Jewish survivor in Kattowitz. Interpreter: Tadeusz Imielski, Iwona Karewicz.

Schmer, Rudek. Member of the Jewish Committee in Gleiwitz.

Shaligin, Yuri. Russian soldier.

Shapell, Nathan. Jewish survivor of Auschwitz.

Steinberg, Paul. Jewish survivor of Auschwitz.

Syska, Rafał. Civilian in Schwientochlowitz. Interpreter: Iwona Karewicz.

Szewczyk, Wilhelm. Member, Silesian Provincial Legislature. Interpreter: Ewa Nowakowska.

Szwarc, Moshe. Jewish survivor in Będzin. Interpreter: Ewa Nowakowska.

Urbisz, Zygmunt. Legal apprentice in Silesia. Interpreter: Ewa Nowakowska.

Witek, Edward. Police lieutenant in Kattowitz. Interpreter: Ewa Nowakowska.

Woitinek, Eva. Now Lischevski. Neighbor of Lola's prison. Interpreter: Doris Diana Dame.

Zideerr, Jan. Jewish survivor in Kattowitz. Interpreter: Tadeusz Imielski.

Historians, journalists, officials:

Biernacki, Stanisław. Director of the Research Department, Main Commission for the Investigation of Crimes Against the Polish Nation, Warsaw. Interpreter: Tadeusz Imielski.

Brehmer, Dietmar. Head of the Deutsche Arbeitsgemeinschaft, Katowice. Interpreters: Iwona Karewicz, Thomas Kleine-Brockhoff.

Brightbart, Aaron. Researcher, Simon Wiesenthal Center for Holocaust Studies, Los Angeles.

Bryś, Piotr. Prosecutor, Provincial Commission for the Investigation of Crimes Against the Polish Nation, Katowice. Interpreters: Tadeusz Imielski, Marilyn Jeanne Odell.

Caspit, Ben. Reporter for *Maariv*, Tel Aviv.

de Zayas, Alfred. Human rights officer, United Nations.

Deak, Istvan. Professor, Columbia University, New York City.

Dziętkowski. Chief of Archives, Provincial Police, Katowice. Interpreter: Ewa Nowakowska.

Filipek, Joachim. Vice President, Provincial Court, Katowice. Interpreter: Ewa Nowakowska.

Gavshon, Michael. Producer for *60 Minutes*.

Gilbo, Patrick. Manager of Historical Resources, American Red Cross, Washington, D.C.

Grodzki, Marek. Prosecutor, Provincial Commission for the Investigation of Crimes Against the Polish Nation, Katowice. Interpreters: Roman Z. Hrabar, Tadeusz Imielski, Iwona Karewicz.

Hrabar, Roman Z. President, Provincial Commission for the Investigation of Crimes Against the Polish Nation, Katowice.

Jankowiak, Gerard. Judge, Katowice. Interpreter: Ewa Nowakowska.

Jaruzelski, Jerzy. Officer, Polish Embassy, Washington, D.C.

Juszkiewicz, Senator Ryszard. Director of the Main Commission for the Investigation of Crimes Against the Polish Nation, Warsaw. Interpreter: Tadeusz Imielski.

Kaim, Waldemar. Director of the Department for the Investigation of Hitlerite Crimes, Main Commission for the Investigation of Crimes Against the Polish Nation, Warsaw. Interpreter: Tadeusz Imielski.

Kaniewski, Stanisław. Director of the Department for the Investigation of Hitlerite Crimes, Main Commission for the Investigation of Crimes Against the Polish Nation, Warsaw. Interpreter: Tadeusz Imielski.

Katuża, Adam. Manager, State Archives, Katowice. Interpreter: Ewa Nowakowska.

Kleine-Brockhoff, Thomas. Editor for *Die Zeit*, Hamburg.

Korbonski, Andre. Professor, UCLA, Los Angeles.

Korbonski, Zofia. Historian, Washington, D.C.

Kowalski, Artur. Historian, San Jose, California.

Kożera, Colonel Wacław. Director, Department of Criminal Institutions, Katowice. Interpreter: Ewa Nowakowska.

Kraska, Krystyna. Assistant District Attorney, Gliwice. Interpreter: Ewa Nowakowska.

Kwarta, Edmund. Deputy Director of Archives, Provincial Police, Katowice. Interpreter: Tadeusz Imielski.

Lerski, Georg. Retired professor, San Francisco State University.

Lisiewicz, Paweł. Member, Provincial Commission for the Investigation of Crimes Against the Polish Nation, Katowice. Interpreters: Tadeusz Imielski, Iwona Karewicz.

Major, Henry. President, Fraternal Order of Bendin-Sosnowicer, New York City.

Motas, Mieczysław. Deputy Director of the Main Commission for the Investigation of Crimes Against the Polish Nation, Warsaw. Interpreter: Tadeusz Imielski.

Musiał, Józef. Vice Minister of Justice, Warsaw. Interpreter: Ewa Nowakowska.

Nasiadko, Leszek. Prosecutor, Provincial Commission for the Investigation of Crimes Against the Polish Nation, Katowice. Interpreters: Tadeusz Imielski, Marilyn Jeanne Odell.

Okulczyk, Aurelia. Secretary, District Attorney's Office, Gliwice. Interpreter: Ewa Nowakowska.

Pomian, Andrew. Historian, Washington, D.C.

Poszado, Stanisław. Manager, Department of Law and Organization, Department of Criminal Institutions, Katowice. Interpreter: Ewa Nowakowska.

Ruciński, Jerzy. Prosecutor, Provincial Commission for the Investigation of Crimes Against the Polish Nation, Katowice. Interpreter: Ewa Nowakowska.

Sawer, Gertruda. Secretary, Provincial Commission for the Investigation of

Crimes Against the Polish Nation, Katowice. Interpreters: Tadeusz Imielski, Iwona Karewicz, Marilyn Jeanne Odell.

Sosinski, Mieczysław. Director of the Department of Administration, Main
Commission for the Investigation of Crimes Against the Polish Nation,
Warsaw. Interpreter: Tadeusz Imielski.

Świątnicka, Stanisława. Judge, Katowice. Interpreter: Ewa Nowakowska.

Swierkosz, Krzysztof. Director, Provincial Commission for the Investigation
of Crimes Against the Polish Nation, Opole. Interviewer: Barbara Zaliwska.

Szczepurek, Major Bogdan. Commandant, Gliwice prison. Interpreter: Ewa
Nowakowska.

Szwarlik, Father Kazimierz. Priest, Church of the Holy Trinity, Będzin.
Interpreter: Zbigniew Podgornik.

Torańska, Teresa. Polish journalist, Washington, D.C. Interpreter: Leszek
Sankowski.

Urban, Thomas. Reporter for *Suddeutsche Zeitung*, Berlin.

Wandycz, Piotr. Professor, Yale University, New Haven, Connecticut.

Watoła, Urszula. Director, Provincial Commission for the Investigation of
Crimes Against the Polish Nation, Katowice. Interpreters: Tadeusz Imielski, Iwona Karewicz, Ewa Nowakowska, Marilyn Jeanne Odell.

Wiesenthal, Simon. Nazi hunter.

Zak, Maurice. President, Provincial Court, Katowice. Interpreters: Iwona
Karewicz, Ewa Nowakowska.

Zaliwska, Barbara. Reporter for *Tak i Nie*, Katowice.

Zawadzki, Tadeusz. Historian, London.

Interview by Teresa Torańska in *Them*

Jewish officers in the Office of State Security, 1945:

Berman, Jacob. Chief of the Office of State Security.

Files of the Office of State Security
(in the Archives of the Provincial Court, Katowice)

Eiserman, Karol. Convicted collaborator in Gleiwitz prison (after September,
1945).

Grzybek, Elżbieta. Convicted collaborator in Gleiwitz prison (from May 6,
1946).

Janicki, Gerhard. Convicted member of Special Section (SD) in Gleiwitz
prison (apparently after 1945).

Janiczek, Emil. Convicted member of Storm Section in Gleiwitz prison (from
January, 1946).

Jarząbek, Franciszek. Convicted member of Storm Section in Gleiwitz prison
(from March 14, 1946).

Karmański, Jan. Accused member of Storm Section in Lola's prison (apparently from August 29, 1945). Later convicted.

Klimek, Gerard. Convicted member of Storm Section in Gleiwitz prison (from February 22, 1946).

Kokoc, Hubert. Accused member of Storm Section in Gleiwitz prison (apparently from August 28, 1946). Later convicted.

Kopółka, Tomasz. Accused collaborator in Lola's prison (from July 18, 1945). Later convicted.

Kozieł, Wilhelm. Convicted member of Storm Section in Gleiwitz prison (from 1946).

Krawczyk, Józef. Accused member of Storm Section in Lola's prison (from July 11, 1945). Later convicted.

Lefniok, Josef. Convict in Gleiwitz prison (in 1947).

Manka, Jan. Accused member of Storm Section in Lola's prison (from July 11, 1945). Later convicted.

Matusiak, Henryk. Convicted murderer in Gleiwitz prison (in 1947 and 1948). Later executed.

Mróz, Paweł. Accused member of Storm Section in Lola's prison (from July 11, 1945). Later convicted.

Pietrzak, Władysław. Convicted anticommunist in Gleiwitz prison (after June 26, 1946).

Pijowczak, Paweł. Accused member of Storm Section in Gleiwitz prison (on September 24, 1945). Later convicted.

Stein, Emanuel. Accused collaborator in Lola's prison (from April 23, 1945). Later convicted.

Szydłowski, Piotr. Accused member of Storm Section in Lola's prison (from July 18, 1945). Later convicted.

Zapora, Małgorzata. Accused member of SS in Lola's prison. Later executed.

Zydek, Henryk. Accused member of Storm Section in Lola's prison (from August 25, 1945). Later convicted.

Statements in the German Federal Archives

Almost all of these statements were photocopied. The photocopies will eventually go to the John Sack Collection at Boston University and will be accessible there.

German prisoners in Blechhammer:

Haldan, Willibald (Ost-Dok. 2/236C/371).
Leistritz, Ernst (Ost-Dok. 2/198/47).

German prisoners in Bunzlau:

Reimann, Eva (Ost-Dok. 2/236C/288).

Germans in Gleiwitz:

Häusler, D. (Ost-Dok. 1/251/3).

N. N. (Ost-Dok. 2/213D/173).
von T. (Ost-Dok. 2/235/128).

German prisoners in Gleiwitz:

Gawlik, Elfriede (Ost-Dok. 2/236C/503).
Griemla, Georg (Ost-Dok. 2/236C/336).
Kowalski, Georg (Ost-Dok. 2/236C/467).
Schymitzek, Angela (Ost-Dok. 2/236D/652).
Urbanke, Karl (Ost-Dok. 2/236D/721).

German prisoners in Kattowitz:

Kroll, Max (Ost-Dok. 2/236B/52).

German prisoners in Lamsdorf:

Aschmann, H. (Ost-Dok. 2/236E/950)
Bech, Johannes (Ost-Dok. 2/233/9)
Donitza, Karl (Ost-Dok. 2/236E/773)
Erbrich, Paul (Ost-Dok. 2/236E/890)
Esser, Dr. Heinz (2/236E/946)
Hoffmann, Ottilie Artelt (Ost-Dok. 2/236E/910)
Hübner, Rudolf (Ost-Dok. 2/228/64)
König, Karl (Ost-Dok. 2/236E/994)
Krell, Gustav (Ost-Dok. 2/236E/802)
Lyga, Erna (Ost-Dok. 2/223/2)
Obst, Erzpriester (Ost-Dok. 2/218/79)
Schneider, Wilhelm (Ost-Dok. 2/236D/713)
Schon, Paul (Ost-Dok. 2/236E/979)
Walke, Magda (Ost-Dok. 2/236E/884)
Willner, Paul (Ost-Dok. 2/236E/407)

German prisoners in Lassowitz:

Zimmermann, Maria (Ost-Dok. 2/215/40).

German prisoners in Myslowitz:

Blacha, Pavil (Ost-Dok. 2/236C/318).
Bronder, Raimund (Ost-Dok. 2/236C/270).
Dohn, Hugo (Ost-Dok. 2/236D/735).
Filippek, Konrad (Ost-Dok. 2/236D/641).
Hemschik, Mathias (Ost-Dok. 2/236B/106).
Kernbach, Florian (Ost-Dok. 2/236D/622, 2/236D/633).
Klaus, Paul (Ost-Dok. 2/236D/746).

Mainka, Franz (Ost-Dok. 2/236B/208).
Michalik, Hedwig (Ost-Dok. 2/236B/48).
Muschalik, Cäcilie (Ost-Dok. 2/236C/309).
Paff, Georg (Ost-Dok. 2/236B/162).
Pielka, Georg (Ost-Dok. 2/236D/637).

German prisoners in Neisse:

Cyrus, Max (Ost-Dok. 2/227/20).
Halke, Maria Rother (Ost-Dok. 2/227/48).
Hesse, Pavil (Ost-Dok. 2/227/62).
Jaeschke, Hubert (Ost-Dok. 2/227/88).
Neuber, Wilhelm (Ost-Dok. 2/236B/132).

German prisoners in Potulice:

Büller, Marta (Ost-Dok. 2/60/11).
Dinkelmann, Heinrich (Ost-Dok. 2/73/32).
Finkgruber, Emil (Ost-Dok. 2/146/98).
Fischer, Margarete (Ost-Dok. 2/137/45).
George, Anna (Ost-Dok. 2/52/29).
Gierszowski, Ella (Ost-Dok. 2/55/7).
Kelm, Sister Erna (Ost-Dok. 2/51/99).
Spandera, Ingeborg (Ost-Dok. 2/131/55).
von Shirach, Christa-Helene Gause (Ost-Dok. 2/148/103).
Zindler, E. (Ost-Dok. 2/64/18).

German prisoners in Schwientochlowitz:

Arondarczyk, Kunigunde (Ost-Dok. 2/236D/724).
Biernot, Heinz (Ost-Dok. 2/236C/431).
Cyl, Paul (Ost-Dok. 2/236D/726).
Cyprian, Albert (Ost-Dok. 2/236C/258).
Freund, Walter (Ost-Dok. 2/236C/351, also published as Number 216 in *Die
    Vertreibung der Deutschen Bevölkerung aus den Gebieten Östlich der
    Oder-Neisse* by Theodor Schieder).
Frystatzki, Johanna (Ost-Dok. 2/230/2, also published as Number 215 in *Die
    Vertreibung der Deutschen Bevölkerung aus den Gebieten Östlich der
    Oder-Neisse* by Theodor Schieder).
Hoinkes, Helena (Ost-Dok. 2/236C/456).
Kempny, Martha Helisch (Ost-Dok. 2/237/162).
Kischel, Erich (Ost-Dok. 2/236B/3, 2/236B/5).
Kubitza, Viktor (Ost-Dok. 2/236B/227).
Kukla, Karl (Ost-Dok. 2/236C/372).
Kworka, Johann (Ost-Dok. 2/236C/388).

Lücke, Hedwig (Ost-Dok. 2/236C/512).
Ogorek, Max (Ost-Dok. 2/236C/362).
Respondek, Hedwig (Ost-Dok. 2/236C/462).
Rotter, Inge (Ost-Dok. 2/236C/391).
Samol, Georg (Ost-Dok. 2/236C/330).
Schnapka, Gertrud Furgol (Ost-Dok. 2/236C/369).
Schwierzok, Leo (Ost-Dok. 2/236D/635).
Schyma, Gertrud (Ost-Dok. 2/236D/704).
Sczakiel, Josef (Ost-Dok. 2/236B/130).
Thiele, Anneliese (Ost-Dok. 2/236D/692).
Urbainski, Ernst (Ost-Dok. 2/236B/100).
Witkowski, Max (Ost-Dok. 2/235/178, 2/235/183, 2/235/185).
Wollny, Günther (Ost-Dok. 2/236C/297).

German prisoners in Ziegenhals:

Langer, Joseph (Ost-Dok. 2/232/18).

Other Germans:

Adam, Fryda (Ost-Dok. 2/233/36).
Aschmann, H. (Ost-Dok. 2/236E/950).
Bech, Elli (Ost-Dok. 2/233/3).
Bech, Johannes (Ost-Dok. 2/233/11).
Drabik (Ost-Dok. 2/236D/680).
Gawoll, Emil (Ost-Dok. 2/236D/667).
Mosler, Josef (Ost-Dok. 2/236C/354).

Statements in *The Tragedy of Silesia* by Dr. Johannes Kaps

Numbers 4, 7, 11, 12, 14, 16, 17, 23, 33, 47, 49, 62, 82, 101, 105, 110, 191, 192, 194 and 196.

Statements in *Die Vertreibung der Deutschen Bevölkerung aus den Gebieten Östlich der Oder-Neisse* by Theodor Schieder

Numbers 140 (F. K.), 143 (Gerlinde Winkler), 166 (Gertrude Schulz), 169 (Anna Schwartz), 171 (Hermann Balzer), 187 (A. B.), 208 (O. M.), 218 (B. F.), 219 (Georg Fritsch), 220 (Adolf Walda), 223 (I. R.), 224 (I. F.), 229 (Paul Seifert), 266 (E. K.), 267 (R. S.), 268 (P. L.), 269 (K. E.), 270 (M.) and 343 (Joseph Buhl).

Statements in *Die Flucht und Vertreibung*
Oberschlesien 1945/46 by Wolfgang Schwarz

Anonymous.
Behrens, Maria.
N.
Sack, Margarete.
Wallura, M.

Archives and Museums

Auschwitz: Auschwitz Museum.
Będzin: City Archives.
Geneva: International Committee of the Red Cross.
Gliwice: City Archives.
Gliwice: District Attorney's Office.
Jerusalem: Yad Vashem.
Katowice: Department of Criminal Institutions.
Katowice: Provincial Commission for the Investigation of Crimes Against the
    Polish Nation.
Katowice: Provincial Court.
Katowice: Provincial Police.
Katowice: State Archives.
Stockholm: Swedish Red Cross.
Tel Aviv: Museum of the Diaspora.
Washington: U.S. National Archives.

Books

On World War II:

Botting, Douglas: *From the Ruins of the Reich.*
Bullock, Adam: *Hitler: A Study in Tyranny.*
Byrnes, James F.: *Speaking Frankly.*
Churchill, Winston: *Closing the Ring.*
Erickson, John: *The Road to Berlin.*
Hitler Youth: *Uns Geht die Sonne Nicht Unter.*
Hyde, H. Montgomery: *Stalin: The History of a Dictator.*
Krakowski, Shmuel: *The War of the Doomed: Jewish Armed Resistance in
    Poland 1942–1944.*
Lucas, James: *War on the Eastern Front.*
Toland, John: *The Last Hundred Days.*
Ulam, Adam B.: *Stalin: The Man and His Era.*

On Będzin:

Vishniac, Roman: *A Vanished World*.

On Auschwitz:

Astor, Gerald: *The Last Nazi*.
Auschwitz Museum: *KL Auschwitz Seen by the SS*.
Delbo, Charlotte: *None of Us Will Return*.
Garliński, Józef: *Fighting Auschwitz*.
Hart, Kitty: *Return to Auschwitz*.
Höss, Rudolf: *Commandant at Auschwitz*.
Kielar, Wiesław: *Anus Mundi*.
Kowalski, Isaac: *Anthology on Armed Jewish Resistance*.
Lengyel, Olga: *Five Chimneys*.
Levi, Primo: *The Drowned and the Saved*.
Manchester, William: *The Arms of Krupp*.
Müller, Filip: *Eyewitness Auschwitz*.
Nomberg-Przytyk, Sara: *Auschwitz*.
Pawełczyńska, Anna: *Values and Violence in Auschwitz*.
Perl, Gisella: *I Was a Doctor in Auschwitz*.
Posner, Gerald L., and John Ware: *Mengele: The Complete Story*.
Suhl, Yuri: *They Fought Back*.
Szmaglewska, Seweryna: *Smoke over Birkenau*.
Wiesel, Elie: *Night*.

On Majdanek:

Rajca, Czesław, and Anna Wiśniewska: *Obóz Koncentracyjny*.

On the SS:

Dicks, Henry V.: *Licensed Mass Murder*.
Graber, G. S.: *History of the SS*.
Grunberger, Richard: *Hitler's SS*.
Krausnick, Helmut, et al.: *Anatomy of the SS State*.
Reitlinger, Gerald: *SS: Alibi of a Nation*.

On Gleiwitz:

Bienek, Horst: *Earth and Fire*.
Bienek, Horst: *The Last Polka*.
Bienek, Horst: *Time Without Bells*.
Pawelitzki, Richard: *Gleiwitz*.

On the Office of State Security:

Błażyński, Zbigniew: *Mówi Józef Światło.*
Korbonski, Stefan: *The Jews and the Poles in World War II.*
Torańska, Teresa: *Them.*

On Germans After World War II:

Anders, Konrad: *Die Arbeitslager in Myslowitz, Schwientochlowitz und Ein- trachthütte* (in *Vermächtnis der Lebenden*)
Bacque, James: *Other Losses.*
Bielke, Pieter: *Schönwald.*
de Zayas, Alfred: *The German Expellees: Victims in War and Peace*
de Zayas, Alfred: *Nemesis at Potsdam.*
Esser, Dr. Heinz: *Die Hölle von Lamsdorf.*
German Federal Archives: *Vertreibung und Vertreibungsverbrechen 1945–1948.*
German Federal Statistical Office: *Die Deutschen Vertriebungsverluste.*
German Red Cross: *Zivilverschollenenliste des Suchdienstes des Deutschen Roten Kreuzes.*
Kaps, Dr. Johannes: *Martyrdom of Silesian Priests.*
Kaps, Dr. Johannes: *The Tragedy of Silesia.*
Maschke, Erich: *Zur Geschichte der Deutschen Kriegsgefangenen des Zweiten Weltkrieges.*
Schieder, Theodor: *Die Vertreibung der Deutschen Bevölkerung aus den Gebieten Östlich der Oder-Neisse.*
Schimitzek, Stanisław: *Truth or Conjecture?*

ACKNOWLEDGMENTS

Of course I thank Lola. Her life was largely a horror story, but she coura-geously chose to retell it and thereby relive it. But what I know about Lola's life comes mostly from other sources, and I also thank the two hundred peo-ple who, often in pain, sometimes in tears, told me about her and the Office of State Security. In particular, I thank two Polish guards in Gleiwitz, Józef Pijarczyk and Lucjan Zenderowski, two German prisoners in Gleiwitz, Gün-ther Ciesla and Josef Wiescholek, and two German prisoners in Schwien-tochlowitz, Heinz "Becker" and Günther Wollny, who appear in this book so ephemerally and anonymously that a reader wouldn't know of their enor-mous contributions.

I thank the good people of Poland. If any reader wonders how an Ameri-can who speaks no Polish in a city that speaks no English discovers which of its 210,000 inhabitants worked in the secret police fifty years ago, the answer is that the American sits on a sofa until the good people of Gliwice call him and tell him in Pidgin English, "We found them!" Eva Polanski, at the Warszawa Restaurant in Santa Monica, California, wrote to her friends in Gliwice asking them to welcome me. Grzegorz and Ewa Bobkowski were waiting when, after being arrested in East Berlin, I arrived at half past three in the morning at Gliwice station. Iwona Karewicz in Sosnowiec, Jan Leassear in Gliwice, and Barbara Zaliwska in Katowice gave me three homes away from home, three meals included. Tadeusz Imielski, Iwona Karewicz, Ewa Nowakowska and Barbara Zaliwska volunteered as my researcher-inter-preters, often declining the fifty cents per hour of a Polish researcher-inter-preter, and Ewa Bobkowska, Grzegorz Bobkowski, Dorota Boreczek, Roman Z. Hrabar, Mordechai Kac, Thomas Kleine-Brockhoff, Wojciech Mrożek, Tadeusz Pfutzner and Zbigniew Podgornik also graciously interpreted for me. Without my knowing it, Edward and Grażyna Jakubowski-Kijonka walked the Gliwice streets, climbed the apartment-house stairs, and knocked on the doors until they discovered the three vital guards from Lola's old prison, and Colonel Wacław Kożera and Major Bogdan Szczepurek allowed me into the prison, even the prisoners' cells, while Poland still was a communist country. Some other warm, always-available, and ever-generous people in Poland who I haven't listed as sources were Ewa Bogdanowska-Jakubowski, Jan Frankiewicz, Anna Lis, Janusz Luks, Mirosław Miernik, Andrzej Niedoba, Dobromira Nowakowska, Zenon Petralwski, Helena Pijarczyk, Anna Roga and Joanna Słowinska, and I thank them all.

I thank the good people of Germany, too. I've said that I went to immense reunions of Germans from Gleiwitz and stopped at the beer-laden tables saying, *"Waren Sie im Gefängnis Gleiwitz?* Were you in Gleiwitz Prison?" I was really a party poop, but my own trip was delightful, thanks to the warm, loving, laughing and ever-helpful people who I found in Germany today. Renate Friedemann, the German consul in Los Angeles, and Frau Simons, of Internaciones in Bonn, generously laid out a trip for me. Doris Diana Dame, Erika Nottebohm, Andrea Seppi and Stefanie von Heygendorff-Hoffken were my cheerful cicerone-interpreters or, as I called them, my nannies, and Karl G. Frank, Thomas Jarosch, Madzia Kukulska and Maximilian Vrecer also kindly interpreted for me. Herren Hagner, Kuse, Lenz and Verlande helped me again and again at the German Federal Archives, in Koblenz, Anka Sarstedt made me at home in Berlin, and Andrea Seppi was my researcher for Germany. Some other warmly remembered people who I haven't listed as sources were Wilfried Ahrens, Winfried Bonse, Herbert Czaya, Reinhard Dinkelmeyer, Jens Ege, Andreas Gundrum, Johann Huth, H. Kalcyk, Karin Kiehn, Bernd Kortmann, Harmut Koschyk, Guntram Kuse, Markus Leuschner, Piotr Mroczyk, Marianne Pietrasch, Sieglinde Roser, Hilde Sachse, Alfred Schickel, Curt Schneider, Siegfried Schrajaks, Bettina Spier, Bernhild Staffen, Helmut Talazko, Barbara Ungeheuer, Petra Waldraff, Hugo Weczerka, Edith Wichary, Gunda Wolter and Hela Ziegler, and I thank them all.

I thank Hanna Lehrmann, my interpreter in Copenhagen, Gunnar Nyby and Stig Wilton in Stockholm, Alfred de Zayas, the great authority on Germans after World War II, in Geneva and Florianne Truninger in Geneva, Richard Sack, my host in Paris, Mary Gantet, my interpreter in Annecy, Maximilian Vrecer, my host in Vienna, Josef Kowalski and Danny Stoppler, my interpreters in Tel Aviv, Isaac Greengrass in Tel Aviv, Sid Halperin in Ashkelon, Chuck and Ruth Milgrom, my hosts in Jerusalem, Barek and Regina Eisenstein, my hosts in Toronto, Linda Winston, my researcher in New York, and Sandy and Lois Edelstein, Georganne Heller, Denny and Edmond Levy, Penny Morell, Tracy Sack, David and Magee Shields, and Linda Winston, my hosts in New York. Back in Los Angeles and later in the Rocky Mountains, I was awash in Polish and Russian, Danish and Swedish, German and Dutch, French and Spanish, and Yiddish and Hebrew, and Igor Automonow, Marlena Bielecki, Jean-Jacques Bohl, Marju Couris, Karl Dietz,

Katharina Ehrhardt, Vera Katz, Jack Lewin, Jerzy Lewinski, Stewart Lyndh, Jody Melamed, Marilyn Jeanne Odell, Eva Polanski, Leszek Sankowski, Shlomo "Singer," Lise-Lotte Stoffel, Annelies van Calsteren-Lek, Andrea van Every, Eric West and Andrez Zysmanowicz helped me to translate letters and documents and to interpret tapes and telephone calls. Some other helpful people in the United States who weren't specifically sources were Peter R. Aikman, Jackie Berry, Adam Bigwood, Cynthia Blatt, Nini Blatt, John Butler, Josef Dugas, Sam Field, Edith Hall, Sherry Hirsch, Adair Klein, Jerry Knoll, Ann Monka, Noah Nunberg, Barbara Pathe, Ted Post, Adam Simms, Aloha South, Helen Walzer, Bernard Weinstein and Eli Zborowski, and, again, I thank them all.

Originally, this book was an article in *California* magazine, and I thank Bob Roe, the Editor, for taming the wild rhetoric that I use in *M* and *Company C* but that would intrude on *An Eye for an Eye.* Another part of this book was an article in the *Village Voice,* and I thank Jonathan Z. Larsen, the Editor, for his courage in bringing it to America's attention. Above all, I thank the courageous people at Basic Books: the Publishers Martin Kessler and Kermit Hummel, my Editor Steve Fraser, and Patty Chang Anker, Linda Carbone, Bill Davis, Shirley Kessel, Ellen Sue Levine, Marilyn Mazur, Michael Mueller, Gary Murphy, Paul Perlow, Gay Salisbury, Helena Schwarz and Lois Shapiro, who felt that this story must be told even when other publishers were calling it "well-written," "extremely well-written," "chilling," "compelling," "disturbing," "dismaying," "shocking," "startling," "astonishing," "mesmerizing," "extraordinary," "important," and were telling me, "I was riveted," "I was bowled over," "I love it," and yet were rejecting it. Some other much-appreciated editors were Art Cooper, Rob Cowley, Richard Goldstein, Harold Hayes, Alyssa Katz, B. J. Moran, Sallie Motsch, Marilyn Jeanne Odell, Murray Polner, Paul Scanlon, Matt Yeomans, and, most of all, Don Hutter, who tragically died in February, 1990, but whose ideas still saturate this book. My tenacious agent was Ellen Levine, my essential attorney was Stephen F. Rohde, my confidante was Paxton Quigley, my devoted assistants were Ewa Nowakowska in Poland and Marilyn Jeanne Odell in the United States, my girlfriend is Catherine Brightful, and I thank these people all. Add the two hundred sources and the two hundred written sources, and *An Eye for an Eye* isn't mine, it's ours.

QUERY

I'll be happy to hear from anyone who was, or who knows anyone who was, a Jewish officer in the UB, the Urząd Bezpieczeństwa Publicznego, the Office of State Security, in Poland in 1945, or from anyone who was a German prisoner in Gleiwitz, Lamsdorf, Neisse or Schwientochlowitz in 1945. I'll also be happy to hear of any errors in this edition, and I'll correct them in future ones.

Please write to John Sack, Basic Books, 10 East 53rd Street, New York, N.Y. 10022, and please give me your address and, if you choose to, your telephone number. If you wish, I'll keep everything confidential.

INDEX